THE LONDON BUS GUIDE

The Routes ~ The Buses
The Garages ~ The Companies

KU-755-569

CONTENTS

Foreword

The move towards reducing emissions in London continues. Over 2000 hybids are being joined by an ever increasing number of electric vehicles. Routes 507 & 521 are now fully electric, the 360 will follow in 2017. The five BYD electric double-deckers will be joined by one from Optare during this year. Also the first hydrogen powered double-decker should hit the streets soon. *Billy Birkett*

The London Bus Guide has become a firm fixture in the bus book publishing world and proved immensely popular with London-based enthusiasts as well as those visiting the capital for the first time.

We always anticipated updating the book every year because the London scene is constantly changing, and this is reflected in a fully-revised Seventh Edition.

To aid its usefulness whilst out and about we have now included an extra section giving the fleet lists of each London operator.

For those who are buying the Guide for the first time, its purpose is to explain the operation of Transport for London's (TfL) bus routes and to make your visits more rewarding and enjoyable. The book is designed to be taken out and used as a quick reference, so the information is presented in a way we find useful when visiting locations for the first time. Your feedback will be welcomed so we can modify and improve future editions.

There is one proviso: Because of the nature of London bus operations (and despite our best efforts to provide an accurate picture), you need to be aware that the scene is constantly changing. What you see today may be completely different tomorrow. The information is correct to 1st April 2017 and we have also highlighted future changes on the opening page of the relevant section. However, no book can hope to give you every quirky little detail. You need to get out and explore for yourself.

I must thank the following:
Mark Mcwalter for his help in compiling the fleet lists. The photographers, for plugging the gaps in my collection. The company staff, for patiently answering our endless questions in the past year. Readers of previous Guides, for their encouraging words.

I hope you find this latest version of the book useful in your exploration of London.

Ken Carr
Boreham, Essex,
April 2017

London Bus Network Overview

The London network is unique in Britain in that it's the only one to be regulated. The buses are organised by TfL's subsidiary London Bus Services Ltd, trading as London Buses (LB). It is this body that decides which routes are run and the service levels to be operated. LB also monitors service quality and is responsible for bus stations, bus stops, fares, revenue protection, radio and vehicle tracking equipment, roadside staff to deal with diversions and major incidents, and the marketing of the London network.

More than 700 routes are operated and more than 100 of those are 24-hour, 7 days a week. Incidentally this is the best night route network in the world. In addition, 600-series routes provide morning and afternoon school journeys in term time, and a declining number of mobility services (900-series routes) operate once a week.

Since the year 2000, there has been a dramatic increase in London bus usage. However, during the last year the number of passenger journeys has started to fall. In 2015/16 journeys fell by 3.3% at 2.29 billion. More journeys take place in London than the rest of England. London's buses travelled 492 million kilometres. It is estimated that 90% of Londoners live within 400 metres of a bus stop, so its not surprising that the bus is so popular.

Contracts

Bus services within the TfL area are operated by private companies under contract to London Buses. Contracts are awarded route by route, normally for a period of five years. However, under the Quality Incentive (QI) scheme, there is an option to extend each route's contract by two years. As the name suggests, the aim is to incentivise operators to provide quality service during the core contract period. Although routes are generally tendered individually, others in the same area often come up for renewal at the same time to make changeovers easier.

The tendering programme is continuous, with between 15% and 20% of the network typically offered each year. Tender evaluation focuses on best value for money, but also takes into account safety and quality as essential features. Contract payments are directly linked to the mileage each route runs and to the overall reliability of the service. Comprehensive quality measurements are in place across all aspects of delivery.

Before offering a tender, London Buses reviews each route to produce a service specification detailing the route that buses will take (including terminal arrangements), service frequency at different times of day and on different days of the

Photo: Ken Carr

only a single return journey each day. Most routes operate from about 04.30 till midnight, but an increasing number run 24 hours a day. Some routes 'morph' into night bus services between midnight and 04.30 (87 becomes N87, for example) with their daytime routes extended or modified.

Within the tender documentation, London Buses also specifies the minimum requirements for the vehicles to be used. The operator may choose the vehicle manufacturer, so long as its vehicles meet the criteria in the specification (like potential operators, new bus models are individually assessed and approved by TfL). Tenders are submitted on a sealed bid basis and must contain all relevant information for London Buses to make an effective evaluation.

The award of Contracts is based on achieving the most economically advantageous outcome within the resources available. The criteria include:

Price Ability - to deliver quality services to the levels specified in the ITT.

Staffing Ability - to recruit, train and retain personnel of a suitable calibre.

Premises - the suitability of an existing depot, and/or the operator's ability to obtain a suitable depot.

Vehicles - the type proposed and any additional features they offer above the tender specification. The operator's ability to maintain vehicles in an acceptable condition throughout the life of the contract is a major consideration.

Financial Status - the operator's resources to fund start-up costs and provide stability over the contract term.

Schedules - compliance with the specifications.

Tender evaluation is led by a Contracts Tendering Manager supported by a small team of skilled technical and commercial staff. Recommendations for contract awards are discussed and approved by the Tender Evaluation Committee, comprising the directors of London Bus Services Ltd.

As mentioned above, there is a nominated gross cost attached to each contract (operating costs plus profit), but the Quality Incentive aspect also provides for performance bonuses and/or deductions, as well as the two-year extension option. Each contract also has a specified Minimum Performance Standard reflecting the particular characteristics of the route. Performance monitoring data obtained by London Buses is normally shared with the operator. The contract price is adjusted each year in line with inflation.

week (including the times of first and last buses), and the type and capacity of vehicle to be used. Operators are then asked to provide a schedule for delivering the specified level of service, along with the base cost of meeting this level plus a profit margin.

Although London Buses operates an approved supplier list, it routinely places advertisements in the Official Journal of the European Union seeking expressions of interest from potential operators. Once a new applicant has been assessed and approved, it is then able to compete in the route-by-route tendering process. Invitations To Tender (ITTs) are normally issued every 2-4 weeks.

Route sizes vary considerably, as does each route's Peak Vehicle Requirement (PVR). This is the number of buses required to operate the service at times of greatest frequency - usually the morning and evening 'rush hours', but not exclusively so - and it ranges from one vehicle to more than fifty. Services are classified as either High Frequency (5 buses or more per hour throughout much of the week) or Low Frequency (4 buses per hour or fewer). About 82% of the network is High Frequency. The highest frequency routes have a bus every 3-4 minutes, the lowest frequency have

The Quality Incentive scheme and performance monitoring are inextricably linked, covering not only service reliability but also driving quality and vehicle condition. The latter two are monitored by a combination of 'mystery traveller' surveys and vehicle inspections at garages. All of this is combined in a set of 'extension threshold' criteria in the tender documentation which, if met, trigger the automatic two-year extension. The operator can choose to decline, in which case the route would be re-tendered immediately at the end of the contract. In the event of acceptance, the extension is on the same basis as the original contract and the route is removed from the tendering renewal process for two years.

Although operators are expected to deliver the full contracted service, this is not always possible. Mechanical breakdowns, staff sickness, roadworks, road closures and other incidents on or near the route can all have a negative effect, hence the minimum performance standard. Any mileage which cannot be operated is split into two categories: Deductible Lost Mileage (loss of route operation considered to be within the Operator's reasonable control, e.g. staff absence, mechanical breakdown) and Non-Deductible Lost Mileage (instances beyond the Operator's reasonable control, such as adverse traffic conditions). Obviously, the Operator is not paid for Deductible Lost Mileage, and the deduction is calculated on a *pro rata* basis. Not surprisingly, the operators and TfL have teams of people who monitor the reasons for lost mileage.

London's environmental issues and poor air quality have been rapidly climbing the list of priorities for tender assessment in recent years. New vehicles have to conform to the latest European emissions standards and operators are also encouraged to introduce higher standards sooner than European law requires. Buses operating on the London network have a minimum standard of Euro-3 which came into effect from 3rd January 2012.

Since late 2009, new vehicle engines for London buses have been manufactured to Euro-5 standard and in 2014 all new buses have to be Euro-6 standard. Each of these progressive steps used to relate (in the main) to the effectiveness of the diesel particulate filters. The Euro-6 standard is far more stringent and demands near-zero emissions of both gases and particulates.

With pollution in mind (and the constant threat of heavy fines being imposed by the EU), Transport for London is trialling the latest advances in vehicle technology, including a batch of hydrogen fuel cell buses which produce no polluting emissions and battery powered electric buses. Diesel-electric hybrids (powered by smaller engines coupled to generators and batteries charged by regenerative braking) also produce lower emissions than a traditional diesel bus. More than 2000 vehicles of various designs were in service by April 2017 - a figure expected to increase rapidly. Plans are now afoot for all single-deck routes in the central area to be electric by 2020. TfL have also identified a number of areas where emissions are dangerously

Golders Green is a major interchange, buses, London Underground and National Express coaches all meet here. *Ken Carr*

TfL are always looking at ways to speed up services. Bus lanes can be found throughout London. In Sutton there is this 'pit-stop' style bus stop on Throwley Way. *Ken Carr*

high and routes running along these roads will be operated by hybrids or electrics. Putney High Street is the first of these to be tackled.

Other Services

London Buses also procures buses for rail replacement journeys on behalf of London Underground. More than 100 such contracts are issued in advance of planned engineering work each year. Some involve only a single bus, others can require fifty or more. The tendering process is similar to that used for normal services and front-line operators such as Abellio and Arriva regularly win these contracts. Smaller companies currently without TfL routes, such as Ensign, also supply vehicles for this work.

London Buses' Dial-a-Ride service is run for the benefit of disabled and elderly people. The service initially used a fleet of Mercedes-Benz minibuses but these are rapidly being replaced by a fleet of Bluebird Tuscanas painted in the familiar TfL red and owned by London Buses itself. Booking one is similar to booking a taxi, although the passenger has to pre-register before being able to use the service. He or she can then phone a call centre with details of the journey they wish to make and they're given a pick-up time, varying 15 minutes either

way. However, they may have to share a vehicle with other passengers on a journey likely to involve pick-ups and set-downs for others. For this reason, there is no guarantee the route will be direct, but the service is free and a commendable addition to London Buses' operations.

The Go-Ahead company in London runs a Commercial Services Fleet, with a variety of older bus types including the much-loved Routemaster. These buses are available for general hire and also appear on special services linked to some of London's big annual events like the Chelsea Flower Show and the Wimbledon Tennis Championships. Regular members of the fleet, identifiable by their gold numbers, are augmented at busy times by vehicles of similar type normally engaged on TfL contracts.

A number of sightseeing-tours operate in the capital. The Original Tour (formerly operated by Arriva and since September 2014 by RATP) and The Big Bus company are the largest. Each uses a mix of older types alongside recently-acquired, purpose-built, tri-axle buses from the Far East. Golden Tours moved into the Central London sightseeing market in the summer of 2011, using a small fleet of ALX400s and some new vehicles.

A digital display on a New Routemaster. This updates throughout the journey and displays the next stop. This one was also informing passengers of the route number change. *Ken Carr*

A new company started in 2015, City Tour, that are using a fleet of open-top Presidents.

In addition to the big players, smaller, self-contained operations exist. Routemasters appear throughout the year on trips operated by Premium Tours, and in the evening, Ghost Bus Tours' black RM runs a couple of 'scary' trips around London.

iBus

Every bus operating a TfL route is fitted with the Automatic Vehicle Location (AVL) system, better known as iBus. It works using a combination of technologies, including the Global Positioning System (GPS) and 'map matching', which receives input from a gyroscope and the bus's speedometer/odometer.

The bus data radio uses GPS to send its location to a central computer system approximately every 30 seconds. This information is available to service controllers monitoring performance along the route and enables them to take action to improve service reliability. It is not uncommon to hear drivers receiving radio messages from controllers instructing them to wait time at a stop to reduce the 'bunching' that can occur when traffic conditions are bad. As well as the driver-generated adjustments, TfL can also send instructions directly to traffic lights, altering the timing of their phases to help speed up buses when congestion occurs.

The bus's on-board computer carries the details of every stop along the route and all of the possible destinations. The computer constantly tracks the bus's position from the AVL information and announces each stop as it occurs, using pre-recorded 'sound bites'. Digital displays on both decks convey the same information to the hearing-impaired. Important locations close to stops, such as hospitals, are also announced visually and aurally.

Centre Comm - London Buses' 24/7 Emergency Command and Control Centre - can also use the bus PA system to communicate directly with passengers in the event of an emergency. Similarly, the driver can make contact with Centre Comm if an accident occurs, allowing the incident to be pin-pointed precisely when emergency assistance is despatched.

The central computer system also predicts the time it will take for buses to arrive at stops.

London United's Fulwell garage iBus room. *Ken Carr*

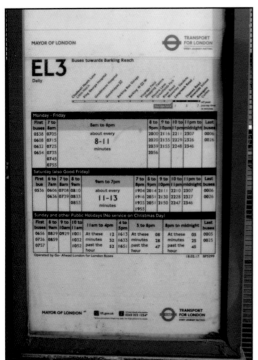

With the Oyster Card 'pay as you go' (formerly Pre-Pay), users are charged a fixed amount for single journeys, but a 'daily cap' limits the maximum deducted from the balance on a card, regardless of how many buses are used that day (a day is measured from 04.30 to 16.30). Weekly and monthly passes can also be purchased and loaded onto an Oyster Card. On boarding the bus, the Oyster Card is held up to a 'reader' which registers the journey and deducts the fare from the credit balance on the card. The process repeats for subsequent journeys until the daily cap (currently £4.20 for buses only, across all zones) is reached.

Children aged under 11 travel free; 11 to 15s travel free if they have an 11-15 Oyster photocard. Further concessions apply to those aged 16 to 18. Over-60s resident in London can apply for a Freedom Pass allowing free off-peak travel on buses and the rail network. A similar scheme is available to the disabled. Most over-60s living outside of London can apply for an English bus pass from their local authority. Since 2008, these passes have been accepted England-wide and provide free travel on all TfL routes after 9.30 am on weekdays and any time at weekends.

For the Enthusiast . . .

London has lots to offer (lots of buses for one thing) and there are a number of 'hot spot' locations where you can enjoy a wide variety of types. If you have never been to central London before, the area between Trafalgar Square and Aldwych is especially recommended. At the latter location, for instance, you can see (on a good day) hydrogen fuel cell buses running alongside heritage Routemasters as well as the standard Alexander-Dennis and Wrightbus models and NRMs. In addition Victoria and Hyde Park Corner are recommended, as is Marble Arch. Please refer to the 'Buses' section of this book for what can be found where.

During the year, various organisations have 'road runs' featuring a variety of older buses retracing routes they served in the dim and distant past. It's also worth keeping an eye out for garage open-days. Bus magazines and other enthusiast publications provide advance details.

We (Visions) run a number of bus tours throughout the year with heritage buses. These vary in content, some are pure garage bashes, others concentrate on photography, we even ran one in 2016 visiting all the locations on the Monopoly board. Full details can be found on our website - *www.visionsinternational.biz*

To enhance your London experience, we recommend the various bus route maps. TfL produces a set of five free maps - a central London

Each bus's arrival can then be displayed on LED countdown indicators at key bus shelters. This 'real time' system is now installed at more than 2,000 locations. The latest development allows passengers to check bus information in real time on their smart-phones.

As a continual process, iBus also provides detailed journey data which operators can use to improve individual routes.

Ticketing

All fares revenue goes directly to TfL and fares are collected in a number of ways. London buses currently accept Travelcards, Oyster Card products, contactless payment cards and bus passes. Since 6th July 2014, cash is no longer accepted and passengers must use one of the options above.

Oyster Card holders are allowed 'one free journey' if their card is empty and fails to register.

When the public consultation was launched, TfL claimed that only 1% of journeys were cash-based and that going cashless would save £24 million by 2020, quite apart from speeding up loading times.

Route W7 was used to trial a 'pre-pay' system in 2003, calling for passengers to buy tickets from machines at stops if they did not have Oyster or a recognised pass. Later, similar machines sprang from the pavements in the central London cashless zone, but all are now out of use.

version and the rest of the area split into four quadrants - north-east, south-west, et cetera. These are also very useful for tracing Overground and Underground railways through the London area. The TfL maps are available from larger Tube stations and Travel Information Centres like the one at Victoria main line station. They can also be downloaded from the web in PDF format. Go to: *http://www.tfl.gov.uk/gettingaround/maps/buses/* and scroll to the bottom of the page.

Alternatively, you can buy a map, especially the one many enthusiasts swear by - Mike Harris's Greater London Bus Map - for around £2.50. A Night Bus version is also available. Further information from: *www.busmap.co.uk*

Further Reading

Visions produce a number of London related books, including David Maxey's excellent Review of the Year - *Red All Over*.

Our *London Bus Club* is now in its third year and continues to grow from strength to strength. Members receive six copies of our glossy bi-monthly, 72 page magazine called *The Londoner* and receive discounts on our products and our *London Bus Tours*. Membership is £19.95 for the year and you can join via our website or by phone on 01245 465974. *The Londoner* magazine is also available from The London Transport Museum in Covent Garden, the Ian Allan shops and from traders at various rallies and shows.

LOTS is the other society in the London area, which it covers in considerable detail in its monthly newsletter *The London Bus*. Further details from: LOTS, Unit N305, Westminster Business Square, 1-45 Durham Street, Vauxhall, London SE11 5JH or via the website: *www.lots.org.uk*

The PSV Circle reports monthly on the London bus scene via news sheets. A year's-worth costs £19.00 and you can start by visiting: *www.psv-circle. org.uk*

The Omnibus Society has a London Historical Research Group. Full details of this can be found at: *www.Omnibussoc.org*

While we're on the web, there are four other sites which are truly excellent.

The first - *www.londonbusroutes.net* - is a useful resource for the most recent/forthcoming changes.

The second - *www.londonbusesbyadam. zenfolio.com* - is a photo site with more than 13,000 images featuring every route in London.

The third is useful if you are looking for a certain bus - *www.londonvf.co.uk*. When you type in the fleet number, LVF will tell you exactly where it is or, if it's not running, when and where it last worked. You can also get a full listing of vehicles on an individual route or even the next half-hour's worth of arrivals at a particular bus stop. Among other features is a history option and a list of current all-over advertising with the relevant bus numbers.

The other very useful website shows where each bus is on a particular route. *http://traintimes.org. uk/map/london-buses*

Titan T1 at North Street garage during *London Bus Tour's* 'Day of the Titan' in March 2017. *Ken Carr*

The Operators

Photo: Ben Youngman

Go-Ahead remains the largest operator in the TfL area with more than 24% of the total peak vehicle requirement. Next is Metroline with an 18% share and Arriva also with 18%. The smallest companies are CT Plus, Quality Line and Sullivan Buses all with less than 1%, while Uno operate a solitary TfL route. Here are potted histories of the main companies, revealing the extent of worldwide financial interest in the running of London's buses:

Abellio is ultimately owned by the Nederlandse Spoorwegen of Holland, originally through its subsidiary NedRailways. In May 2009 the company bought Travel London (and the smaller Travel Surrey) from the National Express Group. Travel London came into being when NatEx bought the French-owned Connex Bus in 2004. A year later it bought Tellings-Golden Miller as well. After the most recent sale, the Travel London designation would have been retained but for NedRailways changing it to Abellio Group in October 2009.

Arriva's first involvement in London was in 1980 when the company was still known as Cowie, after the family who started the company in Sunderland in the 1930s. Cowie bought Grey-Green - basically a fast commuter coach service provider - in 1980. Seven years later, Grey-Green successfully tendered for some London routes. In 1994 the Cowie Group bought Leaside Buses, then the last LBL subsidiary, South London Transport. The group changed its name to Arriva in 1997. Further acquisitions followed

- Kentish Bus in 1997, County Bus in 1998 and London links in 1999. Arriva has the distinction of having been the first to operate the bendybus in London and the last to operate Routemasters in normal daily service (as opposed to heritage). You may have noticed from other London bus publications that Arriva the Shires and Arriva Southern Counties Group (and their bus fleets) are listed separately from Arriva London. This is because they are separate companies operating from different Head Offices. However, Arriva London are in the process of taking over their TfL operations. Legally this process hadn't been completed as we went to press. Therefore, for the last time they appear as separate operators in this edition of the Bus Guide. The company is owned by Deutsche Bahn.

Go-Ahead London is the generic name for all the group's bus operations in the capital. Based in Newcastle, the company's first London venture was the acquisition of London Buses Ltd subsidiary London Central in September 1994. Another former LBL subsidiary, London General, which had initially been a management buy-out, was added in May 1996. The development of both companies since then has been on parallel lines, but they continue to function with separate operating licences.

Metrobus has now been fully amalgamated into Go Ahead's London operation an no longer has its own entry in the Guide. Formed in 1983 from the wreckage of the Orpington & District bus company

collapse. The two garages running TfL routes – Orpington and Croydon – have had their operator licences consolidated under London General.

Go-Ahead had expanded its London operation further in September 2006 when London General bought Docklands Buses. Eight months later, the group acquired the contracted bus operations of Blue Triangle but BT's MD, Roger Wright, understandably retained ownership of the heritage fleet. The East Thames Buses brand was added in 2009, and to complete the present shape of Go-Ahead in London, there have been two separate acquisitions from First Group - Northumberland Park garage in 2012 and part of First's East London operation in 2013.

The Go-Ahead London logo first appeared in August 2008, although the lettering underneath distinguishes between London General, London Central, Docklands and Blue Triangle vehicles. This makes life slightly confusing when New Cross buses transfer to Merton garage.

London United was another LBL subsidiary subject to a management buy-out in 1994. Three years later, the French company Transdev bought it. Sovereign London was acquired in 2002 (re-named London Sovereign from 2004) via the convoluted route of Borehamwood Travel Services (original company name) Blazefield (whose Sovereign subsidiary bought BTS in 1994, whereupon the London tag was added) and Transdev, which bought the whole of Blazefield in 2006. In 2009 the Transdev Group began negotiations with Veolia Environnement with the aim of merging itself with Veolia Transport. In the resulting agreement, made in May 2010,

it was agreed that the RATP Group, which had a minority shareholding in Transdev, would assume ownership of some of Transdev's routes and assets in lieu of cash payment. This had a considerable impact on Transdev's London operations, splitting the company into two, very unequal parts.

London Sovereign's two garages and its routes remained with Transdev as part of the merged Veolia Transdev group, RATP got everything else, i.e. the eight garages of what was originally London United. The agreement took effect in March 2011 and the London United name re-emerged alongside much-reduced RATP Group branding. The small number of buses operating London Sovereign routes still defiantly proclaim themselves to be Transdev.

Now, RATP has acquired the remnants too and the company has renamed itself as RATP-Dev London.

Quality Line - In April 2012, RATP bought Epsom Coaches - a small, family-style firm which had moved into the bus market (rather than solely running coach tours) in the 1980s deregulation. It expanded into London routes in 1997. The bus operation was re-branded as Quality Line in 2003 and, since then, has gradually gained new contracts. The new acquisition operates as an independent division of RATP.

Metroline is another of the LBL companies from 1989, but acquired by the ComfortDelgro Group of Singapore in 2000. By then, Metroline had absorbed Atlas Bus (just after privatisation in 1994) London Northern and R&I Buses in 1998. ComfortDelgro has added Thorpes (2004) and Armchair (2005). 2013's partial purchase of the First Centrewest operation in west London has elevated Metroline to the third largest operator. Although the acquired vehicles have been renumbered in the new owner's series, the five garages operate as a separate entity - Metroline West.

The **Stagecoach** Company's interest in London began in 1994 when it bought LB's East London Bus & Coach Company and the South East London & Kent Bus Company (known as Selkent). Stagecoach pulled out of London in 2006, surprisingly, when it sold its entire operation to the Australian Macquarie

Many companies use withdrawn vehicles to train new drivers. In March 2017 Stagecoach applied this advert to its trainer 17396. *Daniel Neville*

All-over adverts continue to be applied to London's buses. This rather stunning advert appeared on five New Routemasters in 2016. *Peter Edgar*

Bank for £263 million. The new owners reintroduced the East London and Selkent fleetnames and in 2009 created Thameside for its Rainham-based buses. In an equally surprising move, Stagecoach re-acquired the whole lot in October 2010 for only £59 million, whereupon Stagecoach branding was rapidly reinstated.

Tower Transit was a new company formed in 2013 by Transit Systems for the express purpose of operating its partial acquisition of First London. Transit Systems is one of Australia's largest bus and ferry operators.

Hackney Community Transport was established in 1982 when thirty community groups in the London Borough of Hackney formed a pool of six vehicles with a grant from Hackney Borough Council, aimed at providing low cost van and minibus hire for those groups and a door-to-door alternative to public transport for the disabled. HCT gained its first TfL contract in 2001 to operate route 153 under the CT Plus brand. Further contracts followed in 2003. In July 2006 HCT merged with Lambeth and Southwark Community Transport, and in 2008 began running a bendybus service to and from the Olympics 2012 site for construction workers.

Sullivan Buses re-entered the fray in February 2012 after winning the contract for route 298. From September 2012, the company began running a handful of TfL school routes. The company was formed in 1999 and currently runs routes in Hertfordshire, as well as providing rail replacement services to TfL.

Uno operates bus routes in Hertfordshire as well as running the bus service to the University of Hertfordshire. In 2015 it won route 383, which it operates with a fleet of four Enviro200s.

Ensignbus also works rail replacements contracts. Until 1990, the company had some London routes but sold them to Citybus. After a brief return, this came to an end again in 1999.

Finally, a brief word about 'livery' - a much-misused term. Operators running TfL-contracted routes must now paint their buses all-red, apart from modestly-sized fleet names. So, the distinctive blue skirt of Metroline is gradually disappearing, as will the grey/yellow stripes of Go-Ahead's fleet, the 'grey sandwich' of Transdev and Arriva's horns. The white London bus roundel is appearing on the all-over red buses. Apart from that, the only other embellishment is the word 'Hybrid' in green on the latest diesel-electrics, replacing the shower of green leaves on the earlier examples and the claim that they were all the Mayor of London's doing.

In addition, TfL has now decreed that blinds must be lettered in white rather than yellow. This applies to all new vehicle deliveries and refurbishments, although in practice the white-on-blacks are appearing randomly, depending on local requirement or local whim.

Abellio

Abellio's fleet is predominantly made up of ADL (or its predecessors) types. They have thirty-one of the long Enviro200 MMCs for use on the C10 and E7. *Martin Ford*

Garages

QB	Battersea
BC	Beddington
TF	Fulwell
WS	Hayes
WL	Walworth

Fleet Total

717

Double-Deckers - 452
Single-Deckers - 265

PVR = 606

Head Office:
301 Camberwell New Road,
London, SE5 0TF

ROUTES OPERATED

3	49	109	156	159 ●24 hour	172	188 ●24 hour	201
211	290	322	343	344 ●24 hour	345	350	367
381	407	414	415	452	481	484	490
931	969	C2 ●24 hour	C3	C10	E1	E5	E7
E9	H20	H25	H26	H28	K1	K3	N3
N109	N343	N381	P13	R68	R70	S4	U7
U9							

Single-Deckers Operated

Dart - Nimbus
Dart - Pointer
Dart - Pointer 2
Dart SLF - Pointer 2
E20D - Enviro200 (E)
E20D - Enviro200 MMC (E)
E200 Dart - Enviro200

Abellio have eighty-six New Routemasters, all are based at Battersea and operate routes 3, 159 and 211. LT607 crosses the Thames on Westminster Bridge. *Keith Valla*

Double-Deckers Operated

B7TL - Eclipse Gemini
E40D - Enviro400 (E)
E40D - Enviro400 (Euro-6)
E40D - Enviro400 MMC (Euro-6)
E40H - Enviro400 (E)
E40H - Enviro400 (Euro-6)
E40H - Enviro400 MMC (Euro-6)
New Routemaster (LT)
Trident - ALX400
Trident - Enviro400

Arriva

Arriva have a fleet of nine electric Optare MetroCitys. They work route 312 and are based at Croydon garage. *Stephen Day*

Garages

AE	Ash Grove
DT	Dartford
DX	Barking
BN	Brixton
CT	Clapton
TC	Croydon
E	Enfield
EC	Edmonton
GR	Watford
GY	Grays
N	Norwood
AD	Palmers Green
SF	Stamford Hill
AR	Tottenham
TH	Thornton Heath
WN	Wood Green

Fleet Total

1749

Double-Deckers - 1460
Single-Deckers - 289

PVR = 1442

Head Offices:

North: 16 Watsons Road, Wood Green N22 7TZ

South: Bus Garage, Brighton Road, Croydon CR2 6EL

2	19	29	38	41	48	50	59
60	64	66	67	73	78	102 (24 hour)	121
123	128 (24 hour)	133	137	141	142	144	149 (24 hour)
150	157	160	166	173	176 (24 hour)	184	194
197	198	221	229	230	242 (24 hour)	243 (24 hour)	249
250 (24 hour)	253	254	255	258	259	264 (24 hour)	268
279	288	289	303	305	312	313	317
318	319	325	329	333	340	341 (24 hour)	347
349	368	370	375	377	382	393	403
410	412	417	428	450	466	469	492
612	627	631	640	642	673	678	685
690	B12	B13	B15	E10	H2	H3	H18
H19	N2	N19	N29	N38	N41	N73	N76
N133	N137	N253	N279	W3	W6		

Single-Deckers Operated

Dart - Pointer (PDL)
E20D - Enviro200 (E) (EN/ENS/ENX)
E20D - Enviro200 MMC (ENR)
E200 Dart - Enviro200 (EN/ENL/ENS)
MetroCity Electric (EMC)
Optare Solo (OS)
SB120 - Cadet (DWS)
Streetlite (SLS)

Double-Deckers Operated

B5LH - Eclipse Gemini 2 (HV)
B5LH - Eclipse Gemini 2 (E) (HV)
B5LH - Gemini 3 Street (HV)
B7TL - ALX400 (VLA)
B7TL - Eclipse Gemini (VLW)
DB250 - Pulsar Gemini (DW)
E40D - Enviro400 (E) (T)
E40D - Enviro400 (Euro-6) (T)
Enviro400H City (HA)
Gemini 2 DL (DW)
Gemini 2 DL (E) (DW)
Gemini 2 DL (Euro-6) (DW)
New Roumaster (LT)
Streetdeck Gemini 3 (SW)
Trident - Enviro400 (T)

A small batch of Streetdecks with the latest Gemini 3 bodies are allocated to Garston, primarily for use on route 340. No other London operator has gone for this combination.
Tommy Cooling

CT Plus

Hackney Community Transport's CT Plus are the second operator to use ADL's Enviro400H City. They have two batches to work routes 26 & 388. 2523 from the 388 batch, waits to work on route 26 at the stand in Hackney Wick. *Ken Carr*

Garages

| AW | Walthamstow |
| HK | Ash Grove |

Fleet Total

150

Double-Deckers - 46
Single-Deckers - 104

PVR = 120

Head Office:
Mare Street, South Hackney, London E8.

ROUTES OPERATED

26	153	309	385	388	394	397	675
N26	W5	W11	W12	W13	W16	W19	

Single-Deckers Operated

Dart - Nimbus (DCS)
E20D - Enviro200 (DA)
E20D - Enviro200 MMC
E200 Dart - Enviro200 (DA/DAS)
E200 Dart - Esteem (DE)
Optare Solo (OS)

Double-Deckers Operated

E40H - Enviro 400 (E) (HEA)
Enviro400H City
Enviro400 - Olympus (EO)
N230UD - OmniCity (SD)

CT Plus have nine 8.8 metre Optare Solos based at Ash Grove. Six are used on route W12. OS8 nears Walthamstow Bus Station with a service from Coppermill Lane. Ben Youngman

Go-Ahead

Garages

BV	Belvedere
BX	Bexleyheath
Q	Camberwell
C	Croydon
MW	Mandela Way
AL	Merton
NX	New Cross
NP	Northumberland Park
MB	Orpington
PM	Peckham
PL	Plough Lane
AF	Putney
BE	Rainham
SI	Silvertown
SW	Stockwell
A	Sutton
RA	Waterloo

Fleet Total

2389

Double-Deckers - 1664
Single-Deckers - 725

PVR = 1954

Head Office:
18 Merton High Street, London
SW19 1DN

ROUTES OPERATED

1	11	12 *24 hour*	14 *24 hour*	20	21	22	35
36 *24 hour*	37 *24 hour*	39	40	42	44	45	57
63	68	74	76	77	80	87	88 *24 hour*
89	93 *24 hour*	100	101	108 *24 hour*	118	119 *24 hour*	126
127	129	130	132 *24 hour*	135	147	151	152
154 *24 hour*	155	161	162	163	164	170	171
180	181	185	191	192	193	196	200
202	213 *24 hour*	219	225	231	233	244	246
257	270	276	280	284	286	293	299
300	315	320	321 *24 hour*	322	327	337	346
352	353	355	357	358	359	360	363
364	376	379	389	399	401	405	422
424	430	432	434	436	453 *24 hour*	455	464
468	474 *24 hour*	476	485	486 *24 hour*	491	493	507
521	573	574	608	616	624	625	639
646	648	649	650	651	652	654	655
656	657	658	661	663	667	669	670
674	675	679	686	B11	B14	B16	D6
D7	D8	EL1 *24 hour*	EL2	EL3	G1	N1	N11
N21	N22	N35	N44	N63	N64	N68	N74
N87	N89	N155	N171	P5	P12	R1	R2
R3	R4	R6	R8	R9	R11	W4	W10
X68							

Please Note: **Metrobus details have now been integrated into the Go-Ahead listings. Former Metrobus vehicles still carry three digit numbers but they are now treated as part of the overall Go-Ahead fleet.**

The Trident Olympus buses are split between Peckham and Sutton. DOE37 from the latter, runs along Trowley Way, Sutton on an outbound run to Kingston. *Ken Carr*

Single-Deckers Operated

Citaro (MEC)
Dart - Capital (DMN)
Dart - Esteem
Dart - Evolution (ED)
Dart - Pointer (DP/LDP)
Dart - Pointer 2 (LDP)
E20D - Enviro200 (SE/SEN)
E200 Dart - Enviro200 (SE/SEN)
E200 Dart - Esteem (SOE)
E200 Dart - Evolution (ED)
Electrocity (WHY)
Irizar 12e electric (Ei)
KY9E - ADL electric (SEe)
MAN 12.240NL - East Lancs
MAN 14.240NL - Enviro200
MAN 14.240NL - Evolution
N230UB OmniCity
N94UB - Esteem
Optare Solo (OS)
SB180 - Evolution (MDL)
Streetlite (WS)

Double-Deckers Operated

B5LH - Eclipse Gemini 2 (WHV)
B5LH - Eclipse Gemini 2 (E) (WHV)
B5LH - Enviro400 MMC (EHV)
B5LH - Evosetl (MHV)
B5LH - Gemini 3 Street (WHV)
B7TL - Eclipse Gemini (VWL/WVL)
B7TL - President (PVL)
B9TL - Enviro400 (VE)
B9TL - Eclipse Gemini 2 (WVL)
B9TL - Eclipse Gemini 2 (E) (WVL)
E40D - Enviro400 (E) (E)
E40H - Enviro400 (E) (EH)
E40H - Enviro400 MMC (EH)
Gemini 2 DL (WDL)
New Routemaster (LT)
N230UD OmniCity
N230UD OmniDekka
Trident - Enviro400 (E)
Trident - Enviro400H (EH)
Trident - Olympus (DOE)

The stand at Putney Heath is particularly good to see a number of types from the Go-Ahead fleet. One of their early Enviro400s, E34, takes a break with MCV Evoseti, MHV21, which is ten years younger.
Tony Saltwell

Metroline

In January 2017, Metroline took over route 235. A batch of twenty-one 10.9 metre Enviro200 MMCs are allocated to Brentford to work the route. *Tommy Cooling*

Garages

ON	Alperton
AH	Brentford
W	Cricklewood
EW	Edgware
G	Greenford
HD	Harrow Weald
HS	Hayes
HT	Holloway
KC	Kings Cross
PB	Potters Bar
UX	Uxbridge
PA	West Perivale
PV	Perivale East
AC	Willesden
WJ	Willesden Junction

Fleet Total

1741

Double-Deckers - 1301
Single-Deckers - 440

PVR = 1489

Head Office:
Hygeia House, 66 College Road,
Harrow, Middlesex, HA1 1BE

ROUTES OPERATED

4	6 (24 hour)	7	16	17	18	24 (24 hour)	32
34	43 (24 hour)	46	52 (24 hour)	79	83 (24 hour)	90	91
92	95	98	105 (24 hour)	107	112	113	114
117	125	134 (24 hour)	139 (24 hour)	140 (24 hour)	143	168	182
187	189 (24 hour)	190	195	204	206	207	209
210	214 (24 hour)	217	223	224	226	228	232
234	235	237	240	245	260	263	271 (24 hour)
274	282	295 (24 hour)	297 (24 hour)	302	326	307	324
326	331	332	384	390 (24 hour)	395	427	460
482	483	487	603	606	607	609	611
632	634	643	A10	C11	E2	E6	E8
H12	N5	N7	N16	N18	N20	N91	N98
N113	N207	U1	U2	U3	U4	U5	U10
W7	W8						

Single-Deckers Operated

Dart - Pointer (DLD)
Dart - Pointer 2 (DLD)
E20D - Enviro200 (E) (DE/DEL/DEM)
E20D - Enviro200 MMC (E) (DEL)
E200Dart - Enviro200 (DE/DEL/DES)
E200Dart - Evolution (DM)

Double-Deckers Operated

B5LH - Gemini 2 (E) (VWH)
B5LH - Gemini 3 (VWH)
B5LH - Gemini 3 Street (VWH)
B7TL - Gemini (VW)
B7TL - President (VP/VPL)
B9TL - Eclipse Gemini 2 (VW)
B9TL - Eclipse Gemini 2 (E) (VW)
E40D - Enviro400 (E) (TE)
E40H - Enviro400H (E) (TEH)
E40H - Enviro MMC (TEH)
K10 BYD Electric (BYD)
N230UD - Olympus (SEL)
N230UD OmniCity (SN)
New Routemaster (LT)
Trident - ALX400 (TA)
Trident - Enviro400 (TE)
Trident - Enviro400H (TEH)

Less than ten Trident/ALX400s remain operating for Metroline. TA642 waits time at Golders Green on route 210, they can also be found working the 32. If you want to see these, make it soon.
Ken Carr

Quality Line

On 15th April 2017 route X26 transfers to Go-Ahead. What will happen to the single-door Mercedes Citaros currently working the route is unclear. MCL12 heads through Croydon.
Mark Mcwalter

Garages

EB	Epsom

Fleet Total

96

Double-Deckers - 18
Single-Deckers - 78

PVR = 90

Head Office:
Blenheim Road, Longmead Est,
Epsom, Surrey KT19 9AF

ROUTES OPERATED

404	406	411	413	418	463	465	467
470	633	641	K5	S1	S3	X26	

Single-Deckers Operated

Citaro (MCL)
E200Dart - East Lancs (SD)
E200Dart - Enviro 200 (SD)
Optare MetroCity (MCD/OM)
Optare Solo (OS)
Optare Solo SR (OPL)
Optare Versa (OV)
Streetlite (WS)

Double-Deckers Operated

E40D - Enviro400 (DD
Enviro400 (DD)

Quality Line operate a fleet of thirteen Optare MetroCitys that are used on the S1 from Lavender Fields to Banstead. OM05 runs through the centre of Sutton being chased by Go-Ahead's SOE36. *Ken Carr*

RATP-Dev London

From the London United side of RATP-Dev, current fleet member SLE6, leads SP195 along Chiswick High Road. Both are being shadowed by former London United Olympian VA8. *Richard Stiles*

Garages

BT	Edgware
FW	Fulwell
SO	Harrow
AV	Hounslow
HH	Hounslow Heath
PK	Park Royal
S	Shepherd's Bush
V	Stamford Brook
TV	Tolworth
NC	Twickenham

Fleet Total

803

Double-Deckers - 634
Single-Deckers - 269

PVR = 686

Head Office:
Busways House, Wellington Road, Fulwell TW2 5NX

ROUTES OPERATED

9	10 (24 hour)	27 (24 hour)	33 (24 hour)	65 (24 hour)	71	72 (24 hour)	81
85	94 (24 hour)	110	111 (24 hour)	116	120	131	148 (24 hour)
183	203	216	220 (24 hour)	222	251	265	267
272	281 (24 hour)	283	285 (24 hour)	292	326	371	391
398	419	423	440	605	613	635	662
665	671	681	696	697	698	965	C1
E3	E11	H9	H10	H11	H13	H14	H17
H22	H32	H37 (24 hour)	H91	H98	K2	K4	N9

Single-Deckers Operated

Citaro (MCL)
Dart - Pointer (DPS)
Dart - Pointer 2 (DPS)
E20D - Enviro200 MMC (DE)
E200Dart - Enviro200 (DE/DLE/SDE)
E200Dart - Enviro200H (HDE)
Optare MetroCity Electric (OCE)
Optare Tempo (OT)
Optare Versa (OV)

Double-Deckers Operated

B5LH - Eclipse Gemini 2 (E) (VH)
B5LH - Gemini 3 (VH)
B5LH - Gemini 3 Street (VH)
B5LH - SRM (VHR)
B7TL - President (VLP)
B7TL - Vyking (VLE)
E40D - Enviro400 (E) (ADE)
E40H - Enviro400 (E) (ADH)
N94UD OmniCity (SP)
N94UD OmniDekka (SLE)
N230UD OmniCity (SP)
New Routemaster (LT)
Trident - ALX400 (TA/TLA)
Trident - Enviro400H (ADH)

Route 94 is operated by Enviro400 hybrids and newer B5LH Gemini 3s. One of the latter, VH45189, navigates Marble Arch on its way back out of town. *Martin Ford*

Stagecoach

Stagecoach have five Optare Versa's still operational. They can be found on either route 366 or 396.
Michael J. McClelland

Garages

BK	Barking
TB	Bromley
BW	Bow
TL	Catford
T	Leyton
PD	Plumstead
RM	Rainham
NS	Romford
WH	West Ham

Fleet Total

1301

Double-Deckers - 1057
Single-Deckers - 244

PVR = 1101

Head Office:
Stephenson Street, Canning
Town E16 4SA.

ROUTES OPERATED

5	8	15	15H	47	51	53 🕐24 hour	54
55	56	61	62	75	86	96	97
99	103	104	115	122	124	136	145
146	158	165	167	169	174	175	177
178	179	199	205 🕐24 hour	208	215	227	238 🕐24 hour
241	247	248	252	256	261	262	269
273	275	277 🕐24 hour	287	291	294	296	314
323	330	336	354	356	362	365 🕐24 hour	366
372	380	386	396	462	472 🕐24 hour	473	496
498	473	549	588	601	602	621	636
637	638	664	672	677	687	D3	N8
N15	N47	N55	N86	N136	N199	P4	R5
R7	R10						

Single-Deckers Operated

Citaro
Dart - Pointer
E20D - Enviro200 (E)
E20D - Enviro200 MMC (E)
E200 Dart - Enviro200
Optare Versa

Double-Deckers Operated

B5LH - Enviro400 MMC
B5LH - Gemini 3
E40D - Enviro400 (E)
E40D - Enviro400 MMC
E40H - Enviro400H (E)
E40H - Enviro400 MMC
N230UD OmniCity
New Routemaster
Routemaster
Trident - ALX400
Trident - Enviro400

13004 rounds St George's Circus. It is one of thirty-one B5LH/Gemini 3s based at Plumstead. Although when new in 2014 these were allocated to route 53, they are now more likely to be found on the garage's other routes. *Peter Horrex*

Sullivan Buses

Garages

SM   **South Mimms**

Sullivan Buses have retained route 298. They have six Enviro200s to work this route. In early 2017, the company also started to work route W9, eight Enviro200 MMCs were bought to operate it. AE15 works the 298 at Cockfosters. *Peter Horrex*

Fleet Total

42

Double-Deckers - 28
Single-Deckers - 14

PVR = 36

Head Office:
First Floor, Deards House, St Albans Road, South Mimms Service Area, EN6 3NE

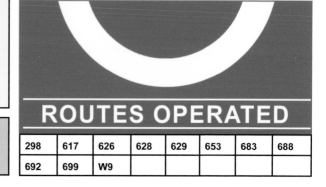

ROUTES OPERATED

298	617	626	628	629	653	683	688
692	699	W9					

Single-Deckers Operated
E20D - Enviro200 (E) (AE)
E20D - Enviro200 MMC (AE)

A PVR increase on the 298 has led to Sullivan's double-deckers making regular appearances on the route. WVL3 heads south at Cockfosters. Later in 2017, the company will start operating route 217. Twelve Enviro400 MMCs are on order for this contract. *Ken Carr*

Double-Deckers Operated
B7TL - Gemini (WVL)
B7TL - Vyking (ELV)
N230UD OmniCity (DS)
Trident - ALX400 (ALX)
Trident - Enviro400 (E)
Trident - President (PDL/TPL)

Tower Transit

Tower Transit are the second operator to go with the B5LH/Evoseti combination. These are for route 82 (to be renumbered as 13). Prior to the start of the contract, early arrivals were put out on route 23. A brand new MV38203 is on diversion at Marble Arch on 11th March 2017. *Martin Ford*

Garages

AS	Atlas Road
LI	Lea Interchange
X	Westbourne Park

Fleet Total

491

Double-Deckers - 372
Single-Deckers - 119

PVR = 386

Head Office:
Great Western Road, London,
W9 3NW.

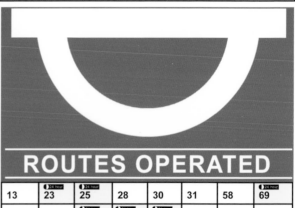

ROUTES OPERATED

13	23 *24 hour*	25 *24 hour*	28	30	31	58	69 *24 hour*
70	212	236 *24 hour*	266 *24 hour*	295 *24 hour*	308	328	339
425	444	488	N28	N31	N97	N550	N551
RV1	W14	W15					

Single-Deckers Operated

E200Dart - Enviro200 (DM/DML)
E20D - Enviro200 (E) (DM/DML/DMV)
SB200 - Pulsar 2 Hydrogen (WSH)
Streetlite (WL/WV)

Double-Deckers Operated

B5LH - Evoseti (MV)
B5LH - Gemini 3 (VH)
B5LH - Gemini 3 Street (VH)
B7TL - Eclipse Gemini (VNW)
B9TL - Eclipse Gemini 2 (VN)
B9TL - Eclipse Gemini 2 (E) (VN)
E40D - Enviro400 (E) (DN)
E40H - Enviro400 (E) (DNH)
E40E - Enviro400 MMC VE (DH)
Gemini 2 DL (WN)
Trident - Enviro400 (DN)

Tower Transit has forty-four of the original Enviro400. These were ordered for routes 26 & 30 in 2011. Having lost route 26, these buses cascaded onto other routes, one of which is the 308. DN33614 departs Stratford Bus Station. *Michael J. McClelland*

UNO

London's smallest operator is Uno. They have four Enviro200s to service the PVR of 3 on route 283. 603 picks-up in Barnet. *Michael J. McClelland*

Garages

HA   Hatfield

Fleet Total

4

Double-Deckers - 0
Single-Deckers - 3

PVR = 3

Head Office:
Gypsy Moth Avenue, Hatfield
Business Park, Hatfield,
Hertfordshire

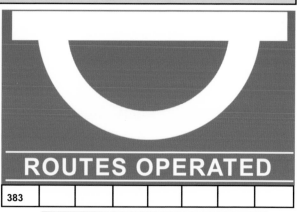

ROUTES OPERATED

383								

Single-Deckers Operated

E20D - Enviro200

The Buses

This section looks at the different types of buses you will find on TfL routes - single-deckers first, then double-deckers. For each type we include details of builder, build dates, operators and the routes on which they can be found. However, this is not an exact science. Some garages vary the types they put out on some routes (or do it on all routes!), while others stick religiously to the type nominated in the contract. It goes without saying that failures and non-availability often conspire to produce other interesting workings.

Since October 2011, all European-manufactured vehicles, including buses, have been built to the ECWVTA (European Community Whole Vehicle Type Approval) specification. These 'whole vehicle' models differ considerably from those that went before and they are listed separately in the Guide. As mentioned earlier, the latest vehicles from Alexander Dennis, Wrightbus and other UK manufacturers also have Euro 6-compliant engines.

London Buses insists that double-deckers (and most single-deckers) have at least two sets of doors, fire suppression systems, environmentally-friendly exhaust traps and double-deckers must also have top deck climate control.

Older types continue to be phased out, while Darts, early Volvos and early Tridents are currently suffering a severe cull.

When an operator orders a new bus, there are numerous choices to make - what type of chassis, with which engine, what type of axles, which body, seat configuration, style of décor, to name but a few. Some manufacturers offer ready-made packages but it is perfectly possible to create a fully custom bus. If you've ever ordered a new car from scratch, rather than buying a vehicle already in the dealer's stock, you'll understand how this process works.

Some manufacturers, such as Alexander Dennis Ltd, produce both chassis and body. They can either be supplied together (often referred to as an 'integral bus') or the body can be fitted to a chassis built by another maker (and, in ADL's case, vice versa).

Others concentrate on one or the other. Volvo produces only a range of chassis for the bus market

The Chinese company BYD have entered into partnership with ADL, to produce a fleet of single-deck electrics. Fifty-one are already in service from Waterloo garage. More are on order for route 360, which should receive them before the end of 2017. *Martin Ford*

while Wrightbus, which had previously concentrated on bodywork, now has a chassis plant too, for its NRM, StreetLite and StreetDeck models.

Optare has been able to supply both chassis and body for single-deckers for the past three years but, until now, has relied on other manufacturers' chassis to support its double-deck bodies. Now, there is a complete double-decker, which is on trial with Go-Ahead but there have been no reports of orders yet from London operators.

2014 saw upgrades to both the Wrightbus Gemini and the ADL Enviro400. 2015 saw further developments. The Gemini 3 now has the Streetdeck style front end, The Enviro400 MMCs (short for Major Model Change) are now available on the Volvo B5LH chassis. A further development was the introduction at the end of 2015 of the Enviro400H City, which features many similar fittings as the NRM.

In 2016, Wrightbus launched the SRM a two-door, single staircase version of the NRM, but available on the Volvo B5LH chassis. RATP Dev London have six and these entered service at the end of 2016.

Volvo have also teamed up with Egyptian manufacturer MCV, the result is the B5LH Evoseti.

The other double-decker currently available is the Wrightbus NRM, or LT type. Over 950 are now in service, with another 50 due this year.

Of the two major suppliers, Alexander Dennis has the greater presence, thanks to the ubiquitous Enviro200 single-decker and the highly-successful Enviro400. However, competition is fierce and the once clear-cut pattern of new vehicle orders is complicated by the 'parachuting' of the LT type onto routes which are not due for contract renewal.

The big change in the single-deck market has been the introduction of the Enviro200 MMC and the fleet of BYD electrics with ADL bodies. An electric bus from Wrightbus is also due very soon in London.

There is a requirement for 300 electric single-deckers in London by 2020, so all the manufacturers are trying to gain a share.

Optare has built nine of its new MetroCity model as fully-electric vehicles and they are with Arriva working route 312, the first to be nominally to be fully operated by electric buses.

A restyled Mercedes Citaro also entered service with Go-Ahead in 2015 and a short version is also now in service.

Despite the addition of new models to the ranges of Wrightbus and Optare, the ADL Enviro200 remains the single-decker of choice for most operators.

2017 will see the completion of the order for the New Routemaster. In February 2016 road closures around the Westminster area resulted to services being terminated on Lambeth Palace Road. *Richard Stiles*

Single-Deckers

Dart SLF / Pointer 8.9m

The remaining six short Darts are still hanging on, all are based at Orpington and can be found on the various single-deck routes, although nominally they are for route R4. *Stephen Day*

Built by: **Transbus**
Operators (routes): **Go-Ahead (R4)**

Introduced: **2004**

Number: **6**

Dart SLF / Pointer 9.3m

The two remaining buses moved from Grays to Thornton Heath in January 2017 and can now be found on route 410. Prior to its move PDL96 picks up at Romford Station. *Thomas Drake*

Built by: **Transbus**
Operators (routes): **Arriva (410)**

Introduced: **2004-2005**

Number: **2**

Dart / Caetano Nimbus 8.9m

CT Plus's short Dart Caetanos are living on borrowed time and could well be withdrawn by the end of April 2017 as CT have retained the contract with new buses. DCS5 shortly after leaving Homerton Hospital in August 2016. *Ben Youngman*

Built by: **TransBus/Caetano**   Introduced: **2003**   Number: **9**
Operators (routes): **CT Plus (394)**

Dart / Caetano Nimbus 10.5m

Another type which is living on borrowed time, the loss to Go-Ahead of route 455 in March 2017 has reduced the numbers further since last year. 8497 heads for Purley in West Croydon. *Mark Mcwalter*

Built by: **TransBus/Caetano, ADL/Caetano**   Introduced: **2001-2005**   Number: **17**
Operators (routes): Abellio **(455, 490, H25)**

Dart / East Lancs Esteem 9.0m

Only four of these Esteem's are left running. The loss of route 336 to Stagecoach in August 2016, started the cull. The survivors are spread across three depots, Bexleyheath, Orpington & Stockwell. In February 2017, 230 was being used on route 170, it departs Putney Heath. *Tony Saltwell*

Built by: **ADL/East Lancs**   Introduced: **2006**   Number: **4**
Operators (routes): **Go-Ahead (379, B14)**

Dart / Marshall Capital 8.9m

The main route to find the elderly short Marshalls operating on, is the 193. There is also usually one each on routes W4 & W10. DMN13 is about to cross Upminster Road in Hornchurch. *Ben Youngman*

Built by: **TransBus/Marshall**   Introduced: **2002**   Number: **13**
Operators (routes): **Go-Ahead (193)**

Dart / MCV Evolution 9.2m

Following Go-Ahead's loss of route W19 in November 2016, four of the Evolutions have moved to Silvertown to work route 300, those remaining at River Road garage can be found on routes 193 & 462. ED10 passes Wanstead Flats last summer. *Ben Youngman*

Built by: **ADL/MCV**   Introduced: **2006**   Number: **9**
Operators (routes): **Go-Ahead (193, 300, 462)**

Dart / Pointer 8.8m

The numbers of this type are dwindling fast, with more due to be withdrawn in 2017. LDP283 shown at Putney Heath is one of six based at Go-Ahead's Putney garage and they will probably last until April 2018, when the route comes up for tender. *Keith Valla*

Built by: **TransBus, ADL**   Introduced: **2003 - 2006**   Number: **21**
Operators (routes): **Abellio (290, E7, K1), Arriva (318, 377), Go-Ahead (424, 464, G1, R1, R3, R4, W4), Stagecoach (291, P4)**

Dart / Pointer 9.3m

Another under fire type, later in 2017, Thornton Heath's allocation of 23, will be probably withdrawn, leaving Arriva with just ten examples at Enfield, which should survive into 2018. *Michael J. McClelland*

Built by: **TransBus, ADL**   Introduced: **2003-2006**   Number: **42**
Operators (routes): **Arriva (166, 410, W6), Stagecoach (291, 386)**

Dart / Pointer 10.1m

A batch of Go-Ahead's 10.1 metre Darts have had their London working life extended due to modifications to reduce emissions. This should see them trough to the end of 2017, at least. One of the 'green ones', LDP254 heads through Brixton in January 2017. *Ken Carr*

Built by: **TransBus, ADL**   Introduced: **2002-2006**   Number: **94**
Operators (routes): **Abellio (490, H28, R68), Arriva (166, 303, 305), Go-Ahead (181, 225, 355, 485, B11, P5, P12), RATP-Dev (72, 216, H22) Metroline (90, 395), Stagecoach (178, 380, P4)**

Dart / Pointer 10.7m

There are twelve 2003-built Pointers at Stockwell for the 170, but they're unlikely to survive the next contract change in December 2017. DP194 on the route's Victoria stand. *David Maxey*

Built by: **TransBus** Introduced: **2003-2004** Number: **22**
Operators (routes): **Go-Ahead (130, 170, 355)**

Dart / Pointer 2 9.3m

Before Go-Ahead took over the contract, Abellio deployed vehicles from this small batch on route 100. 8303, in Moorgate, can still be found working from Walworth depot, but most likely on the 484. *David Maxey*

Built by: **ADL** Introduced: **2004** Number: **1**
Operators (routes): **Abellio (484)**

Dart / Pointer 2 10.1m

The Dart Pointer 2s are still hanging on with their various operators, but it is expected a number will be withdrawn during 2017. *Ken Carr*

Built by: **TransBus, ADL**   Introduced: **1997-2004/06**   Number: **72**
Operators (routes): **Abellio (H25), RATP-Dev (72, 110, 216, 272, 419, C1, H9, H10, H37, H98, K2), Metroline (46, 214, 274)**

Dart / Pointer 2 10.7m

The surviving 10.7 metre Pointer 2 in Go-Ahead's fleet continues to work route 170 alongside the earlier Pointers. DP209 descends St John's Hill on the approach to Clapham Junction. *David Maxey*

Built by: **ADL**   Introduced: **2006**   Number: **1**
Operators (routes): **Go-Ahead (170)**

E200 Dart / Enviro200 8.9m

The single-door, 8.9 metre, Enviro200 has proved popular with most operators. They can mainly be found operating around the outskirts of London. Catford's 36322 departs Lower Sydenham. *Robert Mighton*

Built: **ADL**   Introduced: **2006-11**   Number: **92**
Operators (routes): **Abellio (H25, R68), Arriva (318, 382), CT Plus (394), Go-Ahead (138, 162, 192, 233, B14, P5, R1, R3, R11, W4), RATP-Dev (440, E11, K4), Metroline (384), Quality Ilne (S3), Stagecoach (124, 273, 354, 356, P4)**

E200 Dart / Enviro200 9.3m

The next sized Enviro200 is the least common in London. Tower Transit have just four, they can be found on route 339 and W14. DM44168 heads along Penny Brookes Street in Stratford on the former. *Mark Mcwalter*

Built: **ADL**   Introduced: **2007-2011**   Number: **68**
Operators (routes): **Abellio (484, P13, S4), Arriva (393), Go-Ahead (100, P5), Stagecoach (291, 386), Tower Transit (339, W14, W15)**

E200 Dart / Enviro200 10.2m

The vast majority of the original Enviro200s are the 10.2 metre versions. You will see them all over London. DE1686 was one of 175 of the type Metroline acquired when purchasing First in 2013. *Ken Carr*

Built: **ADL**   Introduced: **2007-2011**   Number: **730**
Operators (routes): **Abellio (152, 201, 235, 290, 350, 407, 433, 455, 481, 490, C10, H28, K3, R68, R70, U7), Arriva (166, 184, 255, 268, 289, 303, 312, 325, 347, 375, 393, 428, 469, B12, B15, H18, H19), Go-Ahead (130, 163, 164, 170, 200, 244, 300, B11, B16), RATP-Dev (33, 72, 216, 265, 283, 326, 371, 391, 398, 440, C1, H9, H10, H11, H13, H14, H17, H22, K2), Metroline (46, 90, 95, 112, 117, 143, 187, 190, 195, 206, 224, 228, 209, 214, 226, 232, 274, 316, 324, 395, 487, A10, C11, E6, U1, U3, U5), Stagecoach (167, 296, 323, 366, 380, 396, 499, D3, P4), Tower Transit (W15)**

E200 Dart / Enviro200 10.8m

The longest version was introduced in 2007. Stagecoach has a batch of twelve, all are based at Catford and are used on a variety of the garage's routes. *Mark Mcwalter*

Built: **ADL**   Introduced: **2007-2011**   Number: **123**
Operators (routes): **Arriva (428, 469, B12), Go-Ahead (80, 170, 244, 276, 364, 376, D6), RATP-Dev (391, 423, H37, H98), Stagecoach (178, 380, P4)**

E200 Dart / Enviro200 Hybrid 10.2m

A batch of five hybrid Enviro200s are operated by London United from Fulwell garage. They can usually be found on route 371 working alongside a fascinating mix of buses. *Ken Carr*

Built: **ADL** Introduced: **2009** Number: **5**
Operators (routes): **London United (371)**

E200 Dart / East Lancs 9.0m

SD52, here working the S3 in North Cheam, is one of a pair of similar type on Quality Line's books. They can appear on any of the Epsom routes, but the S3 is their 'regular'. *David Maxey*

Built: **ADL/East Lancs** Introduced: **2007** Number: **2**
Operators (routes): **Quality Line (S3)**

E200 Dart / East Lancs Esteem 10.4m

Go-Ahead's fleet of forty are split between three garages. Merton has twenty-five, Sutton has ten and there are five at River Road. *Stephen Day*

Built: **ADL/East Lancs & Optare**   Introduced: **2007 & 2009**   Number: **40**
Operators (routes): **Go-Ahead (80, 152, 163, 200, 219, 346, 376, 455)**

E200 Dart / MCV Evolution 10.4m

Route 167 was taken over by Stagecoach in March 2017. The future of Go-Ahead's ten Evolution's is not clear as we went to press. They may have already been consigned to history. ED27 closes in on Ilford at Valentines Park in August 2016. *Ben Youngman*

Built: **ADL/MCV**   Introduced: **2007-2009**   Number: **20**
Operators (routes): **Go-Ahead (300), Metroline (190)**

E20D /Enviro200 8.9m

After improvements to the chassis, an updated version of the Enviro200 started to be introduced from 2011. This model is still available to buy in 2017, although most operators are choosing the newer MMC version. The smallest operator in London is Uno, they have four of the short version for use on their single route. The last of the batch, 604, heads away from New Barnet. *Mark Mcwalter*

Built: **ADL**   Introduced:**2011-2014**   Number: **123**
Operators (routes): **Abellio (K1, S4), Arriva (377, E10), Go-Ahead (138, 162, 233, 322, 352, 424, 434, G1, R1, R2, R4, R6, R11), Quality Line (S3), Stagecoach (124, 314, 336, 354, 356), Uno (383)**

E20D / Enviro200 9.6m

The newest of the 'classic' style Enviro200s entered service in November 2016 with CT Plus. Eighteen have been based at the their new Walthamstow garage primarily for working route W19. *Mark Mcwalter*

Built: **ADL**   Introduced: **2011-2016**   Number: **113**
Operators (routes): **Arriva (410, W6), CT Plus (W19), Go-Ahead (100, 299, 346, R11, W16), Metroline (223, 224, 234, 384), Stagecoach (386), Tower Transit (339, W14, W15)**

E20D / Enviro200 10.2m

Sullivan buses have six of this type for use on route 298. Note the reg, a nice touch by owner Dean Sullivan. The last three letters are the same on all six buses (SUL), the first two are the initials of various members of the Sullivan's team. *Peter Horrex*

Built: **ADL**   Introduced: **2012-2013**   Number: **148**

Operators (routes): **Abellio (290, 490, H28, R68), Go-Ahead (152, 181, 200, 286, 455, 493 P12), Metroline (46, 214, 223, 224, 274, 487), Stagecoach (227, 314), Sullivans (298), Tower Transit (70, W15)**

E20D / Enviro200 10.8m

The longer version has become more popular in recent years. Arriva were the first to take these. ENX8 is one of eight based at Enfield to work route 313. *Peter Horrex*

Built: **ADL**   Introduced: **2011-2015**   Number: **246**

Operators (routes): **Abellio (201, 407, 433, 490, K3, R70), Arriva (289, 313), CT Plus (153), Go-Ahead (39, 80, 126, 163, 164, 181, 246, 284, 286, R9), RATP-Dev (H13), Metroline (112, 206, 316, 331, A10, U2), Stagecoach (165, 256,366, 396), Tower Transit (236, 488, RV1, W14)**

E20D /Enviro200 MMC 9.0m

ADL launched their MMC model in 2015. It uses the E20D chassis with a new style of body. The shortest version available is the 9 metre. Abellio where the first to get these, 8210 picks-up outside The Mall in Bromley High Street. *Mark Mcwalter*

Built: **ADL**   Introduced: **2016**   Number: **70**
Operators (routes): **Abellio (367, 481, E5, H20, H26, U9), Arriva (377), Stagecoach (273, 336, 462)**

E20D /Enviro200 MMC 9.3m

Arriva have seven of the next size up which is also single-door. Based at Dartford they are used on route B13. ENR7 takes time out at Bexleyheath bus station. *Stephen Day*

Built: **ADL**   Introduced: **2016**   Number: **21**
Operators (routes): **Arriva (393, B13)**

E20D /Enviro200 MMC 9.7m

Go-Ahead have two 9.7 metre MMCs for use on the P5. SE291 picks-up in Stockwell. Early 2017 has seen more of this variant entering service with CT Plus. *Thomas Drake*

Built: **ADL** Introduced: **2016** Number: **49**
Operators (routes): **Abellio (P13), CT Plus (309, 397, W11, W16, W19), Go-Ahead (360, P5), Sullivans (W9)**

E20D /Enviro200 MMC 10.9m

The longest MMC is the 10.9 metre version. Abellio's 8861 makes the right turn at Borough station whilst working on route C10. *Ben Youngman*

Built: **ADL** Introduced:**2015-2016** Number: **100**
Operators (routes): **Abellio (C10, E7), Metroline (235, 331, A10, U2, U3), RATP-Dev (265), Stagecoach (362, 499)**

MAN 12.240NL / East Lancs 10.3m

All five of these are based at Orpington and normally work R2. However, they do make appearances on other routes from the garage. 702 pauses in Orpington High Street. *Stephen Day*

Built: **MAN/East Lancs**
Operators (routes): **Go-Ahead (181, 284, R2)**
Introduced: **2007**
Number: **5**

MAN 14.240NL / Enviro200 10.7m

Another small batch is the three MAN powered Enviro200s. These are normally used on route 130. 708 arrives at Crystal Palace on the now double-decked route 202. *Michael J. Mclelland*

Built: **MAN/ADL**
Operators (routes): **Go-Ahead (130)**
Introduced: **2008**
Number: **3**

MAN 14.240NL / MCV Evolution 10.8m

Another type solely used by the Metrobus division of Go-Ahead. Only eight remain and they are split between Croydon & Orpington garages. 712 is based at the former. *Michael J. Mclelland*

Built: **MAN/MCV**   Introduced: **2009**   Number: **8**
Operators (routes): **Go-Ahead (130, 246, 359)**

Mercedes Citaro 12m [single door]

A batch of ten single-door Mercedez were orderd by Quality line for use on the X26 five years ago. However, the route has been won by Go-Ahead from mid-April 2017, so what they will do next remains to be seen. MCl12 arrives at hatton Cross. *Mark Mcwalter*

Built: **Mercedes-Benz**   Introduced: **2012**   Number: **10**
Operators (routes): **Quality Line (X26)**

Mercedes Citaro 12m [dual door]

The number of dual-door Mercedes has reduced since routes 507/521 went over to electric operation. Go-Ahead have refurbished some of the fleet which are now operating on route 108. Others have been to operations outside of London. Stagecoach's fleet continue to work on route 227. *Mark Mcwalter*

Built: **Mercedes-Benz** Introduced: **2009-2012** Number: **40**
Operators (routes): **Go-Ahead (108), RATP-Dev (203, H37), Stagecoach (227)**

Mercedes Citaro 10.8m New Style [dual door]

In December 2016, Quality Line introduced nine 'Baby Mercs' on route 413. MCS03 arrives in Morden on its second day in service on 4th December. *Brian Kemp*

Built: **Mercedes-Benz** Introduced: **2016** Number: **10**
Operators (routes): **Quality Line (413)**

Mercedes Citaro 12m New Style [dual door]

The standard length re-styled Mercs entered service in 2015. Go-Ahead have a fleet of nineteen which are used on route 358. MEC60 departs Crystal Palace. *Brian Kemp*

Built: **Mercedes-Benz**   Introduced: **2015**   Number: **19**
Operators (routes): **Go-Ahead (358)**

Optare MetroCity MC990 9.9m

Quality Line are the sole operator of Optare MetroCity, they have thirteen to work route S1. OM03 runs through Sutton. *Stephen Day*

Built: **Optare**   Introduced: **2014**   Number: **13**
Operators (routes): **Quality Line (S1, 465)**

Optare MetroCity MC1060 10.6m

Quality Line also have a single longer MetroCity, OC1. It tends to alternate between routes 411 & 465. It passes Kingston station working the former. *Brian Kemp*

Built: **Optare**   Introduced: **2014**   Number: **1**
Operators (routes): **Quality Line (411, 465)**

Optare Solo 7.8m

Arriva's short Solo's have all now been renumbered into the main arriva numbering scheme. OS69 (the former 2469) arrives at Golders Green on the H2. *Ken Carr*

Built: **Optare**   Introduced: **2006**   Number: **5**
Operators (routes): **Arriva the Shires (H2, H3)**

Optare Solo 8.8m

CT Plus have nine of these primarily for route W5, they now no longer appear on route 385 as it is operated from CT's new garage at Walthamstow. *Mark Mcwalter*

Built: **Optare**   Introduced: **2009 & 2011**   Number: **20**
Operators (routes): **CT Plus (385, 394, W5), Quality Line (K5, S1)**

Optare Solo 9.6m

A batch of nine of this type were ordered for CT Plus's route 309. OS24 arrives at Canning Town. *Mark Mcwalter*

Built: **Optare**   Introduced: **2012**   Number: **9**
Operators (routes): **CT Plus (309)**

Optare Solo SE 7.1m

Still remaining the shortest buses in London are the pair of SE's based at Orpington. 101 passes the garage heading for the lanes to Biggin Hill. *Ken Carr*

Built: **Optare**   Introduced: **2006**   Number: **2**
Operators (routes): **Go-Ahead (R8)**

Optare Solo SE 7.8m

CT Plus's SE's for route W12 have been joined by an extra bus (an Enviro200 MMC) to cover a PVR increase. OS5 comes off the roundabout at Whipps Cross. *Ben Youngman*

Built: **Optare**   Introduced: **2010**   Number: **7**
Operators (routes): **CT Plus (W5, W12)**

Optare Solo SR 9.0m

The solitary 9 metre Solo SR, Quality Line's OP34, normally works on route 404. Here, it passes through Coulsdon. *Brian Kemp*

Built: **Optare**   Introduced: **2013**   Number: **1**
Operators (routes): **Quality Line (404)**

Optare Solo SR 9.7m

Quality Line also have a small batch of 9.7 metre SRs, which operate route 470. OPL01 picks-up at Morden station. *Peter Horrex*

Built: **Optare**   Introduced: **2012**   Number: **8**
Operators (routes): **Quality Line (470)**

Optare Tempo 12.0m

The Hounslow based Tempos continue to operate on routes 203 & H37. OT7 runs through Richmond on the latter. *Ben Youngman*

Built: **Optare**   Introduced: **2011**   Number: **16**
Operators (routes): **London United (203, H37)**

Optare Versa 10.4m

RATP's Versas work routes 283 & 391. Those for the 391, such as OV3 above, are based at Fulwell. It heads through Richmond before taking up its day's work. *Ben Youngman*

Built: **Optare**   Introduced **2008 & 09**   Number: **41**
Operators (routes): **London United (33, 283, 391), Stagecoach (366, 396)**

Optare Versa 11.1m

Quality Line's long Versas spend their time between routes 411 & 465. OV04 runs through Kingston either to or from West Molesey on the 411.. *Paul Godding*

Built: **Optare**
Operators (routes): **Quality Line (411, 465)**

Introduced: **2010 & 2012**

Number: **13**

Scania N94UB / East Lancs Esteem 10.6m

613 stops in Lewisham on its regular route. These Scanias should be around for at least another year. In March 2016, Go-Ahead gained a two year extension to the route 181 contract. *Mark Mcwalter*

Built: **Scania/East Lancs**
Operators (routes): **Go-Ahead (181, 284)**

Introduced: **2006**

Number: **14**

Scania N230UB OmniCity 12.0m

Seven OmniCitys are still in service, normally you will find them on route 293. Appearances on route 358 are now just a distant memory. 565 awaits departure at The Glades in Bromley. *Mark Mcwalter*

Built: **Scania/East Lancs**   Introduced: **2008**   Number: **7**
Operators (routes): **Go-Ahead (293)**

VDL/DAF SB120 / Wrightbus Cadet 10.2m

The DWLs are still hanging on with Arriva. However nearly two-thirds have been withdrawn over the last year, so you would think the remaining examples are living on borrowed time. *Mark Mcwalter*

Built: **VDL/Wrightbus**   Introduced: **2001 - 2006**   Number: **10**
Operators (routes): **Arriva (288, 303, H18)**

VDL/DAF SB180 / MCV Evolution 10.3m

The single Evolution was displaced from route 549 in March 2017. MDL1 awaits departure from Loughton on its first day on the 549 in October 2016. *Thomas Drake*

Built: **VDL/MCV**   Introduced: **2010**   Number: **1**
Operators (routes): **Go-Ahead ()**

Wrightbus Electrocity 10.4m

The Elecrocitys will more than likely be displaced from route 360 by the end of 2017. The route is the next to receive 100% electric buses. *Mark Mcwalter*

Built: **Wrightbus**   Introduced: **2005 & 2006**   Number: **6**
Operators (routes): **Go-Ahead (360)**

Wrightbus Electrocity 10.3m

WHY7 was the first of the slightly shorter Electrocitys, these will also be displaced by BYD/ADL electrics later this year. *Peter Horrex*

Built: **Wrightbus** Introduced: **2008 & 2011** Number: **7**
Operators (routes): **Go-Ahead (360)**

Wrightbus StreetLite WF 8.8m

Prior to transfer from Go-Ahead to Quality Line in 2016, WS33 heads through Edmonton. This bus is now numbered WS01. *Paul Godding*

Built: **Wrightbus** Introduced: **2012 & 2014** Number:**36**
Operators (routes): **Go-Ahead (192), Quality LIne (463, K5)**

Wrightbus StreetLite DF 9.7m

Arriva ordered a batch of twenty-two 'door forward' StreetLites for the contract renewal of route 450 in October 2016, allocated to Norwood garage rather than Thornton Heath. SLS3 & 4 at West Croydon bus station. *David Maxey*

Built: **Wrightbus**
Operators (routes): **Arriva (450)**

Introduced: **2016**

Number: **22**

Wrightbus StreetLite DF 10.2m

In 2013, Go-Ahead chose the 10.2 metre version for working route 491. WS27 is one of twelve allocated to Northumberland Park for the 491 it takes a breather at Waltham Cross. *Peter Horrex*

Built: **Wrightbus**
Operators (routes): **Go-Ahead (491), Tower Transit (444)**

Introduced: **2012 & 2013**

Number: **13**

Wrightbus StreetLite DF 10.4m

Go-Ahead currently have a 10.4 metre demonstrator in their fleet. It is based at Camberwell and can usually be found on route 360 or P5. Here it passes through Stockwell. *Thomas Drake*

Built: **Wrightbus**　　　　　　　　　　Introduced: **2016**　　　　　　　　　　Number: **1**
Operators (routes): **Go-Ahead (360, P5)**

Wrightbus StreetLite DF 10.8m

Go-Ahead have a batch of eleven of these for use on route 219, they are based at Merton, which is where WS18 is captured taking a breather from its daily chores. *Ken Carr*

Built: **Wrightbus**　　　　　　　　　　Introduced: **2013**　　　　　　　　　　Number: **11**
Operators (routes): **Go-Ahead (219)**

Wrightbus StreetLite DF [Euro-6] 10.8m

Tower Transit also have a batch of eleven 10.8 metre Streetlites, having been bought two years later these are built to Euro-6 spec. WV4601 heads through Chingford Mount on its regular 444 duties. *Mark Mcwalter*

Built: **Wrightbus** Introduced: **2015** Number: **11**
Operators (routes): **Tower Transit (444)**

BYD K9E Electric Bus 10.8m

A third BYD electric demonstrator appeared in 2016. Unlike the previous two which have now departed London, this one is shorter. It passes Elephant & Castle on its regular route the 360. *Martin Ford*

Built: **BYD** Introduced: **2016** Number: **1**
Operators (routes): **Go-Ahead (360)**

BYD K9E/ E200MMC Electric Bus 12.0m

BYD have gone into partnership with ADL for its production models. Fifty-one of these are now operational on routes 507 & 521. A shorter version featuring the same styling is being built for route 360 and these should appear towards the end of 2017. SEe6 is being charged at Waterloo garage. *Ken Carr*

Built: **BYD/ADL**
Operators (routes): **Go-Ahead (507, 521)**

Introduced: **2016**

Number: **51**

Irizar i2e Electric Vehicle 12.0m

With the arrival of the BYDs at Waterloo. The two Irizar demonstrators have moved to New Cross garage and are now being used on route 108. Ei1 poses in the sun alongside the BYD demonstrator EB2 at our 'Londoner Live' show in July 2016. *Stephen Day*

Built: **Irizar**
Operators (routes): **Go-Ahead (108)**

Introduced: **2013**

Number: **2**

Optare MetroCity MC1060EV Electric Bus 10.6m

The other London supplier of electric buses is Optare with their MetroCity. OCE1 is one of four based at Hounslow for use on route H98. *Ken Carr*

Built: **Optare**   Introduced: **2014-2015**   Number: **13**
Operators (routes): **Arriva (312), London United (H98)**

VDL SB200 / Wrightbus Pulsar 2 (Hydrogen Fuel Cell) 11.9m

The hydrogen buses continue to work on route RV1. WSH62996 starts out on another run at Aldgate. *Ken Carr*

Built: **VDL/Wrightbus**   Introduced: **2010-2013**   Number: **8**
Operators (routes): **Tower Transit (RV1)**

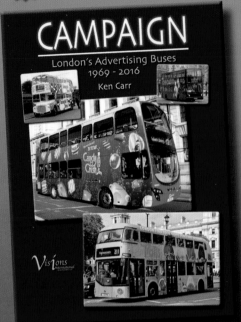

Double-Deckers

Photo: Ben Youngman

ADL Trident / ALX400 9.9m

There are now well under a hundred of the shorter Trident left in service. Around fifty have been withdrawn in the last 12 months. 17976 departs Romford, this is one of just 23 left with Stagecoach. *Mark Mcwalter*

Built: **Dennis/Alexander, TransBus, ADL**   Introduced: **1999-2005**   Number: **71**
Operators (routes): **Abellio (172), Metroline (32, 210), RATP-Dev (131, 267, 281, 285, 371, H32), Stagecoach (115, 247)**

ADL Trident / ALX400 10.5m

Seventy-five of the longer version have been withdrawn in the last year, including TLA24 which is shown at Hounslow Heath garage shortly after withdrawal. RATP have only nine left in operation, the rest are with Stagecoach. *Ken Carr*

Built: **Dennis/Alexander, TransBus, ADL**   Introduced: **1999-2006**   Number: **218**
Operators (routes): **RATP Dev (116, 371, H98), Stagecoach (5, 61, 56, 97, 99, 103, 104, 115, 136, 145, 158, 165, 169, 175, 177, 178, 241, 248, 261, 262, 269, 275, 330, 472)**

ADL Trident / President 9.9m

The solitary remaining short Trident President is operated by Sullivans. When not working school routes it can be found rail replacements. *Michael J. McClelland*

Built: **TransBus**
Operators (routes): **Sulivans (653, 688)**

Introduced: **2000-2002**

Number: **1**

ADL Trident / President 10.5m

Sullivan's have two of the longer versions which are also usedfor schools work. *Stephen Day*

Built: **Dennis/Plaxton, TransBus**
Operators (routes): **Sulivans (653, 688)**

Introduced: **2001-2003**

Number: **2**

ADL Trident / Enviro400 10.1m

It is quite sobering to realise that the very first Enviro400s are now nearly twelve years old! However, some of this type are half that age. TE991 heading along The Broadway in Mill Hill is eight years old, it is likely to stay on this route for another five years. *Ken Carr*

Built: **ADL**   Introduced: **2005-2011**   Number: **912**
Operators (routes): **Abellio** (156, 172, 188, 343, 345, 381, 414, 452, C3, E9), **Arriva** (60, 64, 102, 128, 150, 157, 173, 198, 250, 264, 289, 329, 368, 412, 417, 466)), **Go-Ahead** (36, 37, 44, 45, 57, 63, 118, 132, 147, 163, 191, 196, 200, 237 270, 280, 337, 401, 422, 436 486)), **Metroline** (4, 17, 43, 82, 91, 92, 107, 113, 134, 186, 217, 204, 240, 263, 271, 282, 307, 482,607, U1, U4, W8), **Quality Line** (406, 418, 467), **Stagecoach** (61, 62, 86, 96, 99, 103, 104, 145, 169, 174, 179, 215, 238, 247, 248, 252, 269, 275, 287, 296, 365, 372, 496), **Sullivans** (Schools), **Tower Transit** (25, 30, 69 308, 425)

ADL Trident / Enviro400 10.8m

Only a handful of the longer (standard) version operate in London. This includes Stagecoach's iconic 19000 Spirit of London. When not out working Rainham garage routes, it sometimes appears on specials such as Visions' tour of Stagecoach garages in October 2015. *Ken Carr*

Built: **ADL**   Introduced: **2005 & 2006**   Number: **11**
Operators (routes): **Stagecoach (61, 103, 248, 252)**

ADL Trident / Enviro400H 10.1m

London United's hybrids on route 94 are used quite a lot for advertising campaigns such as ADH8 shown picking-up in Oxford Street displaying an advert for a fashion retailer. *Brian Kemp*

Built: **ADL**   Introduced: **2008-2010**   Number: **42**
Operators (routes): **Go-Ahead (87), London United (27, 94), Metroline (32, 139, 210)**

ADL Trident / Olympus 10.3m

In early 2017 twenty-four of Go-Ahead's DOEs were moved to Peckham garage. They appear on a number of their routes, although mainly the 37 & 63. In February DOE8 had a spin on the 363. *Brian Kemp*

Built: **ADL/East Lancs, ADL/Optare**   Introduced: **2008 & 2009**   Number: **55**
Operators (routes): **CT Plus (W13), Go-Ahead (63, 80, 151, 154, 213)**

ADL E40D / Enviro400 10.2m [EC]

In 2011 an upgraded version of the Enviro400 hits the streets. Built to EC spec, the orange lights running along the lower bodyside help identify these, the buses are Euro-5. *Mark Mcwalter*

Built: **ADL**   Introduced: **2011 - 2013**   Number: **542**
Operators (routes): **Abellio (C2, C3, 156, 345, 381,), Arriva (60, 102, 160, 197, 264, 279, 329, W3), Go-Ahead (36, 45, 77, 89, 127, 147, 185, 213, 321, 353, 401, 422, 468, 486), Metroline (4, 17, 43, 82, 92, 134, 217, 263, 307, W8), Quality Line (406, 418, 467), RATP-Dev (81, 111, 120, 220, 222, H98), Stagecoach (47, 55, 56, 103, 104, 136, 158, 174, 179, 199, 208, 215, 238, 252, 261, 269, 275, 287), Tower Transit (25, 30, 308, 425)**

ADL E40D / Enviro400 10.35m [Euro 6]

In 2012 a Euro-6 version was launched, the number of these on London's streets is quite low as the operators had started to move towards buying hybrids and ADL subsequently launched their MMC model. Stagecoach have nine based at Catford. *Michael J. Mclelland*

Built: **ADL**   Introduced: **2012-2014**   Number: **46**
Operators (routes): **Abellio (345), Arriva (160, 229, 492), Quality Line (406, 418, 467), Stagecoach (47, 54, 136, 199)**

ADL E40H / Enviro400 10.2m [EC]

Metroline uses a batch of the EC spec hybrids based at Cricklewood on route 139. TEH1223 crosses Waterloo bridge on the final leg of its trip from West Hampstead. *Keith Valla*

Built: **ADL**   Introduced: **2011 - 2013**   Number: **199**
Operators (routes): **Abellio (188, 343, 344, 345, 381, C2, C3, E1), CT Plus (388), Go-Ahead (36, 77, 87, 436), Metroline (32, 139, 210), RATP-Dev (27), Stagecoach (55, 56, 215, 275), Tower Transit (23)**

ADL E40H / Enviro400 10.35m [Euro 6]

Abellio's 2446 is one of eight Euro-6 hybrids ordered for route E1, they are now nearly three years into the contract. *Paul Godding*

Built: **ADL** Introduced: **2014** Number: **147**
Operators (routes): **Abellio (49, 452, C2, E1), Stagecoach (47, 54, 75, 96, 136, 205, 277, 472)**

ADL E40D/Enviro400 MMC 10.4m [Euro-6]

The latest style of blinds are shown off by Stagecoach's, Barking based, 10317 whilst working through Ilford. *Mark Mcwalter*

Built: **Alexander Dennis** Introduced: **2014-2017** Number: **51**
Operators (routes): **Abellio (), Stagecoach (62, 145, 175, 294, 498)**

ADL Enviro400H MMC 10.4m [Euro-6]

Go-Ahead's brand new EH57 and EH59 await transfer from Belvedere to Camberwell before taking up duties on routes 35 and 40. *Ken Carr*

Built: **Alexander Dennis**   Introduced: **2015-2017**   Number: **234**
Operators (routes): **Abellio (109, 344, 350, 415), Go-Ahead (14, 22, 35, 40, 42, 45, 74, 185, 363, 430), Metroline (332), Stagecoach (53, 122, 205, 277)**

ADL Enviro400H City 10.4m [Euro-6]

The number of Citys is gradually creeping up, Arriva now have a second batch and CT Plus have two batches. The penultimate member of the first batch, HA18 heads through Aldgate. *Ben Youngman*

Built: **Alexander Dennis**   Introduced: **2015-2017**   Number: **91**
Operators (routes): **Arriva (78, 133, 333), CT Plus (26, 78)**

ADL Enviro400VE MMC 10.5m

The three Virtual Electric Enviros continue to work on route 69. DH38501 arrives at West Ham for 'Londoner Live'. Ironically, the initial plan was for these buses to be allocated to Stagecoach and this was where they were planned to be based, that was until Tower won the tender for the route. *Stephen Day*

Built: **Alexander Dennis**   Introduced: **2015-2016**   Number: **3**
Operators (routes): **Tower Transit (69)**

BYD K10 Electric 10.2m

Another view from 'Londoner Live'. BYD1474 is one of five fully electric double-deckers allocated to Willesden for route 98. Their introduction was stop-start, although whatever problems that were being encountered seem to be largely solved. Normally 3 or 4 tend to be out on the route. *Stephen Day*

Built: **BYD**   Introduced: **2016**   Number: **5**
Operators (routes): **Metroline (98)**

DAF / VDL Wright Pulsar Gemini 10.3m

Another dying breed is the DAF Gemini. They are split between two Arriva garages, South Croydon and Garston. *Mark Mcwalter*

Built: **DAF/Wrightbus, VDL/Wrightbus**   Introduced: **2003-2006**   Number: **48**
Operators (routes): **Arriva (60, 142, 158, 194, 197, 264, 403, 412, 466)**

Scania N94UD OmniDekka 10.6m

RATP-Dev London are the sole operators of these, they are split between London Sovereign' Edgware for route 292 and London United' Fulwell mainly for route 267. They also appear on the 281. *Paul Godding*

Built: **Scania/East Lancs**   Introduced: **2003-2006**   Number: **30**
Operators (routes): **RATP-Dev (267, 281, 292)**

Scania CN94UD OmniCity 10.7m

Two-thirds of these OmniCitys are based at Hounslow, every now and again one may escape onto the 81, such as SP14 running on the route near Heathrow. *Dave McKay*

Built: **Scania** Introduced: **2006** Number: **15**
Operators (routes): **London United (111, 120, 222, H91)**

Scania N230UD OmniCity 10.8m

The large majority of Scanias in London feature the N230UD chassis with the OmniCity body. Metroline acquired thirty-nine when they purchased First, all work route 207 and these were the replacements for the Bendys. *Michael J. Mclelland*

Built: **Scania** Introduced: **2008-2010** Number:
387 Operators (routes): **CT Plus (388, W13), Go-Ahead (320, 353, 405, D7, D8), Metroline (207), RATP-Dev (65, 71, 81, 111, 120, 131, 183, 222, 281, E3, H32, H91, H98) Stagecoach (51, 97, 158, 174, 177, 205, 248, 252, 262, 277365, 372, 473), Sullivans (692, 699)**

Scania N230UD OmniDekka 10.8m

All of these are based at Croydon for route 405 althougth you can find them on route 293 as well. 950 will shortly depart Croydon for a trip which will take it outside of the M25. *Michael J. Mclelland*

Built: **Scania/East Lancs, Scania/Optare**   Introduced: **2007**   Number: **6**
Operators (routes): **Go-Ahead (405)**

Scania N230UD / Olympus 10.8m

Metroline's batch of these are allocated to Perivale for use on routes 90 & 297. SEL743 works on the former at Hatton Cross. *Michael J. Mclelland*

Built: **Scania/East Lancs, Scania/Optare**   Introduced: **2007-2009**   Number: **63**
Operators (routes): **Go-Ahead (320, 161, schools), Metroline (90, 297)**

Volvo B7TL / ALX400 10.1m

The best place to find these is in the East. Barking and Grays have most of the short VLAs. 6121 (now VLA121) heads through Romford on its regular route. *Thomas Drake*

Built: **Volvo/TransBus, Volvo/ADL**   Introduced: **2004-2005**   Number: **62**
Operators (routes): **Arriva (66, 123, 128, 142, 168, 176, 258, 368, 370)**

Volvo B7TL / ALX400 10.6m

The longer buses are allocated to Edmonton and Norwood. As this book is published, route 2 will be changing over to Gemini 3 operation and this will likely see the start of withdrawals at Norwood. Those working route 176, like VLA61 above, will probably go by the end of 2017. *Ken Carr*

Built: **Volvo/TransBus, Volvo/ADL** Introduced: **2003-2005**   Number: **73**
Operators (routes): **Arriva (123, 176, 417)**

Volvo B7TL / President 10.0m

The short Volvo B7TL President, will see drastic reduction in numbers during 2017 as new buses are brought in to to replace them as contracts change or get renewed. Under the plans for reducing the number of buses in Oxford Street, route 98 is one of those that will continue to traverse it. Therefore, it is very likely that the B7TLs will be removed from the route and replaced by hybrids before the new contract on begins in late 2017. *Mark Mcwalter*

Built: **Volvo/Plaxton, Volvo/TransBus, Volvo/ADL**   Introduced: **2000-2005**   Number: **248**
Operators (routes): **Go-Ahead (44, 45, 77, 154, 185, 213, 249, 270, 280, 321, 432, 468), Metroline (4, 17, 43, 98, 260, 271, 302, 460, H12, U3, U4,)**

Volvo B7TL / President 10.6m

London Sovereign have seven of these left based at Edgware. The 183 is the best route to catch them on. VLP26 heads through Harrow. *Mark Mcwalter*

Built: **Volvo/Plaxton, Volvo/TransBus, Volvo/ADL**   Introduced: **2000-2005**   Number: **39**
Operators (routes): **Metroline (4, 17, 43), RATP-Dev (183, 292),**

Volvo B7TL / Eclipse Gemini 10.1m

Earlier examples of this type are beginning to be withdrawn, Arriva's fleet will be decimated in June when the 254 converts to hybrids. Go-Ahead's numbers are also being reduced. WVL202 should last until route 257 is taken over by Stagecoach in October. *Ben Youngman*

Built: **Volvo/Wrightbus**   Introduced: **2001-2005**   Number: **291**
Operators (routes): **Arriva (144, 221, 242, 254, 258, W3), Go-Ahead (36, 45, 87, 127, 132, 161, 180, 185, 196, 231, 249, 257, 280, 320, 353, 401, 422, 468, 474, 476, X68), Metroline (607), Tower Transit (28, 31)**

Volvo B7TL / Eclipse Gemini 10.6m

Abellio's fleet of 10.6 metre Geminis are concentrated at Walworth garage. They can be found on a selection of the garage's routes. 9046 makes its way around Elephant & Castle on the 343. *Ken Carr*

Built: **Volvo/Wrightbus**   Introduced: **2002-2006**   Number: **93**
Operators (routes): **Abellio (172, 188, 343, 381), Arriva (144 221, W3)**

Volvo B7TL / Myllennium Vyking 10.4m

Only four of the short Vykings remain in service. They all work for Sullivans and you will find them on school routes or on rail replacement. ELV6 helps out the Underground at Earls Court. *Michael J. McClelland*

Built: **Volvo/East Lancs**   Introduced: **2002 & 2004**   Number: **4**
Operators (routes): **Sullivans (626, 683)**

Volvo B7TL / Myllennium Vyking 11.0m

RATP-Dev London's Vykings are living on very borrowed time, the remaining couple may be found on route 131. VLE36 rests at Mill Hill Broadway, this bus has now been withdrawn and the chances of a Vyking on the 114 now is zero. Metroline took over the route in September 2016! *Ken Carr*

Built: **Volvo/East Lancs**   Introduced: **2004**   Number: **8**
Operators (routes): **London United (131), Sullivans (626, 683)**

Volvo B9TL / Eclipse Gemini 2 10.4m

The Volvo B9TL Gemini 2s are around starting to approach their half-life stage. Tower Transit's VN36113 entered service in the summer of 2011 on route 25 and it continues to work the route six years later. *Ben Youngman*

Built: **Volvo/Wrightbus**   Introduced: **2009-2011**   Number: **488**
Operators (routes): **Go-Ahead (21, 127, 129, 36, 89, 132, 151, 171, 180, 213, 321, 401, 422, 432, 474, 486, D7), Metroline (18, 79, 83, 90, 105, 237, 245, 427, 483, E2, E8, W7), Tower Transit (25, 30, 58, 69, 212, 266, 308)**

Volvo B9TL / Eclipse Gemini 2 10.5m [EC]

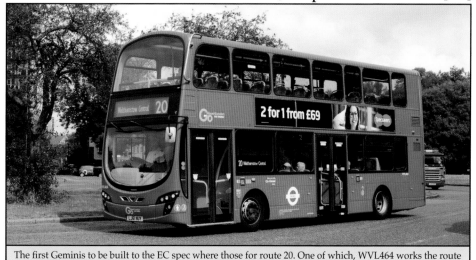

The first Geminis to be built to the EC spec where those for route 20. One of which, WVL464 works the route at Wanstead. *Ken Carr*

Built: **Volvo/Wrightbus**   Introduced: **2012 & 2013**   Number: **227**
Operators (routes): **Go-Ahead (20, 22, 101, 200, 476), Metroline (43, 52, 79, 83, 90, 105, 134, 237, 245, 297, 483, E2, E8, W7), Tower Transit (25, 28, 30, 266)**

Volvo B9TL / Enviro400 10.4m

In the summer of 2016, the three B9 Enviro400s, moved from Putney to Sutton garage after route 85 was lost to RATP-Dev. Now the trio can usually be found on route 213. *Brian Kemp*

Built: **Volvo/Alexander Dennis**   Introduced: **2008**   Number: 3
Operators (routes): **Go-Ahead (213.)**

Volvo B5LH / Eclipse Gemini 2 10.4m

Only Arriva and Go-Ahead took the first version of the hybrid Gemini. Arriva's HV8 was ordered for route 76. However, with this route moving to New Routemaster operation, this bus has now moved south of the River to Brixton. *Stephen Day*

Built: **Volvo/Wrightbus**   Introduced: **2009-2011**   Number: **62**
Operators (routes): **Arriva (50, 67, 133, 319, 333), Go-Ahead (436)**

Volvo B5LH / Eclipse Gemini 10.5m [EC]

The EC spec version is more numerous. Arriva have over one hundred. The 141 is operated by Palmers Green garage, HV59 works the route in Lombard Street. *Ken Carr*

Built: **Volvo/Wrightbus**   Introduced: **2012-2014**   Number: **171**
Operators (routes): **Arriva (29, 50, 67, 141, 144, 243, 329, 319, 341, W3), Go-Ahead (22), Metroline (52), RATP-Dev (183, 292)**

Volvo B5LH / Gemini 3 10.5m [Euro-6]

The Gemini 3 was launched in 2014, of particular note are the smaller windows on the upper-deck and the extra lights on the front. Metroline's VWH2113 navigates Marble Arch on route 6. *Martin Ford*

Built: **Volvo/Wrightbus**   Introduced: **2014-2015**   Number: **167**
Operators (routes): **Metroline (7, 34, 79, 105, 125), RATP-Dev (116, 285), Stagecoach (51, 53, 96, 122, 177, 472), Tower Transit (212)**

Volvo B5LH / Gemini 3 (Streetdeck) 10.6m

In 2015, Wrightbus decided to supply the Gemini 3 with the same front as used on their Streetdeck model. The rather angular WHV154 heads past Elephant & Castle on route 1. *Ken Carr*

Built: **Volvo/Wrightbus**   Introduced: **2015-2017**   Number: **366**
Operators (routes): **Arriva (2, 19, 242, 243, 249, 259, 341), Go-Ahead (1, 14, 74, 93, 119, 127, 155, 202, 270, 405, 430), Metroline (114, 140, 182, 295), RATP-Dev (65, 85, 94, 131, 148), Tower Transit (328)**

Volvo B5LH / Enviro400 MMC 10.5m

ADL's Enviro400 MMC is available on the Volvo B5LH chassis. To date only Go-Ahead and Stagecoach have ordered batches of these. *Martin Ford*

Built: **Volvo/ADL**   Introduced: **2015-2016**   Number: **58**
Operators (routes): **Go-Ahead (135), Stagecoach (47, 53, 177)**

Volvo B5LH / MCV Evoseti

The Egyptian company MCV are offering their Evoseti body on the B5LH chassis. Go-Ahead were the first to try this option. Having just been delivered MHV2 & MHV20 await entry into service. *Ken Car*

Built: **Volvo/MCV**   Introduced: **2016-2017**   Number: **136**
Operators (routes): **Go-Ahead (1, 35, 40, 42, 93, 185, 213, 468), Tower Transit (13)**

Volvo B5TL / Gemini 3 10.6m [Euro-6]

Go-Ahead also operate two former Wrightbus demonstrators which are diesel versions of the Gemini 3. WVL509 heads through Croydon, it can normally be found on the 405. *Mark Mcwalter*

Built: **Volvo/Wrightbus**   Introduced: **2013**   Number: **2**
Operators (routes): **Go-Ahead (127, 405)**

Wright Gemini 2DL 10.4m

Wrightbus used VDL components to create an integral Gemini 2 This is also known as a DB300 Gemini 2. DW221 leaves Homerton Hospital on route 242. *Ben Youngman*

Built: **Wrightbus**   Introduced: **2009-2010**   Number: **143**
Operators (routes): **Arriva (41, 48, 66, 123, 142, 194, 197, 242, 243, 264, 341, 370, 403, 412, 466), Go-Ahead (270), Tower Transit (266)**

Wright Gemini 2DL 10.4m [EC]

Only Arriva have the EC spec version of the integral. DW486 heads through Mill Hill. *Ken Carr*

Built: **Wrightbus (to ECWVTA spec)** Introduced: **2011-2013** Number: **187**
Operators (routes): **Arriva (29, 41, 60, 67, 106, 121, 123, 141, 144, 194, 197, 221, 230, 243, 279, 317, 341, 349, 466)**

Wright Gemini 2DL 10.6m [Euro-6]

DW411, has been converted and increased in length to accommodate a Euro-6 engine. The bus is based at Enfield. *Peter Horrex*

Built: **Wrightbus (to ECWVTA spec)** Introduced: **2011** Number: **1**
Operators (routes): **Arriva (279, 349)**

Wright StreetDeck Gemini 3 10.6m 10.6m [Euro-6]

Only one of the two, Streetdeck chassied demonstrators remains in London. SW1 is now based at Garston. It features the Gemini 3 body. *Mark Mcwalter*

Built: **Wrightbus**   Introduced: **2015**   Number: **1**
Operators (routes): **Arriva (142, 340)**

Wright StreetDeck Gemini 3 (Streetdeck) 10.6m [Euro-6]

Arriva are the only operator to order buses with the Streetdeck chassis, although they have gone with the Gemini 3 body albeit with the Streetdeck style front & rear.. *Mark Mcwalter*

Built: **Wrightbus**   Introduced: **2016**   Number: **9**
Operators (routes): **Arriva (340)**

Wright NRM 11.3m

The New Routemasters are now all single-crewed, following the decision in 2016 to remove all Customer Assistants. In October LT50 was out-shopped in this early London General style livery. *Peter Edgar*

Built: **Wrightbus**   Introduced: **2012-2014**   Number: **306**
Operators (routes): **Arriva (38, 48, 137), Metroline (24, 390), Go-Ahead (11, 88), RATP-Dev (9, 10), Stagecoach (8, 15)**

Wright NRM 11.3m [Euro-6]

The later New Routemasters have been fitted with Euro-6 engines. On the majority of these a new rear door has been also fitted. LT707 crosses Lambeth Bridge on its regular route 3 duties. *Keith Valla*

Built: **Wrightbus**   Introduced: **2014-2017**   Number: **648**
Operators (routes): **Abellio (3, 159, 211), Arriva (59, 73, 137, 149, 253,), Metroline (16, 91, 168, 189), Go-Ahead (11, 12, 21, 68, 76, 88, 168, 453, EL1, EL2, EL3), Stagecoach (8, 15, 55)**

Wright NRM (Short) 10.2m [Euro-6]

Only one of the shortened New Routemasters has been built. ST812 is normally allocated to route 91. here it negotiates the roundabout at Trafalgar Square in early 2017. *Ken Carr*

Built: **Wrightbus**
Introduced: **2016**
Number: **1**
Operators: **Metroline (91)**

Volvo B5LH / Wrightbus SRM 10.6m [Euro-6]

Having originally planned to operate on route 13, the two-door, single-staircase, Volvo powered version of the NRM, now operate a bit out of town on route 183. VHR45205 shows off the nearside differences to its bigger cousin at the start of its journey at Golders Green. *Ken Carr*

Built: **Volvo / Wrightbus**
Introduced: **2016**
Number: **6**
Operators (routes): **London Sovereign (183)**

AEC Routemaster 8.4m

Routemasters continue to work on route 15H. The fleet is going through a refurbishment programme. An un-refurbished RM324, the oldest bus in operational service, tackles the roundabout at Trafalgar Square.
Keith Valla

Built: **AEC**
Operators (routes): **Stagecoach (15H)**

Introduced: **1959-1967**

Number: **10**

Notes

The Garages

Bus garages in the London area come in all shapes, sizes and ages. Some are located on High Streets, others in anonymous industrial parks.

Some are traditional bus garages (i.e. built for buses) such as Sutton, others are former tram and trolleybus depots, like Holloway. This opened as a tram shed, but was then converted to a trolleybus depot before finally becoming a bus garage. Newer garages have been created inside industrial units, such as Beddington Cross.

The biggest garage in London (the biggest in Britain, for that matter) is the new West Ham, opened in 2008 with capacity for more than 300 buses.

Each garage has a one- or two-letter code, used by London Buses for administrative purposes. Operators also give garages their own codes which, in most cases but not always, are the same as the ones assigned by London Buses. Within the book, we've used operators' codes exclusively, as these are the ones you're likely to see on the buses themselves. For the sake of completeness, where the code is different, it's shown in the following listing in parentheses underneath the operator's code.

The continued use of different coding systems from different eras means there is no uniformity. Many were created to a system introduced in the early part of the 20th Century by the London General Omnibus Company, which allocated codes alphabetically - A, B, C, etc., then AA, AB, AC, etc. So, Sutton became A and Camberwell was Q . . . which doesn't make a huge amount of sense. Later codes are a little more user-friendly, for example PM for Peckham.

Some codes have reflected the name of the former owning company. As an example, the Tilling company had three garages at Bromley, Croydon and Lewisham which became TB, TC and TL. So far, so good, but it doesn't explain why TL is referred to as Catford in the modern world. Equally baffling at first sight is Abellio's garage at Battersea – QB – which actually stands for Q-Drive Battersea after the operator when the location was first used.

Some codes have been used for more than one garage over the years, or for different buildings in the same area. A new garage at Peckham, for instance, remained PM. There are other instances of codes lying dormant for many years before resurrection in a completely different area. Readers of a certain age will remember code C as Athol Street, Poplar . . . not Metrobus, Croydon.

Currently, three sites are shared by two companies and . . . yes, you've guessed . . . using different codes:

Edgware is both EW (the original code used by Metroline) and BT (used by London Sovereign).

Fulwell - FW (correct code used by London United) and TF (Abellio).

Ash Grove - AE (Arriva) and HK (CT Plus).

2016 saw two new garages appear, RR (River Road) was opened by Go-Ahead to replace BE (Rainham) which has now been demolished. AW (Walthamstow) has been opened by CT Plus to cope with growing demand, the garage is located near the former greyhound stadium.

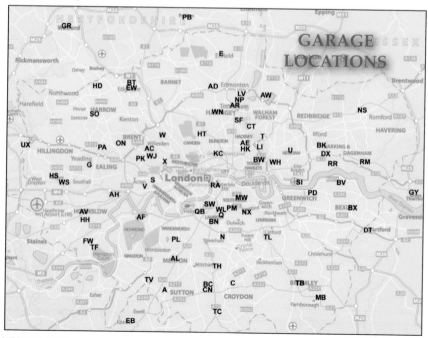

Code	Garage	Address/*Routes Operated*/Buses Allocated	PVR	Operator
A	Sutton	Bushey Road, Sutton, SM1 1QJ *80 93 151 154 164 213 N155* B5LH/Evo, B5LH/Gem3, B9TL/Env400, B9TL/Gem2, Env200 10.8m, Env200/Est, Env400, Tri/Olym	88	Go-Ahead
AC	Willesden	287 High Road, Willesden, London, NW10 2JY *6 52 98 260 302 460 N98* B5LH/Gem2, B5LH/Gem3, B7TL/Pres 10.0m, B9TL/Gem2, BYD D/D	114	Metroline
AD	Palmers Green	Regents Avenue, London, N13 *102 141 329* B5LH5/Gem2, DB250/Gem, Env400,	59	Arriva
AE	Ash Grove	Mare Street, South Hackney, London, E8 *48 78 106 254* B7TL/Gem 10.1m, Env400, Env400H/City, DB300/Gem2, Env200/MMC 9.75, NRM	93	Arriva
AF	Putney	10 Chelverton Road, London, SW15 1RN *14 22 74 337 424 430 639 670 N22 N74* B5LH/Gem2 10.4m, B5LH/Gem3, B7TL/Gem 10.1m, B9TL/Gem2 10.5m, Dart/Point 8.8m, Env400, Env400H/MMC	112	Go-Ahead
AH	Brentford	Commerce Road, Brentford, Middlesex, TW8 8LZ *117 190 209 235 237 E2 E8 609* B9TL/Gem2, Dart/Evo 10.2m, Env200 10.2m, Env200/MMC 10.9	104	Metroline
AL	Merton	High Street, London, SW19 1DN *22 44 57 93 152 155 163 164 200 219 270 280 655 N155* B5LH/Gem3, B7TL/Gem 10.1m, B7TL/Pres 10.0m, B9TL/Gem2, Dart/Point 10.1m, DB300/Gem2, E200/Est 10.4m, Env200 10.2m, Env200 10.8m, Env400, Env400 (E), Street 10.8m	167	Go-Ahead

The cavernous Go-Ahead Merton garage. A good selection of the types based here are on show, including a Routemaster, used by Go-Ahead's Commercial Services division. *Ken Carr*

AR Tottenham
Philip Lane, High Cross, London, N15
19 41 67 123 149 230 243 259 341 N19 N41
B5LH/Gem2, B5LH/Gem3, B7TL/ALX400 10.1m, B7TL/ALX400 10.6m,
DB300/Gem2
184 Arriva

AS Atlas Road
Atlas Road, Harlesden, London, NW10
28 31 266 328 N28 N31
B5LH/Gem3, B7TL/Gem 10.1m, B9TL/Gem 2 (E), DB300/Gem2,
95 Tower Transit

AV Hounslow
Kingsley Road, Hounslow
81 110 111 120 203 222 696 697 H32 H37 H98 N9
Citaro, CN94UD/Omni 10.7m, Dart/Pointer2 10.2m, Env200 10.8m,
Env400, OPMetroCityElec, OPTemp 12.0m, Tri/ALX400 9.9m
140 RATP-Dev

AW Walthamstow Walthamstow Avenue, London, E4 8SP
385 397 W11 W16 W19
Env200 9.6m, Env200/MMC 9.75m
38 CT Plus

BC Beddington
Unit 10, Beddington Cross, Beddington Farm Road, Croydon, CR0 4XH
109 201 367 407 433 931 N109 K1 P13 S4
B7TL/Gem 10.6m, Dart/Nimb 10.5m, Env200 9.3m, Env200 10.2m,
Env200 10.8m, Env200/MMC 9.0, Env400H/MMC,
99 Abellio

BK Barking
205 Longbridge Road, Barking, Essex, IG11 8UE
5 62 145 167 169 362 366 396 462 677 N15
Env200 8.9m, Env200 10.2m, Env400, Env400/MMC, OPVer 10.4m,
Tri/ALX400 9.9m, Tri/ALX400 10.5m.
122 Stagecoach

BN Brixton
39 Streatham Hill, London, SW2
19 50 59 133 137 319 333 N133
B5LH/ Gem2, DB300/Gem2, Env400H/City, NRM
125 Arriva

BT Edgware
Approach Road, Edgware, Middlesex, HA8 7AN
13 183 251 292 326 605 618 619 H14 N13
B5LH/Gem2, B5LH/SRM, B7TL/Pres 10.6m, B7TL/Vyk 11.0m,
Env200 10.2m, N94UD/Omni 10.6m,
76 RATP-Dev

BV Belvedere
Butts Wharf, Crabtree Manorway North, Belvedere, DA17 6BT
180 244 669 N1
B7TL/Gem 10.6m, B7TL/Pres 10.0, Env200 10.2m.
30 Go-Ahead

BW Bow
Fairfield Road, Bow, London, E3 2QP
8 15 205 277 N8 N15 N205
Env 400H, Env400H/MMC, N230UD/Omni 10.8m, NRM.
105 Stagecoach

BX Bexleyheath
Erith Road, Bexleyheath, Kent, DA7 6BX
89 132 401 422 486 625 658 661 669 B11 B14 B16 N21 N89
B7TL/Gem 10.1m, B7TL/Pres 10.0m, B9TL/Gem2, Dart/Est 9.0m
Dart/Point 10.1m, Env200 10.2m, Env400,
99 Go-Ahead

C Croydon
134 Beddington Lane, Beddington, CR9 4ND
119 127 130 202 293 355 359 405 434 455
14.240/Env200 10.7m, 14.240/Evo 10.8m, B5LH/Gem3, Dart/Est 9.0m,
Dart/Point 10.1m, Dart/Point 10.7m, Env200 8.9m, Env200 10.2m,
Env400, N94UD/Omni 10.6m, N230UB/Omni 12m, N230UD/Omni
102 Go-Ahead

CT Clapton
15 Bohemia Place, Mare Street, London, E8
38 242 393 N38
B5LH/Gem3, B7TL/Gem 10.1m, DB300/Gem2, Env200 9.3m,
Env200 10.2m, NRM.
94 Arriva

DT Dartford
Central Road, Dartford, Kent, DA1
160 229 428 469 492 B12 B13 B15 660
Env200 10.2m, Env200 10.8m, Env200 MMC 9.3m, Env400
75 Arriva

DX Barking
638 Ripple Road, Barking, Essex
128 150 173 325 368 673 678
B7TL/ALX400 10.1m, Env200 10.2m, Env400.
71 Arriva

E Enfield
Southbury Road, Ponders End, EN1
121 279 313 317 318 349 377 W6 N279
DB300/Gem2, Env200 8.9m, Env200 10.8m, Env200/MMC 9.0m,
Env400
103 Arriva

Code	Garage	Address/*Routes Operated*/Buses Allocated	PVR	Operator
EB	Epsom	Blenheim Road, Epsom, Surrey, KT19 9AF *404 406 411 413 418 463 465 467 470 633 641 K5 S1 S3 X26* Citaro, E200/Lancs 9.0m, Env200 8.9m, Env400, OPMetroCity, OPSolo 8.8m, OPSolo SR 9.7, OPVer 11.1m, Street 8.8m	90	Quality Line
EC	Edmonton	Unit 1E, Towpath Road, Stonehill Business Park, London N18 *123 382* Dart/Point 9.3m, Env200 8.9m, Env200/MMC 9.3m	28	Arriva
EW	Edgware	Approach Road, Edgware, Middlesex, HA8 7AN *107 113 186 204 240 606 N5 N98 N113* Env400.	73	Metroline
FW	Fulwell	Wellington Road, Fulwell, Middlesex, TW2 5NX *33 65 71 216 267 281 371 391 681* B5LH/Gem3, Env200 10.2m, Env200H 10.2m, N94UD/Omni 10.6m, N230UD/Omni 10.8m, OPVersa 10.4mTri/ALX400 9.9m, Tri/ALX400 10.5m.	129	RATP-Dev

The original Fulwell garage is split by the wall on the right. On this side of the divide is London United's FW, on the other is Abellio's TF. *Ken Carr*

Code	Garage	Address/*Routes Operated*/Buses Allocated	PVR	Operator
G	Greenford	Council Depot, Greenford Road, Greenford *92 95 195 282 482 E6* Env200 10.2m, Env400, Tri/Pres 9.9m.	84	Metroline
GR	Watford	934 St. Albans Road, Watford, Hertfordshire, WD2 6NN *142 258 268 288 303 305 340 631 642 H2 H3 H18 H19* B7TL/ALX400 10.1m, B7TL/Gem 10.1m, Dart/Point 10.1m, DB250/Gem, DB300/Gem2, Env200 10.2m, Env400, OPSolo 7.8m, SB120/Cad 10.2m, Streetdeck	74	Arriva
GY	Grays	Unit 7, Europa Park, London Road, Grays, Essex, RM20 4DB *66 347 370 375* B7TL/ALX400 10.1m, DB300/Gem2, Env200 10.2m,	25	Arriva
HD	Harrow Weald	467 High Road, Harrow Weald, Middlesex, HA3 6EJ *140 182 640 H12 N18* B5LH/Gem3, B7TL/Pres 10.0m.	66	Metroline

Code Garage	Address/*Routes Operated*/Buses Allocated	PVR	Operator
HE Heathrow	Coach travel Centre, Bedfont Road, Stanwell, Middlesex *E10* Env200 (E) 8.9m	**8**	**Arriva**
HF Hertford	Gypsy Moth Ave, Hatfield Business Park, Hatfield, Herts. *383* Env200 (E) 8.9m	**3**	**Uno**
HH Hounslow Heath	Tamian Way, Hounslow, Middlesex, TW4 6BL *116 216 285 423 635 698 H22 H91* B5LH/Gem3, Dart/Point 10.1m, Dart/Point2 10.1m, Env200 10.2m, N94UD/Omni 10.7m, Tri/ALX400 10.5m	**66**	**RATP-Dev**

Pointers are still hanging on at Hounslow Heath. DPS724 and 711 sit in the main shed at the garage. There is a smaller shed on site which has pits for heavier maintenance work. *Ken Carr*

HK Ash Grove	Mare Street, South Hackney, London, E8 *26 153 309 388 394 N26 W5 W12 W13* Dart/Nim 8.9m, E200/Est 10.4m, Env200 8.9m, Env200 10.8m, Env400H, Env400H/City, N230UD/Omni 10.8m, OPSolo 8.8m, OPSolo 9.6m, OP Solo SE 7.8m, Tri/Olym 10.3m,	**82**	**CT Plus**
HS Hayes (HZ)	Swallowfield Way, Hayes *207 427 U5* B9TL/Gem2, Env200 10.2m, Env400, N230UD/Omni 10.8m.	**68**	**Metroline**
HT Holloway	37A Pemberton Gardens, London, N19 5RR *4 17 24 43 91 134 271 390 603 N5 N20 N91 N113 W7* B7TL/Pres 10.0m, B7TL/Pres 10.6m, B9TL/Gem2, Env400, NRM	**202**	**Metroline**
KC King's Cross	Freight Lane, London N1 *46 214 274* Dart/Point2 10.1m, Env200 10.2m	**54**	**Metroline**

LI Lea (HO) **Interchange**	151 Ruckholt Road, Leyton, London, E10 5PB *25 30 58 69 212 236 308 339 425 444 488 N550 N551* *RV1 W14 W15* B5LH/Evo, B5LH/Gem3, B7TL/Gem 10.1B9TL/Gem2, Env200 10.2m, Env200 9.3m, Env200 9.6m, Env200 10.8m, Env400, Env400VE, Puls2Hydro, Street 10.8m	**243 Tower Transit**
MB Orpington	Oak Farm, Farnborough Hill, Green Street Green, Orpington, Kent, BR6 6DA *126 138 161 162 181 233 246 284 320 352 353 358* *464 654 684 R1 R2 R3 R4 R6 R8 R9 R11* 12.240/Lancs 10.3m, 14.240/Evo, B7TL/Gem, Citaro, Dart/Point 8.9m, Dart/Point 10.1m, Env200 8.9m, Env200 10.2m, Env200 10.8m, Env400, N94UB/Est 10.6m, N230UD/Omni 10.8m, OPSolo SE 7.1m.	**158 Go-Ahead**
MW Mandela **Way East**	Mandela Way, SE1 5SS *1 100 453 N1* B5LH/Gem3, Env200 9.3m, Env200 9.6m, NRM	**78 Go-Ahead**
N Norwood	Knights Hill, London, SE27 *2 137 157 176 249 417 450 690 N2 N137* B7TL/ALX400 10.1m, B7TL/ALX400 10.6m, DB300/Gem2, Env400, NRM, Street 9.7m	**139 Arriva**
NP Northumberland **Park**	Marsh Lane, Tottenham, London, N17 *19 20 76 191 192 231 257 299 327 357 379 389 399 476 491* *616 657 675 W4 W10* B7TL/Gem 10.1m, B9TL/Gem2, Dart/Cap 8.9m, Dart/Evo 9.2m, Env200 8.9m, Env200 9.3m, Env200 (E) 9.6m, Env400, NRM, Street 8.8m, Street 10.2m	**171 Go-Ahead**
NS Romford	North Street, Romford, Essex, RM1 1DS *86 103 175 247 256 294 296 496 498 499 N86* Env200 10.2m, Env200 MMC 10.9m, Env400, Env400/MMC, Tri/ALX400 9.9m, Tri/ALX400 10.5m.	**94 Stagecoach**

Stagecoach's 19816 awaits movement to the maintenance area at North Street garage, having failed in service the previous night. *Ken Carr*

Code Garage	Address/*Routes Operated*/Buses Allocated	PVR	Operator
NX New Cross	208 New Cross Road, London, SE14	177	Go-Ahead
	21 36 108 129 171 225 286 321 436 N21 N171		
	B5LH/Gem2, B7TL/Gem 10.1m, B7TL/Pres 10.0m, B9TL/Gem2,		
	Citaro, Dart/Point 10.1m, Env200 10.2m, Env200 10.8m, Env400,		
	Env400H, Irizar Elec, NRM,		
ON Alperton	Ealing Road, Alperton, Middlesex, HA0	73	Metroline
	83 223 224 483 487 N83		
	B9TL/Gem2, Env200 10.2m,		
PA Perivale	Unit 12, Perivale Ind Park, Horsenden Lane Sth, Greenford, UB6 7RL	54	Metroline
(West)	*90 105 297 395 611*		
	B9TL/Gem2, Dart/Point 10.1m, Env200 10.2m, N230/Olym		
PB Potters Bar	High Street, Potters Bar, Herts, EN6 5BE	116	Metroline
	34 125 217 234 263 307 384 634 N20 N91 W8		
	B5LH/Gem3, Env200 8.9m, Env200 (E) 9.6m, Env400		
PD Plumstead	Pettman Crescent, Plumstead, London, SE28 0BJ	175	Stagecoach
	51 53 96 99 122 177 291 386 472 601 602 672		
	B5LH/Gem3, B5LH/MMC, Dart/Point 8.8m, Dart/Point 9.3m,		
	Env200 9.3m, Env200 9.6m, Env400, Env400H, Env400/MMC,		
	N230UD/Omni 10.8m, Tri/ALX400 9.9m, Tri/ALX400 10.5m.		
PK Park Royal	Atlas Road, Harlesden, London, NW10 6DN	56	London United
	220 283 440 E11		
	Env200 8.9m, Env200 10.2m, Env400 (E), OPVer 10.4m,		
	Tri/ALX400 9.9m		
PL Waterside	Waterside Way, London, SW17 0HB	45	Go-Ahead
Way	*39 493 G1*		
	Dart/Point 10.1m, Env200 (E) 8.9m, Env200 (E) 10.2m.		
PM Peckham	Blackpool Road, Peckham, London, SE15 3SE	79	Go-Ahead
	36 37 63 363 N63 P12 X68		
	B5LH/Evo, B9TL/Gem2, Env200 10.2m, Env400, Env400H/MMC,		
	Tri/Olym		
PV Perivale	Alperton Lane, Western Avenue, Greenford, UB6 8DW	51	Metroline
(East)	*7 79 245 N7*		
	B5LH/Gem3, B9TL/Gem2		
Q Camberwell	1 Warner Road, Camberwell, London, SE5 9LU	221	Go-Ahead
	12 35 40 42 45 68 185 360 432 468 624 658 N68 P5 X68		
	B5LH/Evo, B7TL/Gem 10.1m, B7TL/Gem 10.6m, B7TL/Pres 10.0m,		
	B9TL/Gem2, Dart/Point 10.1m, Electy 10.3m, Electy 10.4m, Env200 8.9m,		
	Env200 9.3m, Env200/MMC 9.75m, Env400, Env400H/MMC, NRM.		
QB Battersea	Silverthorne Road, Battersea, London, SW8 3HE	210	Abellio
	3 49 156 159 211 344 414 452 C2 C3 N3		
	B7TL/Gem 10.6m, Env400, Env400H, Env400H/MMC, NRM,		
RA Waterloo	Cornwall Road, London, SE1 8TE	40	Go-Ahead
	507 521		
	BYD/ADL Electric.		
RM Rainham	Unit 2, Albright Ind Estate, Ferry Lane, Rainham, Essex, RM13 9BU	111	Stagecoach
	103 165 174 248 252 256 287 365 372		
	Env200 10.8m, Env400, Env400 10.8m, N230UD/Omni 10.8m,		
	Tri/ALX400 10.5m		
RR River Road	51 River Road, London, IG11 0SW	156	Go-Ahead
	101 147 193 346 364 376 474 608 646 648 649 650		
	651 652 656 667 674 679 686 687 EL1 EL2 EL3		
	B7TL/Gem 10.1m, B9TL/Gem2, Dart/Cap 10.2m, Dart/Evo 9.2m,		
	Dart/Point 10.1m, Dart/Point2 10.7m, Env200 10.2m, Env200 10.8m,		
	Env200 (E) 10.8, Env200/Evo 10.4m, Env400, Street WF.		
S Shepherd's	Wells Road, London, W12	113	London United
Bush	*72 94 148 272 419 C1*		
	B5LH/Gem3, Dart/Point 10.1m, Dart/Point2 10.1m, Env200 10.2m,		
	Env400H, NRM		
SF Stamford	Rookwood Road, London N16	87	Arriva
Hill	*67 73 253 N73 N253*		
	B5LH/Gem2, NRM		

Code Garage	Address/*Routes Operated*/Buses Allocated	PVR	Operator
SI Silvertown	Factory Road, Silvertown, London, E16 *135 276 300 D6 D7 D8* B5LH/MMC, B9TL/Gem2, Dart/Evo 10.4m, Env 200 10.2m, Env200 10.8m, N230UD/Omni, SB180/Evo	**81**	Go-Ahead
SM South Mimms	South Mimms Services, Near Potters Bar, Herts. *298 W9 617 626 628 629 653 683 688 692 699* B7TL/Gem 10.6m, B7TL/Vyk 10.4m, Env200 10.2m, Env200/MMC 9.75m, Env400, N230UD/Omni, Tri/ALX400 9.9m, Tri/Pres 9.9m, Tri/Pres 10.5m.	**36**	Sullivans
SO Harrow	331 Pinner Road, Harrow *183 398 H9 H10 H11 H13 H14 H17* Dart/Point2 10.2m, Env200 10.2m, Env200 10.8m, N94/Omni	**57**	RATP-Dev

Brand new BYD / ADL electrics are parked up beside the battery chargers at Go-Ahead's Waterloo garage. *Ken Carr*

The maintenance area at RATP-Dev London's Shepherd's Bush garage. All the double-deck buses based here are now hybrids. *Ken Carr*

SW Stockwell Binfield Road, London, SW4 6ST
11 77 87 88 118 170 196 315 322 432 N11 N44 N87   **150 Go-Ahead**
B5LH/Gem2, B7TL/Gem 10.1m, B7TL/Pres 10.0m, B9TL/Gem2,
Dart/Est 9.0m, Dart/Point 10.7m, Env200 8.9m, Env200 10.8m,
Env400, Env400H, NRM.

Go-Ahead's two 'celeb' NRMs, LT50 and LT60 are displayed at Stockwell, during the 2016 open day at the garage. *Ken Carr*

T Leyton High Road, Leyton, London, E10 6AD
55 56 97 179 215 275 N55   **88 Stagecoach**
Env400, Env 400H NRM, Tri/ALX400 10.5m.

TB Bromley 111 Hastings Road, Bromley, Kent, BR2 8NH
61 146 208 227 261 269 314 336 636 637 638 664 R5 R7 R10   **96 Stagecoach**
Citaro, Env200 8.9m, Env200 10.8m, Env200 10.2m, Env200/MMC 9.0,
Env400, Env400 10.8m, Tri/ALX400 10.5m.

TC Croydon Brighton Road, Croydon, CR2 6EL
60 166 194 197 264 312 403 412 466 612 627 685   **113 Arriva**
Dart/Point 10.1m, DB250/Gem, DB300/Gem2, Env200 10.2m,
Env400, OpMetroCityElec.

TF Fulwell The Old Tram Depot, Stanley Road, Twickenham, Middlesex, TW2 5NP
290 481 490 969 H20 H25 H26 H28 K3 R68 R70   **87 Abellio**
Dart/Nimb 10.5m, Dart/Point 8.8m, Dart/Point 10.1m,
Dar/Point 2 10.1m, Env200 8.9m, Env200 10.2m, Env200 10.8m,
Env200/MMC 9.0m

TH Thornton 719 London Road, Thornton Heath
    Heath *64 157 198 250 255 289 410 663 689*   **97 Arriva**
Dart/Point 9.3m, Env200 9.6m, Env200 10.2m, Env200 10.8m,
Env400,

TL Catford 180 Bromley Road, Catford, London, SE6 2XA
47 54 75 124 136 178 199 208 273 354 356 380 621 N136 N199 P4   **154 Stagecoach**
B5LH/MMC, Dart/Point 8.8m, Dart/Point 10.1m, Env200 8.9m,
Env200 10.2m, Env200 10.8m, Env200/MMC 9.0m, Env200/MMC 10.9m,
Env400, Env400H, Env400/MMC, Env400H/MMC

Code Garage	Address/*Routes Operated*/Buses Allocated	PVR	Operator
TV Tolworth	Kingston Road, Tolworth *71 85 131 265 613 662 665 671 965 K2 K4* B5LH/Gem3, B7TL/Vyk 11.0m, Dart/Point 10.1m, Dart/Point2 10.1m, Env200 8.9m, Env200 10.2m, Env200/MMC 10.9, N94/Omni Tri/ALX400 9.9m	78	RATP-Dev
UX Uxbridge	Bakers Road, Uxbridge *114 331 607 A10 U1 U2 U3 U4 U10 N207* B5LH/Gem3, B7TL/Gem 10.1m, B7TL/Pres 10.0m, Env200 10.2m, Env200 10.8m, Env200/MMC 10.9m, Env400	95	Metroline
V Stamford Brook	72-74 Chiswick High Road, London, W4 *9 10 27 E3* Env400H, N230UD/Omni, NRM	99	RATP-Dev
W Cricklewood	329 Edgware Road, Dollis Hill, London, NW2 6JP *16 32 112 139 143 168 189 210 232 316 324 332 632 643 C11 N16* Env200 10.2m, Env400H, Env400H/MMC, NRM, Tri/ALX400 9.9m	215	Metroline
WH West Ham	Stephenson Street, Canning Town, London, E16 4SA *15H 86 97 104 115 158 238 241 262 323 330 473 549 D3* Env200 10.2m, Env400, N230UD/Omni, RM, Tri/ALX400 9.9m Tri/ALX400 10.5m	156	Stagecoach
WJ Willesden Junction	Station Road, Harlesden, NW10 *18 187 206 226 228 295 N18* B5LH/Gem3, B9TL/Gem2, Env200 10.2m, Env200 10.8m	120	Metroline
WL Walworth	301 Camberwell New Road, London, SE5 0TF *172 188 343 345 381 415 484 C10 N343 N381* B7TL/Gem 10.6m, Dart/Point2 9.3m, Env 200 9.3m, Env200 10.8m, Env200/MMC 10.9m, Env400, Env400H, Env400H/MMC, Tri/ALX400 9.9m	155	Abellio
WN Wood Green	Jolly Butchers Hill, High Road, London, N22 *29 141 144 184 221 N29 W3* B5LH/Gem2, B5TL/Gem3, B7TL/Gem 10.1m, B7TL/Gem 10.6m, DB300/Gem2, Env200 10.2m, Env400	137	Arriva
WS Hayes	West London Coach Centre, North Hyde Gardens, Hayes, UB3 4QT *350 E1 E5 E7 E9 U7 U9* Dart/Point 8.8m, Env200 10.2m, Env200/MMC 10.9m, Env400H, Env400H/MMC	55	Abellio
X Westbourne Park	Great Western Road, London, W9 *23 82 70* B5LH/Evo, B9TL/Gem2, Env 200 10.2m, Env400, Env400H	72	Tower Transit

The Routes

Photo: *Ben Youngman*

It goes without saying that London has a wonderful variety of bus routes . . . and the capital boasts the best night-time service of any city in the world! As well as the night changeovers to N numbers (e.g. 35 to N35), other routes run 24 hours anyway and retain their usual identity (e.g. 24). The N routes are as a rule extended versions of the day route. Each route has its own Peak Vehicle Requirement based on service frequency, length and passenger numbers. Route 25, for instance, runs from Ilford to Oxford Circus at 3 minute intervals in the rush hour and has the highest PVR of 60 (usually Wrightbus B9TL Geminis, although the odd Enviro400 does appear). The longest routes are X26 from Heathrow to Croydon and N89 from Erith to Charing Cross - both 21 miles. As a general rule, routes running through Central London have higher PVRs.

The following pages take each route in turn and show details of requirements, frequency (Mon-Sat & Sun), operator, buses used and the garages they run from. Bus types shown in italics are not rostered for the route but appear quite frequently.

With roughly a fifth of London routes up for tender each year, there are bound to be numerous changes. This section is correct to 1st April 2017, but as companies helpfully announce changeovers in advance, we've also included details of known alterations in the coming months. New operators are shown where applicable. Some routes receiving new buses will retain their current operator.

There will also be temporary changes caused by roadworks diversions which, in some cases, can also mean a change of frequency and an adjustment to the PVR.

Forthcoming changes...

Route	Date	Change
17	new hybrid d/d	22/7/17
70	RATP Dev existing s/d	24/6/17
120	Metroline new hybrid d/d	24/6/17
131	Go-Ahead existing d/d	30/9/17
195	Abellio with new s/d	15/4/17
217	Sullivan new d/d	3/6/17
236	new s/d	29/4/17
254	Arriva NRM	3/6/17
260	new hybrid d/d	24/6/17
302	new hybrid d/d	24/6/17
382	Metroline existing s/d	15/7/17
394	new s/d	29/4/17
411	new s/d	30/9/17
427	Abellio existing d/d	8/4/17
464	Abellio new s/d	20/5/17
N136	Go-Ahead existing d/d	27/5/17
R68	Abellio with new s/d	24/6/17
R70	Abellio with new s/d	24/6/17
U5	Abellio with new s/d	TBC
X26	Go-Ahead existing d/d	15/4/17

PROPOSED CHANGES TO ROUTES IN CENTRAL LONDON

Plans are afoot to make Oxford Street more pedestrian friendly and possibly, pedestrian only.

In the main these proposals look at cutting the number of buses running down the western end of Oxford Street, the section between Oxford Circus and Marble Arch.

Oxford Street will lose six routes, whilst actually gaining one. The current PVR is 322, if the proposals are carried through it will drop to approximately 140.

The Oxford Street routes to be amended are:

Route 6 - This will run via Piccadilly and Park Lane to Marble Arch before picking up the existing route. This link has never previously been provided.

Route 13 will run to Victoria instead of Aldwych, replacing route 82 which will be withdrawn. However, route 113 will be diverted from Marble Arch along Oxford Street to Oxford Circus.

Route 23 basically becomes a totally different route. It would operate from Lancaster Gate to Wembley Stadium, completely missing out central London.

Route 73 will stop at Oxford Circus and no longer continue to Victoria.

Route 137 will terminate at Marble Arch instead of running on to Oxford Circus. The New Routemasters freed up from the changes on routes 73 & 137 are expected to take over on route 48.

Route 189 will terminate at Marble Arch and not carry on to Oxford Circus.

Other changes would see route 390 (one of those to continue in Oxford Street) run to Victoria instead of Notting Hill Gate

The C2 would terminate at Conduit Street and no longer continue to Victoria. However, route 22 will be diverted from Piccadilly Circus to Oxford Circus covering the route from Green Park vacated by the C2.

Route 3 would no longer run along Regent Street, instead it would go to Russell Square via Charing Cross Road.

Route 242 would terminate at St Pauls instead of Tottenham Court Road.

Route 46 will terminate at Paddington, rather than Lancaster Gate and route 452 will terminate at Harrow Road instead of Kensal Rise.

Route 332 keeps its start and finish points but diverts via Warwick Avenue instead of calling at Edgware Road.

No.	Route	PVR	Freq		Operator	Garage	Type Used
1	Canada Water - Tottenham Court Road Station	17	8	12	Go-Ahead	MW	B5LH/Gem3
2	West Norwood - Marylebone Station	24	8	10	Arriva	N	B5LH/Gem3
3	Crystal Palace - Piccadilly Circus	21	8	12	Abellio	QB	NRM
4	Archway - Waterloo	18	11	12	Metroline	HT	B7TL/Pres Env400
5	Romford - Canning Town	33	7	8	Stagecoach	BK	*Env400* Tri/ALX400
6	Willesden Garage - Aldwych	24	8	10	Metroline	AC	B5LH/Gem3
7	East Acton - Oxford Circus	19	8	12	Metroline	PV	B5LH/Gem3
8	Bow - Tottenham Court Road	30	7	10	Stagecoach	BW	NRM
9	Hammersmith - Aldwych	22	6	10	RATP-Dev	V	NRM
10	Hammersmith - King's Cross	23	9	12	RATP-Dev	V	NRM
11	Fulham - Liverpool Street	26	8	10	Go-Ahead	SW	NRM
12	Dulwich Library - Oxford Circus	34	5	5	Go-Ahead	Q	NRM
13	North Finchley - Victoria (formerly route 82)	28	7	11	Tower Transit	X	B5LH/Evoseti
14	Putney Heath - University College Hospital	35	7	11	Go-Ahead	AF	B5LH/Gem3 E400H MMC
15	Blackwall Station - Trafalgar Square	23	8	8	Stagecoach	BW	NRM
	(Heritage service between Tower Hill & Trafalgar Sq.)	5	20	20	Stagecoach	WH	RM
16	Cricklewood - Victoria	22	6	10	Metroline	W	NRM
17	Archway - London Bridge	18	9	15	Metroline	HT	B7TL/Pres Env400
18	Sudbury - Euston	44	4	7	Metroline	WJ	B9TL/Gem2
19	Battersea Bridge - Finsbury Park	26	8	10	Arriva	AR/BN	B5LH/Gem3
20	Debden - Walthamstow	10	15	30	Go-Ahead	NP	B9TL/Gem2
21	Lewisham - Newington Green	27	7	12	Go-Ahead	NX	NRM
22	Putney Common - Piccadilly Circus	22	8	10	Go-Ahead	AF	*B5LH/Gem2* B7TL/Gem *B9TL/Gem2*
23	Westbourne Park - Liverpool Street	30	8	10	Tower Transit	X	B5LH/Evoseti Env400 Env400H
24	Hampstead Heath - Pimlico	23	8	9	Metroline	HT	NRM
25	Ilford - Oxford Circus	60	8	6	Tower Transit	LI	B9TL/Gem2
26	Hackney Wick - Waterloo	18	11	12	CT Plus	HK	Env400H City
27	Chiswick Business Park - Chalk Farm	28	8	12	RATP-Dev	V	Env400H
28	Wandsworth - Kensal Rise	22	8	10	Tower Transit	AS	B7TL/Gem B9TL/Gem2
29	Wood Green Station - Trafalgar Square	44	5	5	Arriva	WN	B5LH/Gem2
30	Hackney Wick - Marble Arch	23	10	12	Tower Transit	LI	Env400
31	White City - Camden Town	24	7	7	Tower Transit	AS	B7TL/Gem
32	Edgware - Kilburn	17	8	12	Metroline	W	Env400 Tri/ALX400
33	Fulwell Abellio Garage - Hammersmith	18	8	15	RATP-Dev	FW	Env200
34	Barnet - Walthamstow	22	8	12	Metroline	PB	B5LH/Gem3
35	Clapham Junction - Shoreditch	21	10	15	Go-Ahead	Q	B5LH/Evoseti Env400H MMC
36	New Cross Gate - Queens Park	38	6	12	Go-Ahead	NX	B7TL/Pres Env400
37	Putney Heath - Peckham	19	10	12	Go-Ahead	PM	Env400 Tri/Olymp
38	Clapton - Victoria	55	4	5	Arriva	CT	NRM
39	Putney - Clapham Junction	15	8	12	Go-Ahead	PL	Env200 Street DF
40	Dulwich Library - Aldgate	19	8	15	Go-Ahead	Q	B5LH/Evoseti Env400H MMC
41	Tottenham Hale - Archway	22	6	10	Arriva	AR	DB300/Gem2
42	East Dulwich - Bishopsgate	16	10	15	Go-Ahead	Q	B5LH/Evoseti Env400H MMC

Go-Ahead won route 40 from Arriva in 2016. Operated from Camberwell garage a mix of B5LH/Evosetis and Enviro400H MMCs are used on the route. One of the later, EH39 heads into Gracechurch Street at Monument. *Ben Youngman*

No.	Route	PVR	Freq		Operator	Garage	Type Used
43	Friern Barnet - London Bridge	35	8	10	Metroline	HT	B9TL/Gem2
44	Tooting Station - Victoria	20	10	15	Go-Ahead	AL	*B7TL/Gem* *Env400*
45	Clapham Park - King's Cross	23	9	15	Go-Ahead	Q	*B7TL/Gem* B7TL/Pres
46	Lancaster Gate - Smithfield	19	10	15	Metroline	KC	Env200
47	Bellingham Catford Bus Garage - Shoreditch	20	10	15	Stagecoach	TL	B5LH/MMC *Env400*
48	Walthamstow - London Bridge	24	8	12	Arriva	AE	DB300/Gem2 NRM
49	Clapham Junction - White City	20	8	10	Abellio	QB	Env400H
50	Croydon - Stockwell	15	12	20	Arriva	BN	DB250/Gem
51	Orpington - Woolwich	19	10	15	Stagecoach	PD	Env400 N230/Omni
52	Willesden - Victoria	24	7	11	Metroline	AC	B5LH/Gem2 B9TL/Gem2
53	Plumstead Station - Whitehall	34	8	10	Stagecoach	PD	B5LH/Gem3 *Env400* *N230/Omni*
54	Elmers End Station - Woolwich	17	10	15	Stagecoach	TL	Env400H
55	Leyton Green - Oxford Circus	36	6	10	Stagecoach	T	NRM
56	Whipps Cross - Smithfield	22	7	8	Stagecoach	T	Env400H
57	Kingston - Clapham Park	27	8	12	Go-Ahead	AL	Env400
58	East Ham - Walthamstow	17	12	16	Tower Transit	LI	B5LH/Evoseti B9TL/Gem2
59	Streatham Hill - King's Cross	28	7	12	Arriva	BN	NRM
60	Old Coulsdon - Streatham Common	15	13	15	Arriva	TC	Env400

No.	Route	PVR	Freq		Operator	Garage	Type Used
61	Chislehurst Gordon Arms - Bromley	10	15	20	Stagecoach	TB	Env400
62	Marks Gate - Gascoigne Estate	16	12	16	Stagecoach	BK	Env400 MMC Tri/ALX400
63	Honor Oak - King's Cross	32	6	8	Go-Ahead	PM	B5LH/Evoseti Tri/Olymp

Go-Ahead has eighty-five of the the Egyptian built MCV Evosetis. Peckham's allocation work route 63. MHV54, heads through Elephant & Castle in early 2017. *Ken Carr*

64	Vulcan Way - Thornton Heath Bus Garage	21	7	15	Arriva	TH	Env400
65	Kingston - Ealing	27	6	10	RATP-Dev	FW	B5LH/Gem3 N230/Omni
66	Romford - Leytonstone	12	12	20	Arriva	GY	B7TL/ALX400 DB300/Gem2
67	Wood Green Station - Aldgate	17	10	12	Arriva	AR	DB300/Gem2
						SF	B5LH/Gem2
68	West Norwood - Euston	23	8	12	Go-Ahead	Q	NRM
69	Walthamstow - Canning Town	18	8	12	Tower Transit	LI	Env400 Env400 VE
70	Chiswick Business Park - South Kensington	18	10	15	Tower Transit	X	Env200
71	Chessington World of Adventures - Kingston	12	8	12	RATP-Dev	TV	N230/Omni
72	Alton Estate - East Acton	28	8	12	RATP-Dev	S	Dar/Point Env200
73	Stoke Newington - Victoria	53	5	6	Arriva	SF	NRM
74	Putney - Baker Street	21	8	10	Go-Ahead	AF	B5LH/Gem3 Env400H MMC
75	Croydon - Lewisham	14	13	15	Stagecoach	TL	Env400H
76	Tottenham Hale - Waterloo	24	8	12	Go-Ahead	NP	NRM DB300/Gem2
77	Tooting Station - Waterloo	18	10	12	Go-Ahead	SW	*B7TL/Gem* Env400
78	Nunhead - Shoreditch	18	9	12	Arriva	AE	Env400H City
79	Edgware - Alperton	11	12	15	Metroline	PV	*B9TL/Gem2* N230/Olym
80	Belmont Highdown Prison - Hackbridge	16	8	15	Go-Ahead	A	E200/Est Env200

No.	Route	PVR	Freq		Operator	Garage	Type Used
81	Slough - Hounslow	15	12	15	RATP-Dev	AV	Env400 N94/Omni

RATP-Dev London's Hounslow garage works route 81 to Slough. ADE34 takes a breather before another rounder at its home garage. *Ken Carr*

No.	Route	PVR	Freq		Operator	Garage	Type Used
83	Alperton - Golders Green	19	8	10	Metroline	ON	B9TL/Gem2
85	Kingston - Putney	15	8	10	RATP-Dev	TV	B5LH/Gem3
86	Romford - Stratford	34	6	10	Stagecoach	NS	Tri/ALX400
						WH	Tri/ALX400
87	Wandsworth - Aldwych	22	6	12	Go-Ahead	SW	B7TL/Gem Env400
88	Clapham Common - Camden Town	24	8	12	Go-Ahead	SW	NRM
89	Slade Green - Lewisham	17	10	20	Go-Ahead	BX	B9TL/Gem2 Env400
90	Feltham - Northolt	15	10	15	Metroline	PA	B9TL/Gem2 N230/Olym
91	Crouch End - Trafalgar Square	21	8	10	Metroline	HT	NRM
92	Brent Park - Ealing Hospital	18	9	11	Metroline	G	Env400
93	North Cheam - Putney	25	7	10	Go-Ahead	A	B5LH/Evoseti B5LH/Gem3 Tri/Olymp
94	Acton Green - Piccadilly Circus	31	5	8	RATP-Dev	S	B7TL/Gem3 Env400H
95	Southall - Shepherd's Bush	14	12	20	Metroline	G	Env200
96	Bluewater - Woolwich	24	8	12	Stagecoach	PD	Env400 N230/Omni
97	Chingford - Stratford City	22	8	12	Stagecoach	WH/T	Tri/ALX400
98	Willesden - Russell Square	23	7	10	Metroline	AC	B5LH/Gem3 B7TL/Pres BYD D/D

121

No.	Route	PVR	Freq		Operator	Garage	Type Used
99	Bexleyheath - Woolwich	13	12	15	Stagecoach	PD	Env400 Tri/ALX400
100	Shadwell - Elephant & Castle	18	8	12	Go-Ahead	MW	Env200
101	Wanstead - Gallions Reach Shopping Park	12	12	15	Go-Ahead	RR	B9TL/Gem2
102	Edmonton Green - Brent Cross	25	8	12	Arriva	AD	Env400
103	Chase Cross - Rainham	13	10	20	Stagecoach	NS	Tri/ALX400
						RM	Env400
104	Manor Park - Stratford	18	10	15	Stagecoach	WH	Env400 Tri/ALX400
105	Greenford Station - Heathrow Airport Central	17	10	15	Metroline	PA	B9TL/Gem2
106	Finsbury Park - Whitechapel	17	8	10	Arriva	AE	DB300/Gem2

Arriva have at least another year operating route 106. Wrightbus Gemini 2 Integral buses operate the six mile route. DW517 heads along Mare Street, just over halfway into its journey. *Ken Carr*

No.	Route	PVR	Freq		Operator	Garage	Type Used
107	New Barnet Station - Edgware	11	15	20	Metroline	EW	Env400
108	Lewisham - Stratford International Station	17	10	15	Go-Ahead	NX	Citaro Irizar Electric
109	Croydon - Brixton	25	6	10	Abellio	BC	Env400H MMC
110	Hounslow - West Middlesex Hospital	7	20	30	RATP-Dev	AV	Dar/Point Env200
111	Heathrow Airport Central - Kingston	25	10	12	RATP-Dev	AV	N230/Omni
112	Ealing - Brent Cross	9	12	15	Metroline	W	Env200
113	Edgware - Marble Arch	18	10	20	Metroline	EW	Env400H
114	Ruislip - Mill Hill	18	10	12	Metroline	UX	B5LH/Gem3
115	East Ham - Aldgate	19	8	11	Stagecoach	WH	Tri/ALX400
116	Ashford Hospital - Hounslow	7	12	20	RATP-Dev	HH	B5LH/Gem3
117	Staines - West Middlesex Hospital	9	20	30	Metroline	AH	Env200
118	Morden - Brixton	13	13	20	Go-Ahead	SW	Env400

No.	Route	PVR	Freq		Operator	Garage	Type Used
119	Bromley - Purley Way The Colonnades	16	10	15	Go-Ahead	C	B5LH/Gem3
120	Northolt - Hounslow	17	10	12	RATP-Dev	AV	CN94/Omni
							Env400
							N230/Omni
121	Enfield Lock - Turnpike Lane Station	21	10	15	Arriva	E	DB300/Gem2
122	Plumstead Bus Garage - Crystal Palace	18	12	15	Stagecoach	PD	B5LH/Gem3
							Env400H
123	Ilford - Wood Green Station	19	11	15	Arriva	AR/EC	B7TL/ALX400
							DB300/Gem2
124	Eltham - Catford	14	10	15	Stagecoach	TL	Env200
125	Winchmore Hill - Finchley	13	12	17	Metroline	PB	B5LH/Gem3
126	Eltham - Bromley	11	10	20	Go-Ahead	MB	Env200
127	Purley - Tooting	14	13	20	Go-Ahead	C	Env400
128	Claybury - Romford	15	12	20	Arriva	DX	B7TL/ALX400
129	North Greenwich - Greenwich	7	12	20	Go-Ahead	NX	B9TL/Gem2
130	Vulcan Way - Thornton Heath	11	12	30	Go-Ahead	C	Dar/Point
							MAN/Env200
							MAN/Evo
131	Kingston - Tooting	21	8	12	RATP-Dev	TV	B5LH/Gem3
							B7TL/Vyk
							N230/Omni
							Tri/ALX400
132	Bexleyheath - North Greenwich	15	10	15	Go-Ahead	BX	B7TL/Gem
							B9TL/Gem2
							Env400
133	Streatham - Liverpool Street Station	32	7	12	Arriva	BN	B5LH/Gem2
							Env400H City
134	North Finchley - Tottenham Court Road	31	7	8	Metroline	HT	B9TL/Gem2
135	Crossharbour Asda - Old Street Station	16	10	15	Go-Ahead	SI	B5LH/MMC
136	Grove Park - Elephant & Castle	20	10	15	Stagecoach	TL	Env400
							Tri/ALX400
137	Streatham Hill - Oxford Circus	31	6	8	Arriva	BN/N	NRM
138	Coney Hall - Bromley	3	20	30	Go-Ahead	MB	Env200
139	West Hampstead - Waterloo	20	8	12	Metroline	W	Env400
							Env400H
140	Harrow Weald - Heathrow Airport Central	29	8	10	Metroline	HD	B5LH/Gem3
141	Palmers Green - London Bridge	27	7	12	Arriva	AD	B5LH/Gem2
							WN	DB300/Gem2
142	Watford - Brent Cross	15	12	15	Arriva	GR	B7TL/ALX400
							DB250/Gem
143	Brent Cross - Archway	13	12	15	Metroline	W	Env200
144	Edmonton Green - Muswell Hill	18	8	10	Arriva	WN	B5LH/Gem2
							DB300/Gem2
145	Dagenham Asda - Leytonstone	17	12	16	Stagecoach	BK	Env400 MMC
							Tri/ALX400
146	Downe - Bromley	1	60	60	Stagecoach	TB	Env200 MMC
147	Ilford - Canning Town Station	18	8	10	Go-Ahead	RR	Env400
148	Camberwell - Shepherd's Bush	25	8	10	RATP-Dev	S	NRM
149	Edmonton Green - London Bridge	38	8	8	Arriva	AR	NRM
150	Chigwell Row - Becontree Heath	14	12	20	Arriva	DX	Env400
151	Worcester Park - Wallington	14	10	20	Go-Ahead	A	B7TL/Pres
							B9TL/Gem2
							Tri/Olym
152	New Malden - Pollards Hill	15	12	20	Go-Ahead	AL	E200/East Lanc
							Env200
153	Finsbury Park - Moorgate	10	12	15	CT Plus	HK	Env200
154	Morden - Croydon	14	12	15	Go-Ahead	A	B7TL/Pres
							Tri/Olym

No.	Route	PVR	Freq		Operator	Garage	Type Used
155	Tooting - Elephant & Castle	20	8	12	Go-Ahead	AL	B5LH/Gem3
156	Wimbledon - Vauxhall	17	8	12	Abellio	QB	Env400
157	Morden - Crystal Palace	18	12	20	Arriva	N	Env400
158	Chingford Mount - Stratford	19	8	12	Stagecoach	WH	Env400
							Tri/ALX400
159	Streatham - Marble Arch	34	6	12	Abellio	QB	NRM
160	Sidcup - Catford	12	15	20	Arriva	DT	Env400
161	Chislehurst - North Greenwich	16	10	12	Go-Ahead	MB	B7TL/Gem
							Env400
							N94/Omni
162	Eltham Station - Beckenham Junction	11	15	20	Go-Ahead	MB	Env200
163	Morden - Wimbledon	13	8	12	Go-Ahead	AL	E200/Est
164	Sutton - Wimbledon	12	10	15	Go-Ahead	AL	E200/Est
							Env200
165	Abbey Wood Lane - Romford Brewery	12	12	20	Stagecoach	RM	Env200
166	Epsom General Hospital - Croydon	8	20	30	Arriva	TC	*Dar/Point*
							Env200
167	Loughton - Ilford	9	20	30	Stagecoach	BK	E200 MMC
168	Hamsptead Heath - Old Kent Road Tesco	21	7	12	Metroline	W	NRM
169	Clayhall - Barking	14	10	15	Stagecoach	BK	Env400
							Env400 MMC
							Tri/ALX400
170	Roehampton Danebury Avenue - Victoria	20	8	12	Go-Ahead	SW	Dar/Point
							Env200

Danebury Avenue in Roehampton, is the terminating point for route 170. The now unique DP209 (in London terms) waits at the stand before another trip to Victoria via Putney Heath. *Ken Carr*

171	Bellingham Catford Bus Garage - Holborn	25	8	12	Go-Ahead	NX	*B7TL/Pres*
							B9TL/Gem2
172	Brockley Rise - St. Paul's	17	10	15	Abellio	WL	Env400
							Tri/ALX400
173	Little Heath King George Hospital - Beckton Asda	15	10	15	Arriva	DX	Env400

No.	Route	PVR	Freq		Operator	Garage	Type Used
174	Dagnam Park Drive - Dagenham Marsh Way	23	8	15	Stagecoach	RM	Env400
175	Hillrise Estate - Dagenham Ford's Main Works	12	12	20	Stagecoach	NS	Tri/ALX400
176	Penge - Tottenham Court Road Station	28	9	12	Arriva	N	B7TL/ALX400 Env400
177	Thamesmead Town Centre - Peckham	19	10	12	Stagecoach	PD	B5LH/MMC Enviro400H
178	Woolwich - Lewisham	8	15	20	Stagecoach	TL	Dar/Point Env200 Tri/ALX400
179	Chingford - Ilford	12	12	20	Stagecoach	T	Env400
180	Thamesmead East Belvedere Ind. Est. - Lewisham	17	10	15	Go-Ahead	BV	B7TL/Pres B9TL/Gem2
181	Grove Park - Lewisham	13	12	15	Go-Ahead	MB	N94/Est
182	Uxbridge Road - Brent Cross	23	8	12	Metroline	HD	B5LH/Gem3
183	Pinner - Golders Green	23	8	10	RATP-Dev	BT	B5LH/Gem2 B5LH/SRM B7TL/Pres N230/Omni
184	Chipping Barnet - Turnpike Lane Station	19	9	12	Arriva	WN	Env200
185	Lewisham - Victoria	25	8	12	Go-Ahead	Q	B5LH/Evoseti B7TL/Pres Env400H MMC
186	Northwick Park Hospital - Brent Cross	16	12	20	Metroline	EW	Env400
187	Cent. Middlesex Hospital - Finchley Road Sainsbury's	14	10	15	Metroline	WJ	Env200
188	North Greenwich - Russell Square	25	8	12	Abellio	WL	B7TL/Gem Env400H
189	Brent Cross - Oxford Circus	19	8	12	Metroline	W	NRM
190	Richmond - West Brompton	10	15	20	Metroline	AH	E200/Evo
191	Brimsdown - Edmonton Green	18	10	15	Go-Ahead	NP	Env400
192	Enfield - Edmonton Green	14	10	15	Go-Ahead	NP	Street
193	County Park Estate - Queen's Hospital	12	9	20	Go-Ahead	RR	Dar/Cap

Hounslow based Optare Tempo OT9 pulls out of Hatton Cross. Thre route runs from Staines and has a frequency of 20 minutes on weekdays. *Paul Godding*

No.	Route	PVR	Freq		Operator	Garage	Type Used
194	Croydon - Lower Sydenham Sainsbury's	14	12	20	Arriva	TC	DB250/Gem
195	Charville Lane - Brentford	15	12	15	Metroline	G	Env200
196	Norwood Junction - Elephant & Castle	16	12	20	Go-Ahead	SW	Env400
							Env400H
197	Croydon - Peckham	15	12	20	Arriva	TC	DB250/Gem
							Env400
198	Shrublands - Thornton Heath	12	11	20	Arriva	TH	Env400
199	Bellingham Catford Bus Garage - Canada Water	12	12	15	Stagecoach	TL	Env400
							Env400 MMC
200	Raynes Park - Mitcham	16	8	13	Go-Ahead	AL	B7TL/Pres
							Env200
							E200/Est
201	Morden - Herne Hill	10	17	20	Abellio	BC	Env200
202	Blackheath - Crystal Palace	15	10	15	Go-Ahead	C	B5LH/Gem3 St
203	Staines - Hounslow	7	20	30	RATP-Dev	AV	Citaro
							Tempo
204	Edgware - Sudbury	15	10	15	Metroline	EW	Env400
205	Bow - Paddington	28	7	12	Stagecoach	BW	Env400H
							Env400H MMC
206	The Paddocks - Kilburn	12	12	20	Metroline	WJ	Env200
207	Southall Hayes By-Pass - White City	35	6	8	Metroline	HS	N230/Omni
208	Orpington - Lewisham	16	12	15	Stagecoach	TB/TL	Env400
209	Mortlake - Hammersmith	13	6	10	Metroline	AH	Env200
210	Brent Cross - Finsbury Park	16	10	11	Metroline	W	Env400
							Tri/ALX400
211	Hammersmith - Waterloo Station	20	9	12	Abellio	QB	NRM
212	Chingford - Walthamstow St James Street Station	11	10	15	Tower Transit	LI	B5LH/Gem3
213	Sutton Bus Garage - Kingston	19	8	12	Go-Ahead	A	B7TL/Pres
							Env400
214	Highgate - Moorgate	18	8	12	Metroline	KC	Dar/Point
215	Yardley Lane Estate - Walthamstow	5	20	30	Stagecoach	T	Env400
216	Staines - Kingston	10	20	30	RATP-Dev	FW	Dar/Point
						HH	Env200
217	Waltham Cross - Turnpike Lane Station	11	12	20	Metroline	PB	Env400
219	Wimbledon - Clapham Junction Asda	11	12	15	Go-Ahead	AL	Street
220	Harlesden - Wandsworth	25	8	10	RATP-Dev	PK	Env400
							Tri/ALX400
221	Edgware - Turnpike Lane Station	23	12	12	Arriva	WN	B5LH/Gem2
							B7TL/Gem
							DB250/Gem
222	Uxbridge - Hounslow	20	8	12	RATP-Dev	AV	Env400
223	Harrow - Wembley	6	20	30	Metroline	ON	Env200
224	Wembley Stadium Station - St Raphael's Estate	12	15	30	Metroline	ON	Env200
225	Hither Green - Canada Water	8	15	20	Go-Ahead	NX	Dar/Point
226	Ealing - Golders Green	16	12	20	Metroline	WJ	Env200
227	Bromley - Crystal Palace	12	8	12	Stagecoach	TB	Citaro
228	Park Royal - Maida Hill Chippenham Gardens	13	12	20	Metroline	WJ	Env200
229	Thamesmead Town Centre - Sidcup	20	10	15	Arriva	DT	Env400
230	Upper Walthamstow - Wood Green Station	13	12	15	Arriva	AR	DB300/Gem2
231	Enfield - Turnpike Lane Station	7	15	20	Go-Ahead	NP	Env400
232	St. Raphael's Estate - Turnpike Lane Station	13	15	20	Metroline	W	Env200
233	Swanley - Eltham	6	20	30	Go-Ahead	MB	Env200
234	Barnet - East Finchley Sussex Gardens	9	12	20	Metroline	PB	Env200
235	Lower Sunbury - Great West Quarter	22	9	13	Metroline	TF	Env200 MMC
236	Hackney Wick - Finsbury Park	17	8	12	Tower Transit	LI	Env200
237	Hounslow Heath - White City	21	9	13	Metroline	AH	B9TL/Gem2
238	Barking - Stratford	12	10	15	Stagecoach	WH	Env400
							Tri/ALX400
240	Edgware - Golders Green	10	12	20	Metroline	EW	Env400

No.	Route	PVR	Freq		Operator	Garage	Type Used
241	Stratford City - Canning Town	10	10	20	Stagecoach	WH	Tri/ALX400
242	Homerton Hospital - Tottenham Court Road	25	8	10	Arriva	CT	B5LH/Gem3
243	Wood Green Station - Waterloo	32	7	10	Arriva	AR	B5LH/Gem2 DB300/Gem2
244	Abbey Wood - Queen Elizabeth Hospital	12	10	15	Go-Ahead	BV	Env200
245	Alperton - Golders Green	21	8	12	Metroline	PV	B9TL/Gem2
246	Westerham - Bromley	4	30	60	Go-Ahead	MB	MAN/Evo
247	Barkingside - Romford	11	10	20	Stagecoach	NS	Tri/ALX400
248	Cranham - Romford	16	8	15	Stagecoach	RM	N230/Omni
249	Anerley Station - Clapham Common	13	12	15	Arriva	N	B5LH/Gem3
250	Croydon - Brixton	23	8	12	Arriva	TH	Env400
251	Edgware - Arnos Grove	13	12	20	RATP-Dev	BT	Env200
252	Collier Row - Hornchurch	12	10	15	Stagecoach	RM	Env400 N230/Omni
253	Hackney Central Station - Tottenham Court Road	28	6	8	Arriva	SF	NRM
254	Holloway Parkhurst Road - Aldgate	34	6	8	Arriva	AE	B7TL/Gem DB250/Gem
255	Pollards Hill - Balham	10	12	20	Arriva	TH	Env200
256	Noak Hill - Sutton Lane	11	10	20	Stagecoach	RM	Env200
257	Walthamstow - Stratford	15	8	12	Go-Ahead	NP	B7TL/Gem
258	Watford - South Harrow	11	15	30	Arriva Shires	GR	DB250/Gem
259	Edmonton Green - King's Cross	21	8	10	Arriva	AR	B5LH/Gem3
260	Golders Green - White City	17	13	16	Metroline	AC	B7TL/Pres
261	Princess Royal University Hospital - Lewisham	12	12	15	Stagecoach	TB	Env400

Route 262 uses a mix of Trident ALX400s and Scania OmniCitys. This is one of a number of routes that work to supermarkets. 18259 calls in at Stratford on its way to Sainsbury's. *Michael J. McClelland*

262	Beckton Sainsbury's - Stratford	12	10	15	Stagecoach	WH	N230/Omni Tri/ALX400
263	Barnet Hospital - Highbury	18	10	12	Metroline	PB	Env400

No.	Route	PVR	Freq		Operator	Garage	Type Used
264	Croydon - St. George's Hospital	15	11	15	Arriva	TC	DB300/Gem2
265	Tolworth - Putney Bridge	12	12	15	RATP-Dev	TV	Env200
266	Brent Cross - Hammersmith	26	8	11	Tower Transit	AS	B9TL/Gem2
267	Fulwell - Hammersmith	17	10	15	RATP-Dev	FW	N94/Omni
							N230/Omni
268	Golders Green - Finchley Road O2 Centre	8	12	12	Arriva Shires	GR	SB120/Cadet
269	Bexleyheath - Bromley	13	10	15	Stagecoach	TB	Tri/ALX400
270	Mitcham - Putney Bridge	14	11	12	Go-Ahead	AL	B7TL/Gem
							B7TL/Pres
							Env400
271	Highgate - Moorgate	13	9	13	Metroline	HT	Env400
272	Chiswick (Grove Park) - Shepherd's Bush	8	15	15	RATP-Dev	S	Env200
273	Petts Wood - Lewisham Tesco	8	20	30	Stagecoach	TL	Env200 MMC
274	Lancaster Gate - Islington	17	8	8	Metroline	KC	Env200
275	Barkingside - Walthamstow St. James Street Stn.	13	12	20	Stagecoach	T	Env400
276	Stoke Newington - Newham General Hospital	19	12	15	Go-Ahead	SI	Env200
277	Highbury - Crossharbour	25	7	10	Stagecoach	BW	Env400
							N230/Omni
279	Waltham Cross - Manor House	33	6	10	Arriva	E	Env400
280	Belmont - Tooting St. George's Hospital	14	10	12	Go-Ahead	AL	*B7TL/Gem*
							B7TL/Pres
							Env400
281	Tolworth - Hounslow	25	8	12	RATP-Dev	FW	*N94/Omni*
							N230/Omni

Route 281 runs at an 8 minute frequency, the eleven mile route needs twenty-five buses to achieve this. SP88 runs through Surbiton with a run from Hounslow. *Paul Godding*

No.	Route	PVR	Freq		Operator	Garage	Type Used
282	Mount Vernon Hospital - Ealing Hospital	16	12	15	Metroline	G	Env400
283	East Acton - Barn Elms	16	8	12	RATP-Dev	PK	Versa
284	Grove Park Cemetery - Lewisham	12	12	20	Go-Ahead	MB	Env200
285	Heathrow Airport Central - Kingston	19	10	12	RATP-Dev	HH	B5LH/Gem3
286	Sidcup - Greenwich	14	10	15	Go-Ahead	NX	Env200

No.	Route	PVR	Freq		Operator	Garage	Type Used
287	Abbey Wood Lane - Barking	7	15	20	Stagecoach	RM	Env400
288	Broadfields - Queensbury Morrisons	7	10	15	Arriva Shires	GR	SB120/Cadet
289	Purley - Elmers End	10	15	20	Arriva	TH	Env200
290	Staines - Twickenham	7	20	20	Abellio	TF	Env200
291	Woodlands Estate - Queen Elizabeth Hospital	6	10	15	Stagecoach	PD	Dar/Point Env200
292	Rossington Ave - Colindale Asda	9	15	20	RATP-Dev	BT	N94/Omni N230/Omni
293	Epsom General Hospital - Morden	6	20	30	Go-Ahead	C	N230B/Omni
294	Noak Hill - Havering Park	11	12	20	Stagecoach	NS	Env400 MMC
295	Ladbroke Grove - Clapham Junction	21	8	12	Metroline	WJ	B5LH/Gem3 St
296	Romford - Ilford Sainsbury's	6	20	30	Stagecoach	NS	Env200
297	Willesden Garage - Ealing Haven Green	16	10	12	Metroline	PA	B9TL/Gem2 N230/Olym
298	Cranbourne Road - Arnos Grove	6	20	30	Sullivan	SM	Env200
299	Cockfosters - Muswell Hill	7	15	30	Go-Ahead	NP	Env200
300	East Ham - Canning Town	10	15	20	Go-Ahead	SI	Env200
302	Mill Hill - Kensal Rise	16	8	12	Metroline	AC	B7TL/Pres
303	Colindale Asda - Edgware	6	15	20	Arriva Shires	GR	SB120/Cadet
305	Kingsbury - Edgware	4	15	30	Arriva Shires	GR	SB120/Cadet
307	Brimsdown - Barnet Hospital	15	10	20	Stagecoach	PB	Env400
308	Wanstead - Clapton	13	12	20	Tower Transit	LI	Env400
309	Canning Town Station - London Chest Hospital	9	12	15	CT Plus	HK	Env200 MMC Solo
312	South Croydon - Norwood Junction	7	12	20	Arriva	TC	Env200 Metro/EV
313	Potters Bar - Chingford	7	20	30	Arriva	E	Env200
314	New Addington - Eltham	12	15	30	Stagecoach	TB	Env200
315	West Norwood Station - Balham	4	20	30	Go-Ahead	SW	Dar/Point
316	Cricklewood - White City	17	9	13	Metroline	W	Env200
317	Waltham Cross - Enfield	5	20	30	Arriva	E	B7TL/Gem DB250/Gem
318	North Middlesex Hospital - Stamford Hill	7	15	20	Arriva	E	B7TL/Gem DB250/Gem
319	Streatham Hill - Sloane Square	20	9	12	Arriva	BN	B5LH/Gem2 DB300/Gem2
320	Biggin Hill Valley - Catford	12	12	20	Go-Ahead	MB	B7TL/Gem N94/Omni N230/Omni
321	Foots Cray Tesco - New Cross Sainsbury's	20	8	12	Go-Ahead	NX	B7TL/Pres *B9TL/Gem2*
322	Crystal Palace - Clapham Common	10	13	15	Go-Ahead	SW	Env200
323	Canning Town Station - Mile End	4	15	20	Stagecoach	WH	Env200
324	Stanmore - Brent Cross Tesco	6	20	20	Metroline	W	Env200
325	Prince Regent Station - Beckton Sainsbury's	12	12	20	Arriva	DX	Env200
326	Barnet - Brent Cross	14	12	15	RATP-Dev	BT	Env200
327	Waltham Cross - Waltham Cross	1	30	-	Go-Ahead	NP	Street
328	Golders Green - Chelsea	23	8	10	Tower Transit	AS	B5LH/Gem3 St
329	Enfield - Turnpike Lane Station	16	7	8	Arriva	AD	Env400
330	Forest Gate Wanstead Park Station - Canning Town	8	14	22	Stagecoach	WH	Tri/ALX400
331	Ruislip - Uxbridge	8	20	30	Metroline	UX	Env200
332	Neasden Tesco - Paddington	15	10	12	Metroline	W	Env400 MMC
333	Tooting - Elephant & Castle	16	10	12	Arriva	BN	B5LH/Gem2 Env400H City
336	Locksbottom - Catford	10	15	20	Stagecoach	TB	Env200 MMC
337	Richmond - Clapham Junction	11	12	15	Go-Ahead	AF	Env400
339	Leytonstone Station - Shadwell Station	10	15	20	Tower Transit	LI	Env200
340	Edgware - Harrow	9	12	20	Arriva Shires	GR	Streetdeck
341	Lea Valley Tesco - Waterloo County Hall	21	11	12	Arriva	AR	DB300/Gem2

No.	Route	PVR	Freq		Operator	Garage	Type Used
343	New Cross Gate - City Hall	25	7	11	Abellio	WL	B7TL/Gem
							Env400
344	Clapham Junction - Liverpool Street	25	7	8	Abellio	QB	Env400H
							Env400H MMC
345	Peckham - South Kensington	26	8	10	Abellio	WL	Env400
346	Upminster Park Estate - Upminster	3	15	-	Go-Ahead	RR	Env200
347	Ockendon Station - Romford (10am - 4pm only)	1	120	-	Arriva	GY	Env200
349	Ponders End - Stamford Hill	16	8	12	Arriva	E	DB300/Gem2
350	Hayes - Heathrow Airport Terminal 5	8	12	20	Abellio	WS	Env400 MMC
352	Lower Sydenham Sainsbury's - Bromley	6	20	30	Go-Ahead	MB	Env200
353	Ramsden - Forestdale	8	15	30	Go-Ahead	MB	B7TL/Gem
							N94/Omni
354	Penge - Bromley	5	20	30	Stagecoach	TL	Env200
355	Mitcham - Brixton	12	13	15	Go-Ahead	C	Dar/Point
356	Shirley - Upper Sydenham	7	20	30	Stagecoach	TL	Env200
357	Chingford Hatch - Whipps Cross	8	15	30	Go-Ahead	NP	B9TL/Gem2
358	Orpington Station - Crystal Palace	17	12	20	Go-Ahead	MB	Citaro
359	Addington Interchange - Purley	3	30	30	Go-Ahead	C	Man240/Evo
360	Albert Hall - Elephant & Castle	12	12	15	Go-Ahead	Q	BYD Elec
							SB120/Ecity
362	Grange Hill - Little Heath King George Hospital	3	30	30	Stagecoach	BK	Env200 MMC
363	Crystal Palace - Elephant & Castle	13	10	12	Go-Ahead	PM	Env400H MMC
364	Dagenham East - Ilford	14	10	15	Go-Ahead	RR	Env200
365	Orchard Estate - Havering Park	11	12	20	Stagecoach	RM	N230/Omni
366	Redbridge - Beckton Asda	18	10	25	Stagecoach	BK	Env200
367	Bromley - Croydon	9	20	30	Abellio	BC	Env200 MMC
368	Chadwell Heath - Harts Lane Estate	10	10	20	Arriva	DX	Env400
370	Lakeside - Romford	11	15	30	Arriva	GY	B7TL/ALX400
371	Kingston - Richmond Manor Road Sainsbury's	15	9	12	RATP-Dev	FW	*Dar/Point*
							Env200
							Env200H
							N230/Omni
							Tri/ALX400
372	Lakeside - Hornchurch	6	20	30	Stagecoach	RM	Env400
375	Passingford Bridge - Romford	1	90	-	Arriva	GY	Env200
376	Beckton - East Ham	8	15	30	Go-Ahead	RR	Env200
377	Oakwood - Ponders End	4	30	-	Arriva	E	Env200 MMC
379	Yardley Lane Estate - Chingford	3	15	30	Go-Ahead	NP	Dart/Esteem
380	Belmarsh - Lewisham	14	12	15	Stagecoach	TL	Dar/Point
							Env200
381	Peckham - Waterloo County Hall	19	11	12	Abellio	WL	B7TL/Gem
382	Millbrook Park - Southgate	9	15	30	Arriva	EC	Env200
383	Barnet - Woodside Park Station	3	30	-	Uno	HF	Env200
384	Quinta Drive - Cockfosters	9	15	30	Metroline	PB	Env200
385	Chingford - Crooked Billet (10am - 3pm only)	1	70	-	CT Plus	AW	Env200
386	Woolwich - Blackheath Village	11	15	20	Stagecoach	PD	Env200
388	Stratford City - Blackfriars	14	10	12	CT Plus	HK	Env400H City
389	Barnet - Barnet Western Way (11am - 4pm only)	1	60	-	Go-Ahead	NP	Env200
390	Archway - Notting Hill Gate	23	8	12	Metroline	HT	NRM
391	Richmond - Sands End	18	11	13	RATP-Dev	FW	N230/Omni
							Tri/ALX400
							Versa
393	Clapton - Chalk Farm Morrisons	14	12	15	Arriva	CT	Env200
394	Homerton Hospital - Islington Tolpuddle Street	10	12	20	CT Plus	HK	Dar/Nimb
							Env200
395	Westway Cross - Harrow	5	20	30	Metroline	PA	Env200
396	Little Heath King George Hospital - Ilford Sainsbury's	5	20	20	Stagecoach	BK	*Env200*
							Versa
397	Debden - Crooked Billet	5	30	30	CT Plus	AW	Env200 MMC

A number of the TfL routes also run to hospitals. Route 394 links Homerton Hospital to Islington. The elderly Dart Nimbus buses operated on the route by CT Plus will be replaced in May 2017 with Enviro200 MMCs. *Ben Youngman*

No.	Route	PVR	Freq		Operator	Garage	Type Used
398	Ruislip - Wood End	3	30	-	Lon.Sovereign	SO	Dar/Point
399	Hadley Wood - Barnet (10am - 3pm only)	1	60	-	Go-Ahead	NP	Env200
401	Thamesmead Town Centre - Bexleyheath	8	15	30	Go-Ahead	BX	B7TL/Pres B9TL/Gem2 Env400
403	Warlingham - Croydon	7	12	20	Arriva	TC	DB250/Gem
404	Caterham-on-the-Hill - Coulsdon	1	60	-	Quality Line	EB	Solo
405	Redhill - Croydon	10	15	30	Go-Ahead	C	B5LH/Gem3 B9TL/Gem2 N230/Omni
406	Epsom - Kingston	6	20	30	Quality Line	EB	Env400
407	Caterham - Sutton	16	13	21	Abellio	BC	Env200 Env400H MMC
410	Wallington - Crystal Palace	19	9	15	Arriva	TH	Dar/Point SB120/Cadet
411	West Molesey - Kingston	6	20	30	Quality Line	EB	Versa
412	Purley - Croydon	8	15	20	Arriva	TC	DB250/Gem
413	Sutton - Morden	8	15	30	Quality Line	EB	Citaro
414	Putney Bridge Station - Maida Hill	19	9	13	Abellio	QB	Env400
415	Tulse Hill - Old Kent Road Tesco	10	12	20	Abellio	WL	Env400H MMC
417	Crystal Palace - Clapham Common	12	10	15	Arriva	N	DB300/Gem2
418	Epsom - Kingston	7	20	30	Quality Line	EB	Env400

131

No.	Route	PVR	Freq		Operator	Garage	Type Used
419	Richmond - Hammersmith	6	15	30	RATP-Dev	S	Dar/Point
422	Bexleyheath Bus Garage - North Greenwich	16	10	12	Go-Ahead	BX	B9TL/Gem2
							Env400
423	Heathrow Airport (Terminal 5) - Hounslow	7	20	30	RATP-Dev	HH	Env200
424	Putney Heath - Fulham Craven Cottage	5	30	-	Go-Ahead	AF	Dar/Point
425	Clapton Nightingale Road - Stratford	11	12	15	Tower Transit	LI	Env400
427	Uxbridge - Acton	22	8	10	Metroline	HS	B9TL/Gem2
428	Bluewater - Erith	9	15	30	Arriva	DT	Env200
430	Roehampton Danebury Avenue - South Kensington	16	8	10	Go-Ahead	AF	B5LH/Gem3
							Env400H MMC
432	Anerley Station - Brixton	10	12	15	Go-Ahead	SW	B9TL/Gem2
433	Addington Interchange - Croydon	10	8	15	Abellio	BC	Env200
434	Rickman Hill - Whyteleafe Station	3	30	30	Go-Ahead	C	Env200
436	Lewisham - Battersea Park	21	8	12	Go-Ahead	NX	B9TL/Gem2
							Env400H
440	Stonebridge Park Station - Gunnersbury	10	15	20	RATP-Dev	PK	Versa
444	Chingford - Turnpike Lane Station	11	12	15	Tower Transit	LI	Env200
							Street DF
450	Lower Sydenham Sainsbury's - West Croydon	19	8	15	Arriva	N	Street DF
452	Kensal Rise - Vauxhall	23	8	12	Abellio	QB	Env400
453	Deptford - Marylebone Station	36	8	10	Go-Ahead	MW	NRM
455	Old Lodge Lane - Wallington	11	20	30	Go-Ahead	C	Env200
460	North Finchley - Willesden	10	12	15	Metroline	AC	B7TL/Pres

Quality Line introduced eight Streetlites on route 463 in April 2016. From June a ninth joined them, this was transferred in from parent company RATP-Dev and became WS11. Here it loads in Wallington.
Brian Kemp

462	Limes Farm - Ilford	8	15	30	Stagecoach	BK	Env200 MMC
463	Coulsdon South Station - Pollards Hill	9	20	30	Quality Line	EB	Street
464	Tatsfield - New Addington	3	30	60	Go-Ahead	MB	Dar/Point

Route 465 from Kingston to Dorking, at 15 miles, is one of the longer routes operating in London. OV09 heads through Surbiton, on a journey which can take up to an hour and a half. *Paul Godding*

No.	Route	PVR	Freq		Operator	Garage	Type Used
465	Dorking - Kingston	7	30	60	Quality Line	EB	Versa
466	Caterham-on-the-Hill - Addington Interchange	17	10	15	Arriva	TC	DB250/Gem Env400
467	Hook - Epsom	2	60	-	Quality Line	EB	Env400
468	South Croydon - Elephant & Castle	29	8	12	Go-Ahead	Q	B7TL/Gem Env400
469	Erith - Queen Elizabeth Hospital	8	15	20	Arriva	DT	Env200
470	Epsom - Colliers Wood	7	30	-	Quality Line	EB	Solo
472	Thamesmead Town Centre - North Greenwich	22	6	10	Stagecoach	PD	Env400H Env400
473	North Woolwich - Stratford	10	10	15	Stagecoach	WH	N230/Omni
474	Manor Park - Canning Town	12	12	15	Go-Ahead	RR	B9TL/Gem2 Env400
476	Northumberland Park - Euston	23	8	12	Go-Ahead	NP	B9TL/Gem2
481	Isleworth West Middlesex Hospital - Kingston	4	30	60	Abellio	TF	Env200
482	Southall - Heathrow Airport Terminal 5	8	20	30	Metroline	G	Env400
483	Harrow - Ealing Hospital	25	8	10	Metroline	ON	B9TL/Gem2
484	Lewisham - Camberwell	13	10	15	Abellio	WL	Env200
485	Wandsworth - Hammersmith	3	30	-	Go-Ahead	AL	Dar/Point
486	Bexleyheath - North Greenwich	16	8	12	Go-Ahead	BX	*B9TL/Gem2* Env400
487	South Harrow - Willesden Junction Station	9	15	20	Metroline	ON	Env200
488	Dalston Junction - Bromley-by-Bow Tesco	11	12	15	Tower Transit	LI	Env200
490	Heathrow Airport Terminal 5 - Richmond	15	12	20	Abellio	TF	Env200
491	Waltham Cross - North Middlesex Hospital	10	15	30	Go-Ahead	NP	Street
492	Bluewater - Sidcup	6	30	30	Arriva	DT	Env400
493	Richmond Homebase - Tooting St. George's Hospital	17	12	20	Go-Ahead	PL	Env200

133

No.	Route	PVR	Freq		Operator	Garage	Type Used
496	Harold Wood - Romford Queens Hospital	8	15	20	Stagecoach	NS	Env400 Tri/ALX400
498	Brentwood Sainsbury's - Romford Queens Hospital	6	20	30	Stagecoach	NS	Env400 MMC
499	Gallows Corner Tesco - Heath Park Estate	7	20	30	Stagecoach	NS	Env200 MMC
507	Victoria - Waterloo	15	6	12	Go-Ahead	RA	BYD/ADL Elec
521	Waterloo - London Bridge (Mon-Fri only)	31	5	-	Go-Ahead	RA	BYD/ADL Elec
549	Loughton Station - South Woodford	1	60	75	Stagecoach	WH	Env200 MMC
603	Muswell Hill - Swiss Cottage (Mon-Fri only 4 Trips)	2			Metroline	HT	Tri/Pres
607	Uxbridge - White City	20	11	13	Metroline	UX	B7TL/Gem Env400
A10	Uxbridge - Heathrow Airport Central	5	15	30	Metroline	UX	Env200
B11	Thamesmead - Bexleyheath Bus Garage	7	15	30	Go-Ahead	BX	Env200
B12	Joydens Wood - Erith	7	20	30	Arriva	DT	Env200
B13	New Eltham - Bexleyheath	6	15	30	Arriva	DT	Env200 MMC
B14	Orpington - Bexleyheath	5	30	30	Go-Ahead	BX	Env200
B15	Bexleyheath - Horn Park	6	20	30	Arriva	DT	Env200
B16	Kidbrooke Station - Bexleyheath Bus Garage	9	15	30	Go-Ahead	BX	Env200
C1	White City - Victoria	15	11	13	RATP-Dev	S	Env200
C2	Parliament Hill - Victoria	19	8	10	Abellio	QB	Env400 Env400H
C3	Clapham Junction - Earl's Court Tesco	12	8	12	Abellio	QB	Env400 Env400H
C10	Canada Water - Victoria	20	9	12	Abellio	WL	Env200 MMC
C11	Brent Cross - Archway	20	9	12	Metroline	W	Env200
D3	Crossharbour Asda - London Chest Hospital	14	10	15	Stagecoach	WH	Env200
D6	Crossharbour Asda - Cambridge Heath	14	8	15	Go-Ahead	SI	Env200
D7	Poplar - Mile End	14	7	12	Go-Ahead	SI	B9TL/Gem2
D8	Crossharbour Asda - Stratford International	9	12	20	Go-Ahead	SI	N230/Omni
E1	Greenford - Ealing Haven Green	8	10	10	Abellio	WS	Env400H

One of the bigger surprises of 2016, was the announcement that routes EL1, EL2 and EL3 (renumbered from 387) would be getting NRMs. The EL3 was the first to convert. On the first day, 18th February 2017, LT882 (on loan from Northumberland Park) and LT905 wait on the stand at Little Heath. *Tony Saltwell*

No.	Route	PVR	Freq		Operator	Garage	Type Used
E2	Greenford - Brentford	16	8	12	Metroline	AH	B9TL/Gem2
E3	Greenford - Chiswick	26	7	10	RATP-Dev	V	N230/Omni
E5	Toplocks - Perivale Tesco	12	12	20	Abellio	WS	Env200 MMC
E6	Greenford Station - Bulls Bridge Tesco	13	10	15	Metroline	PA	Env200
E7	Ruislip - Ealing	11	12	20	Abellio	WS	Env200 MMC
E8	Hounslow - Ealing	15	8	10	Metroline	AH	Env400
E9	Yeading Barnhill Estate - Ealing Haven Green	8	12	20	Abellio	WS	Env400
E10	Islip Manor - Ealing	8	15	20	Arriva	HE	Env200
E11	Greenford - Warwick Drive	5	20	30	RATP-Dev	PK	Env200
EL1	Barking Reach - Ilford Hill	15	6	10	Go-Ahead	RR	NRM
EL2	Dagenham Dock - Becontree Hill	15	8	15	Go-Ahead	RR	NRM
EL3	Little Heath - Barking Reach	14	10	20	Go-Ahead	RR	NRM
G1	Streatham High Road - Shaftesbury Estate	13	15	20	Go-Ahead	PL	Env200
H2	Golders Green - Golders Green (circular Trip)	3	12	15	Arriva	GR	Solo

OS69 pulls into its dedicated bus stop at Golders Green. The H2 runs every twelve minutes to Hampstead Garden Suburb. *Ken Carr*

No.	Route	PVR	Freq		Operator	Garage	Type Used
H3	Golders Green - Golders Green (circular Trip)	1	60	-	Arriva	GR	Solo
H9	Harrow - Harrow (circular Trip)	8	10	15	RATP-Dev	SO	Env200
H10	Harrow - Harrow (circular Trip)	8	10	15	RATP-Dev	SO	Env200
H11	Mount Vernon Hospital - Harrow	7	15	20	RATP-Dev	SO	Env200
H12	Stanmore - South Harrow	12	10	15	Metroline	HD	B7TL/Pres
H13	St. Vincent's Park - Ruislip Lido	6	20	30	RATP-Dev	SO	Dar/Point Env200
H14	Hatch End - Northwick Park Hospital	8	10	15	RATP-Dev	SO	Env200
H17	Wembley - Harrow	7	15	20	RATP-Dev	SO	Env200
H18	Harrow - Harrow (circular Trip - buses shared with H19)	7	20	30	Arriva	GR	Env200
H19	Harrow - Harrow (circular Trip - buses shared with H18)	7	20	30	Arriva	GR	Env200
H20	Ivybridge Tesco - Hounslow Civic Centre	6	12	20	Abellio	TF	Env200
H22	Hounslow - Richmond Manor Circus	11	12	20	RATP-Dev	HH	Dar/Point
H25	Butts Farm - Hatton Cross	9	15	20	Abellio	TF	Dar/Nimb
H26	Sparrow Farm - Hatton Cross	5	20	30	Abellio	TF	Env200 MMC
H28	Bulls Bridge Tesco - Osterley Tesco	9	20	30	Abellio	TF	Env200
H32	Southall - Hounslow	13	10	15	RATP-Dev	AV	N230/Omni
H37	Hounslow - Richmond Manor Circus	15	6	8	RATP-Dev	AV	Tempo

No.	Route	PVR	Freq		Operator	Garage	Type Used
H91	Hounslow West - Hammersmith	16	10	15	RATP-Dev	HH	N230/Omni
H98	Hayes End Kingsway - Hounslow	16	8	15	RATP-Dev	AV	Env200 Metro/EV
K1	New Malden - Kingston	12	15	20	Abellio	BC	Env200
K2	Hook Library - Kingston Hospital	10	10	15	RATP-Dev	TV	Env200
K3	Esher - Roehampton Vale Asda	11	15	20	Abellio	TF	Env200
K4	Mansfield Estate - Kingston Hospital	4	30	-	RATP-Dev	TV	Env200
K5	Ham - Morden	6	30	-	Quality Line	EB	Solo
P4	Lewisham - Brixton	13	12	12	Stagecoach	TL	Dar/Point Env200
P5	Nine Elms Patmore Estate - Elephant & Castle	10	15	20	Go-Ahead	Q	Env200 Env200 MMC
P12	Brockley Rise - Surrey Quays	15	10	20	Go-Ahead	PM	Env200
P13	Streatham - New Cross Gate Sainsbury's	11	15	20	Abellio	BC	Env200
R1	Green Street Green - Grovelands	7	15	30	Go-Ahead	MB	Env200
R2	Melody Road - Orpington	4	30	-	Go-Ahead	MB	Man240/Est
R3	Orpington - Princess Royal University Hospital	4	30	60	Go-Ahead	MB	Dar/Point
R4	Pauls Cray Hill - Princess Royal University Hospital	6	20	60	Go-Ahead	MB	Dar/Point Env200
R5	Orpington - Orpington (circ. Trip - buses shared with R10)	1	150	-	Stagecoach	TB	Env200

The single bus allocated to route R5 also works route R10, it alternates between the two during the day. 36581 picks-up in Orpington whilst working the former. *Robert Mighton*

R6	Orpington - St Mary Cray	2	30	60	Go-Ahead	MB	Dar/Point
R7	Orpington - Chelsfield	1	70	-	Stagecoach	TB	Env200
R8	Orpington - Biggin Hill	1	80	-	Go-Ahead	MB	Solo
R9	Orpington - Ramsden	3	12	30	Go-Ahead	MB	Env200
R10	Orpington - Orpington (circ. Trip - buses shared with R5)	1	150	-	Stagecoach	TB	Env200
R11	Green Street Green - Sidcup Queen Mary's Hospital	7	15	30	Go-Ahead	MB	Env200
R68	Hampton Court - Kew Retail Park	10	15	15	Abellio	TF	Env200
R70	Richmond Homebase - Nurserylands	11	10	15	Abellio	TF	Env200

The RV1 is the home of the hydrogen buses. They should be joined in 2017 by two new buses built by Van Hool. Here, WSH62991 is on diversion at Tower Gateway during the Tower Bridge closure. *Madeleine Carr*

No.	Route	PVR	Freq		Operator	Garage	Type Used
RV1	Tower Gateway Station - Covent Garden	10	12	12	Tower Transit	LI	Env200 HYDRO
S1	Banstead - Lavender Fields	11	16	20	Quality Line	EB	Metrocity
S3	Sutton Hospital - Malden Manor Station	8	20	-	Quality Line	EB	Env200 Solo
S4	Roundshaw - St. Helier Station	6	30	-	Abellio	BC	Env200
U1	West Drayton - Ruislip	8	15	30	Metroline	UX	Env200
U2	Brunel University - Uxbridge	9	10	20	Metroline	UX	Env200
U3	Heathrow Airport Central - Uxbridge	11	12	20	Metroline	UX	Env200 Tri/Pres
U4	Prologis Park - Uxbridge	14	8	15	Metroline	UX	Env400 Tri/Pres
U5	Hayes - Uxbridge	11	12	20	Metroline	HS	Env200
U7	Hayes Sainsbury's - Uxbridge	5	30	30	Abellio	WS	Env200
U9	Harefield Hospital - Uxbridge	3	20	60	Abellio	WS	Env200 MMC
U10	Heathfield Rise - Uxbridge	2	60	-	Metroline	UX	Env200
W3	Northumberland Park - Finsbury Park	23	6	10	Arriva	WN	Env400
W4	Oakthorpe Park - Jarrow Road	13	10	15	Go-Ahead	NP	Env200
W5	Archway - Harringay Sainsbury's	8	12	20	CT Plus	HK	Env200 Solo
W6	Southgate - Edmonton Green	9	10	15	Arriva	E	Dar/Point
W7	Muswell Hill - Finsbury Park	17	6	8	Metroline	HT	B9TL/Gem2
W8	Chase Farm Hospital - Picketts Lock	15	8	12	Metroline	PB	Env400
W9	Chase Farm Hospital - Southgate	8	15	30	Sullivan	SM	Env200 MMC
W10	Crews Hill - Enfield (11am-3pm)	1	60	-	Go-Ahead	NP	Env200
W11	Chingford Hall Estate - Walthamstow	8	10	15	CT Plus	AW	Env200 MMC
W12	Wanstead - Coppermill Lane	6	20	30	CT Plus	HK	Solo

Two recent wins for CT Plus are routes W16 & W19, both from Go-Ahead. Both routes operate out of the new Walthamstow garage. In a surprising move for the W19 the original style of Enviro200s were ordered whereas the W16 has got MMCs. One of each meet at Leytonstone Station. *Michael J. McClelland*

No.	Route	PVR	Freq		Operator	Garage	Type Used
W13	Woodford Wells - Leytonstone	5	15	30	CT Plus	HK	E200 MMC
W14	Woodford Bridge - Leyton Asda	10	15	20	Tower Transit	LI	Env200
W15	Cogan Avenue - Hackney	21	8	12	Tower Transit	LI	Env200
W16	Chingford Mount - Leytonstone Station	9	12	20	CT Plus	AW	Env200 MMC
W19	Ilford - Argyll Avenue Industrial Estate	15	13	20	CT Plus	AW	Env200
X26	West Croydon - Heathrow Airport Central	10	30	30	Quality Line	EB	Citaro
X68	West Croydon - Russell Square (Mon-Fri peak hours)	7	20	-	Go-Ahead	Q	B7TL/Gem
							Env400
						PM	B7TL/Pres

Night Buses

No.	Route	PVR	Freq mf	sat	Operator	Garage	Type Used
N1	Thamesmead - Tottenham Court Road	9	30	20	Go-Ahead	BV	BTL9/Gem2
						MW	B5LH/Gem3
N2	Crystal Palace - Trafalgar Square	6	30	20	Arriva	N	B7TL/ALX400
							Env400
N3	Bromley - Oxford Circus	13	30	15	Abellio	QB	NRM
N5	Edgware - Trafalgar Square	16	15	10	Metroline	EW	Env400
						HT	B9TL/Gem2
6	Willesden Garage - Aldwych	10	15	12	Metroline	AC	B5LH/Gem3
							B7TL/Pres
N7	Northolt - Oxford Cicus	6	30	30	Metroline	PV	B5LH/Gem3

No.	Route	PVR	Freq mf	sat	Operator	Garage	Type Used
N8	Hainault - Oxford Circus	21	20	8	Stagecoach	BW	NRM
N9	Heathrow Airport Terminal 5 - Aldwych	18	20	10	RATP-Dev	AV	N230/Omni
10	Hammersmith - King's Cross	4	30	30	RATP-Dev	V	NRM
N11	Ealing - Liverpool Street	7	30	30	Go-Ahead	SW	NRM
12	Dulwich Library - Oxford Circus	8	30	15	Go-Ahead	Q	NRM
14	Putney Heath - University College Hospital	13	15	10	Go-Ahead	AF	B5LH/Gem3 E400H MMC
N15	Romford - Trafalgar Square	29	10	8	Stagecoach	BK	Env400
						BW	Env400H
N16	Edgware - Victoria	7	20	20	Metroline	W	NRM
N18	Harrow Weald - Trafalgar Square	14	15	10	Metroline	WJ	B5LH/Gem3 B9TL/Gem2
N19	Clapham Junction - Finsbury Park	8	30	20	Go-Ahead	SW	B5LH/Gem3 B9TL/Gem2
N20	Barnet - Trafalgar Square	16	30	10	Metroline	HT	B9TL/Gem2
						PB	Env400
N21	Bexleyheath - Trafalgar Square	9	30	20	Go-Ahead	BX/NX	B9TL/Gem2
N22	Fulwell - Piccadilly Circus	8	30	20	Go-Ahead	AF	B7TL/Gem
23	Westbourne Park - Liverpool Street	5	30	30	Tower Transit	X	Env400 Env400H
24	Hampstead Heath - Pimlico	8	15	15	Metroline	HT	NRM
25	Ilford - Oxford Circus	31	8	6	Tower Transit	LI	B9TL/Gem2
N26	Chingford - Trafalgar Square	16	20	12	CT Plus	HK	Env400 City
27	Chiswick Business Park - Camden Town	4	30	30	RATP-Dev	V	Env400H
N28	Wandsworth - Camden Town	5	30	30	Tower Transit	AS	B7TL/Gem
N29	Enfield - Trafalgar Square	37	8	4	Arriva	WN	B5LH/Gem3
N31	Clapham Junction - Camden Town	5	30	30	Tower Transit	AS	B7TL/Gem
33	Fulwell - Hammersmith	3	30	30	RATP-Dev	FW	Env200
34	Barnet - Walthamstow	3	-	30	Metroline	PB	B5LH/Gem3
N35	Clapham Junction - Tottenham Court Road Station	15	20	8	Go-Ahead	Q	Env400H
36	New Cross Gate - Queens Park	7	30	20	Go-Ahead	PM	B9TL/Gem2
37	Putney Heath - Peckham	4	30	30	Go-Ahead	PM	Env400
N38	Walthamstow - Victoria	26	12	12	Arriva	CT	NRM
N41	Tottenham Hale - Trafalgar Square	8	30	20	Arriva	AR	DB300/Gem2
43	Friern Barnet - London Bridge	7	30	20	Metroline	HT	B9TL/Gem2
N44	Sutton - Aldwych	9	30	20	Go-Ahead	SW	B7TL/Gem Env400H
47	Catford Bus Garage - Shoreditch	4	30	30	Stagecoach	TL	B5LH/E400MMC Env400H
52	Willesden - Victoria	3	30	30	Metroline	AC	B5LH/Gem2 B9TL/Gem2
53	Plumstead Station - Whitehall	12	20	12	Stagecoach	PD	B5LH/Gem2 Env400H
N55	Woodford Wells - Oxford Circus	15	30	12	Stagecoach	T	NRM
57	Kingston - Clapham Park	4	30	30	Go-Ahead	AL	Env400
N63	Crystal Palace - King's Cross	8	30	15	Go-Ahead	PM	B9TL/Gem2
64	Vulcan Way - Thornton Heath Bus Garage	4	30	30	Arriva	TH	Env400
65	Chessington World of Adventures - Ealing	6	30	30	RATP-Dev	FW	N230/Omni
N68	Camberwell - Tottenham Court Road Station	7	30	20	Go-Ahead	Q	B7TL/Gem
69	Walthamstow - Canning Town	3	30	30	Tower Transit	LI	Env400
72	Alton Estate - East Acton	3	30	30	RATP-Dev	S	Dart/Pointer
N73	Walthamstow - Victoria	14	30	12	Arriva	SF	B5LH/Gem2
N74	Danebury Avenue - Baker Street	5	30	30	Go-Ahead	AF	B5LH/Gem3
76	Tottenham Hale - Waterloo	6	30	30	Arriva	AR	B5LH/Gem2
83	Ealing Hospital - Golders Green	4	30	30	Metroline	ON	B9TL/Gem2
85	Kingston - Putney	3	30	30	RATP-Dev	TV	B5LH/Gem3
N86	Dagnam Park Drive - Stratford	9	30	15	Stagecoach	NS	Env400 Tri/ALX400

No.	Route	PVR	Freq mf	sat	Operator	Garage	Type Used
N87	Kingston - Aldwych	16	15	10	Go-Ahead	SW	B7TL/Gem Env400H
88	Clapham Common - Camden Town	7	30	20	Go-Ahead	SW	NRM
N89	Erith - Trafalgar Square	13	30	20	Go-Ahead	BX	B9TL/Gem2
N91	Cockfosters - Trafalgar Square	13	30	15	Metroline	HT PB	B9TL/Gem2 Env400
93	North Cheam - Putney	3	30	30	Go-Ahead	A	Tri/Olym
94	Acton Green - Piccadilly Circus	6	30	15	RATP-Dev	S	Env400H
N97	Hammersmith - Trafalgar Square	9	20	10	Tower Transit	AS	B5LH/Gem3
N98	Stanmore - Russell Square	13	15	10	Metroline	AC EW	B7TL/Pres Env400
102	Edmonton Green - Golders Green	4	30	30	Arriva	AD	Env400
105	Greenford Station - Heathrow Airport Central	3	30	30	Metroline	PA	B9TL/Gem2
108	Lewisham - Stratford	3	30	30	Go-Ahead	NX	Citaro
N109	Croydon - Oxford Circus	10	20	20	Abellio	BC	E400H MMC
111	Heathrow Airport Central - Kingston	4	30	30	RATP-Dev	AV	N230/Omni
N113	Mitcham - Trafalgar Square	4	30	30	Metroline	EW	Env400
119	Bromley - Purley Way	3	30	30	Go-Ahead	C	B5LH/Gem3
123	Ilford - Wood Green	4	-	30	Arriva	AR	B7TL/ALX400
128	Claybury - Romford	5	30	30	Arriva	DX	Env400
132	Bexleyheath - North Greenwich	4	-	30	Go-Ahead	BX	B7TL/Pres
N133	Edgware - Liverpool Street Station	8	20	20	Arriva	N	Env400H City
134	North Finchley - Tottenham Court Road	10	15	12	Metroline	HT	B9TL/Gem2
N136	Chislehurst War Memorial - Oxford Circus	10	30	20	Stagecoach	TL	Env400 Env400H
N137	Crystal Palace - Oxford Circus	11	30	15	Arriva	N	Env400
139	West Hampstead - Waterloo	4	30	30	Metroline	W	Env400H
140	Harrow Weald - Heathrow Airport Central	4	30	30	Metroline	HD	B5LH/Gem3
145	Dagenham - Leytonstone	4	-	30	Stagecoach	BK	Env400 Env400 MMC
148	Camberwell - White City	6	20	20	RATP-Dev	S	NRM
149	Edmonton Green - London Bridge	9	30	15	Arriva	AR	NRM
154	Morden - Croydon	3	-	30	Go-Ahead	A	Tri/Olym
N155	Morden -Aldwych	18	15	8	Go-Ahead	A AL	Tri/Olym B5LH/Gem3
158	Chingford Mount - Stratford	3	-	30	Stagecoach	WH	Env400 Tri/ALX400
159	Streatham - Marble Arch	7	20	20	Abellio	QB	NRM
N171	Hither Green - Tottenham Court Road	5	30	30	Go-Ahead	NX	B9TL/Gem2
176	Penge - Tottenham Court Road Station	12	30	15	Arriva	N	*B7TL/ALX400* Env400
183	Pinner - Golders Green	3	-	30	Lon Sov	SO	
188	North Greenwich - Russell Square	5	30	30	Abellio	WL	Env400H
189	Brent Cross - Oxford Circus	4	30	30	Metroline	W	NRM
N199	St Mary's Cray - Trafalgar Square	12	30	20	Stagecoach	TL	Env400 Env400H
N205	Leyton - Paddington	9	30	20	Stagecoach	BW	Env400H
N207	Uxbridge - Holborn	21	15	8	Metroline	UX	N230/Omni
213	Sutton Bus Garage - Kingston	3	30	30	Go-Ahead	A	B7TL/Pres
214	Highgate - Moorgate	10	20	10	Metroline	KC	Env200
220	Harlesden - Wandsworth	3	30	30	RATP-Dev	S	Env400H
222	Uxbridge - Hounslow	4	30	30	RATP-Dev	AV	Env400
238	Barking - Stratford	3	30	30	Stagecoach	BK	Env400
242	Homerton Hospital - Tottenham Court Road	9	20	15	Arriva	CT	DB300/Gem2
243	Wood Green Station - Waterloo	11	30	15	Arriva	AR	B5LH/Gem2 *DB300/Gem2*
250	Croydon - Brixton	5	30	30	Arriva	TH	Env400
N253	Aldgate - Tottenham Court Road Station	14	15	12	Arriva	SF	B5LH/Gem

No.	Route	PVR mf	Freq sat		Operator	Garage	Type Used
264	Croydon - St. George's Hospital	3	30	30	Arriva	TC	DB300/Gem
266	Brent Cross - Hammersmith	5	30	30	Tower Transit	AS	B9TL/Gem2
271	Highgate - Moorgate	2	30	30	Metroline	HT	B9TL/Gem2
277	Highbury - Leamouth	5	30	30	Stagecoach	BW	N230/Omni
N279	Waltham Cross - Trafalgar Square	17	20	12	Arriva	E	Env400
281	Tolworth - Hounslow	4	30	30	RATP-Dev	FW	N230/Omni
285	Heathrow Airport Central - Kingston	4	30	30	RATP-Dev	HH	B5LH/Gem3
295	Ladbroke Grove - Clapham Junction	4	30	30	Metroline	WJ	B5LH/Gem3
296	Romford - Ilford	3	-	30	Stagecoach	NS	Env200
297	Willesden Garage - Ealing Haven Green	4	30	30	Metroline	PA	B5LH/Gem3
321	Foots Cray - New Cross	3	30	30	Go-Ahead	NX	B9TL/Gem2
341	Lea Valley - Waterloo County Hall	5	30	30	Arriva	AR	Env400
N343	New Cross Gate - Trafalgar Square	5	30	30	Abellio	WL	Env400 Env400H
344	Clapham Junction - Liverpool Street	4	30	30	Abellio	QB	Env400H MMC
345	Peckham - South Kensington	4	30	30	Abellio	WL	Env400
365	Orchard Estate - Havering Park	4	30	30	Stagecoach	NS	Env400
N381	Peckham - Trafalgar Square	4	30	30	Abellio	WL	B7TL/Gem
390	Archway - Notting Hill Gate	5	30	30	Metroline	HT	NRM
453	Deptford - Marylebone Station	11	20	12	Go-Ahead	MW	NRM
472	Thamesmead - North Greenwich	3	30	30	Stagecoach	PD	Env400H
474	Manor Park - Canning Town	3	30	30	Go-Ahead	RR	B9TL/Gem2 Env400
486	Bexleyheath - North Greenwich	3	-	30	Go-Ahead	BX	Env400
N550	Canning Town - Trafalgar Square	7	30	30	Tower Transit	LI	Env400
N551	Gallions Reach - Trafalgar Square	8	30	30	Tower Transit	LI	Env400
C2	Parliament Hill - Victoria	4	30	30	Abellio	QB	Env400
E1	Greenford - Ealing	4	30	30	Abellio	QB	Env400H Env400H MMC
EL1	Barking Reach - Ilford Hill	2	30	30	Go-Ahead	RR	NRM
H32	Southall - Hounslow	2	30	30	RATP-Dev	AV	N230/Omni
H37	Hounslow - Richmond	2	-	30	RATP-Dev	AV	Tempo
W3	Northumberland Park - Finsbury Park	3	-	30	Arriva	WN	Env400
W7	Muswell Hill - Finsbury Park	2	-	20	Metroline	HT	B9TL/Gem2

School Buses

No.	Route	PVR	Operator	Garage	Type Used

Additional School Runs On Existing Routes

No.	Route	PVR	Operator	Garage	Type Used
143	Archway - East Finchley	5	Metroline	HT	Tri/Pres
				W	Env200
150	Gants Hill - Beacontree Heath	1	Go-Ahead	RR	N230/Olym
163	Morden - Wimbledon	1	Go-Ahead	AL	B7TL/Gem B7TL/Pres
184	Bells Hill - Alexander Park School	1	Arriva	WN	B7TL/Gem
293	Epsom - Morden	1	Go-Ahead	C	N230/Omni
313	Chingford - Dame Alice Owen's School	1	Arriva	E	Env400
405	West Croydon - Purley	2	Arriva	TC	DB250/Gem

Route	PVR	Operator	Garage	Type Used

Specific School Only Routes

Route		PVR	Operator	Garage	Type Used
601	Thamesmead - Dartford Heath	7	Stagecoach	PD	N230/Omni
					Tri/ALX400
602	Thamesmead - Bexleyheath Grammar School	2	Stagecoach	PD	N230/Omni
605	Edgware - Mill Hill County School	2	Lon.Sovereign	BT	B7TL/Pres
606	Queensbury - Ravenscroft School	3	Metroline	EW	*Env400*
608	Gallows Corner - Shenfield High School	3	Go-Ahead	RR	N230/Olym
609	Hammersmith - Harrodian School	1	Metroline	AH	Env200
611	Stonebridge Park - East Finchley Cemetery	1	Metroline	PA	N230/Olym
612	Sanderstead - Wallington County Grammar School	2	Arriva	TC	DB250/Gem
613	Worcester Park - Glenthorne High School	1	RATP-Dev	TV	Tri/ALX400
616	Green Dragon Lane - Edmonton Green	2	Go-Ahead	NP	B7TL/Pres
617	Turnpike Lane Station - St. Ignatius College	2	Sullivans	SM	B7TL/Gem
					B7TL/Vyk
					Env400
					Tri/ALX400
					Tri/Pres
618	Mill Hill - Avanti House School	2	Lon.Sovereign	BT	B7TL/Pres
619	Edgware - Avanti House School	1	Lon.Sovereign	BT	N230/Omni
621	Lewisham - Crown Woods School	1	Stagecoach	TL	Tri/ALX400
624	Grove Park - Crown Woods School	2	Go-Ahead	Q	B7TL/Gem
					Env400
625	Plumstead Common - Chislehurst	2	Go-Ahead	BX	B7TL/Gem
626	Finchley - Potters Bar Dame Alice Owen's School	4	Sullivans	SM	*B7TL/Gem*
					B7TL/Vyk
					Tri/ALX400
					Tri/Pres
627	Worcester Park - Wallington High School	2	Arriva	TC	DB250/Gem
628	Kingsbury - Southgate	3	Sullivans	SM	B7TL/Gem
					B7TL/Vyk
					Env400
					Tri/ALX400
					Tri/Pres
629	Wood Green Station - St. Ignatius College	2	Sullivans	SM	B7TL/Gem
					B7TL/Vyk
					Env400
					Tri/ALX400
					Tri/Pres
631	Golders Green - Henrietta Barnett School	1	Arriva Shires	GR	Solo
632	Kilburn Park - Grahame Park Corner Mead	3	Metroline	W	Env400H
					Tri/ALX400
633	Coulsdon - Pollards Hill	1	Quality Line	EB	Env400
634	Muswell Hill - Barnet Hospital	1	Metroline	PB	Env400
635	Brentford - Sunbury St. Paul's School	3	RATP-Dev	HH	Tri/ALX400
636	Kemnal College - Bromley South	1	Stagecoach	TB	Tri/ALX400
637	Kemnal College - Bromley South	1	Stagecoach	TB	Tri/ALX400
638	Coney Hall - Kemnal College	7	Stagecoach	TB	Tri/ALX400
639	Clapham Junction - Putney Heath John Paul II School	1	Go-Ahead	AF	B5LH/Gem3
					Env400H MMC
640	South Harrow - Clamp Hill	2	Metroline	HD	B9TL/Gem2
641	West Molesey - Teddington School	1	Quality Line	EB	Versa
642	West Hendon - Canons Corner	3	Arriva Shires	GR	B7TL/ALX400
					Env400
643	Brent Cross - East Finchley Cemetery	2	Metroline	W	Tri/ALX400
646	Noak Hill - Cranham	3	Go-Ahead	RR	Dar/Cap
					Env200
648	Romford - Cranham	2	Go-Ahead	RR	Dart/Cap
649	Romford - County Park Campion School	2	Go-Ahead	RR	N230/Olym

No.	Route	PVR	Operator	Garage	Type Used
650	Romford - Emerson Park School	3	Go-Ahead	RR	N230/Olym
651	Romford - Chase Cross	2	Go-Ahead	RR	N230/Olym
652	Abbey Wood Lane - Upminster Station	2	Go-Ahead	RR	N230/Olym
653	Muswell Hill - Kingsbury	3	Sullivans	SM	B7TL/Gem
					B7TL/Vyk
					Env400
					Tri/ALX400
					Tri/Pres
654	Addington Interchange - Ramsden Priory School	1	Go-Ahead	MB	N94/Omni
655	Mitcham - Raynes Park High School	1	Go-Ahead	AL	B7TL/Gem
					B7TL/ Pres
656	Gallows Corner - Emerson Park School	2	Go-Ahead	RR	N230/Olym
657	Crooked Billet - Woodford Wells Bancroft's School	1	Go-Ahead	NP	B9TL/Gem2
658	Woolwich - Crown Woods School	3	Go-Ahead	BX	B9TL/Gem2
				Q	B7TL/Gem
					Env400
660	Bellingham - Crown Woods School	1	Arriva	DT	Env400
661	Petts Wood Station - Mottingham Eltham College	1	Go-Ahead	BX	N230/Olym
662	Surbiton - Holy Cross School	1	RATP-Dev	TV	Tri/ALX400
663	Thornton Heath - Pampisford Road	1	Arriva	TH	DB250/Gem
664	Homestead Way - Biggin Hill Charles Darwin School	2	Stagecoach	TB	Tri/ALX400
665	Surbiton - Holy Cross School	1	RATP-Dev	TV	Dar/Point
667	Ilford - West Hatch School	2	Go-Ahead	RR	N230/Olym
669	Thamesmead - Albany Park Cleeve Park School	2	Go-Ahead	BV	N230/Olym
				BX	N230/Olym
670	Clapham Junction - Putney Heath John Paul II School	1	Go-Ahead	AF	B5LH/Gem3
671	Chessington South Station - Tiffin Girls' School	1	RATP-Dev	TV	Tri/ALX400
672	Thamesmead Woolwich Polytechnic School - Woolwich	2	Stagecoach	PD	Tri/ALX400
673	Warren School - Beckton	1	Arriva	DX	Env400
674	Dagnam Park Drive - Romford	1	Go-Ahead	RR	N230/Olym
675	Walthamstow - Woodbridge High School	1	Go-Ahead	NP	B7TL/Pres
677	Ilford - Debden	1	Stagecoach	BK	Env400 MMC

A new route was introduced in March 2017, to cover the school element of route 167 which now no longer runs to Debden. Operated by Stagecoach, there is one run from Ilford to Debden in the morning and the return operates in the afternoon. *Michael J. McClelland*

No.	Route	PVR	Operator	Garage	Type Used
678	Beckton - Stratford	4	Arriva	DX	B7TL/ALX400
679	Goodmayes - Woodford Wells	4	Go-Ahead	RR	N230/Olym
681	Hounslow - Teddington School	2	RATP-Dev	FW	N230/Omni
683	Friern Barnet - Kingsbury	2	Sullivans	SM	B7TL/Gem
					B7TL/Vyk
					Env400
					Tri/ALX400
					Tri/Pres
684	Orpington - Charles Darwin School	1	Go-Ahead	MB	B7TL/Gem
685	Warlingham School - Selsdon	1	Arriva	TC	DB250/Gem
686	Romford Station - St. Edward's School	2	Go-Ahead	RR	N230/Olym
687	Dagenham Park School - Barking	1	Go-Ahead	RR	Env400
688	Southgate - Kingsbury	6	Sullivans	SM	B7TL/Gem
					Tri/ALX400
					Tri/Pres
689	Croydon - The Glade	1	Arriva	TH	Env400
690	West Norwood - Burntwood School	2	Arriva	N	B7TL/ALX400
692	Potters Bar Dame Alice Owen's School - Green Dragon Lane	1	Sullivans	SM	N230/Omni
696	Carnarvon Drive - Bishop Ramsey School	2	RATP-Dev	AV	Tri/ALX400
697	Kinghill Avenue - Ickenham	4	RATP-Dev	AV	N230/Omni
698	West Drayton - Ickenham	5	RATP-Dev	HH	Env200
					CN94/Omni
699	Green Dragon Lane - Potters Bar Dame Alice Owen's School	3	Sullivans	SM	N230/Omni
W13	Leytonstone - Woodford Wells	1	CT Plus	HK	Tri/Olym

900 series Mobility Routes

No.	Route	Operator	Garage	Type Used
931	Crystal Palace - Lewisham (Fridays only)	Abellio	BC	Env200
965	Riverhill - Kingston Sainsbury's (Mondays & Fridays only)	RATP-Dev	TV	Env200
969	Whitton - Roehampton Vale Asda (Tuesday & Fridays only)	Abellio	TF	Env200

Fleet Lists

Abellio

No.	G.	Type	No.	G.	Type	No.	G.	Type
2400	BC	E40D/E400MMC 10.35	2470	QB	E40H/E400 (E6) 10.35	2540	QB	E40H/E400MMC 10.35
2401	WL	E40H/E400 (EC) 10.2	2471	QB	E40H/E400 (E6) 10.35	2541	QB	E40H/E400MMC 10.35
2402	WL	E40H/E400 (EC) 10.2	2472	QB	E40H/E400 (E6) 10.35	2542	QB	E40H/E400MMC 10.35
2403	WL	E40H/E400 (EC) 10.2	2473	QB	E40H/E400 (E6) 10.35	2543	QB	E40H/E400MMC 10.35
2404	WL	E40H/E400 (EC) 10.2	2474	QB	E40H/E400 (E6) 10.35	2544	QB	E40H/E400MMC 10.35
2405	WL	E40H/E400 (EC) 10.2	2475	QB	E40H/E400 (E6) 10.35	2545	QB	E40H/E400MMC 10.35
2406	WL	E40H/E400 (EC) 10.2	2476	QB	E40H/E400 (E6) 10.35	2546	QB	E40H/E400MMC 10.35
2407	WL	E40H/E400 (EC) 10.2	2477	QB	E40H/E400 (E6) 10.35	2547	QB	E40H/E400MMC 10.35
2408	WL	E40H/E400 (EC) 10.2	2478	QB	E40H/E400 (E6) 10.35	2548	QB	E40H/E400MMC 10.35
2409	WL	E40H/E400 (EC) 10.2	2479	QB	E40H/E400 (E6) 10.35	2549	QB	E40H/E400MMC 10.35
2410	WL	E40H/E400 (EC) 10.2	2480	QB	E40H/E400 (E6) 10.35	2550	QB	E40H/E400MMC 10.35
2411	WL	E40H/E400 (EC) 10.2	2481	QB	E40H/E400 (E6) 10.35	2551	QB	E40H/E400MMC 10.35
2412	WL	E40H/E400 (EC) 10.2	2482	QB	E40H/E400 (E6) 10.35	8020	TF	Dart/Pointer 8.8
2413	WL	E40H/E400 (EC) 10.2	2483	QB	E40H/E400 (E6) 10.35	8024	WS	Dart/Pointer 8.8
2414	QB	E40H/E400 (EC) 10.2	2484	QB	E40H/E400 (E6) 10.35	8037	TF	Dart/Pointer 8.8
2415	QB	E40H/E400 (EC) 10.2	2485	QB	E40H/E400 (E6) 10.35	8065	TF	Dart/Pointer 8.8
2416	QB	E40H/E400 (EC) 10.2	2486	QB	E40H/E400 (E6) 10.35	8103	TF	E200/E200 8.9
2417	QB	E40H/E400 (EC) 10.2	2487	BC	E40H/E400MMC 10.35	8104	TF	E200/E200 8.9
2418	QB	E40H/E400 (EC) 10.2	2488	BC	E40H/E400MMC 10.35	8105	TF	E200/E200 8.9
2419	QB	E40H/E400 (EC) 10.2	2489	BC	E40H/E400MMC 10.35	8106	TF	E200/E200 8.9
2420	QB	E40H/E400 (EC) 10.2	2490	BC	E40H/E400MMC 10.35	8113	WS	Dart/Pointer 8.8
2421	QB	E40H/E400 (EC) 10.2	2491	BC	E40H/E400MMC 10.35	8114	WS	Dart/Pointer 8.8
2422	QB	E40H/E400 (EC) 10.2	2492	BC	E40H/E400MMC 10.35	8118	TF	E20D/E200 8.9
2423	WL	E40H/E400 (EC) 10.2	2493	BC	E40H/E400MMC 10.35	8119	TF	E20D/E200 8.9
2424	WL	E40H/E400 (EC) 10.2	2494	BC	E40H/E400MMC 10.35	8120	TF	E20D/E200 8.9
2425	WL	E40H/E400 (EC) 10.2	2495	BC	E40H/E400MMC 10.35	8121	TF	E20D/E200 8.9
2426	WL	E40H/E400 (EC) 10.2	2496	BC	E40H/E400MMC 10.35	8122	TF	E20D/E200 8.9
2427	WL	E40H/E400 (EC) 10.2	2497	BC	E40H/E400MMC 10.35	8123	TF	E20D/E200 8.9
2428	WL	E40H/E400 (EC) 10.2	2498	BC	E40H/E400MMC 10.35	8124	TF	E20D/E200 8.9
2429	WL	E40H/E400 (EC) 10.2	2499	BC	E40H/E400MMC 10.35	8125	TF	E20D/E200 8.9
2430	WL	E40H/E400 (EC) 10.2	2500	BC	E40H/E400MMC 10.35	8126	TF	E20D/E200 8.9
2431	WL	E40H/E400 (EC) 10.2	2501	BC	E40H/E400MMC 10.35	8127	TF	E20D/E200 8.9
2432	WL	E40H/E400 (EC) 10.2	2502	BC	E40H/E400MMC 10.35	8138	TF	E20D/E200MMC 9.0
2433	WL	E40H/E400 (EC) 10.2	2503	BC	E40H/E400MMC 10.35	8139	TF	E20D/E200MMC 9.0
2434	WL	E40H/E400 (EC) 10.2	2504	BC	E40H/E400MMC 10.35	8140	TF	E20D/E200MMC 9.0
2435	WL	E40H/E400 (EC) 10.2	2505	BC	E40H/E400MMC 10.35	8141	TF	E20D/E200MMC 9.0
2436	WL	E40H/E400 (EC) 10.2	2506	BC	E40H/E400MMC 10.35	8142	WS	E20D/E200MMC 9.0
2437	WL	E40H/E400 (EC) 10.2	2507	BC	E40H/E400MMC 10.35	8143	WS	E20D/E200MMC 9.0
2438	QB	E40H/E400 (EC) 10.2	2508	BC	E40H/E400MMC 10.35	8144	WS	E20D/E200MMC 9.0
2439	QB	E40H/E400 (EC) 10.2	2509	BC	E40H/E400MMC 10.35	8145	WS	E20D/E200MMC 9.0
2440	QB	E40H/E400 (EC) 10.2	2510	BC	E40H/E400MMC 10.35	8146	WS	E20D/E200MMC 9.0
2441	QB	E40H/E400 (EC) 10.2	2511	BC	E40H/E400MMC 10.35	8147	WS	E20D/E200MMC 9.0
2442	QB	E40H/E400 (EC) 10.2	2512	BC	E40H/E400MMC 10.35	8148	WS	E20D/E200MMC 9.0
2443	QB	E40H/E400 (EC) 10.2	2513	BC	E40H/E400MMC 10.35	8149	WS	E20D/E200MMC 9.0
2444	WS	E40H/E400 (E6) 10.35	2514	WL	E40H/E400MMC 10.35	8150	WS	E20D/E200MMC 9.0
2445	WS	E40H/E400 (E6) 10.35	2515	WL	E40H/E400MMC 10.35	8151	WS	E20D/E200MMC 9.0
2446	WS	E40H/E400 (E6) 10.35	2516	WL	E40H/E400MMC 10.35	8152	WS	E20D/E200MMC 9.0
2447	WS	E40H/E400 (E6) 10.35	2517	WL	E40H/E400MMC 10.35	8153	WS	E20D/E200MMC 9.0
2448	WS	E40H/E400 (E6) 10.35	2518	WL	E40H/E400MMC 10.35	8154	WS	E20D/E200MMC 9.0
2449	WS	E40H/E400 (E6) 10.35	2519	WL	E40H/E400MMC 10.35	8155	TF	E20D/E200MMC 9.0
2450	WS	E40H/E400 (E6) 10.35	2520	WL	E40H/E400MMC 10.35	8156	TF	E20D/E200MMC 9.0
2451	WS	E40H/E400 (E6) 10.35	2521	WL	E40H/E400MMC 10.35	8157	TF	E20D/E200MMC 9.0
2452	QB	E40H/E400 (E6) 10.35	2522	WL	E40H/E400MMC 10.35	8158	TF	E20D/E200MMC 9.0
2453	QB	E40H/E400 (E6) 10.35	2523	WS	E40H/E400MMC 10.35	8159	TF	E20D/E200MMC 9.0
2454	QB	E40H/E400 (E6) 10.35	2524	WS	E40H/E400MMC 10.35	8160	TF	E20D/E200MMC 9.0
2455	QB	E40H/E400 (E6) 10.35	2525	WS	E40H/E400MMC 10.35	8161	TF	E20D/E200MMC 9.0
2456	QB	E40H/E400 (E6) 10.35	2526	WS	E40H/E400MMC 10.35	8162	WS	E20D/E200MMC 9.0
2457	QB	E40H/E400 (E6) 10.35	2527	WS	E40H/E400MMC 10.35	8163	WS	E20D/E200MMC 9.0
2458	QB	E40H/E400 (E6) 10.35	2528	WS	E40H/E400MMC 10.35	8164	WS	E20D/E200MMC 9.0
2459	QB	E40H/E400 (E6) 10.35	2529	WS	E40H/E400MMC 10.35	8165	WS	E20D/E200MMC 9.0
2460	QB	E40H/E400 (E6) 10.35	2530	WS	E40H/E400MMC 10.35	8166	TF	E20D/E200MMC 9.0
2461	QB	E40H/E400 (E6) 10.35	2531	WS	E40H/E400MMC 10.35	8167	TF	E20D/E200MMC 9.0
2462	QB	E40H/E400 (E6) 10.35	2532	WL	E40H/E400MMC 10.35	8168	TF	E20D/E200MMC 9.0
2463	QB	E40H/E400 (E6) 10.35	2533	WL	E40H/E400MMC 10.35	8169	TF	E20D/E200MMC 9.0
2464	QB	E40H/E400 (E6) 10.35	2534	QB	E40H/E400MMC 10.35	8170	TF	E20D/E200MMC 9.0
2465	QB	E40H/E400 (E6) 10.35	2535	QB	E40H/E400MMC 10.35	8201	TF	E20D/E200 8.9
2466	QB	E40H/E400 (E6) 10.35	2536	QB	E40H/E400MMC 10.35	8202	TF	E20D/E200 8.9
2467	QB	E40H/E400 (E6) 10.35	2537	QB	E40H/E400MMC 10.35	8203	TF	E20D/E200 8.9
2468	QB	E40H/E400 (E6) 10.35	2538	QB	E40H/E400MMC 10.35	8204	TF	E20D/E200 8.9
2469	QB	E40H/E400 (E6) 10.35	2539	QB	E40H/E400MMC 10.35	8205	TF	E20D/E200 8.9

No.	G.	Type	No.	G.	Type	No.	G.	Type
8206	TF	E20D/E200 8.9	8521	TF	E200/E200 10.2	8815	TF	E20D/E200 10.8
8207	TF	E20D/E200 8.9	8522	BC	E200/E200 10.2	8816	TF	E20D/E200 10.8
8210	BC	E20D/E200MMC 9.0	8523	BC	E200/E200 10.2	8817	TF	E20D/E200 10.8
8211	BC	E20D/E200MMC 9.0	8524	BC	E200/E200 10.2	8820	BC	E20D/E200 10.8
8212	BC	E20D/E200MMC 9.0	8525	TF	E200/E200 10.2	8821	BC	E20D/E200 10.8
8213	BC	E20D/E200MMC 9.0	8526	BC	E200/E200 10.2	8822	BC	E20D/E200 10.8
8214	BC	E20D/E200MMC 9.0	8527	TF	E200/E200 10.2	8823	BC	E20D/E200 10.8
8215	BC	E20D/E200MMC 9.0	8529	TF	E200/E200 10.2	8824	BC	E20D/E200 10.8
8216	BC	E20D/E200MMC 9.0	8530	TF	E200/E200 10.2	8825	BC	E20D/E200 10.8
8217	BC	E20D/E200MMC 9.0	8531	TF	E200/E200 10.2	8826	BC	E20D/E200 10.8
8218	BC	E20D/E200MMC 9.0	8532	TF	E200/E200 10.2	8827	BC	E20D/E200 10.8
8219	BC	E20D/E200MMC 9.0	8533	TF	E200/E200 10.2	8828	BC	E20D/E200 10.8
8303	WL	Dart/Pointer2 9.3	8534	TF	E200/E200 10.2	8829	BC	E20D/E200 10.8
8321	BC	E200/E200 9.3	8535	TF	E200/E200 10.2	8830	BC	E20D/E200 10.8
8322	BC	E200/E200 9.3	8536	TF	E200/E200 10.2	8831	BC	E20D/E200 10.8
8323	BC	E200/E200 9.3	8537	TF	E200/E200 10.2	8832	BC	E20D/E200 10.8
8324	BC	E200/E200 9.3	8538	TF	E200/E200 10.2	8833	BC	E20D/E200 10.8
8325	BC	E200/E200 9.3	8539	TF	E200/E200 10.2	8834	BC	E20D/E200 10.8
8326	BC	E200/E200 9.3	8540	TF	E200/E200 10.2	8835	BC	E20D/E200 10.8
8327	BC	E200/E200 9.3	8541	TF	E200/E200 10.2	8836	BC	E20D/E200 10.8
8328	WL	E200/E200 9.3	8542	TF	E200/E200 10.2	8837	BC	E20D/E200 10.8
8329	WL	E200/E200 9.3	8543	TF	E200/E200 10.2	8838	BC	E20D/E200 10.8
8330	WL	E200/E200 9.3	8544	TF	E200/E200 10.2	8839	BC	E20D/E200 10.8
8331	WL	E200/E200 9.3	8545	TF	E200/E200 10.2	8840	BC	E20D/E200 10.8
8332	WL	E200/E200 9.3	8546	TF	E200/E200 10.2	8841	BC	E20D/E200 10.8
8333	WL	E200/E200 9.3	8547	TF	E200/E200 10.2	8842	BC	E20D/E200 10.8
8334	WL	E200/E200 9.3	8548	TF	E200/E200 10.2	8843	BC	E20D/E200 10.8
8335	WL	E200/E200 9.3	8549	TF	E200/E200 10.2	8844	WL	E20D/E200MMC 10.9
8336	WL	E200/E200 9.3	8550	TF	E200/E200 10.2	8845	WL	E20D/E200MMC 10.9
8337	WL	E200/E200 9.3	8551	TF	E200/E200 10.2	8846	WL	E20D/E200MMC 10.9
8338	WL	E200/E200 9.3	8567	WS	E200/E200 10.2	8847	WL	E20D/E200MMC 10.9
8339	WL	E200/E200 9.3	8568	WS	E200/E200 10.2	8848	WL	E20D/E200MMC 10.9
8340	WL	E200/E200 9.3	8569	TF	E200/E200 10.2	8849	WL	E20D/E200MMC 10.9
8341	WL	E200/E200 9.3	8570	WS	E200/E200 10.2	8850	WL	E20D/E200MMC 10.9
8343	BC	E20D/E200MMC 9.75	8577	TF	E20D/E200 10.2	8851	WL	E20D/E200MMC 10.9
8344	BC	E20D/E200MMC 9.75	8578	TF	E20D/E200 10.2	8852	WL	E20D/E200MMC 10.9
8345	BC	E20D/E200MMC 9.75	8579	TF	E20D/E200 10.2	8853	WL	E20D/E200MMC 10.9
8346	BC	E20D/E200MMC 9.75	8580	TF	E20D/E200 10.2	8854	WL	E20D/E200MMC 10.9
8347	BC	E20D/E200MMC 9.75	8581	TF	E20D/E200 10.2	8855	WL	E20D/E200MMC 10.9
8440	TF	Dart/Pointer 2 10.2	8582	TF	E20D/E200 10.2	8856	WL	E20D/E200MMC 10.9
8442	WL	E200/E200 9.3	8583	TF	E20D/E200 10.2	8857	WL	E20D/E200MMC 10.9
8447	TF	Dart/Pointer 10.1	8584	TF	E20D/E200 10.2	8858	WL	E20D/E200MMC 10.9
8448	TF	Dart/Pointer 10.1	8585	TF	E20D/E200 10.2	8859	WL	E20D/E200MMC 10.9
8450	TF	Dart/Pointer 10.1	8586	TF	E20D/E200 10.2	8860	WL	E20D/E200MMC 10.9
8451	TF	Dart/Pointer 10.1	8587	TF	E20D/E200 10.2	8861	WL	E20D/E200MMC 10.9
8460	TF	Dart/Nimbus 10.5	8588	TF	E20D/E200 10.2	8862	WL	E20D/E200MMC 10.9
8461	TF	Dart/Nimbus 10.5	8589	TF	E20D/E200 10.2	8863	WL	E20D/E200MMC 10.9
8462	TF	Dart/Nimbus 10.5	8590	TF	E20D/E200 10.2	8864	WL	E20D/E200MMC 10.9
8468	TF	Dart/Nimbus 10.5	8591	TF	E20D/E200 10.2	8866	WS	E20D/E200MMC 10.9
8469	TF	Dart/Nimbus 10.5	8777	BC	E20D/E200 10.8	8867	WS	E20D/E200MMC 10.9
8470	TF	Dart/Nimbus 10.5	8778	BC	E20D/E200 10.8	8868	WS	E20D/E200MMC 10.9
8471	TF	Dart/Nimbus 10.5	8779	BC	E20D/E200 10.8	8869	WS	E20D/E200MMC 10.9
8472	TF	Dart/Nimbus 10.5	8780	BC	E20D/E200 10.8	8870	WS	E20D/E200MMC 10.9
8488	TF	Dart/Nimbus 10.5	8781	BC	E20D/E200 10.8	8871	WS	E20D/E200MMC 10.9
8491	BC	Dart/Nimbus 10.5	8782	BC	E20D/E200 10.8	8872	WS	E20D/E200MMC 10.9
8492	BC	Dart/Nimbus 10.5	8783	BC	E20D/E200 10.8	8873	WS	E20D/E200MMC 10.9
8493	BC	Dart/Nimbus 10.5	8784	BC	E20D/E200 10.8	8874	WS	E20D/E200MMC 10.9
8494	BC	Dart/Nimbus 10.5	8785	BC	E20D/E200 10.8	8875	WS	E20D/E200MMC 10.9
8495	BC	Dart/Nimbus 10.5	8786	BC	E20D/E200 10.8	9001	WL	B7TL/Gemini 10.6
8496	BC	Dart/Nimbus 10.5	8787	BC	E20D/E200 10.8	9002	WL	B7TL/Gemini 10.6
8497	BC	Dart/Nimbus 10.5	8788	TF	E20D/E200 10.8	9003	WL	B7TL/Gemini 10.6
8498	BC	Dart/Nimbus 10.5	8789	TF	E20D/E200 10.8	9004	WL	B7TL/Gemini 10.6
8507	TF	E200/E200 10.2	8790	TF	E20D/E200 10.8	9005	WL	B7TL/Gemini 10.6
8508	TF	E200/E200 10.2	8791	TF	E20D/E200 10.8	9006	WL	B7TL/Gemini 10.6
8509	TF	E200/E200 10.2	8792	TF	E20D/E200 10.8	9007	WL	B7TL/Gemini 10.6
8510	TF	E200/E200 10.2	8793	TF	E20D/E200 10.8	9008	WL	B7TL/Gemini 10.6
8511	TF	E200/E200 10.2	8806	TF	E20D/E200 10.8	9009	WL	B7TL/Gemini 10.6
8512	TF	E200/E200 10.2	8807	TF	E20D/E200 10.8	9010	WL	B7TL/Gemini 10.6
8513	TF	E200/E200 10.2	8808	TF	E20D/E200 10.8	9011	WL	B7TL/Gemini 10.6
8514	TF	E200/E200 10.2	8809	TF	E20D/E200 10.8	9012	WL	B7TL/Gemini 10.6
8515	TF	E200/E200 10.2	8810	TF	E20D/E200 10.8	9013	WL	B7TL/Gemini 10.6
8517	WS	E200/E200 10.2	8811	TF	E20D/E200 10.8	9014	WL	B7TL/Gemini 10.6
8518	BC	E200/E200 10.2	8812	TF	E20D/E200 10.8	9015	WL	B7TL/Gemini 10.6
8519	BC	E200/E200 10.2	8813	TF	E20D/E200 10.8	9016	WL	B7TL/Gemini 10.6
8520	WS	E200/E200 10.2	8814	TF	E20D/E200 10.8	9017	WL	B7TL/Gemini 10.6

Abellio

No.	G.	Type	No.	G.	Type	No.	G.	Type
9018	WL	B7TL/Gemini 10.6	9422	QB	Trident/E400 10.1	9516	QB	Trident/E400 10.1
9019	WL	B7TL/Gemini 10.6	9423	QB	Trident/E400 10.1	9517	QB	Trident/E400 10.1
9020	WL	B7TL/Gemini 10.6	9424	QB	Trident/E400 10.1	9518	QB	Trident/E400 10.1
9021	WL	B7TL/Gemini 10.6	9425	QB	Trident/E400 10.1	9519	QB	Trident/E400 10.1
9022	WL	B7TL/Gemini 10.6	9426	QB	Trident/E400 10.1	9520	QB	Trident/E400 10.1
9023	WL	B7TL/Gemini 10.6	9427	QB	Trident/E400 10.1	9521	QB	Trident/E400 10.1
9025	WL	B7TL/Gemini 10.6	9428	WL	Trident/E400 10.1	9522	QB	Trident/E400 10.1
9028	WL	B7TL/Gemini 10.6	9429	WL	Trident/E400 10.1	9523	QB	Trident/E400 10.1
9029	BC	B7TL/Gemini 10.6	9430	WL	Trident/E400 10.1	9524	QB	E40D/E400 (EC) 10.2
9030	QB	B7TL/Gemini 10.6	9431	WL	Trident/E400 10.1	9525	QB	E40D/E400 (EC) 10.2
9031	QB	B7TL/Gemini 10.6	9432	WL	Trident/E400 10.1	9526	QB	E40D/E400 (EC) 10.2
9033	WL	B7TL/Gemini 10.6	9433	WL	Trident/E400 10.1	9527	QB	E40D/E400 (EC) 10.2
9034	WL	B7TL/Gemini 10.6	9434	WL	Trident/E400 10.1	9528	QB	E40D/E400 (EC) 10.2
9035	WL	B7TL/Gemini 10.6	9435	WL	Trident/E400 10.1	9529	QB	E40D/E400 (EC) 10.2
9036	WL	B7TL/Gemini 10.6	9436	WL	Trident/E400 10.1	9530	QB	E40D/E400 (EC) 10.2
9037	WL	B7TL/Gemini 10.6	9437	WL	Trident/E400 10.1	9531	QB	E40D/E400 (EC) 10.2
9038	WL	B7TL/Gemini 10.6	9438	WL	Trident/E400 10.1	9532	QB	E40D/E400 (EC) 10.2
9039	WL	B7TL/Gemini 10.6	9439	WL	Trident/E400 10.1	9533	QB	E40D/E400 (EC) 10.2
9040	WL	B7TL/Gemini 10.6	9440	WL	Trident/E400 10.1	9534	QB	E40D/E400 (EC) 10.2
9041	WL	B7TL/Gemini 10.6	9441	WL	Trident/E400 10.1	9535	QB	E40D/E400 (EC) 10.2
9042	WL	B7TL/Gemini 10.6	9442	WL	Trident/E400 10.1	9536	QB	E40D/E400 (EC) 10.2
9043	WL	B7TL/Gemini 10.6	9443	WL	Trident/E400 10.1	9537	QB	E40D/E400 (EC) 10.2
9044	WL	B7TL/Gemini 10.6	9444	WL	Trident/E400 10.1	9538	QB	E40D/E400 (EC) 10.2
9045	WL	B7TL/Gemini 10.6	9445	WL	Trident/E400 10.1	9539	QB	E40D/E400 (EC) 10.2
9046	WL	B7TL/Gemini 10.6	9446	WL	Trident/E400 10.1	9540	QB	E40D/E400 (EC) 10.2
9047	WL	B7TL/Gemini 10.6	9447	WL	Trident/E400 10.1	9541	QB	E40D/E400 (EC) 10.2
9048	WL	B7TL/Gemini 10.6	9448	WL	Trident/E400 10.1	9542	QB	E40D/E400 (EC) 10.2
9049	WL	B7TL/Gemini 10.6	9449	WL	Trident/E400 10.1	9543	QB	E40D/E400 (EC) 10.2
9050	WL	B7TL/Gemini 10.6	9450	WL	Trident/E400 10.1	9544	WL	E40D/E400 (E6) 10.35
9051	WL	B7TL/Gemini 10.6	9451	WL	Trident/E400 10.1	9545	WL	E40D/E400 (EC)10.2
9052	WL	B7TL/Gemini 10.6	9452	WL	Trident/E400 10.1	9546	WL	E40D/E400 (EC)10.2
9053	WL	B7TL/Gemini 10.6	9453	WL	Trident/E400 10.1	9547	WL	E40D/E400 (EC)10.2
9054	WL	B7TL/Gemini 10.6	9454	WL	Trident/E400 10.1	9548	WL	E40D/E400 (EC)10.2
9055	WL	B7TL/Gemini 10.6	9455	WL	Trident/E400 10.1	9549	WL	E40D/E400 (EC)10.2
9056	WL	B7TL/Gemini 10.6	9456	WS	Trident/E400 10.1	9550	WL	E40D/E400 (EC)10.2
9057	WL	B7TL/Gemini 10.6	9457	WS	Trident/E400 10.1	9551	WL	E40D/E400 (EC)10.2
9058	WL	B7TL/Gemini 10.6	9458	WS	Trident/E400 10.1	9552	WL	E40D/E400 (EC)10.2
9059	WL	B7TL/Gemini 10.6	9459	WS	Trident/E400 10.1	9553	WL	E40D/E400 (EC)10.2
9060	WL	B7TL/Gemini 10.6	9460	WS	Trident/E400 10.1	9554	WL	E40D/E400 (EC)10.2
9061	WL	B7TL/Gemini 10.6	9461	WS	Trident/E400 10.1	9555	QB	E40D/E400 (EC)10.2
9062	WL	B7TL/Gemini 10.6	9462	WS	Trident/E400 10.1	9556	QB	E40D/E400 (EC)10.2
9063	WL	B7TL/Gemini 10.6	9463	WS	Trident/E400 10.1	9557	QB	E40D/E400 (EC)10.2
9064	WL	B7TL/Gemini 10.6	9464	WS	Trident/E400 10.1	9558	QB	E40D/E400 (EC)10.2
9065	WL	B7TL/Gemini 10.6	9465	WL	Trident/E400 10.1	9826	WL	Trident/ALX400 9.9
9067	BC	B7TL/Gemini 10.6	9466	QB	Trident/E400 10.1	9828	WL	Trident/ALX400 9.9
9069	WL	B7TL/Gemini 10.6	9487	QB	Trident/E400 10.1	9835	WL	Trident/ALX400 9.9
9070	WL	B7TL/Gemini 10.6	9488	QB	Trident/E400 10.1	9836	WL	Trident/ALX400 9.9
9071	WL	B7TL/Gemini 10.6	9489	QB	Trident/E400 10.1	9839	WL	Trident/ALX400 9.9
9071	WL	B7TL/Gemini 10.6	9490	QB	Trident/E400 10.1	9842	WL	Trident/ALX400 9.9
9072	WL	B7TL/Gemini 10.6	9491	QB	Trident/E400 10.1	LT602	QB	NRM (E6) 11.3
9072	WL	B7TL/Gemini 10.6	9492	QB	Trident/E400 10.1	LT603	QB	NRM (E6) 11.3
9073	WL	B7TL/Gemini 10.6	9493	QB	Trident/E400 10.1	LT604	QB	NRM (E6) 11.3
9073	WL	B7TL/Gemini 10.6	9494	QB	Trident/E400 10.1	LT605	QB	NRM (E6) 11.3
9401	QB	Trident/E400 10.1	9495	QB	Trident/E400 10.1	LT606	QB	NRM (E6) 11.3
9402	QB	Trident/E400 10.1	9496	QB	Trident/E400 10.1	LT607	QB	NRM (E6) 11.3
9403	QB	Trident/E400 10.1	9497	QB	Trident/E400 10.1	LT608	QB	NRM (E6) 11.3
9404	QB	Trident/E400 10.1	9498	QB	Trident/E400 10.1	LT609	QB	NRM (E6) 11.3
9405	QB	Trident/E400 10.1	9499	QB	Trident/E400 10.1	LT610	QB	NRM (E6) 11.3
9406	QB	Trident/E400 10.1	9500	QB	Trident/E400 10.1	LT611	QB	NRM (E6) 11.3
9407	QB	Trident/E400 10.1	9501	QB	Trident/E400 10.1	LT612	QB	NRM (E6) 11.3
9408	QB	Trident/E400 10.1	9502	QB	Trident/E400 10.1	LT613	QB	NRM (E6) 11.3
9409	QB	Trident/E400 10.1	9503	QB	Trident/E400 10.1	LT614	QB	NRM (E6) 11.3
9410	QB	Trident/E400 10.1	9504	QB	Trident/E400 10.1	LT615	QB	NRM (E6) 11.3
9411	QB	Trident/E400 10.1	9505	QB	Trident/E400 10.1	LT616	QB	NRM (E6) 11.3
9412	QB	Trident/E400 10.1	9506	QB	Trident/E400 10.1	LT617	QB	NRM (E6) 11.3
9413	QB	Trident/E400 10.1	9507	QB	Trident/E400 10.1	LT618	QB	NRM (E6) 11.3
9414	QB	Trident/E400 10.1	9508	QB	Trident/E400 10.1	LT619	QB	NRM (E6) 11.3
9415	QB	Trident/E400 10.1	9509	QB	Trident/E400 10.1	LT620	QB	NRM (E6) 11.3
9416	QB	Trident/E400 10.1	9510	QB	Trident/E400 10.1	LT621	QB	NRM (E6) 11.3
9417	QB	Trident/E400 10.1	9511	QB	Trident/E400 10.1	LT622	QB	NRM (E6) 11.3
9418	QB	Trident/E400 10.1	9512	QB	Trident/E400 10.1	LT623	QB	NRM (E6) 11.3
9419	QB	Trident/E400 10.1	9513	QB	Trident/E400 10.1	LT624	QB	NRM (E6) 11.3
9420	QB	Trident/E400 10.1	9514	QB	Trident/E400 10.1	LT625	QB	NRM (E6) 11.3
9421	QB	Trident/E400 10.1	9515	QB	Trident/E400 10.1	LT626	QB	NRM (E6) 11.3

No.	G.	Type	No.	G.	Type	No.	G.	Type
LT627	QB	NRM (E6) 11.3	LT698	QB	NRM (E6) 11.3	LT770	QB	NRM (E6) 11.3
LT628	QB	NRM (E6) 11.3	LT699	QB	NRM (E6) 11.3	LT771	QB	NRM (E6) 11.3
LT629	QB	NRM (E6) 11.3	LT700	QB	NRM (E6) 11.3	LT772	QB	NRM (E6) 11.3
LT630	QB	NRM (E6) 11.3	LT701	QB	NRM (E6) 11.3	LT773	QB	NRM (E6) 11.3
LT631	QB	NRM (E6) 11.3	LT702	QB	NRM (E6) 11.3	LT774	QB	NRM (E6) 11.3
LT632	QB	NRM (E6) 11.3	LT703	QB	NRM (E6) 11.3	LT775	QB	NRM (E6) 11.3
LT633	QB	NRM (E6) 11.3	LT704	QB	NRM (E6) 11.3	LT776	QB	NRM (E6) 11.3
LT634	QB	NRM (E6) 11.3	LT705	QB	NRM (E6) 11.3	LT777	QB	NRM (E6) 11.3
LT635	QB	NRM (E6) 11.3	LT706	QB	NRM (E6) 11.3	LT778	QB	NRM (E6) 11.3
LT636	QB	NRM (E6) 11.3	LT707	QB	NRM (E6) 11.3	LT779	QB	NRM (E6) 11.3
LT637	QB	NRM (E6) 11.3	LT708	QB	NRM (E6) 11.3	LT780	QB	NRM (E6) 11.3
LT638	QB	NRM (E6) 11.3	LT709	QB	NRM (E6) 11.3	LT781	QB	NRM (E6) 11.3
LT639	QB	NRM (E6) 11.3	LT710	QB	NRM (E6) 11.3	LT782	QB	NRM (E6) 11.3
LT640	QB	NRM (E6) 11.3	LT711	QB	NRM (E6) 11.3	LT783	QB	NRM (E6) 11.3
LT691	QB	NRM (E6) 11.3	LT712	QB	NRM (E6) 11.3	LT784	QB	NRM (E6) 11.3
LT692	QB	NRM (E6) 11.3	LT713	QB	NRM (E6) 11.3	LT785	QB	NRM (E6) 11.3
LT693	QB	NRM (E6) 11.3	LT714	QB	NRM (E6) 11.3	LT786	QB	NRM (E6) 11.3
LT694	QB	NRM (E6) 11.3	LT715	QB	NRM (E6) 11.3	LT787	QB	NRM (E6) 11.3
LT695	QB	NRM (E6) 11.3	LT716	QB	NRM (E6) 11.3	LT788	QB	NRM (E6) 11.3
LT696	QB	NRM (E6) 11.3	LT768	QB	NRM (E6) 11.3			
LT697	QB	NRM (E6) 11.3	LT769	QB	NRM (E6) 11.3			

A flashback to 2012. Brand new Euro spec Enviro400s 9547 & 9546 sit in the yard at Battersea garage. Originally ordered for use on route 3, the arrival of New Routemasters for that route led to them being transferred to Walworth. *Dave McKay*

Arriva

No.	G.	Type	No.	G.	Type	No.	G.	Type
DW31	AD	DB250/Gemini 10.3	DW221	CT	Gemini 2DL 10.4	DW290	AR	Gemini 2DL 10.4
DW32	AD	DB250/Gemini 10.3	DW222	CT	Gemini 2DL 10.4	DW291	AR	Gemini 2DL 10.4
DW35	TC	DB250/Gemini 10.3	DW223	CT	Gemini 2DL 10.4	DW292	GR	Gemini 2DL 10.4
DW36	TC	DB250/Gemini 10.3	DW224	AE	Gemini 2DL 10.4	DW293	AR	Gemini 2DL 10.4
DW37	TC	DB250/Gemini 10.3	DW225	AE	Gemini 2DL 10.4	DW294	AR	Gemini 2DL 10.4
DW38	TC	DB250/Gemini 10.3	DW226	AE	Gemini 2DL 10.4	DW295	AR	Gemini 2DL 10.4
DW39	TC	DB250/Gemini 10.3	DW227	AE	Gemini 2DL 10.4	DW296	AR	Gemini 2DL 10.4
DW40	TC	DB250/Gemini 10.3	DW228	AE	Gemini 2DL 10.4	DW297	GR	Gemini 2DL 10.4
DW41	TC	DB250/Gemini 10.3	DW229	AE	Gemini 2DL 10.4	DW298	AR	Gemini 2DL 10.4
DW42	TC	DB250/Gemini 10.3	DW230	AE	Gemini 2DL 10.4	DW299	AR	Gemini 2DL 10.4
DW43	TC	DB250/Gemini 10.3	DW231	AE	Gemini 2DL 10.4	DW300	GR	Gemini 2DL 10.4
DW44	TC	DB250/Gemini 10.3	DW232	BN	Gemini 2DL 10.4	DW301	AR	Gemini 2DL 10.4
DW92	TC	DB250/Gemini 10.3	DW233	AE	Gemini 2DL 10.4	DW302	AR	Gemini 2DL 10.4
DW94	TC	DB250/Gemini 10.3	DW234	AE	Gemini 2DL 10.4	DW303	AR	Gemini 2DL 10.4
DW95	TC	DB250/Gemini 10.3	DW235	AE	Gemini 2DL 10.4	DW304	AR	Gemini 2DL 10.4
DW96	TC	DB250/Gemini 10.3	DW236	AE	Gemini 2DL 10.4	DW305	AR	Gemini 2DL 10.4
DW97	TC	DB250/Gemini 10.3	DW237	AE	Gemini 2DL 10.4	DW306	AR	Gemini 2DL 10.4
DW98	TC	DB250/Gemini 10.3	DW238	AE	Gemini 2DL 10.4	DW307	AR	Gemini 2DL 10.4
DW99	TC	DB250/Gemini 10.3	DW239	N	Gemini 2DL 10.4	DW308	AR	Gemini 2DL 10.4
DW101	TC	DB250/Gemini 10.3	DW240	AE	Gemini 2DL 10.4	DW309	AR	Gemini 2DL 10.4
DW102	TC	DB250/Gemini 10.3	DW241	AE	Gemini 2DL 10.4	DW310	AR	Gemini 2DL 10.4
DW103	TC	DB250/Gemini 10.3	DW242	AE	Gemini 2DL 10.4	DW311	AR	Gemini 2DL 10.4
DW104	TC	DB250/Gemini 10.3	DW243	N	Gemini 2DL 10.4	DW312	AR	Gemini 2DL 10.4
DW105	TC	DB250/Gemini 10.3	DW244	AE	Gemini 2DL 10.4	DW313	AR	Gemini 2DL 10.4
DW106	TC	DB250/Gemini 10.3	DW245	AE	Gemini 2DL 10.4	DW314	AR	Gemini 2DL 10.4
DW107	TC	DB250/Gemini 10.3	DW246	AE	Gemini 2DL 10.4	DW315	AR	Gemini 2DL 10.4
DW108	TC	DB250/Gemini 10.3	DW247	AE	Gemini 2DL 10.4	DW316	AR	Gemini 2DL 10.4
DW109	TC	DB250/Gemini 10.3	DW248	TC	Gemini 2DL 10.4	DW317	AR	Gemini 2DL 10.4
DW110	TC	DB250/Gemini 10.3	DW249	N	Gemini 2DL 10.4	DW318	AR	Gemini 2DL 10.4
DW111	TC	DB250/Gemini 10.3	DW250	TC	Gemini 2DL 10.4	DW319	AR	Gemini 2DL 10.4
DW112	TC	DB250/Gemini 10.3	DW251	TC	Gemini 2DL 10.4	DW320	AR	Gemini 2DL 10.4
DW113	TC	DB250/Gemini 10.3	DW252	TC	Gemini 2DL 10.4	DW321	AR	Gemini 2DL 10.4
DW114	TC	DB250/Gemini 10.3	DW253	TC	Gemini 2DL 10.4	DW322	AR	Gemini 2DL 10.4
DW115	TC	DB250/Gemini 10.3	DW254	TC	Gemini 2DL 10.4	DW323	AR	Gemini 2DL 10.4
DW116	TC	DB250/Gemini 10.3	DW255	TC	Gemini 2DL 10.4	DW324	AR	Gemini 2DL 10.4
DW117	TC	DB250/Gemini 10.3	DW256	TC	Gemini 2DL 10.4	DW325	AR	Gemini 2DL 10.4
DW134	GR	DB250/Gemini 10.3	DW257	TC	Gemini 2DL 10.4	DW326	AR	Gemini 2DL 10.4
DW135	GR	DB250/Gemini 10.3	DW258	TC	Gemini 2DL 10.4	DW327	AR	Gemini 2DL 10.4
DW136	GR	DB250/Gemini 10.3	DW259	TC	Gemini 2DL 10.4	DW328	AR	Gemini 2DL 10.4
DW137	GR	DB250/Gemini 10.3	DW260	TC	Gemini 2DL 10.4	DW329	AR	Gemini 2DL 10.4
DW138	GR	DB250/Gemini 10.3	DW261	TC	Gemini 2DL 10.4	DW330	AR	Gemini 2DL 10.4
DW139	GR	DB250/Gemini 10.3	DW262	TC	Gemini 2DL 10.4	DW331	AR	Gemini 2DL 10.4
DW140	GR	DB250/Gemini 10.3	DW263	TC	Gemini 2DL 10.4	DW332	AR	Gemini 2DL 10.4
DW141	GR	DB250/Gemini 10.3	DW264	TC	Gemini 2DL 10.4	DW333	AR	Gemini 2DL 10.4
DW142	GR	DB250/Gemini 10.3	DW265	TC	Gemini 2DL 10.4	DW334	AR	Gemini 2DL 10.4
DW143	GR	DB250/Gemini 10.3	DW266	TC	Gemini 2DL 10.4	DW335	AR	Gemini 2DL 10.4
DW144	GR	DB250/Gemini 10.3	DW267	TC	Gemini 2DL 10.4	DW336	N	Gemini 2DL 10.4
DW145	GR	DB250/Gemini 10.3	DW268	TC	Gemini 2DL 10.4	DW401	E	Gemini 2DL (EC) 10.4
DW190	GR	Gemini 2DL 10.4	DW269	TC	Gemini 2DL 10.4	DW402	E	Gemini 2DL (EC) 10.4
DW191	GR	Gemini 2DL 10.4	DW270	TC	Gemini 2DL 10.4	DW403	E	Gemini 2DL (EC) 10.4
DW201	GY	Gemini 2DL 10.4	DW271	TC	Gemini 2DL 10.4	DW404	E	Gemini 2DL (EC) 10.4
DW202	GY	Gemini 2DL 10.4	DW272	TC	Gemini 2DL 10.4	DW405	E	Gemini 2DL (EC) 10.4
DW203	GY	Gemini 2DL 10.4	DW273	TC	Gemini 2DL 10.4	DW406	E	Gemini 2DL (EC) 10.4
DW204	GY	Gemini 2DL 10.4	DW274	TC	Gemini 2DL 10.4	DW407	E	Gemini 2DL (EC) 10.4
DW205	GY	Gemini 2DL 10.4	DW275	TC	Gemini 2DL 10.4	DW408	E	Gemini 2DL (EC) 10.4
DW206	GY	Gemini 2DL 10.4	DW276	TC	Gemini 2DL 10.4	DW409	E	Gemini 2DL (EC) 10.4
DW207	GY	Gemini 2DL 10.4	DW277	N	Gemini 2DL 10.4	DW410	E	Gemini 2DL (EC) 10.4
DW208	GY	Gemini 2DL 10.4	DW278	N	Gemini 2DL 10.4	DW411	E	Gemini 2DL (EC) 10.4
DW209	GY	Gemini 2DL 10.4	DW279	N	Gemini 2DL 10.4	DW412	E	Gemini 2DL (EC) 10.4
DW210	GY	Gemini 2DL 10.4	DW280	N	Gemini 2DL 10.4	DW413	E	Gemini 2DL (EC) 10.4
DW211	GY	Gemini 2DL 10.4	DW281	TC	Gemini 2DL 10.4	DW414	E	Gemini 2DL (EC) 10.4
DW212	GY	Gemini 2DL 10.4	DW282	N	Gemini 2DL 10.4	DW415	E	Gemini 2DL (EC) 10.4
DW213	GY	Gemini 2DL 10.4	DW283	N	Gemini 2DL 10.4	DW416	E	Gemini 2DL (EC) 10.4
DW214	CT	Gemini 2DL 10.4	DW284	TC	Gemini 2DL 10.4	DW417	E	Gemini 2DL (EC) 10.4
DW215	CT	Gemini 2DL 10.4	DW285	N	Gemini 2DL 10.4	DW418	E	Gemini 2DL (EC) 10.4
DW216	CT	Gemini 2DL 10.4	DW286	N	Gemini 2DL 10.4	DW419	E	Gemini 2DL (EC) 10.4
DW217	CT	Gemini 2DL 10.4	DW287	N	Gemini 2DL 10.4	DW420	E	Gemini 2DL (EC) 10.4
DW218	CT	Gemini 2DL 10.4	DW288	N	Gemini 2DL 10.4	DW421	E	Gemini 2DL (EC) 10.4
DW219	CT	Gemini 2DL 10.4	DW289	N	Gemini 2DL 10.4	DW422	E	Gemini 2DL (EC) 10.4
DW220	CT	Gemini 2DL 10.4						

No.	G.	Type	No.	G.	Type	No.	G.	Type
DW423	E	Gemini 2DL (EC) 10.4	DW496	WN	Gemini 2DL (EC) 10.4	DW570	E	Gemini 2DL (EC) 10.4
DW424	AR	Gemini 2DL (EC) 10.4	DW497	WN	Gemini 2DL (EC) 10.4	DW571	E	Gemini 2DL (EC) 10.4
DW425	AR	Gemini 2DL (EC) 10.4	DW498	WN	Gemini 2DL (EC) 10.4	DW572	E	Gemini 2DL (EC) 10.4
DW426	AR	Gemini 2DL (EC) 10.4	DW499	WN	Gemini 2DL (EC) 10.4	DW573	E	Gemini 2DL (EC) 10.4
DW427	AR	Gemini 2DL (EC) 10.4	DW500	TC	Gemini 2DL (EC) 10.4	DW574	E	Gemini 2DL (EC) 10.4
DW428	AR	Gemini 2DL (EC) 10.4	DW501	TC	Gemini 2DL (EC) 10.4	DW575	E	Gemini 2DL (EC) 10.4
DW429	AR	Gemini 2DL (EC) 10.4	DW502	TC	Gemini 2DL (EC) 10.4	DW576	E	Gemini 2DL (EC) 10.4
DW430	AR	Gemini 2DL (EC) 10.4	DW503	TC	Gemini 2DL (EC) 10.4	DW577	E	Gemini 2DL (EC) 10.4
DW431	AR	Gemini 2DL (EC) 10.4	DW504	TC	Gemini 2DL (EC) 10.4	DW578	E	Gemini 2DL (EC) 10.4
DW432	AR	Gemini 2DL (EC) 10.4	DW505	TC	Gemini 2DL (EC) 10.4	DW579	AR	Gemini 2DL (EC) 10.4
DW433	AR	Gemini 2DL (EC) 10.4	DW506	TC	Gemini 2DL (EC) 10.4	DW580	AR	Gemini 2DL (EC) 10.4
DW434	AR	Gemini 2DL (EC) 10.4	DW507	TC	Gemini 2DL (EC) 10.4	DW581	AR	Gemini 2DL (EC) 10.4
DW435	AR	Gemini 2DL (EC) 10.4	DW508	TC	Gemini 2DL (EC) 10.4	DW582	AR	Gemini 2DL (EC) 10.4
DW436	AR	Gemini 2DL (EC) 10.4	DW509	TC	Gemini 2DL (EC) 10.4	DW583	AR	Gemini 2DL (EC) 10.4
DW437	AR	Gemini 2DL (EC) 10.4	DW510	TC	Gemini 2DL (EC) 10.4	DW584	AR	Gemini 2DL (EC) 10.4
DW438	AR	Gemini 2DL (EC) 10.4	DW511	TC	Gemini 2DL (EC) 10.4	DW585	AR	Gemini 2DL (EC) 10.4
DW439	AR	Gemini 2DL (EC) 10.4	DW512	TC	Gemini 2DL (EC) 10.4	DW586	AR	Gemini 2DL (EC) 10.4
DW440	AR	Gemini 2DL (EC) 10.4	DW513	TC	Gemini 2DL (EC) 10.4	DWL56	GR	SB120/Cadet 10.2
DW441	AR	Gemini 2DL (EC) 10.4	DW514	TC	Gemini 2DL (EC) 10.4	DWL75	GR	SB120/Cadet 10.2
DW442	AR	Gemini 2DL (EC) 10.4	DW515	TC	Gemini 2DL (EC) 10.4	DWL79	GR	SB120/Cadet 10.2
DW443	AR	Gemini 2DL (EC) 10.4	DW516	AE	Gemini 2DL (EC) 10.4	DWL80	GR	SB120/Cadet 10.2
DW444	AR	Gemini 2DL (EC) 10.4	DW517	AE	Gemini 2DL (EC) 10.4	DWL81	GR	SB120/Cadet 10.2
DW445	AR	Gemini 2DL (EC) 10.4	DW518	AE	Gemini 2DL (EC) 10.4	DWL82	GR	SB120/Cadet 10.2
DW446	AR	Gemini 2DL (EC) 10.4	DW519	AE	Gemini 2DL (EC) 10.4	DWL85	GR	SB120/Cadet 10.2
DW447	AR	Gemini 2DL (EC) 10.4	DW520	AE	Gemini 2DL (EC) 10.4	DWL89	GR	SB120/Cadet 10.2
DW448	AR	Gemini 2DL (EC) 10.4	DW521	AE	Gemini 2DL (EC) 10.4	DWL92	GR	SB120/Cadet 10.2
DW449	AR	Gemini 2DL (EC) 10.4	DW522	AE	Gemini 2DL (EC) 10.4	DWL96	GR	SB120/Cadet 10.2
DW450	AR	Gemini 2DL (EC) 10.4	DW523	AE	Gemini 2DL (EC) 10.4	EMC1	TC	MetroCity EV 10.6
DW451	AR	Gemini 2DL (EC) 10.4	DW524	AE	Gemini 2DL (EC) 10.4	EMC2	TC	MetroCity EV 10.6
DW452	AR	Gemini 2DL (EC) 10.4	DW525	AE	Gemini 2DL (EC) 10.4	EMC3	TC	MetroCity EV 10.6
DW453	AR	Gemini 2DL (EC) 10.4	DW526	AE	Gemini 2DL (EC) 10.4	EMC4	TC	MetroCity EV 10.6
DW454	AR	Gemini 2DL (EC) 10.4	DW527	AE	Gemini 2DL (EC) 10.4	EMC5	TC	MetroCity EV 10.6
DW455	AR	Gemini 2DL (EC) 10.4	DW528	AE	Gemini 2DL (EC) 10.4	EMC6	TC	MetroCity EV 10.6
DW456	AR	Gemini 2DL (EC) 10.4	DW529	AE	Gemini 2DL (EC) 10.4	EMC7	TC	MetroCity EV 10.6
DW457	AR	Gemini 2DL (EC) 10.4	DW530	AE	Gemini 2DL (EC) 10.4	EMC8	TC	MetroCity EV 10.6
DW458	AR	Gemini 2DL (EC) 10.4	DW531	AE	Gemini 2DL (EC) 10.4	EMC9	TC	MetroCity EV 10.6
DW459	AR	Gemini 2DL (EC) 10.4	DW532	AE	Gemini 2DL (EC) 10.4	EN1	EC	E200/E200 8.9
DW460	AR	Gemini 2DL (EC) 10.4	DW533	AE	Gemini 2DL (EC) 10.4	EN2	EC	E200/E200 8.9
DW461	AR	Gemini 2DL (EC) 10.4	DW534	AE	Gemini 2DL (EC) 10.4	EN3	EC	E200/E200 8.9
DW462	AR	Gemini 2DL (EC) 10.4	DW535	AR	Gemini 2DL (EC) 10.4	EN4	EC	E200/E200 8.9
DW463	AR	Gemini 2DL (EC) 10.4	DW536	AR	Gemini 2DL (EC) 10.4	EN5	EC	E200/E200 8.9
DW464	AR	Gemini 2DL (EC) 10.4	DW537	AR	Gemini 2DL (EC) 10.4	EN6	EC	E200/E200 8.9
DW465	AR	Gemini 2DL (EC) 10.4	DW538	AR	Gemini 2DL (EC) 10.4	EN7	EC	E200/E200 8.9
DW466	AR	Gemini 2DL (EC) 10.4	DW539	AR	Gemini 2DL (EC) 10.4	EN8	EC	E200/E200 8.9
DW467	AR	Gemini 2DL (EC) 10.4	DW540	AR	Gemini 2DL (EC) 10.4	EN9	EC	E200/E200 8.9
DW468	AR	Gemini 2DL (EC) 10.4	DW541	AR	Gemini 2DL (EC) 10.4	EN10	EC	E200/E200 8.9
DW469	AR	Gemini 2DL (EC) 10.4	DW542	AR	Gemini 2DL (EC) 10.4	EN11	EC	E200/E200 8.9
DW470	AR	Gemini 2DL (EC) 10.4	DW543	AR	Gemini 2DL (EC) 10.4	EN12	E	E200/E200 8.9
DW470	AR	Gemini 2DL (EC) 10.4	DW544	AR	Gemini 2DL (EC) 10.4	EN13	E	E200/E200 8.9
DW471	AR	Gemini 2DL (EC) 10.4	DW545	AR	Gemini 2DL (EC) 10.4	EN14	E	E20D/E200 8.9
DW472	WN	Gemini 2DL (EC) 10.4	DW546	AR	Gemini 2DL (EC) 10.4	EN15	E	E200/E200 8.9
DW473	WN	Gemini 2DL (EC) 10.4	DW547	AR	Gemini 2DL (EC) 10.4	EN16	E	E200/E200 8.9
DW474	WN	Gemini 2DL (EC) 10.4	DW548	AR	Gemini 2DL (EC) 10.4	EN17	E	E200/E200 8.9
DW475	WN	Gemini 2DL (EC) 10.4	DW549	AR	Gemini 2DL (EC) 10.4	EN18	E	E200/E200 8.9
DW476	WN	Gemini 2DL (EC) 10.4	DW550	AR	Gemini 2DL (EC) 10.4	EN19	E	E200/E200 8.9
DW477	WN	Gemini 2DL (EC) 10.4	DW551	AR	Gemini 2DL (EC) 10.4	EN20	E	E200/E200 8.9
DW478	WN	Gemini 2DL (EC) 10.4	DW552	AR	Gemini 2DL (EC) 10.4	EN21	E	E200/E200 8.9
DW479	WN	Gemini 2DL (EC) 10.4	DW553	AR	Gemini 2DL (EC) 10.4	EN22	E	E200/E200 8.9
DW480	WN	Gemini 2DL (EC) 10.4	DW554	AR	Gemini 2DL (EC) 10.4	EN25	HE	E20D/E200 8.9
DW481	WN	Gemini 2DL (EC) 10.4	DW555	AR	Gemini 2DL (EC) 10.4	EN26	HE	E20D/E200 8.9
DW482	WN	Gemini 2DL (EC) 10.4	DW556	E	Gemini 2DL (EC) 10.4	EN27	HE	E20D/E200 8.9
DW483	WN	Gemini 2DL (EC) 10.4	DW557	E	Gemini 2DL (EC) 10.4	EN28	HE	E20D/E200 8.9
DW484	WN	Gemini 2DL (EC) 10.4	DW558	E	Gemini 2DL (EC) 10.4	EN29	HE	E20D/E200 8.9
DW485	WN	Gemini 2DL (EC) 10.4	DW559	E	Gemini 2DL (EC) 10.4	EN30	HE	E20D/E200 8.9
DW486	WN	Gemini 2DL (EC) 10.4	DW560	E	Gemini 2DL (EC) 10.4	EN31	HE	E20D/E200 8.9
DW487	WN	Gemini 2DL (EC) 10.4	DW561	E	Gemini 2DL (EC) 10.4	EN32	HE	E20D/E200 8.9
DW488	WN	Gemini 2DL (EC) 10.4	DW562	E	Gemini 2DL (EC) 10.4	EN33	HE	E20D/E200 8.9
DW489	WN	Gemini 2DL (EC) 10.4	DW563	E	Gemini 2DL (EC) 10.4	EN34	E	E20D/E200MMC 9.0
DW490	WN	Gemini 2DL (EC) 10.4	DW564	E	Gemini 2DL (EC) 10.4	EN35	E	E20D/E200MMC 9.0
DW491	WN	Gemini 2DL (EC) 10.4	DW565	E	Gemini 2DL (EC) 10.4	EN36	E	E20D/E200MMC 9.0
DW492	WN	Gemini 2DL (EC) 10.4	DW566	E	Gemini 2DL (EC) 10.4	EN37	E	E20D/E200MMC 9.0
DW493	WN	Gemini 2DL (EC) 10.4	DW567	E	Gemini 2DL (EC) 10.4	EN38	E	E20D/E200MMC 9.0
DW494	WN	Gemini 2DL (EC) 10.4	DW568	E	Gemini 2DL (EC) 10.4	ENL1	WN	E200/E200 10.2
DW495	WN	Gemini 2DL (EC) 10.4	DW569	E	Gemini 2DL (EC) 10.4	ENL2	TC	E200/E200 10.2

Arriva

No.	G.	Type	No.	G.	Type	No.	G.	Type
ENL3	GY	E200/E200 10.2	ENL80	DT	E200/E200 10.2	ENX13	TH	E20D/E200 10.8
ENL4	TC	E200/E200 10.2	ENL81	DT	E200/E200 10.2	ENX14	TH	E20D/E200 10.8
ENL5	GY	E200/E200 10.2	ENL82	DT	E200/E200 10.2	ENX15	TH	E20D/E200 10.8
ENL6	CT	E200/E200 10.2	ENL83	DT	E200/E200 10.2	ENX16	TH	E20D/E200 10.8
ENL7	CT	E200/E200 10.2	ENL84	DT	E200/E200 10.2	ENX17	TH	E20D/E200 10.8
ENL8	DT	E200/E200 10.2	ENL85	DT	E200/E200 10.2	ENX18	TH	E20D/E200 10.8
ENL9	DT	E200/E200 10.2	ENL86	DT	E200/E200 10.2	ENX19	TH	E20D/E200 10.8
ENL10	DT	E200/E200 10.2	ENL87	DT	E200/E200 10.2	ENX20	DT	E200/E200 10.8
ENL11	GR	E200/E200 10.2	ENL88	DT	E200/E200 10.2	ENX21	DT	E200/E200 10.8
ENL12	GR	E200/E200 10.2	ENL89	GR	E200/E200 10.2	ENX22	DT	E200/E200 10.8
ENL13	GR	E200/E200 10.2	ENL90	GY	E200/E200 10.2	ENX23	DT	E200/E200 10.8
ENL14	GR	E200/E200 10.2	ENL91	DT	E200/E200 10.2	ENX24	DT	E200/E200 10.8
ENL15	GR	E200/E200 10.2	ENL92	DT	E200/E200 10.2	ENX25	DT	E200/E200 10.8
ENL16	GR	E200/E200 10.2	ENL93	DT	E200/E200 10.2	ENX26	DT	E200/E200 10.8
ENL17	GR	E200/E200 10.2	ENL94	DT	E200/E200 10.2	ENX27	DT	E200/E200 10.8
ENL18	CT	E200/E200 10.2	ENL95	DT	E200/E200 10.2	ENX28	DT	E200/E200 10.8
ENL19	CT	E200/E200 10.2	ENL101	GR	E200/E200 10.2	ENX29	DT	E200/E200 10.8
ENL20	WN	E200/E200 10.2	ENL102	GR	E200/E200 10.2	ENX30	DT	E200/E200 10.8
ENL21	TC	E200/E200 10.2	ENL103	GR	E200/E200 10.2	HA1	AE	E40H/E400 City 10.4
ENL22	TC	E200/E200 10.2	ENL104	GR	E200/E200 10.2	HA2	AE	E40H/E400 City 10.4
ENL23	TC	E200/E200 10.2	ENL105	GR	E200/E200 10.2	HA3	AE	E40H/E400 City 10.4
ENL24	TC	E200/E200 10.2	ENL106	GR	E200/E200 10.2	HA4	AE	E40H/E400 City 10.4
ENL25	TC	E200/E200 10.2	ENL107	GR	E200/E200 10.2	HA5	AE	E40H/E400 City 10.4
ENL26	TC	E200/E200 10.2	ENL108	GR	E200/E200 10.2	HA6	AE	E40H/E400 City 10.4
ENL27	TC	E200/E200 10.2	ENL109	GR	E200/E200 10.2	HA7	AE	E40H/E400 City 10.4
ENL29	TC	E200/E200 10.2	ENL110	GR	E200/E200 10.2	HA8	AE	E40H/E400 City 10.4
ENL30	WN	E200/E200 10.2	ENL111	GR	E200/E200 10.2	HA9	AE	E40H/E400 City 10.4
ENL31	WN	E200/E200 10.2	ENL112	GR	E200/E200 10.2	HA10	AE	E40H/E400 City 10.4
ENL32	WN	E200/E200 10.2	ENR1	DT	E20D/E200MMC 9.3	HA11	AE	E40H/E400 City 10.4
ENL33	WN	E200/E200 10.2	ENR2	DT	E20D/E200MMC 9.3	HA12	AE	E40H/E400 City 10.4
ENL34	WN	E200/E200 10.2	ENR3	DT	E20D/E200MMC 9.3	HA13	AE	E40H/E400 City 10.4
ENL35	WN	E200/E200 10.2	ENR4	DT	E20D/E200MMC 9.3	HA14	AE	E40H/E400 City 10.4
ENL36	WN	E200/E200 10.2	ENR5	DT	E20D/E200MMC 9.3	HA15	AE	E40H/E400 City 10.4
ENL37	WN	E200/E200 10.2	ENR6	DT	E20D/E200MMC 9.3	HA16	AE	E40H/E400 City 10.4
ENL38	WN	E200/E200 10.2	ENR7	DT	E20D/E200MMC 9.3	HA17	AE	E40H/E400 City 10.4
ENL39	WN	E200/E200 10.2	ENS1	CT	E200/E200 9.3	HA18	AE	E40H/E400 City 10.4
ENL40	WN	E200/E200 10.2	ENS2	CT	E200/E200 9.3	HA19	AE	E40H/E400 City 10.4
ENL41	WN	E200/E200 10.2	ENS3	CT	E200/E200 9.3	HA20	BN	E40H/E400 City 10.4
ENL42	WN	E200/E200 10.2	ENS4	CT	E200/E200 9.3	HA21	BN	E40H/E400 City 10.4
ENL43	WN	E200/E200 10.2	ENS5	CT	E200/E200 9.3	HA22	BN	E40H/E400 City 10.4
ENL44	WN	E200/E200 10.2	ENS6	CT	E200/E200 9.3	HA23	BN	E40H/E400 City 10.4
ENL45	WN	E200/E200 10.2	ENS7	CT	E200/E200 9.3	HA24	BN	E40H/E400 City 10.4
ENL46	WN	E200/E200 10.2	ENS8	CT	E200/E200 9.3	HA25	BN	E40H/E400 City 10.4
ENL47	WN	E200/E200 10.2	ENS9	CT	E200/E200 9.3	HA26	BN	E40H/E400 City 10.4
ENL48	WN	E200/E200 10.2	ENS10	CT	E200/E200 9.3	HA27	BN	E40H/E400 City 10.4
ENL49	TH	E200/E200 10.2	ENS11	CT	E200/E200 9.3	HA28	BN	E40H/E400 City 10.4
ENL50	TH	E200/E200 10.2	ENS12	CT	E200/E200 9.3	HA29	BN	E40H/E400 City 10.4
ENL51	TH	E200/E200 10.2	ENS13	CT	E200/E200 9.3	HA30	BN	E40H/E400 City 10.4
ENL52	TH	E200/E200 10.2	ENS14	EC	E200/E200 9.3	HA31	BN	E40H/E400 City 10.4
ENL53	TH	E200/E200 10.2	ENS15	TH	E20D/E200 9.6	HA32	BN	E40H/E400 City 10.4
ENL54	TH	E200/E200 10.2	ENS16	TH	E20D/E200 9.6	HA33	BN	E40H/E400 City 10.4
ENL55	TH	E200/E200 10.2	ENS17	TH	E20D/E200 9.6	HA34	BN	E40H/E400 City 10.4
ENL56	TH	E200/E200 10.2	ENS18	TH	E20D/E200 9.6	HA35	BN	E40H/E400 City 10.4
ENL57	TH	E200/E200 10.2	ENS19	TH	E20D/E200 9.6	HA36	BN	E40H/E400 City 10.4
ENL58	TH	E200/E200 10.2	ENS20	TH	E20D/E200 9.6	HA37	BN	E40H/E400 City 10.4
ENL59	TH	E200/E200 10.2	ENS21	TH	E20D/E200 9.6	HA38	BN	E40H/E400 City 10.4
ENL60	TH	E200/E200 10.2	ENS22	TH	E20D/E200 9.6	HA39	BN	E40H/E400 City 10.4
ENL61	DX	E200/E200 10.2	ENS23	TH	E20D/E200 9.6	HA40	BN	E40H/E400 City 10.4
ENL62	DX	E200/E200 10.2	ENS24	TH	E20D/E200 9.6	HA41	BN	E40H/E400 City 10.4
ENL63	DX	E200/E200 10.2	ENS25	TH	E20D/E200 9.6	HA42	BN	E40H/E400 City 10.4
ENL64	DX	E200/E200 10.2	ENS26	TH	E20D/E200 9.6	HA43	BN	E40H/E400 City 10.4
ENL65	DX	E200/E200 10.2	ENS27	TH	E20D/E200 9.6	HA44	BN	E40H/E400 City 10.4
ENL66	DX	E200/E200 10.2	ENS28	TH	E20D/E200 9.6	HA45	BN	E40H/E400 City 10.4
ENL67	DX	E200/E200 10.2	ENX1	E	E20D/E200 10.8	HA46	BN	E40H/E400 City 10.4
ENL68	DX	E200/E200 10.2	ENX2	E	E20D/E200 10.8	HA47	BN	E40H/E400 City 10.4
ENL69	DX	E200/E200 10.2	ENX3	E	E20D/E200 10.8	HA48	BN	E40H/E400 City 10.4
ENL70	DX	E200/E200 10.2	ENX4	E	E20D/E200 10.8	HA49	BN	E40H/E400 City 10.4
ENL71	DX	E200/E200 10.2	ENX5	E	E20D/E200 10.8	HA50	BN	E40H/E400 City 10.4
ENL72	DX	E200/E200 10.2	ENX6	E	E20D/E200 10.8	HA51	BN	E40H/E400 City 10.4
ENL73	DX	E200/E200 10.2	ENX7	E	E20D/E200 10.8	HA52	BN	E40H/E400 City 10.4
ENL74	DX	E200/E200 10.2	ENX8	E	E20D/E200 10.8	HA53	BN	E40H/E400 City 10.4
ENL77	DT	E200/E200 10.2	ENX9	TH	E20D/E200 10.8	HV1	BN	B5LH/Gemini 2 10.4
ENL78	DT	E200/E200 10.2	ENX10	TH	E20D/E200 10.8	HV2	BN	B5LH/Gemini 2 10.4
ENL79	DT	E200/E200 10.2	ENX11	TH	E20D/E200 10.8	HV3	BN	B5LH/Gemini 2 10.4
			ENX12	TH	E20D/E200 10.8			

No.	G.	Type	No.	G.	Type	No.	G.	Type
HV4	BN	B5LH/Gemini 2 10.4	HV79	WN	B5LH/Gemini 2 (EC) 10.5	HV202	AR	B5LH/Gemini 3 ST 10.6
HV5	BN	B5LH/Gemini 2 10.4	HV80	WN	B5LH/Gemini 2 (EC) 10.5	HV203	AR	B5LH/Gemini 3 ST 10.6
HV6	BN	B5LH/Gemini 2 10.4	HV81	WN	B5LH/Gemini 2 (EC) 10.5	HV204	AR	B5LH/Gemini 3 ST 10.6
HV7	BN	B5LH/Gemini 2 10.4	HV82	WN	B5LH/Gemini 2 (EC) 10.5	HV205	AR	B5LH/Gemini 3 ST 10.6
HV8	AR	B5LH/Gemini 2 10.4	HV83	WN	B5LH/Gemini 2 (EC) 10.5	HV206	AR	B5LH/Gemini 3 ST 10.6
HV9	BN	B5LH/Gemini 2 10.4	HV84	WN	B5LH/Gemini 2 (EC) 10.5	HV207	AR	B5LH/Gemini 3 ST 10.6
HV10	AR	B5LH/Gemini 2 10.4	HV85	WN	B5LH/Gemini 2 (EC) 10.5	HV208	AR	B5LH/Gemini 3 ST 10.6
HV11	BN	B5LH/Gemini 2 10.4	HV86	WN	B5LH/Gemini 2 (EC) 10.5	HV209	AR	B5LH/Gemini 3 ST 10.6
HV12	AR	B5LH/Gemini 2 10.4	HV87	WN	B5LH/Gemini 2 (EC) 10.5	HV210	AR	B5LH/Gemini 3 ST 10.6
HV13	BN	B5LH/Gemini 2 10.4	HV88	WN	B5LH/Gemini 2 (EC) 10.5	HV211	AR	B5LH/Gemini 3 ST 10.6
HV14	BN	B5LH/Gemini 2 10.4	HV89	WN	B5LH/Gemini 2 (EC) 10.5	HV212	AR	B5LH/Gemini 3 ST 10.6
HV15	BN	B5LH/Gemini 2 10.4	HV90	WN	B5LH/Gemini 2 (EC) 10.5	HV213	AR	B5LH/Gemini 3 ST 10.6
HV16	BN	B5LH/Gemini 2 10.4	HV91	WN	B5LH/Gemini 2 (EC) 10.5	HV214	AR	B5LH/Gemini 3 ST 10.6
HV17	AR	B5LH/Gemini 2 10.4	HV92	WN	B5LH/Gemini 2 (EC) 10.5	HV215	AR	B5LH/Gemini 3 ST 10.6
HV18	AR	B5LH/Gemini 2 10.4	HV93	WN	B5LH/Gemini 2 (EC) 10.5	HV216	AR	B5LH/Gemini 3 ST 10.6
HV19	BN	B5LH/Gemini 2 10.4	HV94	WN	B5LH/Gemini 2 (EC) 10.5	HV217	AR	B5LH/Gemini 3 ST 10.6
HV20	AR	B5LH/Gemini 2 10.4	HV95	WN	B5LH/Gemini 2 (EC) 10.5	HV218	AR	B5LH/Gemini 3 ST 10.6
HV21	AR	B5LH/Gemini 2 10.4	HV96	WN	B5LH/Gemini 2 (EC) 10.5	HV219	AR	B5LH/Gemini 3 ST 10.6
HV22	BN	B5LH/Gemini 2 10.4	HV97	WN	B5LH/Gemini 2 (EC) 10.5	HV220	AR	B5LH/Gemini 3 ST 10.6
HV23	BN	B5LH/Gemini 2 10.4	HV98	WN	B5LH/Gemini 2 (EC) 10.5	HV221	AR	B5LH/Gemini 3 ST 10.6
HV24	BN	B5LH/Gemini 2 10.4	HV99	WN	B5LH/Gemini 2 (EC) 10.5	HV222	AR	B5LH/Gemini 3 ST 10.6
HV25	BN	B5LH/Gemini 2 10.4	HV100	WN	B5LH/Gemini 2 (EC) 10.5	HV223	AR	B5LH/Gemini 3 ST 10.6
HV26	BN	B5LH/Gemini 2 10.4	HV101	WN	B5LH/Gemini 2 (EC) 10.5	HV224	AR	B5LH/Gemini 3 ST 10.6
HV27	BN	B5LH/Gemini 2 10.4	HV102	WN	B5LH/Gemini 2 (EC) 10.5	HV225	AR	B5LH/Gemini 3 ST 10.6
HV28	BN	B5LH/Gemini 2 10.4	HV103	WN	B5LH/Gemini 2 (EC) 10.5	HV226		B5LH/Gemini 3 ST 10.6
HV29	BN	B5LH/Gemini 2 10.4	HV104	WN	B5LH/Gemini 2 (EC) 10.5	HV227		B5LH/Gemini 3 ST 10.6
HV30	BN	B5LH/Gemini 2 10.4	HV105	WN	B5LH/Gemini 2 (EC) 10.5	HV228	CT	B5LH/Gemini 3 ST 10.6
HV31	BN	B5LH/Gemini 2 10.4	HV106	WN	B5LH/Gemini 2 (EC) 10.5	HV229	CT	B5LH/Gemini 3 ST 10.6
HV32	BN	B5LH/Gemini 2 10.4	HV107	WN	B5LH/Gemini 2 (EC) 10.5	HV230	CT	B5LH/Gemini 3 ST 10.6
HV33	BN	B5LH/Gemini 2 10.4	HV108	WN	B5LH/Gemini 2 (EC) 10.5	HV231	CT	B5LH/Gemini 3 ST 10.6
HV34	BN	B5LH/Gemini 2 10.4	HV109	WN	B5LH/Gemini 2 (EC) 10.5	HV232	CT	B5LH/Gemini 3 ST 10.6
HV35	BN	B5LH/Gemini 2 10.4	HV110	WN	B5LH/Gemini 2 (EC) 10.5	HV233	CT	B5LH/Gemini 3 ST 10.6
HV36	BN	B5LH/Gemini 2 10.4	HV111	WN	B5LH/Gemini 2 (EC) 10.5	HV234	CT	B5LH/Gemini 3 ST 10.6
HV37	BN	B5LH/Gemini 2 10.4	HV112	WN	B5LH/Gemini 2 (EC) 10.5	HV235	CT	B5LH/Gemini 3 ST 10.6
HV38	BN	B5LH/Gemini 2 10.4	HV113	WN	B5LH/Gemini 2 (EC) 10.5	HV236	CT	B5LH/Gemini 3 ST 10.6
HV39	BN	B5LH/Gemini 2 10.4	HV114	WN	B5LH/Gemini 2 (EC) 10.5	HV237	CT	B5LH/Gemini 3 ST 10.6
HV40	BN	B5LH/Gemini 2 10.4	HV115	WN	B5LH/Gemini 2 (EC) 10.5	HV238	CT	B5LH/Gemini 3 ST 10.6
HV41	AR	B5LH/Gemini 2 10.4	HV116	WN	B5LH/Gemini 2 (EC) 10.5	HV239		B5LH/Gemini 3 ST 10.6
HV42	WN	B5LH/Gemini 2 10.4	HV117	WN	B5LH/Gemini 2 (EC) 10.5	HV240		B5LH/Gemini 3 ST 10.6
HV43	WN	B5LH/Gemini 2 10.4	HV118	WN	B5LH/Gemini 2 (EC) 10.5	HV241		B5LH/Gemini 3 ST 10.6
HV44	SF	B5LH/Gemini 2 10.4	HV119	WN	B5LH/Gemini 2 (EC) 10.5	HV242		B5LH/Gemini 3 ST 10.6
HV45	AR	B5LH/Gemini 2 10.4	HV120	WN	B5LH/Gemini 2 (EC) 10.5	HV243		B5LH/Gemini 3 ST 10.6
HV46	BN	B5LH/Gemini 2 10.4	HV121	WN	B5LH/Gemini 2 (EC) 10.5	HV244		B5LH/Gemini 3 ST 10.6
HV47	BN	B5LH/Gemini 2 (EC) 10.5	HV122	WN	B5LH/Gemini 2 (EC) 10.5	HV245		B5LH/Gemini 3 ST 10.6
HV48	AR	B5LH/Gemini 2 (EC) 10.5	HV123	WN	B5LH/Gemini 2 (EC) 10.5	HV246		B5LH/Gemini 3 ST 10.6
HV49	AR	B5LH/Gemini 2 (EC) 10.5	HV124	WN	B5LH/Gemini 2 (EC) 10.5	HV247		B5LH/Gemini 3 ST 10.6
HV50	AR	B5LH/Gemini 2 (EC) 10.5	HV125	WN	B5LH/Gemini 2 (EC) 10.5	HV248		B5LH/Gemini 3 ST 10.6
HV51	AR	B5LH/Gemini 2 (EC) 10.5	HV126	WN	B5LH/Gemini 2 (EC) 10.5	HV295		B5LH/Gemini 3 ST 10.6
HV52	AR	B5LH/Gemini 2 (EC) 10.5	HV127	WN	B5LH/Gemini 2 (EC) 10.5	HV296		B5LH/Gemini 3 ST 10.6
HV53	AR	B5LH/Gemini 2 (EC) 10.5	HV128	WN	B5LH/Gemini 2 (EC) 10.5	HV297		B5LH/Gemini 3 ST 10.6
HV54	AR	B5LH/Gemini 2 (EC) 10.5	HV129	WN	B5LH/Gemini 2 (EC) 10.5	HV298		B5LH/Gemini 3 ST 10.6
HV55	SF	B5LH/Gemini 2 (EC) 10.5	HV130	WN	B5LH/Gemini 2 (EC) 10.5	HV299		B5LH/Gemini 3 ST 10.6
HV56	AR	B5LH/Gemini 2 (EC) 10.5	HV131	WN	B5LH/Gemini 2 (EC) 10.5	HV300		B5LH/Gemini 3 ST 10.6
HV57	AD	B5LH/Gemini 2 (EC) 10.5	HV132	BN	B5LH/Gemini 2 (EC) 10.5	HV301		B5LH/Gemini 3 ST 10.6
HV58	AD	B5LH/Gemini 2 (EC) 10.5	HV133	BN	B5LH/Gemini 2 (EC) 10.5	HV302		B5LH/Gemini 3 ST 10.6
HV59	AD	B5LH/Gemini 2 (EC) 10.5	HV134	BN	B5LH/Gemini 2 (EC) 10.5	HV303		B5LH/Gemini 3 ST 10.6
HV60	AD	B5LH/Gemini 2 (EC) 10.5	HV135	BN	B5LH/Gemini 2 (EC) 10.5	HV304		B5LH/Gemini 3 ST 10.6
HV61	AD	B5LH/Gemini 2 (EC) 10.5	HV136	BN	B5LH/Gemini 2 (EC) 10.5	HV305		B5LH/Gemini 3 ST 10.6
HV62	AD	B5LH/Gemini 2 (EC) 10.5	HV137	BN	B5LH/Gemini 2 (EC) 10.5	HV306		B5LH/Gemini 3 ST 10.6
HV63	AD	B5LH/Gemini 2 (EC) 10.5	HV138	BN	B5LH/Gemini 2 (EC) 10.5	HV307		B5LH/Gemini 3 ST 10.6
HV64	AD	B5LH/Gemini 2 (EC) 10.5	HV139	BN	B5LH/Gemini 2 (EC) 10.5	HV308		B5LH/Gemini 3 ST 10.6
HV65	AD	B5LH/Gemini 2 (EC) 10.5	HV140	BN	B5LH/Gemini 2 (EC) 10.5	HV309		B5LH/Gemini 3 ST 10.6
HV66	AD	B5LH/Gemini 2 (EC) 10.5	HV141	BN	B5LH/Gemini 2 (EC) 10.5	HV310		B5LH/Gemini 3 ST 10.6
HV67	AD	B5LH/Gemini 2 (EC) 10.5	HV142	BN	B5LH/Gemini 2 (EC) 10.5	HV311		B5LH/Gemini 3 ST 10.6
HV68	AD	B5LH/Gemini 2 (EC) 10.5	HV143	BN	B5LH/Gemini 2 (EC) 10.5	LT1	CT	NRM 11.3
HV69	AD	B5LH/Gemini 2 (EC) 10.5	HV144	BN	B5LH/Gemini 2 (EC) 10.5	LT2	CT	NRM 11.3
HV70	AD	B5LH/Gemini 2 (EC) 10.5	HV145	BN	B5LH/Gemini 2 (EC) 10.5	LT3	CT	NRM 11.3
HV71	AD	B5LH/Gemini 2 (EC) 10.5	HV146	BN	B5LH/Gemini 2 (EC) 10.5	LT4	CT	NRM 11.3
HV72	AD	B5LH/Gemini 2 (EC) 10.5	HV147	BN	B5LH/Gemini 2 (EC) 10.5	LT5	CT	NRM 11.3
HV73	AD	B5LH/Gemini 2 (EC) 10.5	HV148	BN	B5LH/Gemini 2 (EC) 10.5	LT6	CT	NRM 11.3
HV74	AD	B5LH/Gemini 2 (EC) 10.5	HV149	BN	B5LH/Gemini 2 (EC) 10.5	LT7	CT	NRM 11.3
HV75	AD	B5LH/Gemini 2 (EC) 10.5	HV150	BN	B5LH/Gemini 2 (EC) 10.5	LT172	SF	NRM (E6) 11.3
HV76	AD	B5LH/Gemini 2 (EC) 10.5	HV151	BN	B5LH/Gemini 2 (EC) 10.5	LT173	SF	NRM (E6) 11.3
HV77	WN	B5LH/Gemini 2 (EC) 10.5	HV152	BN	B5LH/Gemini 2 (EC) 10.5	LT176	CT	NRM 11.3
HV78	WN	B5LH/Gemini 2 (EC) 10.5	HV201	AR	B5LH/Gemini 3 ST 10.6	LT177	CT	NRM 11.3

Arriva

No.	G.	Type	No.	G.	Type	No.	G.	Type
LT178	CT	NRM 11.3	LT333	N	NRM 11.3	LT536	SF	NRM (E6) 11.3
LT179	CT	NRM 11.3	LT334	N	NRM 11.3	LT537	SF	NRM (E6) 11.3
LT180	CT	NRM 11.3	LT335	N	NRM 11.3	LT538	SF	NRM (E6) 11.3
LT181	CT	NRM 11.3	LT336	N	NRM 11.3	LT539	SF	NRM (E6) 11.3
LT182	CT	NRM 11.3	LT337	N	NRM 11.3	LT540	SF	NRM (E6) 11.3
LT183	CT	NRM 11.3	LT338	N	NRM 11.3	LT541	SF	NRM (E6) 11.3
LT184	CT	NRM 11.3	LT339	N	NRM 11.3	LT542	SF	NRM (E6) 11.3
LT185	CT	NRM 11.3	LT340	N	NRM 11.3	LT564	AR	NRM (E6) 11.3
LT186	CT	NRM 11.3	LT341	N	NRM 11.3	LT565	AR	NRM (E6) 11.3
LT187	CT	NRM 11.3	LT342	N	NRM 11.3	LT566	AR	NRM (E6) 11.3
LT188	SF	NRM (E6) 11.3	LT343	N	NRM 11.3	LT567	AR	NRM (E6) 11.3
LT191	CT	NRM 11.3	LT344	N	NRM 11.3	LT568	AR	NRM (E6) 11.3
LT192	CT	NRM 11.3	LT345	N	NRM 11.3	LT569	AR	NRM (E6) 11.3
LT193	CT	NRM 11.3	LT346	N	NRM 11.3	LT570	AR	NRM (E6) 11.3
LT194	CT	NRM 11.3	LT347	N	NRM 11.3	LT571	AR	NRM (E6) 11.3
LT195	CT	NRM 11.3	LT348	N	NRM 11.3	LT572	AR	NRM (E6) 11.3
LT196	CT	NRM 11.3	LT349	N	NRM 11.3	LT573	AR	NRM (E6) 11.3
LT197	CT	NRM 11.3	LT350	N	NRM 11.3	LT574	AR	NRM (E6) 11.3
LT198	CT	NRM 11.3	LT351	N	NRM 11.3	LT575	AR	NRM (E6) 11.3
LT199	CT	NRM 11.3	LT352	N	NRM 11.3	LT576	AR	NRM (E6) 11.3
LT200	CT	NRM 11.3	LT353	SF	NRM 11.3	LT577	AR	NRM (E6) 11.3
LT201	CT	NRM 11.3	LT354	SF	NRM 11.3	LT578	AR	NRM (E6) 11.3
LT202	CT	NRM 11.3	LT355	SF	NRM 11.3	LT579	AR	NRM (E6) 11.3
LT203	CT	NRM 11.3	LT356	SF	NRM 11.3	LT580	AR	NRM (E6) 11.3
LT204	CT	NRM 11.3	LT464	SF	NRM (E6) 11.3	LT581	AR	NRM (E6) 11.3
LT205	CT	NRM 11.3	LT465	SF	NRM (E6) 11.3	LT582	AR	NRM (E6) 11.3
LT206	CT	NRM 11.3	LT466	SF	NRM (E6) 11.3	LT583	AR	NRM (E6) 11.3
LT207	CT	NRM 11.3	LT467	SF	NRM (E6) 11.3	LT584	AR	NRM (E6) 11.3
LT208	CT	NRM 11.3	LT468	SF	NRM (E6) 11.3	LT585	AR	NRM (E6) 11.3
LT209	CT	NRM 11.3	LT469	SF	NRM (E6) 11.3	LT586	AR	NRM (E6) 11.3
LT210	CT	NRM 11.3	LT470	SF	NRM (E6) 11.3	LT587	AR	NRM (E6) 11.3
LT211	CT	NRM 11.3	LT471	SF	NRM (E6) 11.3	LT588	AR	NRM (E6) 11.3
LT212	CT	NRM 11.3	LT472	SF	NRM (E6) 11.3	LT589	AR	NRM (E6) 11.3
LT213	CT	NRM 11.3	LT473	SF	NRM (E6) 11.3	LT590	AR	NRM (E6) 11.3
LT214	CT	NRM 11.3	LT474	SF	NRM (E6) 11.3	LT591	AR	NRM (E6) 11.3
LT215	CT	NRM 11.3	LT475	SF	NRM (E6) 11.3	LT592	AR	NRM (E6) 11.3
LT216	CT	NRM 11.3	LT476	SF	NRM (E6) 11.3	LT593	AR	NRM (E6) 11.3
LT217	CT	NRM 11.3	LT477	SF	NRM (E6) 11.3	LT594	AR	NRM (E6) 11.3
LT218	CT	NRM 11.3	LT488	SF	NRM (E6) 11.3	LT595	AR	NRM (E6) 11.3
LT219	CT	NRM 11.3	LT489	SF	NRM (E6) 11.3	LT596	AR	NRM (E6) 11.3
LT220	CT	NRM 11.3	LT490	SF	NRM (E6) 11.3	LT597	AR	NRM (E6) 11.3
LT221	CT	NRM 11.3	LT491	SF	NRM (E6) 11.3	LT598	AR	NRM (E6) 11.3
LT222	CT	NRM 11.3	LT492	SF	NRM (E6) 11.3	LT599	AR	NRM (E6) 11.3
LT223	CT	NRM 11.3	LT493	SF	NRM (E6) 11.3	LT600	AR	NRM (E6) 11.3
LT224	CT	NRM 11.3	LT494	SF	NRM (E6) 11.3	LT601	AR	NRM (E6) 11.3
LT225	CT	NRM 11.3	LT495	SF	NRM (E6) 11.3	LT716	BN	NRM (E6) 11.3
LT226	CT	NRM 11.3	LT496	SF	NRM (E6) 11.3	LT717	BN	NRM (E6) 11.3
LT227	CT	NRM 11.3	LT497	SF	NRM (E6) 11.3	LT718	BN	NRM (E6) 11.3
LT228	CT	NRM 11.3	LT498	SF	NRM (E6) 11.3	LT719	BN	NRM (E6) 11.3
LT229	CT	NRM 11.3	LT499	SF	NRM (E6) 11.3	LT720	BN	NRM (E6) 11.3
LT230	CT	NRM 11.3	LT500	SF	NRM (E6) 11.3	LT721	BN	NRM (E6) 11.3
LT231	CT	NRM 11.3	LT513	AR	NRM (E6) 11.3	LT722	BN	NRM (E6) 11.3
LT232	CT	NRM 11.3	LT514	AR	NRM (E6) 11.3	LT723	BN	NRM (E6) 11.3
LT233	CT	NRM 11.3	LT515	AR	NRM (E6) 11.3	LT724	BN	NRM (E6) 11.3
LT234	AE	NRM 11.3	LT516	AR	NRM (E6) 11.3	LT725	BN	NRM (E6) 11.3
LT235	AE	NRM 11.3	LT517	SF	NRM (E6) 11.3	LT726	BN	NRM (E6) 11.3
LT236	AE	NRM 11.3	LT518	SF	NRM (E6) 11.3	LT727	BN	NRM (E6) 11.3
LT237	AE	NRM 11.3	LT519	SF	NRM (E6) 11.3	LT728	BN	NRM (E6) 11.3
LT238	AE	NRM 11.3	LT520	SF	NRM (E6) 11.3	LT729	BN	NRM (E6) 11.3
LT317	BN	NRM 11.3	LT521	SF	NRM (E6) 11.3	LT730	BN	NRM (E6) 11.3
LT318	BN	NRM 11.3	LT522	SF	NRM (E6) 11.3	LT731	BN	NRM (E6) 11.3
LT319	BN	NRM 11.3	LT523	SF	NRM (E6) 11.3	LT732	BN	NRM (E6) 11.3
LT320	BN	NRM 11.3	LT524	SF	NRM (E6) 11.3	LT733	BN	NRM (E6) 11.3
LT321	BN	NRM 11.3	LT525	SF	NRM (E6) 11.3	LT734	BN	NRM (E6) 11.3
LT322	BN	NRM 11.3	LT526	SF	NRM (E6) 11.3	LT735	BN	NRM (E6) 11.3
LT323	BN	NRM 11.3	LT527	SF	NRM (E6) 11.3	LT736	BN	NRM (E6) 11.3
LT324	BN	NRM 11.3	LT528	SF	NRM (E6) 11.3	LT737	BN	NRM (E6) 11.3
LT325	BN	NRM 11.3	LT529	SF	NRM (E6) 11.3	LT738	BN	NRM (E6) 11.3
LT326	BN	NRM 11.3	LT530	SF	NRM (E6) 11.3	LT739	BN	NRM (E6) 11.3
LT327	BN	NRM 11.3	LT531	SF	NRM (E6) 11.3	LT740	BN	NRM (E6) 11.3
LT328	BN	NRM 11.3	LT532	SF	NRM (E6) 11.3	LT741	BN	NRM (E6) 11.3
LT329	BN	NRM 11.3	LT533	SF	NRM (E6) 11.3	LT742	BN	NRM (E6) 11.3
LT330	N	NRM 11.3	LT534	SF	NRM (E6) 11.3	LT743	BN	NRM (E6) 11.3
LT331	N	NRM 11.3	LT535	SF	NRM (E6) 11.3	LT744	BN	NRM (E6) 11.3
LT332	N	NRM 11.3				LT813	SF	NRM (E6) 11.3

No.	G.	Type	No.	G.	Type	No.	G.	Type
LT814	SF	NRM (E6) 11.3	PDL136	TH	Dart Pointer 9.3	T42	AD	Trident/E400 10.1
LT815	SF	NRM (E6) 11.3	PDL152	GR	Dart/Pointer 10.1	T43	AD	Trident/E400 10.1
LT816	SF	NRM (E6) 11.3	SLS1	N	Streetlite DF 9.7	T44	TC	Trident/E400 10.1
LT817	SF	NRM (E6) 11.3	SLS2	N	Streetlite DF 9.7	T45	TC	Trident/E400 10.1
LT818	SF	NRM (E6) 11.3	SLS3	N	Streetlite DF 9.7	T46	TC	Trident/E400 10.1
LT819	SF	NRM (E6) 11.3	SLS4	N	Streetlite DF 9.7	T47	TC	Trident/E400 10.1
LT820	SF	NRM (E6) 11.3	SLS5	N	Streetlite DF 9.7	T48	TC	Trident/E400 10.1
LT821	SF	NRM (E6) 11.3	SLS6	N	Streetlite DF 9.7	T49	TC	Trident/E400 10.1
LT822	SF	NRM (E6) 11.3	SLS7	N	Streetlite DF 9.7	T50	TC	Trident/E400 10.1
LT823	SF	NRM (E6) 11.3	SLS8	N	Streetlite DF 9.7	T51	TC	Trident/E400 10.1
LT824	SF	NRM (E6) 11.3	SLS9	N	Streetlite DF 9.7	T52	TC	Trident/E400 10.1
LT825	SF	NRM (E6) 11.3	SLS10	N	Streetlite DF 9.7	T53	TC	Trident/E400 10.1
LT826	SF	NRM (E6) 11.3	SLS11	N	Streetlite DF 9.7	T54	TC	Trident/E400 10.1
LT827	SF	NRM (E6) 11.3	SLS12	N	Streetlite DF 9.7	T55	TC	Trident/E400 10.1
LT828	SF	NRM (E6) 11.3	SLS13	N	Streetlite DF 9.7	T56	TC	Trident/E400 10.1
LT829	SF	NRM (E6) 11.3	SLS13	N	Streetlite DF 9.7	T57	TC	Trident/E400 10.1
LT830	SF	NRM (E6) 11.3	SLS15	N	Streetlite DF 9.7	T58	TC	Trident/E400 10.1
LT831	SF	NRM (E6) 11.3	SLS16	N	Streetlite DF 9.7	T59	TC	Trident/E400 10.1
LT832	SF	NRM (E6) 11.3	SLS17	N	Streetlite DF 9.7	T60	TC	Trident/E400 10.1
LT833	SF	NRM (E6) 11.3	SLS18	N	Streetlite DF 9.7	T61	TC	Trident/E400 10.1
LT834	SF	NRM (E6) 11.3	SLS19	N	Streetlite DF 9.7	T62	TC	Trident/E400 10.1
LT835	SF	NRM (E6) 11.3	SLS20	N	Streetlite DF 9.7	T63	TC	Trident/E400 10.1
LT836	SF	NRM (E6) 11.3	SLS21	N	Streetlite DF 9.7	T64	TC	Trident/E400 10.1
LT837	SF	NRM (E6) 11.3	SLS22	N	Streetlite DF 9.7	T65	DX	Trident/E400 10.1
LT838	SF	NRM (E6) 11.3	SW1	GR	Streetdeck/Gemini 3 10.6	T66	DX	Trident/E400 10.6
LT839	SF	NRM (E6) 11.3	SW2	GR	Streetdeck/Gem3ST 10.6	T67	DX	Trident/E400 10.1
LT840	SF	NRM (E6) 11.3	SW3	GR	Streetdeck/Gem3ST 10.6	T68	DX	Trident/E400 10.1
LT841	SF	NRM (E6) 11.3	SW4	GR	Streetdeck/Gem3ST 10.6	T69	DX	Trident/E400 10.1
LT842	SF	NRM (E6) 11.3	SW5	GR	Streetdeck/Gem3ST 10.6	T70	DX	Trident/E400 10.1
LT843	SF	NRM (E6) 11.3	SW6	GR	Streetdeck/Gem3ST 10.6	T71	DX	Trident/E400 10.1
LT844	SF	NRM (E6) 11.3	SW7	GR	Streetdeck/Gem3ST 10.6	T72	DX	Trident/E400 10.1
OS68	GR	Solo 7.8	SW8	GR	Streetdeck/Gem3ST 10.6	T73	DX	Trident/E400 10.1
OS69	GR	Solo 7.8	SW9	GR	Streetdeck/Gem3ST 10.6	T74	DX	Trident/E400 10.1
OS70	GR	Solo 7.8	SW10	GR	Streetdeck/Gem3ST 10.6	T75	DX	Trident/E400 10.1
OS71	GR	Solo 7.8	T1	AD	Trident/E400 10.1	T76	DX	Trident/E400 10.1
OS72	GR	Solo 7.8	T2	AD	Trident/E400 10.1	T77	DX	Trident/E400 10.1
PDL95	TH	Dart/Pointer 9.3	T3	AD	Trident/E400 10.1	T78	DX	Trident/E400 10.1
PDL96	TH	Dart/Pointer 9.3	T4	AD	Trident/E400 10.1	T79	DX	Trident/E400 10.1
PDL97	TH	Dart/Pointer 9.3	T5	AD	Trident/E400 10.1	T80	DX	Trident/E400 10.1
PDL98	TH	Dart/Pointer 9.3	T6	AD	Trident/E400 10.1	T81	DX	Trident/E400 10.1
PDL99	TH	Dart/Pointer 9.3	T7	AD	Trident/E400 10.1	T82	DX	Trident/E400 10.1
PDL100	TH	Dart/Pointer 9.3	T8	AD	Trident/E400 10.1	T83	DX	Trident/E400 10.1
PDL101	EC	Dart/Pointer 9.3	T9	AD	Trident/E400 10.1	T84	N	Trident/E400 10.1
PDL102	EC	Dart/Pointer 9.3	T10	AD	Trident/E400 10.1	T85	N	Trident/E400 10.1
PDL103	EC	Dart/Pointer 9.3	T11	AD	Trident/E400 10.1	T86	N	Trident/E400 10.1
PDL104	EC	Dart/Pointer 9.3	T12	TH	Trident/E400 10.1	T87	N	Trident/E400 10.1
PDL105	EC	Dart/Pointer 9.3	T13	TH	Trident/E400 10.1	T88	N	Trident/E400 10.1
PDL106	EC	Dart/Pointer 9.3	T14	TH	Trident/E400 10.1	T89	N	Trident/E400 10.1
PDL107	EC	Dart/Pointer 9.3	T15	TH	Trident/E400 10.1	T90	N	Trident/E400 10.1
PDL108	EC	Dart/Pointer 9.3	T16	TH	Trident/E400 10.1	T91	N	Trident/E400 10.1
PDL109	EC	Dart/Pointer 9.3	T17	TH	Trident/E400 10.1	T92	N	Trident/E400 10.1
PDL110	EC	Dart/Pointer 9.3	T18	TH	Trident/E400 10.1	T93	N	Trident/E400 10.1
PDL111	EC	Dart/Pointer 9.3	T19	TH	Trident/E400 10.1	T94	N	Trident/E400 10.1
PDL112	EC	Dart/Pointer 9.3	T20	TH	Trident/E400 10.1	T95	N	Trident/E400 10.1
PDL113	EC	Dart/Pointer 9.3	T21	TH	Trident/E400 10.1	T96	N	Trident/E400 10.1
PDL114	EC	Dart/Pointer 9.3	T22	TH	Trident/E400 10.1	T97	N	Trident/E400 10.1
PDL115	EC	Dart/Pointer 9.3	T23	TH	Trident/E400 10.1	T98	N	Trident/E400 10.1
PDL116	EC	Dart/Pointer 9.3	T24	TH	Trident/E400 10.1	T99	N	Trident/E400 10.1
PDL117	GR	Dart/Pointer 10.1	T25	TH	Trident/E400 10.1	T100	N	Trident/E400 10.1
PDL118	GR	Dart/Pointer 10.1	T26	TH	Trident/E400 10.1	T101	N	Trident/E400 10.1
PDL119	GR	Dart/Pointer 10.1	T27	AD	Trident/E400 10.1	T102	N	Trident/E400 10.1
PDL121	TC	Dart/Pointer 10.1	T28	AD	Trident/E400 10.1	T103	N	Trident/E400 10.1
PDL123	GR	Dart/Pointer 10.1	T29	AD	Trident/E400 10.1	T104	N	Trident/E400 10.1
PDL124	TH	Dart/Pointer 9.3	T30	AD	Trident/E400 10.1	T105	N	Trident/E400 10.1
PDL125	TH	Dart/Pointer 9.3	T31	AD	Trident/E400 10.1	T106	N	Trident/E400 10.1
PDL126	TH	Dart/Pointer 9.3	T32	AD	Trident/E400 10.1	T107	N	Trident/E400 10.1
PDL127	TH	Dart/Pointer 9.3	T33	AD	Trident/E400 10.1	T108	N	Trident/E400 10.1
PDL128	TH	Dart/Pointer 9.3	T34	AD	Trident/E400 10.1	T109	N	Trident/E400 10.1
PDL129	TH	Dart/Pointer 9.3	T35	AD	Trident/E400 10.1	T110	N	Trident/E400 10.1
PDL130	TH	Dart/Pointer 9.3	T36	AD	Trident/E400 10.1	T111	N	Trident/E400 10.1
PDL131	TH	Dart/Pointer 9.3	T37	AD	Trident/E400 10.1	T112	N	Trident/E400 10.1
PDL132	TH	Dart/Pointer 9.3	T38	AD	Trident/E400 10.1	T113	N	Trident/E400 10.1
PDL133	TH	Dart/Pointer 9.3	T39	AD	Trident/E400 10.1	T114	N	Trident/E400 10.1
PDL134	TH	Dart/Pointer 9.3	T40	AD	Trident/E400 10.1	T115	N	Trident/E400 10.1
PDL135	TH	Dart/Pointer 9.3	T41	AD	Trident/E400 10.1	T116	N	Trident/E400 10.1

Arriva

No.	G.	Type	No.	G.	Type	No.	G.	Type
T117	N	Trident/E400 10.1	T191	DX	Trident/E400 10.1	T271	WN	E40D/E400 (EC) 10.2
T118	N	Trident/E400 10.1	T192	DX	Trident/E400 10.1	T272	WN	E40D/E400 (EC) 10.2
T119	TH	Trident/E400 10.1	T193	DX	Trident/E400 10.1	T273	WN	E40D/E400 (EC) 10.2
T120	TH	Trident/E400 10.1	T199	GR	Trident/E400 10.1	T274	WN	E40D/E400 (EC) 10.2
T121	TH	Trident/E400 10.1	T201	WN	E40D/E400 (EC) 10.2	T275	WN	E40D/E400 (EC) 10.2
T122	TH	Trident/E400 10.1	T202	WN	E40D/E400 (EC) 10.2	T276	WN	E40D/E400 (EC) 10.2
T123	TH	Trident/E400 10.1	T203	WN	E40D/E400 (EC) 10.2	T277	WN	E40D/E400 (EC) 10.2
T124	TH	Trident/E400 10.1	T204	WN	E40D/E400 (EC) 10.2	T278	WN	E40D/E400 (EC) 10.2
T125	TH	Trident/E400 10.1	T205	WN	E40D/E400 (EC) 10.2	T279	TC	E40D/E400 (EC) 10.2
T126	TH	Trident/E400 10.1	T206	WN	E40D/E400 (EC) 10.2	T280	TC	E40D/E400 (EC) 10.2
T127	TH	Trident/E400 10.1	T207	WN	E40D/E400 (EC) 10.2	T281	TC	E40D/E400 (EC) 10.2
T128	N	Trident/E400 10.1	T208	WN	E40D/E400 (EC) 10.2	T282	TC	E40D/E400 (EC) 10.2
T129	N	Trident/E400 10.1	T209	WN	E40D/E400 (EC) 10.2	T283	TC	E40D/E400 (EC) 10.2
T130	TH	Trident/E400 10.1	T210	WN	E40D/E400 (EC) 10.2	T284	TC	E40D/E400 (EC) 10.2
T131	TH	Trident/E400 10.1	T211	WN	E40D/E400 (EC) 10.2	T285	TC	E40D/E400 (EC) 10.2
T132	TH	Trident/E400 10.1	T212	WN	E40D/E400 (EC) 10.2	T286	TC	E40D/E400 (EC) 10.2
T133	TH	Trident/E400 10.1	T213	WN	E40D/E400 (EC) 10.2	T287	TC	E40D/E400 (EC) 10.2
T134	TH	Trident/E400 10.1	T214	WN	E40D/E400 (EC) 10.2	T288	DT	E40D/E400 (EC) 10.2
T135	TH	Trident/E400 10.1	T215	WN	E40D/E400 (EC) 10.2	T289	DT	E40D/E400 (EC) 10.2
T136	TH	Trident/E400 10.1	T216	WN	E40D/E400 (EC) 10.2	T290	DT	E40D/E400 (EC) 10.2
T137	TH	Trident/E400 10.1	T217	WN	E40D/E400 (EC) 10.2	T291	DT	E40D/E400 (EC) 10.2
T138	TH	Trident/E400 10.1	T218	WN	E40D/E400 (EC) 10.2	T292	DT	E40D/E400 (EC) 10.2
T139	TH	Trident/E400 10.1	T219	WN	E40D/E400 (EC) 10.2	T293	DT	E40D/E400 (EC) 10.2
T140	TH	Trident/E400 10.1	T220	WN	E40D/E400 (EC) 10.2	T294	DT	E40D/E400 (EC) 10.2
T141	TH	Trident/E400 10.1	T221	WN	E40D/E400 (EC) 10.2	T295	DT	E40D/E400 (EC) 10.2
T142	TH	Trident/E400 10.1	T222	WN	E40D/E400 (EC) 10.2	T296	DT	E40D/E400 (EC) 10.2
T143	TH	Trident/E400 10.1	T223	WN	E40D/E400 (EC) 10.2	T297	DT	E40D/E400 (EC) 10.2
T144	TH	Trident/E400 10.1	T224	E	E40D/E400 (EC) 10.2	T298	DT	E40D/E400 (EC) 10.2
T145	TH	Trident/E400 10.1	T225	E	E40D/E400 (EC) 10.2	T299	DT	E40D/E400 (EC) 10.2
T146	TH	Trident/E400 10.1	T226	E	E40D/E400 (EC) 10.2	T300	DT	E40D/E400 (EC) 10.2
T147	TH	Trident/E400 10.1	T227	E	E40D/E400 (EC) 10.2	T301	DT	E40D/E400 (E6) 10.35
T148	TH	Trident/E400 10.1	T228	E	E40D/E400 (EC) 10.2	T302	DT	E40D/E400 (E6) 10.35
T149	TH	Trident/E400 10.1	T229	E	E40D/E400 (EC) 10.2	T303	DT	E40D/E400 (E6) 10.35
T150	TH	Trident/E400 10.1	T230	E	E40D/E400 (EC) 10.2	T304	DT	E40D/E400 (E6) 10.35
T151	TH	Trident/E400 10.1	T231	E	E40D/E400 (EC) 10.2	T305	DT	E40D/E400 (E6) 10.35
T152	TH	Trident/E400 10.1	T232	E	E40D/E400 (EC) 10.2	T306	DT	E40D/E400 (E6) 10.35
T153	TH	Trident/E400 10.1	T233	E	E40D/E400 (EC) 10.2	T307	DT	E40D/E400 (E6) 10.35
T154	TH	Trident/E400 10.1	T234	E	E40D/E400 (EC) 10.2	T308	DT	E40D/E400 (E6) 10.35
T155	TH	Trident/E400 10.1	T235	E	E40D/E400 (EC) 10.2	T309	DT	E40D/E400 (E6) 10.35
T156	TH	Trident/E400 10.1	T236	E	E40D/E400 (EC) 10.2	T310	DT	E40D/E400 (E6) 10.35
T157	TH	Trident/E400 10.1	T237	E	E40D/E400 (EC) 10.2	T311	DT	E40D/E400 (E6) 10.35
T158	TH	Trident/E400 10.1	T238	E	E40D/E400 (EC) 10.2	T312	DT	E40D/E400 (E6) 10.35
T159	TH	Trident/E400 10.1	T239	E	E40D/E400 (EC) 10.2	T313	DT	E40D/E400 (E6) 10.35
T160	TH	Trident/E400 10.1	T240	E	E40D/E400 (EC) 10.2	T314	DT	E40D/E400 (E6) 10.35
T161	TH	Trident/E400 10.1	T241	E	E40D/E400 (EC) 10.2	T315	DT	E40D/E400 (E6) 10.35
T162	TH	Trident/E400 10.1	T242	E	E40D/E400 (EC) 10.2	T316	DT	E40D/E400 (E6) 10.35
T163	TH	Trident/E400 10.1	T243	E	E40D/E400 (EC) 10.2	T317	DT	E40D/E400 (E6) 10.35
T164	TH	Trident/E400 10.1	T244	E	E40D/E400 (EC) 10.2	T318	DT	E40D/E400 (E6) 10.35
T165	TH	Trident/E400 10.1	T245	E	E40D/E400 (EC) 10.2	T319	DT	E40D/E400 (E6) 10.35
T166	TH	Trident/E400 10.1	T246	E	E40D/E400 (EC) 10.2	T320	DT	E40D/E400 (E6) 10.35
T167	TH	Trident/E400 10.1	T247	E	E40D/E400 (EC) 10.2	T321	DT	E40D/E400 (E6) 10.35
T168	DX	Trident/E400 10.1	T248	E	E40D/E400 (EC) 10.2	T322	DT	E40D/E400 (E6) 10.35
T169	DX	Trident/E400 10.1	T249	E	E40D/E400 (EC) 10.2	T323	DT	E40D/E400 (E6) 10.35
T170	DX	Trident/E400 10.1	T250	E	E40D/E400 (EC) 10.2	T324	DT	E40D/E400 (E6) 10.35
T171	DX	Trident/E400 10.1	T251	E	E40D/E400 (EC) 10.2	T325	DT	E40D/E400 (E6) 10.35
T172	DX	Trident/E400 10.1	T252	E	E40D/E400 (EC) 10.2	T326	DT	E40D/E400 (E6) 10.35
T173	DX	Trident/E400 10.1	T253	E	E40D/E400 (EC) 10.2	T327	DT	E40D/E400 (E6) 10.35
T174	DX	Trident/E400 10.1	T254	E	E40D/E400 (EC) 10.2	T328	DT	E40D/E400 (E6) 10.35
T175	DX	Trident/E400 10.1	T255	E	E40D/E400 (EC) 10.2	T329	DT	E40D/E400 (E6) 10.35
T176	DX	Trident/E400 10.1	T256	E	E40D/E400 (EC) 10.2	T330	DT	E40D/E400 (E6) 10.35
T177	DX	Trident/E400 10.1	T257	E	E40D/E400 (EC) 10.2	T331	DT	E40D/E400 (E6) 10.35
T178	DX	Trident/E400 10.1	T258	E	E40D/E400 (EC) 10.2	VLA1	AR	B7TL/ALX400 10.6
T179	DX	Trident/E400 10.1	T259	E	E40D/E400 (EC) 10.2	VLA2	AR	B7TL/ALX400 10.6
T180	DX	Trident/E400 10.1	T260	WN	E40D/E400 (EC) 10.2	VLA3	AR	B7TL/ALX400 10.6
T181	DX	Trident/E400 10.1	T261	WN	E40D/E400 (EC) 10.2	VLA4	AR	B7TL/ALX400 10.6
T182	DX	Trident/E400 10.1	T262	WN	E40D/E400 (EC) 10.2	VLA5	AR	B7TL/ALX400 10.6
T183	DX	Trident/E400 10.1	T263	WN	E40D/E400 (EC) 10.2	VLA6	AR	B7TL/ALX400 10.6
T184	DX	Trident/E400 10.1	T264	WN	E40D/E400 (EC) 10.2	VLA7	AR	B7TL/ALX400 10.6
T185	DX	Trident/E400 10.1	T265	WN	E40D/E400 (EC) 10.2	VLA8	AR	B7TL/ALX400 10.6
T186	DX	Trident/E400 10.1	T266	WN	E40D/E400 (EC) 10.2	VLA9	AR	B7TL/ALX400 10.6
T187	DX	Trident/E400 10.1	T267	WN	E40D/E400 (EC) 10.2	VLA10	AR	B7TL/ALX400 10.6
T188	DX	Trident/E400 10.1	T268	WN	E40D/E400 (EC) 10.2	VLA11	AR	B7TL/ALX400 10.6
T189	DX	Trident/E400 10.1	T269	WN	E40D/E400 (EC) 10.2	VLA12	AR	B7TL/ALX400 10.6
T190	DX	Trident/E400 10.1	T270	WN	E40D/E400 (EC) 10.2	VLA13	AR	B7TL/ALX400 10.6

No.	G.	Type
VLA14	AR	B7TL/ALX400 10.6
VLA15	AR	B7TL/ALX400 10.6
VLA16	AR	B7TL/ALX400 10.6
VLA17	N	B7TL/ALX400 10.6
VLA18	N	B7TL/ALX400 10.6
VLA19	N	B7TL/ALX400 10.6
VLA20	N	B7TL/ALX400 10.6
VLA21	N	B7TL/ALX400 10.6
VLA22	N	B7TL/ALX400 10.6
VLA23	N	B7TL/ALX400 10.6
VLA24	N	B7TL/ALX400 10.6
VLA25	N	B7TL/ALX400 10.6
VLA26	N	B7TL/ALX400 10.6
VLA27	N	B7TL/ALX400 10.6
VLA28	N	B7TL/ALX400 10.6
VLA29	N	B7TL/ALX400 10.6
VLA30	N	B7TL/ALX400 10.6
VLA31	N	B7TL/ALX400 10.6
VLA32	N	B7TL/ALX400 10.6
VLA33	N	B7TL/ALX400 10.6
VLA34	N	B7TL/ALX400 10.6
VLA35	N	B7TL/ALX400 10.6
VLA36	N	B7TL/ALX400 10.6
VLA37	N	B7TL/ALX400 10.6
VLA38	N	B7TL/ALX400 10.6
VLA39	N	B7TL/ALX400 10.6
VLA40	N	B7TL/ALX400 10.6
VLA41	N	B7TL/ALX400 10.6
VLA42	N	B7TL/ALX400 10.6
VLA43	N	B7TL/ALX400 10.6
VLA44	N	B7TL/ALX400 10.6
VLA45	N	B7TL/ALX400 10.6
VLA46	N	B7TL/ALX400 10.6
VLA47	N	B7TL/ALX400 10.6
VLA48	N	B7TL/ALX400 10.6
VLA49	N	B7TL/ALX400 10.6
VLA50	N	B7TL/ALX400 10.6
VLA51	N	B7TL/ALX400 10.6
VLA52	N	B7TL/ALX400 10.6
VLA53	N	B7TL/ALX400 10.6
VLA54	N	B7TL/ALX400 10.6
VLA55	N	B7TL/ALX400 10.6
VLA56	N	B7TL/ALX400 10.6
VLA57	N	B7TL/ALX400 10.6
VLA58	N	B7TL/ALX400 10.6
VLA59	N	B7TL/ALX400 10.6
VLA60	N	B7TL/ALX400 10.6
VLA61	N	B7TL/ALX400 10.6
VLA62	N	B7TL/ALX400 10.6
VLA63	N	B7TL/ALX400 10.6
VLA64	N	B7TL/ALX400 10.6
VLA65	N	B7TL/ALX400 10.6
VLA66	N	B7TL/ALX400 10.6
VLA67	N	B7TL/ALX400 10.6
VLA68	N	B7TL/ALX400 10.6
VLA69	N	B7TL/ALX400 10.6
VLA70	N	B7TL/ALX400 10.6
VLA71	N	B7TL/ALX400 10.6
VLA72	N	B7TL/ALX400 10.6
VLA73	N	B7TL/ALX400 10.6
VLA74	N	B7TL/ALX400 10.1
VLA75	N	B7TL/ALX400 10.1
VLA76	N	B7TL/ALX400 10.1
VLA77	N	B7TL/ALX400 10.1
VLA101	AR	B7TL/ALX400 10.1
VLA102	AR	B7TL/ALX400 10.1
VLA103	AR	B7TL/ALX400 10.1
VLA104	AR	B7TL/ALX400 10.1
VLA105	GY	B7TL/ALX400 10.1

No.	G.	Type
VLA106	GY	B7TL/ALX400 10.1
VLA107	DX	B7TL/ALX400 10.1
VLA108	GY	B7TL/ALX400 10.1
VLA109	N	B7TL/ALX400 10.1
VLA110	GY	B7TL/ALX400 10.1
VLA111	GY	B7TL/ALX400 10.1
VLA112	GY	B7TL/ALX400 10.1
VLA113	GY	B7TL/ALX400 10.1
VLA114	GY	B7TL/ALX400 10.1
VLA115	GY	B7TL/ALX400 10.1
VLA116	GY	B7TL/ALX400 10.1
VLA117	GY	B7TL/ALX400 10.1
VLA118	GY	B7TL/ALX400 10.1
VLA119	GY	B7TL/ALX400 10.1
VLA120	GY	B7TL/ALX400 10.1
VLA121	GY	B7TL/ALX400 10.1
VLA122	N	B7TL/ALX400 10.1
VLA123	N	B7TL/ALX400 10.1
VLA124	DX	B7TL/ALX400 10.1
VLA125	DX	B7TL/ALX400 10.1
VLA126	DX	B7TL/ALX400 10.1
VLA127	DX	B7TL/ALX400 10.1
VLA128	DX	B7TL/ALX400 10.1
VLA129	DX	B7TL/ALX400 10.1
VLA130	DX	B7TL/ALX400 10.1
VLA131	DX	B7TL/ALX400 10.1
VLA132	DX	B7TL/ALX400 10.1
VLA133	DX	B7TL/ALX400 10.1
VLA134	DX	B7TL/ALX400 10.1
VLA135	DX	B7TL/ALX400 10.1
VLA136	DX	B7TL/ALX400 10.1
VLA137	DX	B7TL/ALX400 10.1
VLA138	DX	B7TL/ALX400 10.1
VLA139	DX	B7TL/ALX400 10.1
VLA140	DX	B7TL/ALX400 10.1
VLA141	DX	B7TL/ALX400 10.1
VLA142	DX	B7TL/ALX400 10.1
VLA143	DX	B7TL/ALX400 10.1
VLA164	GR	B7TL/ALX400 10.1
VLA165	GR	B7TL/ALX400 10.1
VLA166	GR	B7TL/ALX400 10.1
VLA167	GR	B7TL/ALX400 10.1
VLA168	GR	B7TL/ALX400 10.1
VLA169	GR	B7TL/ALX400 10.1
VLA170	GR	B7TL/ALX400 10.1
VLA171	GR	B7TL/ALX400 10.1
VLA172	GR	B7TL/ALX400 10.1
VLA173	GR	B7TL/ALX400 10.1
VLA174	GR	B7TL/ALX400 10.1
VLA175	GR	B7TL/ALX400 10.1
VLA176	GR	B7TL/ALX400 10.1
VLA177	GR	B7TL/ALX400 10.1
VLA178	GR	B7TL/ALX400 10.1
VLA179	GR	B7TL/ALX400 10.1
VLW80	WN	B7TL/Gemini 10.1
VLW81	WN	B7TL/Gemini 10.1
VLW86	CT	B7TL/Gemini 10.1
VLW87	CT	B7TL/Gemini 10.1
VLW88	CT	B7TL/Gemini 10.1
VLW89	CT	B7TL/Gemini 10.1
VLW91	CT	B7TL/Gemini 10.1
VLW92	CT	B7TL/Gemini 10.1
VLW93	CT	B7TL/Gemini 10.1
VLW94	CT	B7TL/Gemini 10.1
VLW95	GR	B7TL/Gemini 10.1
VLW96	CT	B7TL/Gemini 10.1
VLW126	CT	B7TL/Gemini 10.1
VLW128	GR	B7TL/Gemini 10.1
VLW129	GR	B7TL/Gemini 10.1
VLW130	CT	B7TL/Gemini 10.1

No.	G.	Type
VLW131	GR	B7TL/Gemini 10.1
VLW132	AE	B7TL/Gemini 10.1
VLW133	AE	B7TL/Gemini 10.1
VLW134	AE	B7TL/Gemini 10.1
VLW135	AE	B7TL/Gemini 10.1
VLW136	AE	B7TL/Gemini 10.1
VLW137	AE	B7TL/Gemini 10.1
VLW138	AE	B7TL/Gemini 10.1
VLW139	AE	B7TL/Gemini 10.1
VLW140	AE	B7TL/Gemini 10.1
VLW141	AE	B7TL/Gemini 10.1
VLW142	AE	B7TL/Gemini 10.1
VLW143	AE	B7TL/Gemini 10.1
VLW144	AE	B7TL/Gemini 10.1
VLW145	AE	B7TL/Gemini 10.1
VLW146	AE	B7TL/Gemini 10.1
VLW147	AE	B7TL/Gemini 10.1
VLW148	AE	B7TL/Gemini 10.1
VLW149	AE	B7TL/Gemini 10.1
VLW150	AE	B7TL/Gemini 10.1
VLW151	AE	B7TL/Gemini 10.1
VLW152	AE	B7TL/Gemini 10.1
VLW153	AE	B7TL/Gemini 10.1
VLW154	AE	B7TL/Gemini 10.1
VLW155	AE	B7TL/Gemini 10.1
VLW156	AE	B7TL/Gemini 10.1
VLW157	AE	B7TL/Gemini 10.1
VLW158	AE	B7TL/Gemini 10.1
VLW159	AE	B7TL/Gemini 10.1
VLW160	AE	B7TL/Gemini 10.1
VLW161	AE	B7TL/Gemini 10.1
VLW162	AE	B7TL/Gemini 10.1
VLW163	AE	B7TL/Gemini 10.1
VLW164	AE	B7TL/Gemini 10.1
VLW165	AE	B7TL/Gemini 10.1
VLW166	AE	B7TL/Gemini 10.1
VLW167	AE	B7TL/Gemini 10.1
VLW168	AE	B7TL/Gemini 10.1
VLW169	AE	B7TL/Gemini 10.1
VLW170	AE	B7TL/Gemini 10.1
VLW171	AE	B7TL/Gemini 10.1
VLW172	WN	B7TL/Gemini 10.1
VLW173	WN	B7TL/Gemini 10.1
VLW174	WN	B7TL/Gemini 10.1
VLW175	WN	B7TL/Gemini 10.1
VLW176	WN	B7TL/Gemini 10.1
VLW177	WN	B7TL/Gemini 10.1
VLW178	WN	B7TL/Gemini 10.1
VLW179	WN	B7TL/Gemini 10.1
VLW180	WN	B7TL/Gemini 10.6
VLW181	WN	B7TL/Gemini 10.6
VLW182	WN	B7TL/Gemini 10.6
VLW183	WN	B7TL/Gemini 10.6
VLW184	WN	B7TL/Gemini 10.6
VLW185	WN	B7TL/Gemini 10.6
VLW186	WN	B7TL/Gemini 10.6
VLW187	WN	B7TL/Gemini 10.6
VLW188	WN	B7TL/Gemini 10.6
VLW190	WN	B7TL/Gemini 10.6
VLW191	WN	B7TL/Gemini 10.6
VLW192	WN	B7TL/Gemini 10.6
VLW193	WN	B7TL/Gemini 10.6
VLW194	WN	B7TL/Gemini 10.6
VLW195	WN	B7TL/Gemini 10.6
VLW196	WN	B7TL/Gemini 10.6
VLW197	WN	B7TL/Gemini 10.6
VLW198	WN	B7TL/Gemini 10.6
VLW199	WN	B7TL/Gemini 10.6

CT Plus

No.	G.	Type	No.	G.	Type	No.	G.	Type
1220	HK	E20D/E200 8.9	1273	HK	E20D/E200MMC 9.0	DA4	HK	E20D/E200 10.8
1221	AW	E20D/E200 9.6	1274	HK	E20D/E200MMC 9.0	DA5	HK	E20D/E200 10.8
1222	AW	E20D/E200 9.6	1275	HK	E20D/E200MMC 9.0	DA6	HK	E20D/E200 10.8
1223	AW	E20D/E200 9.6	1276	HK	E20D/E200MMC 9.0	DA7	HK	E20D/E200 10.8
1224	AW	E20D/E200 9.6	1277	HK	E20D/E200MMC 9.0	DA8	HK	E20D/E200 10.8
1225	AW	E20D/E200 9.6	1278	HK	E20D/E200MMC 9.0	DA9	HK	E20D/E200 10.8
1226	AW	E20D/E200 9.6	1279	HK	E20D/E200MMC 9.0	DA10	HK	E20D/E200 10.8
1227	AW	E20D/E200 9.6	1280	HK	E20D/E200MMC 9.0	DA11	HK	E20D/E200 10.8
1228	AW	E20D/E200 9.6	1281	HK	E20D/E200MMC 9.0	DA12	HK	E20D/E200 10.8
1229	AW	E20D/E200 9.6	1282	HK	E20D/E200MMC 9.0	DAS1	HK	E200/E200 8.9
1230	AW	E20D/E200 9.6	1282	HK	E20D/E200MMC 9.0	DAS2	HK	E200/E200 8.9
1231	AW	E20D/E200 9.6	2501	HK	E40H/E400 City 10.4	DCS1	HK	Dart/Nimbus 8.9
1232	AW	E20D/E200 9.6	2502	HK	E40H/E400 City 10.4	DCS2	HK	Dart/Nimbus 8.9
1234	AW	E20D/E200 9.6	2503	HK	E40H/E400 City 10.4	DCS3	HK	Dart/Nimbus 8.9
1235	AW	E20D/E200 9.6	2504	HK	E40H/E400 City 10.4	DCS4	HK	Dart/Nimbus 8.9
1236	AW	E20D/E200 9.6	2505	HK	E40H/E400 City 10.4	DCS5	HK	Dart/Nimbus 8.9
1237	AW	E20D/E200 9.6	2506	HK	E40H/E400 City 10.4	DCS6	HK	Dart/Nimbus 8.9
1238	AW	E20D/E200MMC 9.75	2507	HK	E40H/E400 City 10.4	DCS7	HK	Dart/Nimbus 8.9
1239	AW	E20D/E200MMC 9.75	2508	HK	E40H/E400 City 10.4	DCS8	HK	Dart/Nimbus 8.9
1240	AW	E20D/E200MMC 9.75	2509	HK	E40H/E400 City 10.4	DCS9	HK	Dart/Nimbus 8.9
1241	AW	E20D/E200MMC 9.75	2510	HK	E40H/E400 City 10.4	HEA1	HK	E40H/400 10.2
1242	AW	E20D/E200MMC 9.75	2511	HK	E40H/E400 City 10.4	OS2	HK	Solo SE 7.8
1243	AW	E20D/E200MMC 9.75	2512	HK	E40H/E400 City 10.4	OS3	HK	Solo SE 7.8
1244	AW	E20D/E200MMC 9.75	2513	HK	E40H/E400 City 10.4	OS4	HK	Solo SE 7.8
1245	AW	E20D/E200MMC 9.75	2514	HK	E40H/E400 City 10.4	OS5	HK	Solo SE 7.8
1246	AW	E20D/E200MMC 9.75	2515	HK	E40H/E400 City 10.4	OS6	HK	Solo SE 7.8
1247	AW	E20D/E200MMC 9.75	2516	HK	E40H/E400 City 10.4	OS7	HK	Solo SE 7.8
1248	AW	E20D/E200MMC 9.75	2517	HK	E40H/E400 City 10.4	OS8	HK	Solo SE 7.8
1249	AW	E20D/E200MMC 9.75	2518	HK	E40H/E400 City 10.4	OS9	HK	Solo 8.8
1250	AW	E20D/E200MMC 9.75	2519	HK	E40H/E400 City 10.4	OS10	HK	Solo 8.8
1251	AW	E20D/E200MMC 9.75	2520	HK	E40H/E400 City 10.4	OS11	HK	Solo 8.8
1252	AW	E20D/E200MMC 9.75	2521	HK	E40H/E400 City 10.4	OS12	HK	Solo 8.8
1253	AW	E20D/E200MMC 9.75	2522	HK	E40H/E400 City 10.4	OS13	HK	Solo 8.8
1254	AW	E20D/E200MMC 9.75	2523	HK	E40H/E400 City 10.4	OS14	HK	Solo 8.8
1255	AW	E20D/E200MMC 9.75	2524	HK	E40H/E400 City 10.4	OS15	HK	Solo 8.8
1256	AW	E20D/E200MMC 9.75	2525	HK	E40H/E400 City 10.4	OS16	HK	Solo 8.8
1257	AW	E20D/E200MMC 9.75	2526	HK	E40H/E400 City 10.4	OS18	HK	Solo 8.8
1258	AW	E20D/E200MMC 9.75	2527	HK	E40H/E400 City 10.4	OS19	HK	Solo 8.8
1259	AW	E20D/E200MMC 9.75	2528	HK	E40H/E400 City 10.4	OS20	HK	Solo 9.6
1260	AW	E20D/E200MMC 9.75	2529	HK	E40H/E400 City 10.4	OS21	HK	Solo 9.6
1261	AW	E20D/E200MMC 9.75	2530	HK	E40H/E400 City 10.4	OS22	HK	Solo 9.6
1262	AW	E20D/E200MMC 9.75	2531	HK	E40H/E400 City 10.4	OS23	HK	Solo 9.6
1263	AW	E20D/E200MMC 9.75	2532	HK	E40H/E400 City 10.4	OS24	HK	Solo 9.6
1264	AW	E20D/E200MMC 9.75	2533	HK	E40H/E400 City 10.4	OS25	HK	Solo 9.6
1265	HK	E20D/E200MMC 10.9	2534	HK	E40H/E400 City 10.4	OS26	HK	Solo 9.6
1266	HK	E20D/E200MMC 10.9	2535	HK	E40H/E400 City 10.4	OS27	HK	Solo 9.6
1267	HK	E20D/E200MMC 10.9	2536	HK	E40H/E400 City 10.4	SD1	HK	N230/OmniCity 10.8
1268	HK	E20D/E200MMC 10.9	2537	HK	E40H/E400 City 10.4	SD2	HK	N230/OmniCity 10.8
1269	HK	E20D/E200MMC 10.9	2538	HK	E40H/E400 City 10.4	SD3	HK	N230/OmniCity 10.8
1270	HK	E20D/E200MMC 10.9	2539	HK	E40H/E400 City 10.4	SD4	HK	N230/OmniCity 10.8
1271	HK	E20D/E200MMC 10.9	DA2	HK	E20D/E200 10.8	SD5	HK	N230/OmniCity 10.8
1272	HK	E20D/E200MMC 9.0	DA3	HK	E20D/E200 10.8	SD6	HK	N230/OmniCity 10.8

Go-Ahead

No.	G.	Type	No.	G.	Type	No.	G.	Type
101	MB	Solo SE 7.1	275	MB	Dart/Pointer 8.9	871	RR	N230/Olympus 10.8
102	MB	Solo SE 7.1	276	MB	Dart/Pointer 8.9	872	RR	N230/Olympus 10.8
142	NP	Dart/Capital 8.9	277	MB	Dart/Pointer 8.9	873	RR	N230/Olympus 10.8
148	Q	E200/E200 8.9	278	MB	Dart/Pointer 8.9	874	RR	N230/Olympus 10.8
149	BX	E200/E200 8.9	279	NP	Dart/Pointer 8.9	875	RR	N230/Olympus 10.8
150	BX	E200/E200 8.9	561	C	N230/OmniCity 12.0	876	RR	N230/Olympus 10.8
151	BX	E200/E200 8.9	562	C	N230/OmniCity 12.0	877	RR	N230/Olympus 10.8
152	BX	E200/E200 8.9	563	C	N230/OmniCity 12.0	878	RR	N230/Olympus 10.8
153	BX	E200/E200 8.9	564	C	N230/OmniCity 12.0	879	MB	N230/Olympus 10.8
154	MB	E200/E200 8.9	565	C	N230/OmniCity 12.0	880	MB	N230/Olympus 10.8
155	MB	E200/E200 8.9	566	C	N230/OmniCity 12.0	881	MB	N230/Olympus 10.8
156	MB	E200/E200 8.9	567	C	N230/OmniCity 12.0	882	MB	N230/Olympus 10.8
157	MB	E200/E200 8.9	601	MB	N94/Esteem 10.6	883	RR	N230/Olympus 10.8
158	MB	E200/E200 8.9	602	MB	N94/Esteem 10.6	884	RR	N230/Olympus 10.8
159	MB	E200/E200 8.9	603	MB	N94/Esteem 10.6	885	RR	N230/Olympus 10.8
160	MB	E200/E200 8.9	604	MB	N94/Esteem 10.6	886	RR	N230/Olympus 10.8
161	MB	E200/E200 8.9	605	MB	N94/Esteem 10.6	887	RR	N230/Olympus 10.8
162	MB	E200/E200 8.9	606	MB	N94/Esteem 10.6	889	RR	N230/Olympus 10.8
163	MB	E20D/E200 8.9	607	MB	N94/Esteem 10.6	890	RR	N230/Olympus 10.8
164	MB	E20D/E200 8.9	608	MB	N94/Esteem 10.6	891	RR	N230/Olympus 10.8
165	MB	E20D/E200 8.9	609	MB	N94/Esteem 10.6	892	RR	N230/Olympus 10.8
166	MB	E20D/E200 8.9	610	MB	N94/Esteem 10.6	893	RR	N230/Olympus 10.8
167	MB	E20D/E200 8.9	611	MB	N94/Esteem 10.6	894	RR	N230/Olympus 10.8
168	MB	E20D/E200 8.9	612	MB	N94/Esteem 10.6	895	RR	N230/Olympus 10.8
169	MB	E20D/E200 8.9	613	MB	N94/Esteem 10.6	896	RR	N230/Olympus 10.8
170	MB	E20D/E200 8.9	614	MB	N94/Esteem 10.6	897	MB	N230/Olympus 10.8
171	MB	E20D/E200 8.9	701	MB	12.240/East Lancs 10.3	898	MB	N230/Olympus 10.8
172	MB	E20D/E200 8.9	702	MB	12.240/East Lancs 10.3	899	MB	N230/Olympus 10.8
173	MB	E20D/E200 8.9	703	MB	12.240/East Lancs 10.3	947	C	N230/OmniDekka 10.8
174	MB	E20D/E200 8.9	704	MB	12.240/East Lancs 10.3	948	C	N230/OmniDekka 10.8
175	MB	E20D/E200 8.9	705	MB	12.240/East Lancs 10.3	949	C	N230/OmniDekka 10.8
176	MB	E20D/E200 8.9	706	C	14.240/E200 10.7	950	C	N230/OmniDekka 10.8
177	MB	E20D/E200 8.9	707	C	14.240/E200 10.7	951	C	N230/OmniDekka 10.8
178	MB	E20D/E200 8.9	708	C	14.240/E200 10.7	952	C	N230/OmniDekka 10.8
179	MB	E20D/E200 8.9	709	MB	14.240/Evoultion 10.8	955	C	N230/OmniCity 10.8
180	MB	E20D/E200 8.9	712	C	14.240/Evoultion 10.8	956	C	N230/OmniCity 10.8
181	MB	E20D/E200 8.9	713	C	14.240/Evoultion 10.8	957	C	N230/OmniCity 10.8
182	MB	E20D/E200 8.9	715	MB	14.240/Evoultion 10.8	958	SI	N230/OmniCity 10.8
183	MB	E20D/E200 8.9	717	MB	14.240/Evoultion 10.8	959	SI	N230/OmniCity 10.8
184	MB	E20D/E200 8.9	718	C	14.240/Evoultion 10.8	960	SI	N230/OmniCity 10.8
185	MB	E20D/E200 8.9	720	MB	14.240/Evoultion 10.8	961	SI	N230/OmniCity 10.8
186	MB	E20D/E200 8.9	721	C	14.240/Evoultion 10.8	962	SI	N230/OmniCity 10.8
187	MB	E20D/E200 8.9	723	MB	14.240/Evoultion 10.8	963	SI	N230/OmniCity 10.8
188	MB	E20D/E200 8.9	731	MB	E200/E200 10.2	964	SI	N230/OmniCity 10.8
189	C	E20D/E200 8.9	732	MB	E200/E200 10.2	965	SI	N230/OmniCity 10.8
190	C	E20D/E200 8.9	733	MB	E200/E200 10.2	966	SI	N230/OmniCity 10.8
191	C	E20D/E200 8.9	740	MB	E20D/E200 10.8	967	SI	N230/OmniCity 10.8
210	C	Dart/Pointer 10.7	741	MB	E20D/E200 10.8	968	SI	N230/OmniCity 10.8
211	C	Dart/Pointer 10.7	742	MB	E20D/E200 10.8	969	SI	N230/OmniCity 10.8
212	C	Dart/Pointer 10.7	743	MB	E20D/E200 10.8	970	SI	N230/OmniCity 10.8
213	C	Dart/Pointer 10.7	744	MB	E20D/E200 10.8	971	SI	N230/OmniCity 10.8
214	C	Dart/Pointer 10.7	745	MB	E20D/E200 10.8	972	SI	N230/OmniCity 10.8
215	C	Dart/Pointer 10.7	746	MB	E20D/E200 10.8	973	SI	N230/OmniCity 10.8
216	C	Dart/Pointer 10.7	747	MB	E20D/E200 10.8	974	MB	N230/OmniCity 10.8
219	C	Dart/Pointer 10.7	748	MB	E20D/E200 10.8	975	MB	N230/OmniCity 10.8
228	NP	Dart/Esteem 9.0	749	MB	E20D/E200 10.8	976	MB	N230/OmniCity 10.8
229	NP	Dart/Esteem 9.0	750	MB	E20D/E200 10.8	977	MB	N230/OmniCity 10.8
230	SW	Dart/Esteem 9.0	751	MB	E20D/E200 10.8	978	MB	N230/OmniCity 10.8
231	RR	Dart/Esteem 9.0	752	MB	E20D/E200 10.8	DMN1	NP	Dart/Capital 8.9m
232	RR	Dart/Esteem 9.0	753	MB	E20D/E200 10.8	DMN4	RR	Dart/Capital 10.2
251	MB	Dart/Pointer 8.9	754	MB	E20D/E200 10.8	DMN7	RR	Dart/Capital 8.9m
252	MB	Dart/Pointer 8.9	755	MB	E20D/E200 10.8	DMN8	RR	Dart/Capital 8.9m
253	MB	Dart/Pointer 8.9	756	MB	E20D/E200 10.8	DMN9	RR	Dart/Capital 8.9m
254	MB	Dart/Pointer 8.9	757	MB	E20D/E200 10.8	DMN10	RR	Dart/Capital 8.9m
255	MB	Dart/Pointer 8.9	758	MB	E20D/E200 10.8	DMN11	RR	Dart/Capital 8.9m
256	MB	Dart/Pointer 8.9	759	MB	E20D/E200 10.8	DMN12	RR	Dart/Capital 8.9m
271	MB	Dart/Pointer 8.9	760	MB	E20D/E200 10.8	DMN13	RR	Dart/Capital 8.9m
272	MB	Dart/Pointer 8.9	761	MB	E20D/E200 10.8	DMN15	RR	Dart/Capital 8.9m
273	MB	Dart/Pointer 8.9	762	MB	E20D/E200 10.8	DMN16	RR	Dart/Capital 8.9m
274	MB	Dart/Pointer 8.9	870	RR	N230/Olympus 10.8	DMN17	RR	Dart/Capital 8.9m

Go-Ahead

No.	G.	Type	No.	G.	Type	No.	G.	Type
DMN18	RR	Dart/Capital 8.9m	E5	SW	Trident/E400 10.1	E79	AL	Trident/E400 10.1
DOE1	PM	Trident/Olympus 10.3	E6	SW	Trident/E400 10.1	E80	AL	Trident/E400 10.1
DOE2	PM	Trident/Olympus 10.3	E7	SW	Trident/E400 10.1	E81	AL	Trident/E400 10.1
DOE3	PM	Trident/Olympus 10.3	E8	SW	Trident/E400 10.1	E82	AL	Trident/E400 10.1
DOE4	PM	Trident/Olympus 10.3	E9	SW	Trident/E400 10.1	E83	AL	Trident/E400 10.1
DOE5	PM	Trident/Olympus 10.3	E10	SW	Trident/E400 10.1	E84	AL	Trident/E400 10.1
DOE6	PM	Trident/Olympus 10.3	E11	SW	Trident/E400 10.1	E85	AL	Trident/E400 10.1
DOE7	PM	Trident/Olympus 10.3	E12	SW	Trident/E400 10.1	E86	AL	Trident/E400 10.1
DOE8	PM	Trident/Olympus 10.3	E13	SW	Trident/E400 10.1	E87	AL	Trident/E400 10.1
DOE9	RR	Trident/Olympus 10.3	E14	SW	Trident/E400 10.1	E88	AL	Trident/E400 10.1
DOE10	PM	Trident/Olympus 10.3	E15	SW	Trident/E400 10.1	E89	AL	Trident/E400 10.1
DOE11	PM	Trident/Olympus 10.3	E16	PM	Trident/E400 10.1	E90	AL	Trident/E400 10.1
DOE12	PM	Trident/Olympus 10.3	E17	PM	Trident/E400 10.1	E91	AL	Trident/E400 10.1
DOE13	PM	Trident/Olympus 10.3	E18	PM	Trident/E400 10.1	E92	AL	Trident/E400 10.1
DOE14	A	Trident/Olympus 10.3	E19	PM	Trident/E400 10.1	E93	AL	Trident/E400 10.1
DOE15	A	Trident/Olympus 10.3	E20	PM	Trident/E400 10.1	E94	NX	Trident/E400 10.1
DOE16	PM	Trident/Olympus 10.3	E21	PM	Trident/E400 10.1	E95	NX	Trident/E400 10.1
DOE17	PM	Trident/Olympus 10.3	E22	PM	Trident/E400 10.1	E96	NX	Trident/E400 10.1
DOE18	A	Trident/Olympus 10.3	E23	PM	Trident/E400 10.1	E97	NX	Trident/E400 10.1
DOE19	PM	Trident/Olympus 10.3	E24	PM	Trident/E400 10.1	E98	NX	Trident/E400 10.1
DOE20	A	Trident/Olympus 10.3	E25	PM	Trident/E400 10.1	E99	NX	Trident/E400 10.1
DOE21	A	Trident/Olympus 10.3	E26	PM	Trident/E400 10.1	E100	AL	Trident/E400 10.1
DOE22	A	Trident/Olympus 10.3	E27	PM	Trident/E400 10.1	E101	AL	Trident/E400 10.1
DOE23	A	Trident/Olympus 10.3	E28	PM	Trident/E400 10.1	E102	AL	Trident/E400 10.1
DOE24	A	Trident/Olympus 10.3	E29	PM	Trident/E400 10.1	E103	AL	Trident/E400 10.1
DOE25	A	Trident/Olympus 10.3	E30	PM	Trident/E400 10.1	E104	AL	Trident/E400 10.1
DOE26	A	Trident/Olympus 10.3	E31	PM	Trident/E400 10.1	E105	AL	Trident/E400 10.1
DOE27	A	Trident/Olympus 10.3	E32	PM	Trident/E400 10.1	E106	AL	Trident/E400 10.1
DOE28	A	Trident/Olympus 10.3	E33	PM	Trident/E400 10.1	E107	AL	Trident/E400 10.1
DOE29	A	Trident/Olympus 10.3	E34	PM	Trident/E400 10.1	E108	AL	Trident/E400 10.1
DOE30	PM	Trident/Olympus 10.3	E35	PM	Trident/E400 10.1	E109	AL	Trident/E400 10.1
DOE31	PM	Trident/Olympus 10.3	E36	PM	Trident/E400 10.1	E110	AL	Trident/E400 10.1
DOE32	A	Trident/Olympus 10.3	E37	PM	Trident/E400 10.1	E111	AL	Trident/E400 10.1
DOE33	A	Trident/Olympus 10.3	E38	SW	Trident/E400 10.1	E112	AL	Trident/E400 10.1
DOE34	A	Trident/Olympus 10.3	E39	BX	Trident/E400 10.1	E113	AL	Trident/E400 10.1
DOE35	A	Trident/Olympus 10.3	E40	NP	Trident/E400 10.1	E114	AL	Trident/E400 10.1
DOE36	A	Trident/Olympus 10.3	E41	BX	Trident/E400 10.1	E115	AL	Trident/E400 10.1
DOE37	A	Trident/Olympus 10.3	E42	BX	Trident/E400 10.1	E116	AL	Trident/E400 10.1
DOE38	A	Trident/Olympus 10.3	E43	BX	Trident/E400 10.1	E117	AL	Trident/E400 10.1
DOE39	PM	Trident/Olympus 10.3	E44	BX	Trident/E400 10.1	E118	AL	Trident/E400 10.1
DOE40	PM	Trident/Olympus 10.3	E45	BX	Trident/E400 10.1	E119	AL	Trident/E400 10.1
DOE41	PM	Trident/Olympus 10.3	E46	BX	Trident/E400 10.1	E120	AL	Trident/E400 10.1
DOE42	PM	Trident/Olympus 10.3	E47	BX	Trident/E400 10.1	E121	AL	Trident/E400 10.1
DOE43	PM	Trident/Olympus 10.3	E48	BX	Trident/E400 10.1	E122	AL	Trident/E400 10.1
DOE44	A	Trident/Olympus 10.3	E49	BX	Trident/E400 10.1	E123	AL	Trident/E400 10.1
DOE45	PM	Trident/Olympus 10.3	E50	BX	Trident/E400 10.1	E124	AL	Trident/E400 10.1
DOE46	A	Trident/Olympus 10.3	E51	BX	Trident/E400 10.1	E125	AL	Trident/E400 10.1
DOE47	A	Trident/Olympus 10.3	E52	BX	Trident/E400 10.1	E126	AL	Trident/E400 10.1
DOE48	A	Trident/Olympus 10.3	E53	BX	Trident/E400 10.1	E127	AL	Trident/E400 10.1
DOE49	A	Trident/Olympus 10.3	E54	BX	Trident/E400 10.1	E128	AL	Trident/E400 10.1
DOE50	A	Trident/Olympus 10.3	E55	BX	Trident/E400 10.1	E129	BX	Trident/E400 10.1
DOE51	A	Trident/Olympus 10.3	E56	BX	Trident/E400 10.1	E130	BX	Trident/E400 10.1
DOE52	A	Trident/Olympus 10.3	E57	AL	Trident/E400 10.1	E131	BX	Trident/E400 10.1
DOE53	A	Trident/Olympus 10.3	E58	Q	Trident/E400 10.1	E132	BX	Trident/E400 10.1
DOE54	A	Trident/Olympus 10.3	E59	Q	Trident/E400 10.1	E133	BX	Trident/E400 10.1
DP192	NX	Dart/Pointer 10.7	E60	Q	Trident/E400 10.1	E134	BX	Trident/E400 10.1
DP193	SW	Dart/Pointer 10.7	E61	AL	Trident/E400 10.1	E135	BX	Trident/E400 10.1
DP194	SW	Dart/Pointer 10.7	E62	BX	Trident/E400 10.1	E136	MB	Trident/E400 10.1
DP195	SW	Dart/Pointer 10.7	E63	BX	Trident/E400 10.1	E137	BX	Trident/E400 10.1
DP196	SW	Dart/Pointer 10.7	E64	BX	Trident/E400 10.1	E138	SW	Trident/E400 10.1
DP197	SW	Dart/Pointer 10.7	E65	BX	Trident/E400 10.1	E139	SW	Trident/E400 10.1
DP198	SW	Dart/Pointer 10.7	E66	BX	Trident/E400 10.1	E140	SW	Trident/E400 10.1
DP199	SW	Dart/Pointer 10.7	E67	NP	Trident/E400 10.1	E141	SW	Trident/E400 10.1
DP200	SW	Dart/Pointer 10.7	E68	AL	Trident/E400 10.1	E142	SW	Trident/E400 10.1
DP201	SW	Dart/Pointer 10.7	E69	AL	Trident/E400 10.1	E143	SW	Trident/E400 10.1
DP202	SW	Dart/Pointer 10.7	E70	AL	Trident/E400 10.1	E144	SW	Trident/E400 10.1
DP203	SW	Dart/Pointer 10.7	E71	AL	Trident/E400 10.1	E145	SW	Trident/E400 10.1
DP204	SW	Dart/Pointer 10.7	E72	AL	Trident/E400 10.1	E146	SW	Trident/E400 10.1
DP205	SW	Dart/Pointer 10.7	E73	AL	Trident/E400 10.1	E147	SW	Trident/E400 10.1
DP209	SW	Dart/Pointer 10.7	E74	AL	Trident/E400 10.1	E148	SW	Trident/E400 10.1
E1	SW	Trident/E400 10.1	E75	AL	Trident/E400 10.1	E149	SW	Trident/E400 10.1
E2	SW	Trident/E400 10.1	E76	AL	Trident/E400 10.1	E150	SW	Trident/E400 10.1
E3	SW	Trident/E400 10.1	E77	AL	Trident/E400 10.1	E151	AL	Trident/E400 10.1
E4	SW	Trident/E400 10.1	E78	AL	Trident/E400 10.1	E152	AF	Trident/E400 10.1

No.	G.	Type	No.	G.	Type	No.	G.	Type
E153	AF	Trident/E400 10.1	E228	NX	E40D/E400 (EC) 10.2	EH4	SW	Trident/E400H 10.1
E154	AF	Trident/E400 10.1	E229	BX	E40D/E400 (EC) 10.2	EH5	SW	Trident/E400H 10.1
E155	AF	Trident/E400 10.1	E230	BX	E40D/E400 (EC) 10.2	EH6	NX	E40H/E400 (EC) 10.2
E156	AF	Trident/E400 10.1	E231	BX	E40D/E400 (EC) 10.2	EH7	NX	E40H/E400 (EC) 10.2
E157	AF	Trident/E400 10.1	E232	BX	E40D/E400 (EC) 10.2	EH8	NX	E40H/E400 (EC) 10.2
E158	AF	Trident/E400 10.1	E233	BX	E40D/E400 (EC) 10.2	EH9	NX	E40H/E400 (EC) 10.2
E159	AF	Trident/E400 10.1	E234	BX	E40D/E400 (EC) 10.2	EH10	NX	E40H/E400 (EC) 10.2
E160	AF	Trident/E400 10.1	E235	BX	E40D/E400 (EC) 10.2	EH11	NX	E40H/E400 (EC) 10.2
E161	AF	Trident/E400 10.1	E236	BX	E40D/E400 (EC) 10.2	EH12	NX	E40H/E400 (EC) 10.2
E162	AF	Trident/E400 10.1	E237	BX	E40D/E400 (EC) 10.2	EH13	NX	E40H/E400 (EC) 10.2
E163	RR	E40D/E400 (EC) 10.2	E238	BX	E40D/E400 (EC) 10.2	EH14	NX	E40H/E400 (EC) 10.2
E164	RR	E40D/E400 (EC) 10.2	E239	BX	E40D/E400 (EC) 10.2	EH15	NX	E40H/E400 (EC) 10.2
E165	RR	E40D/E400 (EC) 10.2	E240	BX	E40D/E400 (EC) 10.2	EH16	NX	E40H/E400 (EC) 10.2
E166	RR	E40D/E400 (EC) 10.2	E241	BX	E40D/E400 (EC) 10.2	EH17	NX	E40H/E400 (EC) 10.2
E167	RR	E40D/E400 (EC) 10.2	E242	BX	E40D/E400 (EC) 10.2	EH18	NX	E40H/E400 (EC) 10.2
E168	RR	E40D/E400 (EC) 10.2	E243	BX	E40D/E400 (EC) 10.2	EH19	SW	E40H/E400 (EC) 10.2
E169	RR	E40D/E400 (EC) 10.2	E244	BX	E40D/E400 (EC) 10.2	EH20	SW	E40H/E400 (EC) 10.2
E170	RR	E40D/E400 (EC) 10.2	E245	BX	E40D/E400 (EC) 10.2	EH21	SW	E40H/E400 (EC) 10.2
E171	RR	E40D/E400 (EC) 10.2	E246	NX	E40D/E400 (EC) 10.2	EH22	SW	E40H/E400 (EC) 10.2
E172	RR	E40D/E400 (EC) 10.2	E247	NX	E40D/E400 (EC) 10.2	EH23	SW	E40H/E400 (EC) 10.2
E173	RR	Trident/E400 10.1	E248	NX	E40D/E400 (EC) 10.2	EH24	SW	E40H/E400 (EC) 10.2
E174	RR	E40D/E400 (EC) 10.2	E249	NX	E40D/E400 (EC) 10.2	EH25	SW	E40H/E400 (EC) 10.2
E175	RR	E40D/E400 (EC) 10.2	E250	NX	E40D/E400 (EC) 10.2	EH26	SW	E40H/E400 (EC) 10.2
E176	RR	E40D/E400 (EC) 10.2	E251	NX	E40D/E400 (EC) 10.2	EH27	SW	E40H/E400 (EC) 10.2
E177	RR	E40D/E400 (EC) 10.2	E252	NX	E40D/E400 (EC) 10.2	EH28	SW	E40H/E400 (EC) 10.2
E178	RR	E40D/E400 (EC) 10.2	E253	NX	E40D/E400 (EC) 10.2	EH29	SW	E40H/E400 (EC) 10.2
E179	RR	E40D/E400 (EC) 10.2	E254	NX	E40D/E400 (EC) 10.2	EH30	SW	E40H/E400 (EC) 10.2
E180	RR	E40D/E400 (EC) 10.2	E255	NX	E40D/E400 (EC) 10.2	EH31	SW	E40H/E400 (EC) 10.2
E181	RR	E40D/E400 (EC) 10.2	E256	NX	E40D/E400 (EC) 10.2	EH32	SW	E40H/E400 (EC) 10.2
E182	RR	E40D/E400 (EC) 10.2	E257	NX	E40D/E400 (EC) 10.2	EH33	SW	E40H/E400 (EC) 10.2
E183	RR	E40D/E400 (EC) 10.2	E258	NX	E40D/E400 (EC) 10.2	EH34	SW	E40H/E400 (EC) 10.2
E184	RR	E40D/E400 (EC) 10.2	E259	NX	E40D/E400 (EC) 10.2	EH35	SW	E40H/E400 (EC) 10.2
E185	RR	E40D/E400 (EC) 10.2	E260	NX	E40D/E400 (EC) 10.2	EH36	SW	E40H/E400 (EC) 10.2
E186	AL	E40D/E400 (EC) 10.2	E261	NX	E40D/E400 (EC) 10.2	EH37	SW	E40H/E400 (EC) 10.2
E187	AL	E40D/E400 (EC) 10.2	E262	NX	E40D/E400 (EC) 10.2	EH38	SW	E40H/E400 (EC) 10.2
E188	AL	E40D/E400 (EC) 10.2	E263	NX	E40D/E400 (EC) 10.2	EH39	Q	E40H/E400MMC 10.35
E189	Q	E40D/E400 (EC) 10.2	E264	NX	E40D/E400 (EC) 10.2	EH40	Q	E40H/E400MMC 10.35
E190	Q	E40D/E400 (EC) 10.2	E265	NX	E40D/E400 (EC) 10.2	EH41	Q	E40H/E400MMC 10.35
E191	Q	E40D/E400 (EC) 10.2	E266	NX	E40D/E400 (EC) 10.2	EH42	Q	E40H/E400MMC 10.35
E192	Q	E40D/E400 (EC) 10.2	E267	NX	E40D/E400 (EC) 10.2	EH43	Q	E40H/E400MMC 10.35
E193	Q	E40D/E400 (EC) 10.2	E268	NX	E40D/E400 (EC) 10.2	EH44	Q	E40H/E400MMC 10.35
E194	Q	E40D/E400 (EC) 10.2	E269	NX	E40D/E400 (EC) 10.2	EH45	Q	E40H/E400MMC 10.35
E195	Q	E40D/E400 (EC) 10.2	E270	NX	E40D/E400 (EC) 10.2	EH46	Q	E40H/E400MMC 10.35
E196	Q	E40D/E400 (EC) 10.2	E271	NX	E40D/E400 (EC) 10.2	EH47	Q	E40H/E400MMC 10.35
E197	Q	E40D/E400 (EC) 10.2	E272	NX	E40D/E400 (EC) 10.2	EH48	Q	E40H/E400MMC 10.35
E198	Q	E40D/E400 (EC) 10.2	E273	NX	E40D/E400 (EC) 10.2	EH49	Q	E40H/E400MMC 10.35
E199	Q	E40D/E400 (EC) 10.2	E274	NX	E40D/E400 (EC) 10.2	EH50	Q	E40H/E400MMC 10.35
E200	Q	E40D/E400 (EC) 10.2	E275	NX	E40D/E400 (EC) 10.2	EH51	Q	E40H/E400MMC 10.35
E201	Q	E40D/E400 (EC) 10.2	E276	NP	E40D/E400 (EC) 10.2	EH52	Q	E40H/E400MMC 10.35
E202	RR	E40D/E400 (EC) 10.2	E277	SW	E40D/E400 (EC) 10.2	EH53	Q	E40H/E400MMC 10.35
E203	BX	E40D/E400 (EC) 10.2	E278	SW	E40D/E400 (EC) 10.2	EH54	Q	E40H/E400MMC 10.35
E204	BX	E40D/E400 (EC) 10.2	E279	SW	E40D/E400 (EC) 10.2	EH55	Q	E40H/E400MMC 10.35
E205	BX	E40D/E400 (EC) 10.2	E280	SW	E40D/E400 (EC) 10.2	EH56	Q	E40H/E400MMC 10.35
E206	BX	E40D/E400 (EC) 10.2	ED9	SI	Dart/Evolution 9.2	EH57	Q	E40H/E400MMC 10.35
E207	BX	E40D/E400 (EC) 10.2	ED10	RR	Dart/Evolution 9.2	EH58	Q	E40H/E400MMC 10.35
E208	MB	E40D/E400 (EC) 10.2	ED11	RR	Dart/Evolution 9.2	EH59	Q	E40H/E400MMC 10.35
E209	MB	E40D/E400 (EC) 10.2	ED12	SI	Dart/Evolution 9.2	EH60	Q	E40H/E400MMC 10.35
E210	MB	E40D/E400 (EC) 10.2	ED13	RR	Dart/Evolution 9.2	EH61	PM	E40H/E400MMC 10.35
E211	MB	E40D/E400 (EC) 10.2	ED14	RR	Dart/Evolution 9.2	EH62	PM	E40H/E400MMC 10.35
E212	MB	E40D/E400 (EC) 10.2	ED15	RR	Dart/Evolution 9.2	EH63	PM	E40H/E400MMC 10.35
E213	MB	E40D/E400 (EC) 10.2	ED16	NP	Dart/Evolution 9.2	EH64	PM	E40H/E400MMC 10.35
E214	MB	E40D/E400 (EC) 10.2	ED17	SI	Dart/Evolution 9.2	EH65	PM	E40H/E400MMC 10.35
E215	C	E40D/E400 (EC) 10.2	ED18	RR	E200/Evolution 10.4	EH66	PM	E40H/E400MMC 10.35
E216	C	E40D/E400 (EC) 10.2	ED19	RR	E200/Evolution 10.4	EH67	PM	E40H/E400MMC 10.35
E217	C	E40D/E400 (EC) 10.2	ED20	RR	E200/Evolution 10.4	EH68	PM	E40H/E400MMC 10.35
E218	C	E40D/E400 (EC) 10.2	ED21	RR	E200/Evolution 10.4	EH69	PM	E40H/E400MMC 10.35
E219	C	E40D/E400 (EC) 10.2	ED22	RR	E200/Evolution 10.4	EH70	PM	E40H/E400MMC 10.35
E220	C	E40D/E400 (EC) 10.2	ED24	RR	E200/Evolution 10.4	EH71	PM	E40H/E400MMC 10.35
E221	C	E40D/E400 (EC) 10.2	ED25	RR	E200/Evolution 10.4	EH72	PM	E40H/E400MMC 10.35
E222	C	E40D/E400 (EC) 10.2	ED26	RR	E200/Evolution 10.4	EH73	PM	E40H/E400MMC 10.35
E223	C	E40D/E400 (EC) 10.2	ED27	RR	E200/Evolution 10.4	EH74	AF	E40H/E400MMC 10.35
E224	SW	E40D/E400 (EC) 10.2	ED28	SI	E200/Evolution 10.4	EH75	AF	E40H/E400MMC 10.35
E225	AL	E40D/E400 (EC) 10.2	EH1	SW	Trident/E400H 10.1	EH76	AF	E40H/E400MMC 10.35
E226	SW	E40D/E400 (EC) 10.2	EH2	SW	Trident/E400H 10.1	EH77	AF	E40H/E400MMC 10.35
E227	AL	E40D/E400 (EC) 10.2	EH3	SW	Trident/E400H 10.1	EH78	AF	E40H/E400MMC 10.35

Go-Ahead

No.	G.	Type	No.	G.	Type	No.	G.	Type
EH79	AF	E40H/E400MMC 10.35	EN5	NP	Trident/E400 10.1	LT50	SW	NRM 11.3
EH80	AF	E40H/E400MMC 10.35	EN6	NP	Trident/E400 10.1	LT51	SW	NRM 11.3
EH81	AF	E40H/E400MMC 10.35	EN7	NP	Trident/E400 10.1	LT52	SW	NRM 11.3
EH82	AF	E40H/E400MMC 10.35	EN8	NP	Trident/E400 10.1	LT53	SW	NRM 11.3
EH83	AF	E40H/E400MMC 10.35	EN9	NP	Trident/E400 10.1	LT54	SW	NRM 11.3
EH84	AF	E40H/E400MMC 10.35	EN10	NP	Trident/E400 10.1	LT55	SW	NRM 11.3
EH85	AF	E40H/E400MMC 10.35	EN11	NP	Trident/E400 10.1	LT56	SW	NRM 11.3
EH86	AF	E40H/E400MMC 10.35	EN12	NP	Trident/E400 10.1	LT57	SW	NRM 11.3
EH87	AF	E40H/E400MMC 10.35	EN13	NP	Trident/E400 10.1	LT58	SW	NRM 11.3
EH88	AF	E40H/E400MMC 10.35	EN14	NP	Trident/E400 10.1	LT59	SW	NRM 11.3
EH89	AF	E40H/E400MMC 10.35	EN15	NP	Trident/E400 10.1	LT60	SW	NRM 11.3
EH90	AF	E40H/E400MMC 10.35	EN16	NP	Trident/E400 10.1	LT61	SW	NRM 11.3
EH91	AF	E40H/E400MMC 10.35	EN17	NP	Trident/E400 10.1	LT62	SW	NRM 11.3
EH92	AF	E40H/E400MMC 10.35	EN18	NP	Trident/E400 10.1	LT63	SW	NRM 11.3
EH93	AF	E40H/E400MMC 10.35	EN19	NP	Trident/E400 10.1	LT64	SW	NRM 11.3
EH94	AF	E40H/E400MMC 10.35	EN20	NP	Trident/E400 10.1	LT65	SW	NRM 11.3
EH95	AF	E40H/E400MMC 10.35	EN21	NP	Trident/E400 10.1	LT66	SW	NRM 11.3
EH96	AF	E40H/E400MMC 10.35	EN22	NP	Trident/E400 10.1	LT67	SW	NRM 11.3
EH97	AF	E40H/E400MMC 10.35	EN23	NP	Trident/E400 10.1	LT68	SW	NRM 11.3
EH98	AF	E40H/E400MMC 10.35	EN24	NP	Trident/E400 10.1	LT118	SW	NRM 11.3
EH99	AF	E40H/E400MMC 10.35	EN25	BX	Trident/E400 10.1	LT119	SW	NRM 11.3
EH100	AF	E40H/E400MMC 10.35	EN26	BX	Trident/E400 10.1	LT189	SW	NRM (E6) 11.3
EH101	AF	E40H/E400MMC 10.35	EN27	BX	Trident/E400 10.1	LT273	MW	NRM (E6) 11.3
EH102	AF	E40H/E400MMC 10.35	LDP191	RR	Dart/Pointer 10.1	LT274	MW	NRM (E6) 11.3
EH103	AF	E40H/E400MMC 10.35	LDP192	MB	Dart/Pointer 10.1	LT275	MW	NRM (E6) 11.3
EH104	AF	E40H/E400MMC 10.35	LDP193	BX	Dart/Pointer 10.1	LT276	MW	NRM (E6) 11.3
EH105	AF	E40H/E400MMC 10.35	LDP194	BX	Dart/Pointer 10.1	LT277	MW	NRM (E6) 11.3
EH106	AF	E40H/E400MMC 10.35	LDP198	RR	Dart/Pointer 10.1	LT278	MW	NRM (E6) 11.3
EH107	AF	E40H/E400MMC 10.35	LDP200	PM	Dart/Pointer 10.1	LT279	MW	NRM (E6) 11.3
EH108	AF	E40H/E400MMC 10.35	LDP205	MB	Dart/Pointer 10.1	LT280	MW	NRM (E6) 11.3
EH109	AF	E40H/E400MMC 10.35	LDP206	BX	Dart/Pointer 10.1	LT281	MW	NRM (E6) 11.3
EH110	AF	E40H/E400MMC 10.35	LDP207	Q	Dart/Pointer 10.1	LT282	MW	NRM (E6) 11.3
EH111	AF	E40H/E400MMC 10.35	LDP208	NX	Dart/Pointer 10.1	LT283	MW	NRM (E6) 11.3
EH112	AF	E40H/E400MMC 10.35	LDP209	NX	Dart/Pointer 10.1	LT284	MW	NRM (E6) 11.3
EH113	Q	E40H/E400MMC 10.35	LDP210	NX	Dart/Pointer 10.1	LT285	MW	NRM (E6) 11.3
EH114	Q	E40H/E400MMC 10.35	LDP249	C	Dart/Pointer 10.1	LT286	MW	NRM (E6) 11.3
EH115	Q	E40H/E400MMC 10.35	LDP250	C	Dart/Pointer 10.1	LT287	MW	NRM (E6) 11.3
EH116	Q	E40H/E400MMC 10.35	LDP252	C	Dart/Pointer 10.1	LT288	MW	NRM (E6) 11.3
EH117	Q	E40H/E400MMC 10.35	LDP253	C	Dart/Pointer 10.1	LT289	MW	NRM (E6) 11.3
EH118	Q	E40H/E400MMC 10.35	LDP254	C	Dart/Pointer 10.1	LT290	MW	NRM (E6) 11.3
EH119	Q	E40H/E400MMC 10.35	LDP255	C	Dart/Pointer 10.1	LT291	MW	NRM (E6) 11.3
EH120	Q	E40H/E400MMC 10.35	LDP256	C	Dart/Pointer 10.1	LT292	MW	NRM (E6) 11.3
EH121	Q	E40H/E400MMC 10.35	LDP257	C	Dart/Pointer 10.1	LT293	MW	NRM (E6) 11.3
EH122	Q	E40H/E400MMC 10.35	LDP258	C	Dart/Pointer 10.1	LT294	MW	NRM (E6) 11.3
EH123	Q	E40H/E400MMC 10.35	LDP259	C	Dart/Pointer 10.1	LT295	MW	NRM (E6) 11.3
EH124	Q	E40H/E400MMC 10.35	LDP260	C	Dart/Pointer 10.1	LT296	MW	NRM (E6) 11.3
EH125	Q	E40H/E400MMC 10.35	LDP261	C	Dart/Pointer 10.1	LT297	MW	NRM (E6) 11.3
EH126	Q	E40H/E400MMC 10.35	LDP262	C	Dart/Pointer 10.1	LT298	MW	NRM (E6) 11.3
EH127	Q	E40H/E400MMC 10.35	LDP273	NX	Dart/Pointer 10.1	LT299	MW	NRM (E6) 11.3
EH128	Q	E40H/E400MMC 10.35	LDP274	NX	Dart/Pointer 10.1	LT300	MW	NRM (E6) 11.3
EH129	Q	E40H/E400MMC 10.35	LDP275	NX	Dart/Pointer 10.1	LT301	MW	NRM (E6) 11.3
EH130	Q	E40H/E400MMC 10.35	LDP276	NX	Dart/Pointer 10.1	LT302	MW	NRM (E6) 11.3
EHV1	SI	B5LH/E400MMC 10.5	LDP277	NX	Dart/Pointer 10.1	LT303	MW	NRM (E6) 11.3
EHV2	SI	B5LH/E400MMC 10.5	LDP278	NX	Dart/Pointer 10.1	LT304	MW	NRM (E6) 11.3
EHV3	SI	B5LH/E400MMC 10.5	LDP279	NX	Dart/Pointer 10.1	LT305	MW	NRM (E6) 11.3
EHV4	SI	B5LH/E400MMC 10.5	LDP280	NX	Dart/Pointer 10.1	LT306	MW	NRM (E6) 11.3
EHV5	SI	B5LH/E400MMC 10.5	LDP281	PL	Dart/Pointer 8.8	LT307	MW	NRM (E6) 11.3
EHV6	SI	B5LH/E400MMC 10.5	LDP282	PL	Dart/Pointer 8.8	LT308	MW	NRM (E6) 11.3
EHV7	SI	B5LH/E400MMC 10.5	LDP283	PL	Dart/Pointer 8.8	LT309	MW	NRM (E6) 11.3
EHV8	SI	B5LH/E400MMC 10.5	LDP284	PL	Dart/Pointer 8.8	LT310	MW	NRM (E6) 11.3
EHV9	SI	B5LH/E400MMC 10.5	LDP285	PL	Dart/Pointer 8.8	LT311	MW	NRM (E6) 11.3
EHV10	SI	B5LH/E400MMC 10.5	LDP286	AF	Dart/Pointer 8.8	LT417	Q	NRM (E6) 11.3
EHV11	SI	B5LH/E400MMC 10.5	LDP292	AL	Dart/Pointer 10.1	LT418	Q	NRM (E6) 11.3
EHV12	SI	B5LH/E400MMC 10.5	LDP293	AL	Dart/Pointer 10.1	LT419	Q	NRM (E6) 11.3
EHV13	SI	B5LH/E400MMC 10.5	LDP294	AL	Dart/Pointer 10.1	LT420	Q	NRM (E6) 11.3
EHV14	SI	B5LH/E400MMC 10.5	LT41	SW	NRM 11.3	LT421	Q	NRM (E6) 11.3
EHV15	SI	B5LH/E400MMC 10.5	LT42	SW	NRM 11.3	LT422	Q	NRM (E6) 11.3
EHV16	SI	B5LH/E400MMC 10.5	LT43	SW	NRM 11.3	LT423	Q	NRM (E6) 11.3
EI1	NX	i2e Electric 12.0	LT44	SW	NRM 11.3	LT424	Q	NRM (E6) 11.3
EI2	NX	i2e Electric 12.0	LT45	SW	NRM 11.3	LT425	Q	NRM (E6) 11.3
EN1	NP	Trident/E400 10.1	LT46	SW	NRM 11.3	LT426	Q	NRM (E6) 11.3
EN2	NP	Trident/E400 10.1	LT47	SW	NRM 11.3	LT427	Q	NRM (E6) 11.3
EN3	NP	Trident/E400 10.1	LT48	SW	NRM 11.3	LT428	Q	NRM (E6) 11.3
EN4	NP	Trident/E400 10.1	LT49	SW	NRM 11.3	LT429	Q	NRM (E6) 11.3

No.	G.	Type	No.	G.	Type	No.	G.	Type
LT430	Q	NRM (E6) 11.3	LT687	Q	NRM (E6) 11.3	LT915	RR	NRM (E6) 11.3
LT431	Q	NRM (E6) 11.3	LT688	Q	NRM (E6) 11.3	LT916	RR	NRM (E6) 11.3
LT432	Q	NRM (E6) 11.3	LT689	Q	NRM (E6) 11.3	LT917	RR	NRM (E6) 11.3
LT433	Q	NRM (E6) 11.3	LT690	Q	NRM (E6) 11.3	LT918	RR	NRM (E6) 11.3
LT434	Q	NRM (E6) 11.3	LT845	NX	NRM (E6) 11.3	LT919	RR	NRM (E6) 11.3
LT435	Q	NRM (E6) 11.3	LT846	NX	NRM (E6) 11.3	LT920	RR	NRM (E6) 11.3
LT436	Q	NRM (E6) 11.3	LT847	NX	NRM (E6) 11.3	LT921	RR	NRM (E6) 11.3
LT437	Q	NRM (E6) 11.3	LT848	NX	NRM (E6) 11.3	LT922	RR	NRM (E6) 11.3
LT438	Q	NRM (E6) 11.3	LT849	NX	NRM (E6) 11.3	LT923	RR	NRM (E6) 11.3
LT439	Q	NRM (E6) 11.3	LT850	NX	NRM (E6) 11.3	LT924	RR	NRM (E6) 11.3
LT440	Q	NRM (E6) 11.3	LT851	NX	NRM (E6) 11.3	LT925	RR	NRM (E6) 11.3
LT441	Q	NRM (E6) 11.3	LT852	NX	NRM (E6) 11.3	LT926	RR	NRM (E6) 11.3
LT442	Q	NRM (E6) 11.3	LT853	NX	NRM (E6) 11.3	LT927	RR	NRM (E6) 11.3
LT443	Q	NRM (E6) 11.3	LT854	NX	NRM (E6) 11.3	LT928	RR	NRM (E6) 11.3
LT444	Q	NRM (E6) 11.3	LT855	NX	NRM (E6) 11.3	LT929	RR	NRM (E6) 11.3
LT445	Q	NRM (E6) 11.3	LT856	NX	NRM (E6) 11.3	LT930	RR	NRM (E6) 11.3
LT446	Q	NRM (E6) 11.3	LT857	NX	NRM (E6) 11.3	LT931	RR	NRM (E6) 11.3
LT447	Q	NRM (E6) 11.3	LT858	NX	NRM (E6) 11.3	LT932	RR	NRM (E6) 11.3
LT448	Q	NRM (E6) 11.3	LT859	NX	NRM (E6) 11.3	LT933	RR	NRM (E6) 11.3
LT449	Q	NRM (E6) 11.3	LT860	NX	NRM (E6) 11.3	LT934	RR	NRM (E6) 11.3
LT450	Q	NRM (E6) 11.3	LT861	NX	NRM (E6) 11.3	LT935	RR	NRM (E6) 11.3
LT451	Q	NRM (E6) 11.3	LT862	NX	NRM (E6) 11.3	LT936	RR	NRM (E6) 11.3
LT452	Q	NRM (E6) 11.3	LT863	NX	NRM (E6) 11.3	LT937	RR	NRM (E6) 11.3
LT453	Q	NRM (E6) 11.3	LT864	NX	NRM (E6) 11.3	LT938	RR	NRM (E6) 11.3
LT454	Q	NRM (E6) 11.3	LT865	NX	NRM (E6) 11.3	LT939	RR	NRM (E6) 11.3
LT455	Q	NRM (E6) 11.3	LT866	NX	NRM (E6) 11.3	LT940	RR	NRM (E6) 11.3
LT456	MW	NRM (E6) 11.3	LT867	NX	NRM (E6) 11.3	LT941	RR	NRM (E6) 11.3
LT457	SW	NRM (E6) 11.3	LT868	NX	NRM (E6) 11.3	LT942	RR	NRM (E6) 11.3
LT458	SW	NRM (E6) 11.3	LT869	NX	NRM (E6) 11.3	LT943	RR	NRM (E6) 11.3
LT459	SW	NRM (E6) 11.3	LT870	NX	NRM (E6) 11.3	LT944	RR	NRM (E6) 11.3
LT478	SW	NRM (E6) 11.3	LT871	NX	NRM (E6) 11.3	LT945	RR	NRM (E6) 11.3
LT479	SW	NRM (E6) 11.3	LT872	NX	NRM (E6) 11.3	LT946	RR	NRM (E6) 11.3
LT480	SW	NRM (E6) 11.3	LT873	NX	NRM (E6) 11.3	LT947	RR	NRM (E6) 11.3
LT481	SW	NRM (E6) 11.3	LT874	NX	NRM (E6) 11.3	LT948	RR	NRM (E6) 11.3
LT482	SW	NRM (E6) 11.3	LT875	NP	NRM (E6) 11.3	LT949	RR	NRM (E6) 11.3
LT483	SW	NRM (E6) 11.3	LT876	NP	NRM (E6) 11.3	LT950	RR	NRM (E6) 11.3
LT484	SW	NRM (E6) 11.3	LT877	NP	NRM (E6) 11.3	LT951	RR	NRM (E6) 11.3
LT485	SW	NRM (E6) 11.3	LT878	NP	NRM (E6) 11.3	LT952	RR	NRM (E6) 11.3
LT486	SW	NRM (E6) 11.3	LT879	NP	NRM (E6) 11.3	LT953	RR	NRM (E6) 11.3
LT487	SW	NRM (E6) 11.3	LT880	NP	NRM (E6) 11.3	**MDL1**	SI	SB180/Evoultion 10.3
LT501	SW	NRM (E6) 11.3	LT881	NP	NRM (E6) 11.3	**MEC1**	NX	Citaro 12.0
LT502	SW	NRM (E6) 11.3	LT882	NP	NRM (E6) 11.3	**MEC2**	NX	Citaro 12.0
LT503	SW	NRM (E6) 11.3	LT883	NP	NRM (E6) 11.3	**MEC3**	NX	Citaro 12.0
LT504	SW	NRM (E6) 11.3	LT884	NP	NRM (E6) 11.3	**MEC4**	NX	Citaro 12.0
LT505	SW	NRM (E6) 11.3	LT885	NP	NRM (E6) 11.3	**MEC5**	NX	Citaro 12.0
LT506	SW	NRM (E6) 11.3	LT886	NP	NRM (E6) 11.3	**MEC6**	NX	Citaro 12.0
LT507	SW	NRM (E6) 11.3	LT887	NP	NRM (E6) 11.3	**MEC7**	NX	Citaro 12.0
LT508	SW	NRM (E6) 11.3	LT888	NP	NRM (E6) 11.3	**MEC8**	NX	Citaro 12.0
LT509	SW	NRM (E6) 11.3	LT889	NP	NRM (E6) 11.3	**MEC9**	NX	Citaro 12.0
LT510	SW	NRM (E6) 11.3	LT890	NP	NRM (E6) 11.3	**MEC10**	NX	Citaro 12.0
LT511	SW	NRM (E6) 11.3	LT891	NP	NRM (E6) 11.3	**MEC12**	NX	Citaro 12.0
LT512	SW	NRM (E6) 11.3	LT892	NP	NRM (E6) 11.3	**MEC14**	NX	Citaro 12.0
LT664	Q	NRM (E6) 11.3	LT893	NP	NRM (E6) 11.3	**MEC17**	NX	Citaro 12.0
LT665	Q	NRM (E6) 11.3	LT894	NP	NRM (E6) 11.3	**MEC20**	NX	Citaro 12.0
LT666	Q	NRM (E6) 11.3	LT895	NP	NRM (E6) 11.3	**MEC27**	NX	Citaro 12.0
LT667	Q	NRM (E6) 11.3	LT896	NP	NRM (E6) 11.3	**MEC30**	NX	Citaro 12.0
LT668	Q	NRM (E6) 11.3	LT897	NP	NRM (E6) 11.3	**MEC32**	NX	Citaro 12.0
LT669	Q	NRM (E6) 11.3	LT898	NP	NRM (E6) 11.3	**MEC37**	NX	Citaro 12.0
LT670	Q	NRM (E6) 11.3	LT899	NP	NRM (E6) 11.3	**MEC46**	NX	Citaro 12.0
LT671	Q	NRM (E6) 11.3	LT900	NP	NRM (E6) 11.3	**MEC50**	NX	Citaro 12.0
LT672	Q	NRM (E6) 11.3	LT901	NP	NRM (E6) 11.3	**MEC51**	MB	Citaro New Style 12.0
LT673	Q	NRM (E6) 11.3	LT902	NP	NRM (E6) 11.3	**MEC52**	MB	Citaro New Style 12.0
LT674	Q	NRM (E6) 11.3	LT903	RR	NRM (E6) 11.3	**MEC53**	MB	Citaro New Style 12.0
LT675	Q	NRM (E6) 11.3	LT904	RR	NRM (E6) 11.3	**MEC54**	MB	Citaro New Style 12.0
LT676	Q	NRM (E6) 11.3	LT905	RR	NRM (E6) 11.3	**MEC55**	MB	Citaro New Style 12.0
LT677	Q	NRM (E6) 11.3	LT906	RR	NRM (E6) 11.3	**MEC56**	MB	Citaro New Style 12.0
LT678	Q	NRM (E6) 11.3	LT907	RR	NRM (E6) 11.3	**MEC57**	MB	Citaro New Style 12.0
LT679	Q	NRM (E6) 11.3	LT908	RR	NRM (E6) 11.3	**MEC58**	MB	Citaro New Style 12.0
LT680	Q	NRM (E6) 11.3	LT909	RR	NRM (E6) 11.3	**MEC59**	MB	Citaro New Style 12.0
LT681	Q	NRM (E6) 11.3	LT910	RR	NRM (E6) 11.3	**MEC60**	MB	Citaro New Style 12.0
LT682	Q	NRM (E6) 11.3	LT911	RR	NRM (E6) 11.3	**MEC61**	MB	Citaro New Style 12.0
LT683	Q	NRM (E6) 11.3	LT912	RR	NRM (E6) 11.3	**MEC62**	MB	Citaro New Style 12.0
LT684	Q	NRM (E6) 11.3	LT913	RR	NRM (E6) 11.3	**MEC63**	MB	Citaro New Style 12.0
LT685	Q	NRM (E6) 11.3	LT914	RR	NRM (E6) 11.3	**MEC64**	MB	Citaro New Style 12.0
LT686	Q	NRM (E6) 11.3	LT915	RR	NRM (E6) 11.3	**MEC65**	MB	Citaro New Style 12.0

Go-Ahead

No.	G.	Type	No.	G.	Type	No.	G.	Type
MEC66	MB	Citaro New Style 12.0	MHV71	Q	B5LH/Evosetti 10.6	PVL363	BX	B7TL/President 10.0
MEC67	MB	Citaro New Style 12.0	MHV72	Q	B5LH/Evosetti 10.6	PVL364	BX	B7TL/President 10.0
MEC68	MB	Citaro New Style 12.0	MHV73	Q	B5LH/Evosetti 10.6	PVL365	BX	B7TL/President 10.0
MEC69	MB	Citaro New Style 12.0	MHV74	Q	B5LH/Evosetti 10.6	PVL366	BX	B7TL/President 10.0
MHV1	Q	B5LH/Evosetti 10.6	MHV75	Q	B5LH/Evosetti 10.6	PVL371	BV	B7TL/President 10.0
MHV2	Q	B5LH/Evosetti 10.6	MHV76	Q	B5LH/Evosetti 10.6	PVL372	BV	B7TL/President 10.0
MHV3	Q	B5LH/Evosetti 10.6	MHV77	Q	B5LH/Evosetti 10.6	PVL373	BV	B7TL/President 10.0
MHV4	Q	B5LH/Evosetti 10.6	MHV78	Q	B5LH/Evosetti 10.6	PVL374	BX	B7TL/President 10.0
MHV5	Q	B5LH/Evosetti 10.6	MHV79	Q	B5LH/Evosetti 10.6	PVL375	SW	B7TL/President 10.0
MHV6	Q	B5LH/Evosetti 10.6	MHV80	Q	B5LH/Evosetti 10.6	PVL376	SW	B7TL/President 10.0
MHV7	Q	B5LH/Evosetti 10.6	MHV81	Q	B5LH/Evosetti 10.6	PVL377	C	B7TL/President 10.0
MHV8	Q	B5LH/Evosetti 10.6	MHV82	Q	B5LH/Evosetti 10.6	PVL378	SW	B7TL/President 10.0
MHV9	Q	B5LH/Evosetti 10.6	MHV83	Q	B5LH/Evosetti 10.6	PVL379	SW	B7TL/President 10.0
MHV10	Q	B5LH/Evosetti 10.6	MHV84	Q	B5LH/Evosetti 10.6	PVL380	SW	B7TL/President 10.0
MHV11	Q	B5LH/Evosetti 10.6	MHV85	Q	B5LH/Evosetti 10.6	PVL381	SW	B7TL/President 10.0
MHV12	Q	B5LH/Evosetti 10.6	PVL272	Q	B7TL/President 10.0	PVL382	SW	B7TL/President 10.0
MHV13	Q	B5LH/Evosetti 10.6	PVL281	AL	B7TL/President 10.0	PVL383	SW	B7TL/President 10.0
MHV14	Q	B5LH/Evosetti 10.6	PVL282	AL	B7TL/President 10.0	PVL385	SW	B7TL/President 10.0
MHV15	Q	B5LH/Evosetti 10.6	PVL283	AL	B7TL/President 10.0	PVL386	SW	B7TL/President 10.0
MHV16	Q	B5LH/Evosetti 10.6	PVL284	AL	B7TL/President 10.0	PVL387	SW	B7TL/President 10.0
MHV17	Q	B5LH/Evosetti 10.6	PVL285	AL	B7TL/President 10.0	PVL388	AL	B7TL/President 10.0
MHV18	Q	B5LH/Evosetti 10.6	PVL286	AL	B7TL/President 10.0	PVL389	SW	B7TL/President 10.0
MHV19	Q	B5LH/Evosetti 10.6	PVL287	AL	B7TL/President 10.0	PVL390	AL	B7TL/President 10.0
MHV20	Q	B5LH/Evosetti 10.6	PVL288	SW	B7TL/President 10.0	PVL391	AL	B7TL/President 10.0
MHV21	A	B5LH/Evosetti 10.6	PVL289	AL	B7TL/President 10.0	PVL392	AL	B7TL/President 10.0
MHV22	A	B5LH/Evosetti 10.6	PVL290	AL	B7TL/President 10.0	PVL393	AL	B7TL/President 10.0
MHV23	A	B5LH/Evosetti 10.6	PVL291	AL	B7TL/President 10.0	PVL394	AL	B7TL/President 10.0
MHV24	A	B5LH/Evosetti 10.6	PVL292	AL	B7TL/President 10.0	PVL395	AL	B7TL/President 10.0
MHV25	A	B5LH/Evosetti 10.6	PVL293	AL	B7TL/President 10.0	PVL396	AL	B7TL/President 10.0
MHV26	A	B5LH/Evosetti 10.6	PVL294	AL	B7TL/President 10.0	PVL397	AL	B7TL/President 10.0
MHV27	A	B5LH/Evosetti 10.6	PVL295	AL	B7TL/President 10.0	PVL398	AL	B7TL/President 10.0
MHV28	A	B5LH/Evosetti 10.6	PVL296	AL	B7TL/President 10.0	PVL399	AL	B7TL/President 10.0
MHV29	A	B5LH/Evosetti 10.6	PVL297	AL	B7TL/President 10.0	PVL400	AL	B7TL/President 10.0
MHV30	A	B5LH/Evosetti 10.6	PVL298	Q	B7TL/President 10.0	PVL401	AL	B7TL/President 10.0
MHV31	A	B5LH/Evosetti 10.6	PVL299	Q	B7TL/President 10.0	PVL402	AL	B7TL/President 10.0
MHV32	A	B5LH/Evosetti 10.6	PVL300	Q	B7TL/President 10.0	PVL403	AL	B7TL/President 10.0
MHV33	A	B5LH/Evosetti 10.6	PVL301	Q	B7TL/President 10.0	PVL404	AL	B7TL/President 10.0
MHV34	A	B5LH/Evosetti 10.6	PVL302	Q	B7TL/President 10.0	PVL405	SW	B7TL/President 10.0
MHV35	A	B5LH/Evosetti 10.6	PVL303	Q	B7TL/President 10.0	PVL406	SW	B7TL/President 10.0
MHV36	A	B5LH/Evosetti 10.6	PVL304	Q	B7TL/President 10.0	PVL407	SW	B7TL/President 10.0
MHV37	A	B5LH/Evosetti 10.6	PVL305	Q	B7TL/President 10.0	PVL408	SW	B7TL/President 10.0
MHV38	A	B5LH/Evosetti 10.6	PVL306	Q	B7TL/President 10.0	PVL409	SW	B7TL/President 10.0
MHV39	A	B5LH/Evosetti 10.6	PVL307	Q	B7TL/President 10.0	PVL410	SW	B7TL/President 10.0
MHV40	A	B5LH/Evosetti 10.6	PVL308	Q	B7TL/President 10.0	PVL411	SW	B7TL/President 10.0
MHV41	A	B5LH/Evosetti 10.6	PVL309	Q	B7TL/President 10.0	PVL412	SW	B7TL/President 10.0
MHV42	A	B5LH/Evosetti 10.6	PVL310	Q	B7TL/President 10.0	PVL413	SW	B7TL/President 10.0
MHV43	A	B5LH/Evosetti 10.6	PVL311	Q	B7TL/President 10.0	PVL414	SW	B7TL/President 10.0
MHV44	A	B5LH/Evosetti 10.6	PVL312	Q	B7TL/President 10.0	PVL415	SW	B7TL/President 10.0
MHV45	PM	B5LH/Evosetti 10.6	PVL313	Q	B7TL/President 10.0	PVL416	SW	B7TL/President 10.0
MHV46	PM	B5LH/Evosetti 10.6	PVL314	Q	B7TL/President 10.0	PVL417	SW	B7TL/President 10.0
MHV47	PM	B5LH/Evosetti 10.6	PVL315	Q	B7TL/President 10.0	PVL418	SW	B7TL/President 10.0
MHV48	PM	B5LH/Evosetti 10.6	PVL316	Q	B7TL/President 10.0	PVL419	SW	B7TL/President 10.0
MHV49	PM	B5LH/Evosetti 10.6	PVL317	Q	B7TL/President 10.0	SE1	AL	E200/E200 10.2
MHV50	PM	B5LH/Evosetti 10.6	PVL318	Q	B7TL/President 10.0	SE2	AL	E200/E200 10.2
MHV51	PM	B5LH/Evosetti 10.6	PVL319	NX	B7TL/President 10.0	SE3	AL	E200/E200 10.2
MHV52	PM	B5LH/Evosetti 10.6	PVL320	NX	B7TL/President 10.0	SE4	AL	E200/E200 10.2
MHV53	PM	B5LH/Evosetti 10.6	PVL321	NX	B7TL/President 10.0	SE5	AL	E200/E200 10.2
MHV54	PM	B5LH/Evosetti 10.6	PVL322	NX	B7TL/President 10.0	SE6	AL	E200/E200 10.2
MHV55	PM	B5LH/Evosetti 10.6	PVL323	NX	B7TL/President 10.0	SE7	AL	E200/E200 10.2
MHV56	Q	B5LH/Evosetti 10.6	PVL326	Q	B7TL/President 10.0	SE8	AL	E200/E200 10.2
MHV57	Q	B5LH/Evosetti 10.6	PVL327	Q	B7TL/President 10.0	SE9	AL	E200/E200 10.2
MHV58	Q	B5LH/Evosetti 10.6	PVL328	Q	B7TL/President 10.0	SE10	AL	E200/E200 10.2
MHV59	Q	B5LH/Evosetti 10.6	PVL343	NX	B7TL/President 10.0	SE11	AL	E200/E200 10.2
MHV60	Q	B5LH/Evosetti 10.6	PVL344	NX	B7TL/President 10.0	SE12	AL	E200/E200 10.2
MHV61	Q	B5LH/Evosetti 10.6	PVL345	NX	B7TL/President 10.0	SE13	AL	E200/E200 10.2
MHV62	Q	B5LH/Evosetti 10.6	PVL347	NX	B7TL/President 10.0	SE14	AL	E200/E200 10.2
MHV63	Q	B5LH/Evosetti 10.6	PVL348	NX	B7TL/President 10.0	SE15	AL	E200/E200 10.2
MHV64	Q	B5LH/Evosetti 10.6	PVL349	NX	B7TL/President 10.0	SE16	AL	E200/E200 10.2
MHV65	Q	B5LH/Evosetti 10.6	PVL351	NX	B7TL/President 10.0	SE17	SI	E200/E200 10.2
MHV66	Q	B5LH/Evosetti 10.6	PVL352	NX	B7TL/President 10.0	SE18	RR	E200/E200 10.8
MHV67	Q	B5LH/Evosetti 10.6	PVL353	NX	B7TL/President 10.0	SE19	RR	E200/E200 10.8
MHV68	Q	B5LH/Evosetti 10.6	PVL354	NX	B7TL/President 10.0	SE20	RR	E200/E200 10.8
MHV69	Q	B5LH/Evosetti 10.6	PVL355	NX	B7TL/President 10.0	SE21	RR	E200/E200 10.8
MHV70	Q	B5LH/Evosetti 10.6	PVL362	BX	B7TL/President 10.0	SE22	RR	E200/E200 10.8

No.	G.	Type	No.	G.	Type	No.	G.	Type
SE23	RR	E200/E200 10.8	SE99	RR	E200/E200 10.8	SE174	C	E20D/E200 10.2
SE24	RR	E200/E200 10.8	SE100	RR	E200/E200 10.8	SE175	PL	E20D/E200 10.2
SE25	RR	E200/E200 10.8	SE101	RR	E200/E200 10.8	SE176	PL	E20D/E200 10.2
SE26	RR	E200/E200 10.8	SE102	RR	E200/E200 10.8	SE177	PL	E20D/E200 10.2
SE27	RR	E200/E200 10.8	SE103	RR	E200/E200 10.8	SE178	PL	E20D/E200 10.2
SE28	RR	E200/E200 10.8	SE104	SI	E200/E200 10.8	SE179	PL	E20D/E200 10.2
SE29	RR	E200/E200 10.8	SE105	SI	E200/E200 10.8	SE180	PL	E20D/E200 10.2
SE30	RR	E200/E200 10.8	SE106	SI	E200/E200 10.8	SE181	PL	E20D/E200 10.2
SE31	RR	E200/E200 10.8	SE107	SI	E200/E200 10.8	SE182	PL	E20D/E200 10.2
SE32	RR	E200/E200 10.8	SE108	SI	E200/E200 10.8	SE183	PL	E20D/E200 10.2
SE33	RR	E200/E200 10.8	SE109	SI	E200/E200 10.8	SE184	PL	E20D/E200 10.2
SE34	RR	E200/E200 10.8	SE110	SI	E200/E200 10.8	SE185	PL	E20D/E200 10.2
SE35	RR	E200/E200 10.8	SE111	SI	E200/E200 10.8	SE186	PL	E20D/E200 10.2
SE36	RR	E200/E200 10.8	SE112	SI	E200/E200 10.8	SE187	PL	E20D/E200 10.2
SE38	SI	E200/E200 10.2	SE113	SI	E200/E200 10.8	SE188	PL	E20D/E200 10.2
SE39	SI	E200/E200 10.2	SE114	SI	E200/E200 10.8	SE189	PL	E20D/E200 10.2
SE40	SI	E200/E200 10.2	SE115	SI	E200/E200 10.8	SE190	PL	E20D/E200 10.2
SE41	SI	E200/E200 10.2	SE116	SI	E200/E200 10.8	SE191	PL	E20D/E200 10.2
SE42	SI	E200/E200 10.2	SE117	SI	E200/E200 10.8	SE192	PL	E20D/E200 10.2
SE43	SI	E200/E200 10.2	SE118	SI	E200/E200 10.8	SE193	PL	E20D/E200 10.2
SE44	SI	E200/E200 10.2	SE119	SI	E200/E200 10.8	SE198	NX	E20D/E200 10.8
SE45	SI	E200/E200 10.2	SE120	A	E200/E200 10.8	SE199	NX	E20D/E200 10.8
SE46	SI	E200/E200 10.2	SE121	SI	E200/E200 10.8	SE200	NX	E20D/E200 10.8
SE47	SW	E200/E200 10.8	SE122	SI	E200/E200 10.8	SE201	NX	E20D/E200 10.8
SE48	SW	E200/E200 10.8	SE123	SI	E200/E200 10.8	SE202	NX	E20D/E200 10.8
SE49	SW	E200/E200 10.8	SE124	SI	E200/E200 10.8	SE203	NX	E20D/E200 10.8
SE50	SW	E200/E200 10.8	SE125	SI	E200/E200 10.8	SE204	NX	E20D/E200 10.8
SE51	SW	E200/E200 10.8	SE126	SI	E200/E200 10.8	SE205	NX	E20D/E200 10.8
SE52	SW	E200/E200 10.8	SE127	SI	E200/E200 10.8	SE206	NX	E20D/E200 10.8
SE53	SW	E200/E200 10.8	SE128	SI	E200/E200 10.8	SE207	NX	E20D/E200 10.8
SE54	SW	E200/E200 10.8	SE129	SI	E200/E200 10.8	SE208	NX	E20D/E200 10.8
SE55	BV	E200/E200 10.2	SE130	SI	E200/E200 10.8	SE209	NX	E20D/E200 10.8
SE56	BV	E200/E200 10.2	SE131	SI	E200/E200 10.8	SE210	NX	E20D/E200 10.8
SE57	BV	E200/E200 10.2	SE132	SI	E200/E200 10.8	SE211	NX	E20D/E200 10.8
SE58	BV	E200/E200 10.2	SE133	SI	E200/E200 10.8	SE212	NX	E20D/E200 10.8
SE59	BV	E200/E200 10.2	SE134	SI	E200/E200 10.8	SE213	MW	E20D/E200 9.6
SE60	BV	E200/E200 10.2	SE135	SI	E200/E200 10.8	SE214	MW	E20D/E200 9.6
SE61	BV	E200/E200 10.2	SE136	SI	E200/E200 10.8	SE215	MW	E20D/E200 9.6
SE62	BV	E200/E200 10.2	SE137	SI	E200/E200 10.8	SE216	MW	E20D/E200 9.6
SE63	BV	E200/E200 10.2	SE138	SI	E200/E200 10.8	SE217	MW	E20D/E200 9.6
SE64	BV	E200/E200 10.2	SE139	SI	E200/E200 10.8	SE218	MW	E20D/E200 9.6
SE65	BV	E200/E200 10.2	SE140	SI	E200/E200 10.8	SE219	MW	E20D/E200 9.6
SE66	BV	E200/E200 10.2	SE141	SI	E200/E200 10.8	SE220	MW	E20D/E200 9.6
SE67	BV	E200/E200 10.2	SE142	PM	E20D/E200 10.2	SE221	MW	E20D/E200 9.6
SE68	BX	E200/E200 10.2	SE143	PM	E20D/E200 10.2	SE222	MW	E20D/E200 9.6
SE69	BX	E200/E200 10.2	SE144	PM	E20D/E200 10.2	SE223	MW	E20D/E200 9.6
SE70	BX	E200/E200 10.2	SE145	AL	E20D/E200 10.2	SE224	MW	E20D/E200 9.6
SE71	BX	E200/E200 10.2	SE146	AL	E20D/E200 10.2	SE225	MW	E20D/E200 9.6
SE72	BX	E200/E200 10.2	SE147	AL	E20D/E200 10.2	SE226	MW	E20D/E200 9.6
SE73	BX	E200/E200 10.2	SE148	AL	E20D/E200 10.2	SE227	MW	E20D/E200 9.6
SE74	BX	E200/E200 10.2	SE149	AL	E20D/E200 10.2	SE228	MW	E20D/E200 9.6
SE75	BX	E200/E200 10.2	SE150	AL	E20D/E200 10.2	SE229	MW	E20D/E200 9.6
SE76	BX	E200/E200 10.2	SE151	MB	E20D/E200 10.2	SE230	MW	E20D/E200 9.6
SE77	BX	E200/E200 10.2	SE152	NX	E20D/E200 10.2	SE231	MW	E20D/E200 9.6
SE78	BX	E200/E200 10.2	SE153	PM	E20D/E200 10.2	SE232	RR	E20D/E200 9.6
SE79	BX	E200/E200 10.2	SE154	PM	E20D/E200 10.2	SE233	RR	E20D/E200 9.6
SE80	BX	E200/E200 10.2	SE155	PM	E20D/E200 10.2	SE234	MW	E20D/E200 9.6
SE81	BX	E200/E200 10.2	SE156	PM	E20D/E200 10.2	SE235	SW	E20D/E200 8.9
SE82	BX	E200/E200 10.2	SE157	PM	E20D/E200 10.2	SE236	SW	E20D/E200 8.9
SE83	BX	E200/E200 10.2	SE158	PM	E20D/E200 10.2	SE237	SW	E20D/E200 8.9
SE84	BX	E200/E200 10.2	SE159	PM	E20D/E200 10.2	SE238	SW	E20D/E200 8.9
SE85	Q	E200/E200 9.3	SE160	PM	E20D/E200 10.2	SE239	SW	E20D/E200 8.9
SE86	Q	E200/E200 9.3	SE161	PM	E20D/E200 10.2	SE240	SW	E20D/E200 8.9
SE87	Q	E200/E200 9.3	SE162	PM	E20D/E200 10.2	SE241	SW	E20D/E200 8.9
SE88	Q	E200/E200 9.3	SE163	PM	E20D/E200 10.2	SE242	SW	E20D/E200 8.9
SE89	Q	E200/E200 9.3	SE164	PM	E20D/E200 10.2	SE243	SW	E20D/E200 8.9
SE90	Q	E200/E200 9.3	SE165	PM	E20D/E200 10.2	SE244	SW	E20D/E200 8.9
SE91	Q	E200/E200 9.3	SE166	PM	E20D/E200 10.2	SE245	SW	E20D/E200 8.9
SE92	MW	E200/E200 9.3	SE167	C	E20D/E200 10.2	SE246	AF	E20D/E200 8.9
SE93	Q	E200/E200 9.3	SE168	C	E20D/E200 10.2	SE247	AF	E20D/E200 8.9
SE94	A	E200/E200 10.8	SE169	C	E20D/E200 10.2	SE248	AF	E20D/E200 8.9
SE95	RR	E200/E200 10.8	SE170	C	E20D/E200 10.2	SE249	AF	E20D/E200 8.9
SE96	RR	E200/E200 10.8	SE171	C	E20D/E200 10.2	SE251	PL	E20D/E200 8.9
SE97	RR	E200/E200 10.8	SE172	C	E20D/E200 10.2	SE252	PL	E20D/E200 8.9
SE98	RR	E200/E200 10.8	SE173	C	E20D/E200 10.2	SE253	PL	E20D/E200 8.9

Go-Ahead

No.	G.	Type	No.	G.	Type	No.	G.	Type
SE254	PL	E20D/E200 8.9	SEe36	RA	K9E Electric ADL 12.0	SOE22	AL	E200/East Lancs 10.4
SE255	PL	E20D/E200 8.9	SEe37	RA	K9E Electric ADL 12.0	SOE23	RR	E200/East Lancs 10.4
SE256	PL	E20D/E200 8.9	SEe38	RA	K9E Electric ADL 12.0	SOE24	RR	E200/East Lancs 10.4
SE257	PL	E20D/E200 8.9	SEe39	RA	K9E Electric ADL 12.0	SOE25	RR	E200/East Lancs 10.4
SE258	PL	E20D/E200 8.9	SEe40	RA	K9E Electric ADL 12.0	SOE26	RR	E200/East Lancs 10.4
SE259	PL	E20D/E200 8.9	SEe41	RA	K9E Electric ADL 12.0	SOE27	RR	E200/East Lancs 10.4
SE260	PL	E20D/E200 8.9	SEe42	RA	K9E Electric ADL 12.0	SOE28	AL	E200/East Lancs 10.4
SE261	MB	E20D/E200 8.9	SEe43	RA	K9E Electric ADL 12.0	SOE29	AL	E200/East Lancs 10.4
SE262	MB	E20D/E200 8.9	SEe44	RA	K9E Electric ADL 12.0	SOE30	AL	E200/East Lancs 10.4
SE263	MB	E20D/E200 8.9	SEe45	RA	K9E Electric ADL 12.0	SOE31	C	E200/East Lancs 10.4
SE264	MB	E20D/E200 8.9	SEe46	RA	K9E Electric ADL 12.0	SOE32	C	E200/East Lancs 10.4
SE265	MB	E20D/E200 8.9	SEe47	RA	K9E Electric ADL 12.0	SOE33	C	E200/East Lancs 10.4
SE266	MB	E20D/E200 8.9	SEe48	RA	K9E Electric ADL 12.0	SOE34	C	E200/East Lancs 10.4
SE267	MB	E20D/E200 8.9	SEe49	RA	K9E Electric ADL 12.0	SOE35	A	E200/East Lancs 10.4
SE268	A	E20D/E200 10.8	SEe50	RA	K9E Electric ADL 12.0	SOE36	A	E200/East Lancs 10.4
SE269	A	E20D/E200 10.8	SEe51	RA	K9E Electric ADL 12.0	SOE37	A	E200/East Lancs 10.4
SE270	A	E20D/E200 10.8	SEN1	NP	E200/E200 8.9	SOE38	A	E200/East Lancs 10.4
SE271	A	E20D/E200 10.8	SEN2	NP	E200/E200 8.9	SOE39	A	E200/East Lancs 10.4
SE272	A	E20D/E200 10.8	SEN3	NP	E200/E200 8.9	SOE40	A	E200/East Lancs 10.4
SE273	A	E20D/E200 10.8	SEN4	NP	E200/E200 8.9	VE1	A	B9TL/E400 10.4
SE274	PL	E20D/E200 10.8	SEN5	NP	E200/E200 8.9	VE2	A	B9TL/E400 10.4
SE275	PL	E20D/E200 10.8	SEN6	NP	E200/E200 8.9	VE3	A	B9TL/E400 10.4
SE276	PL	E20D/E200 10.8	SEN7	NP	E200/E200 8.9	VWL10	Q	B7TL/Gemini 10.6
SE277	PL	E20D/E200 10.8	SEN8	NP	E200/E200 8.9	WD1	AL	Gemini 2DL 10.4
SE278	PL	E20D/E200 10.8	SEN9	NP	E200/E200 8.9	WHV1	NX	B5LH/Gemini 2 10.4
SE279	PL	E20D/E200 10.8	SEN10	NP	E200/E200 8.9	WHV2	NX	B5LH/Gemini 2 10.4
SE280	PL	E20D/E200 10.8	SEN11	NP	E200/E200 8.9	WHV3	NX	B5LH/Gemini 2 10.4
SE281	PL	E20D/E200 10.8	SEN12	NP	E200/E200 8.9	WHV4	NX	B5LH/Gemini 2 10.4
SE282	AL	E20D/E200 10.8	SEN13	NP	E200/E200 9.3	WHV5	NX	B5LH/Gemini 2 10.4
SE283	AL	E20D/E200 10.8	SEN14	NP	E200/E200 9.3	WHV6	NX	B5LH/Gemini 2 10.4
SE284	AL	E20D/E200 10.8	SEN15	NP	E200/E200 9.3	WHV7	NX	B5LH/Gemini 2 10.4
SE285	AL	E20D/E200 10.8	SEN16	NP	E200/E200 9.3	WHV8	NX	B5LH/Gemini 2 10.4
SE286	AL	E20D/E200 10.8	SEN17	NP	E200/E200 9.3	WHV9	NX	B5LH/Gemini 2 10.4
SE287	AL	E20D/E200 10.8	SEN18	NP	E200/E200 9.3	WHV10	NX	B5LH/Gemini 2 10.4
SE288	MB	E20D/E200 8.9	SEN19	NP	E200/E200 9.3	WHV11	NX	B5LH/Gemini 2 10.4
SE289	MB	E20D/E200 8.9	SEN20	NP	E200/E200 9.3	WHV12	NX	B5LH/Gemini 2 10.4
SE290	MB	E20D/E200 8.9	SEN21	NP	E20D/E200 9.6	WHV13	NX	B5LH/Gemini 2 10.4
SE291	Q	E20D/E200MMC 9.75	SEN22	NP	E20D/E200 9.6	WHV14	NX	B5LH/Gemini 2 10.4
SE292	Q	E20D/E200MMC 9.75	SEN23	NP	E20D/E200 9.6	WHV15	NX	B5LH/Gemini 2 10.4
SEe1	RA	K9E Electric ADL 12.0	SEN24	MB	E20D/E200 9.6	WHV16	NX	B5LH/Gemini 2 10.4
SEe2	RA	K9E Electric ADL 12.0	SEN25	MB	E20D/E200 9.6	WHV17	SW	B5LH/Gemini 2 (EC) 10.5
SEe3	RA	K9E Electric ADL 12.0	SEN26	MB	E20D/E200 9.6	WHV18	SW	B5LH/Gemini 2 (EC) 10.5
SEe4	RA	K9E Electric ADL 12.0	SEN27	NP	E20D/E200 9.6	WHV19	SW	B5LH/Gemini 2 (EC) 10.5
SEe5	RA	K9E Electric ADL 12.0	SEN28	NP	E20D/E200 9.6	WHV20	SW	B5LH/Gemini 2 (EC) 10.5
SEe6	RA	K9E Electric ADL 12.0	SEN29	NP	E20D/E200 9.6	WHV21	SW	B5LH/Gemini 2 (EC) 10.5
SEe7	RA	K9E Electric ADL 12.0	SEN30	AL	E20D/E200 10.8	WHV22	SW	B5LH/Gemini 2 (EC) 10.5
SEe8	RA	K9E Electric ADL 12.0	SEN31	AL	E20D/E200 10.8	WHV23	SW	B5LH/Gemini 2 (EC) 10.5
SEe9	RA	K9E Electric ADL 12.0	SEN32	AL	E20D/E200 10.8	WHV24	SW	B5LH/Gemini 2 (EC) 10.5
SEe10	RA	K9E Electric ADL 12.0	SEN33	AL	E20D/E200 10.8	WHV25	SW	B5LH/Gemini 2 (EC) 10.5
SEe11	RA	K9E Electric ADL 12.0	SEN34	AL	E20D/E200 10.8	WHV26	SW	B5LH/Gemini 2 (EC) 10.5
SEe12	RA	K9E Electric ADL 12.0	SEN35	AL	E20D/E200 10.8	WHV27	SW	B5LH/Gemini 2 (EC) 10.5
SEe13	RA	K9E Electric ADL 12.0	SEN36	AL	E20D/E200 10.8	WHV28	SW	B5LH/Gemini 2 (EC) 10.5
SEe14	RA	K9E Electric ADL 12.0	SEN37	AL	E20D/E200 10.8	WHV29	SW	B5LH/Gemini 2 (EC) 10.5
SEe15	RA	K9E Electric ADL 12.0	SOE1	AL	E200/East Lancs 10.4	WHV30	SW	B5LH/Gemini 2 (EC) 10.5
SEe16	RA	K9E Electric ADL 12.0	SOE2	AL	E200/East Lancs 10.4	WHV31	SW	B5LH/Gemini 2 (EC) 10.5
SEe17	RA	K9E Electric ADL 12.0	SOE3	AL	E200/East Lancs 10.4	WHV32	SW	B5LH/Gemini 2 (EC) 10.5
SEe18	RA	K9E Electric ADL 12.0	SOE4	AL	E200/East Lancs 10.4	WHV33	AF	B5LH/Gemini 2 (EC) 10.5
SEe19	RA	K9E Electric ADL 12.0	SOE5	AL	E200/East Lancs 10.4	WHV34	AF	B5LH/Gemini 2 (EC) 10.5
SEe20	RA	K9E Electric ADL 12.0	SOE6	AL	E200/East Lancs 10.4	WHV35	AF	B5LH/Gemini 2 (EC) 10.5
SEe21	RA	K9E Electric ADL 12.0	SOE7	AL	E200/East Lancs 10.4	WHV36	AF	B5LH/Gemini 2 (EC) 10.5
SEe22	RA	K9E Electric ADL 12.0	SOE8	AL	E200/East Lancs 10.4	WHV37	AF	B5LH/Gemini 2 (EC) 10.5
SEe23	RA	K9E Electric ADL 12.0	SOE9	AL	E200/East Lancs 10.4	WHV38	AF	B5LH/Gemini 2 (EC) 10.5
SEe24	RA	K9E Electric ADL 12.0	SOE10	AL	E200/East Lancs 10.4	WHV39	AF	B5LH/Gemini 2 (EC) 10.5
SEe25	RA	K9E Electric ADL 12.0	SOE11	AL	E200/East Lancs 10.4	WHV40	AF	B5LH/Gemini 2 (EC) 10.5
SEe26	RA	K9E Electric ADL 12.0	SOE12	AL	E200/East Lancs 10.4	WHV41	AF	B5LH/Gemini 2 (EC) 10.5
SEe27	RA	K9E Electric ADL 12.0	SOE13	AL	E200/East Lancs 10.4	WHV42	C	B5LH/Gemini 3 ST 10.6
SEe28	RA	K9E Electric ADL 12.0	SOE14	AL	E200/East Lancs 10.4	WHV43	C	B5LH/Gemini 3 ST 10.6
SEe29	RA	K9E Electric ADL 12.0	SOE15	AL	E200/East Lancs 10.4	WHV44	C	B5LH/Gemini 3 ST 10.6
SEe30	RA	K9E Electric ADL 12.0	SOE16	AL	E200/East Lancs 10.4	WHV45	C	B5LH/Gemini 3 ST 10.6
SEe31	RA	K9E Electric ADL 12.0	SOE17	AL	E200/East Lancs 10.4	WHV46	C	B5LH/Gemini 3 ST 10.6
SEe32	RA	K9E Electric ADL 12.0	SOE18	AL	E200/East Lancs 10.4	WHV47	C	B5LH/Gemini 3 ST 10.6
SEe33	RA	K9E Electric ADL 12.0	SOE19	AL	E200/East Lancs 10.4	WHV48	C	B5LH/Gemini 3 ST 10.6
SEe34	RA	K9E Electric ADL 12.0	SOE20	AL	E200/East Lancs 10.4	WHV49	C	B5LH/Gemini 3 ST 10.6
SEe35	RA	K9E Electric ADL 12.0	SOE21	AL	E200/East Lancs 10.4	WHV50	C	B5LH/Gemini 3 ST 10.6

No.	G.	Type	No.	G.	Type	No.	G.	Type
WHV51	C	B5LH/Gemini 3 ST 10.6	WHV126	AF	B5LH/Gemini 3 ST 10.6	WS21	NP	Streetlite DF 10.2
WHV52	C	B5LH/Gemini 3 ST 10.6	WHV127	AF	B5LH/Gemini 3 ST 10.6	WS22	NP	Streetlite DF 10.2
WHV53	C	B5LH/Gemini 3 ST 10.6	WHV128	AF	B5LH/Gemini 3 ST 10.6	WS23	NP	Streetlite DF 10.2
WHV54	C	B5LH/Gemini 3 ST 10.6	WHV129	AF	B5LH/Gemini 3 ST 10.6	WS24	NP	Streetlite DF 10.2
WHV55	C	B5LH/Gemini 3 ST 10.6	WHV130	AF	B5LH/Gemini 3 ST 10.6	WS25	NP	Streetlite DF 10.2
WHV56	C	B5LH/Gemini 3 ST 10.6	WHV131	AF	B5LH/Gemini 3 ST 10.6	WS26	NP	Streetlite DF 10.2
WHV57	C	B5LH/Gemini 3 ST 10.6	WHV132	AF	B5LH/Gemini 3 ST 10.6	WS27	NP	Streetlite DF 10.2
WHV58	C	B5LH/Gemini 3 ST 10.6	WHV133	AF	B5LH/Gemini 3 ST 10.6	WS28	NP	Streetlite DF 10.2
WHV59	C	B5LH/Gemini 3 ST 10.6	WHV134	AF	B5LH/Gemini 3 ST 10.6	WS29	NP	Streetlite DF 10.2
WHV60	C	B5LH/Gemini 3 ST 10.6	WHV135	AF	B5LH/Gemini 3 ST 10.6	WS30	NP	Streetlite DF 10.2
WHV61	C	B5LH/Gemini 3 ST 10.6	WHV136	AF	B5LH/Gemini 3 ST 10.6	WS31	NP	Streetlite DF 10.2
WHV62	C	B5LH/Gemini 3 ST 10.6	WHV137	AF	B5LH/Gemini 3 ST 10.6	WS32	NP	Streetlite DF 10.2
WHV63	C	B5LH/Gemini 3 ST 10.6	WHV138	AF	B5LH/Gemini 3 ST 10.6	WS49	NP	Streetlite WF 8.8
WHV64	C	B5LH/Gemini 3 ST 10.6	WHV139	AF	B5LH/Gemini 3 ST 10.6	WS50	NP	Streetlite WF 8.8
WHV65	C	B5LH/Gemini 3 ST 10.6	WHV140	AF	B5LH/Gemini 3 ST 10.6	WS51	NP	Streetlite WF 8.8
WHV66	C	B5LH/Gemini 3 ST 10.6	WHV141	AF	B5LH/Gemini 3 ST 10.6	WS52	NP	Streetlite WF 8.8
WHV67	C	B5LH/Gemini 3 ST 10.6	WHV142	AF	B5LH/Gemini 3 ST 10.6	WS53	NP	Streetlite WF 8.8
WHV68	C	B5LH/Gemini 3 ST 10.6	WHV143	MW	B5LH/Gemini 3 ST 10.6	WS54	NP	Streetlite WF 8.8
WHV69	C	B5LH/Gemini 3 ST 10.6	WHV144	MW	B5LH/Gemini 3 ST 10.6	WS55	NP	Streetlite WF 8.8
WHV70	C	B5LH/Gemini 3 ST 10.6	WHV145	MW	B5LH/Gemini 3 ST 10.6	WS56	NP	Streetlite WF 8.8
WHV71	C	B5LH/Gemini 3 ST 10.6	WHV146	MW	B5LH/Gemini 3 ST 10.6	WS57	NP	Streetlite WF 8.8
WHV72	C	B5LH/Gemini 3 ST 10.6	WHV147	MW	B5LH/Gemini 3 ST 10.6	WS58	NP	Streetlite WF 8.8
WHV73	C	B5LH/Gemini 3 ST 10.6	WHV148	MW	B5LH/Gemini 3 ST 10.6	WS59	NP	Streetlite WF 8.8
WHV74	C	B5LH/Gemini 3 ST 10.6	WHV149	MW	B5LH/Gemini 3 ST 10.6	WS60	NP	Streetlite WF 8.8
WHV75	C	B5LH/Gemini 3 ST 10.6	WHV150	MW	B5LH/Gemini 3 ST 10.6	WS61	NP	Streetlite WF 8.8
WHV76	C	B5LH/Gemini 3 ST 10.6	WHV151	MW	B5LH/Gemini 3 ST 10.6	WS62	NP	Streetlite WF 8.8
WHV77	C	B5LH/Gemini 3 ST 10.6	WHV152	MW	B5LH/Gemini 3 ST 10.6	WS63	NP	Streetlite WF 8.8
WHV78	C	B5LH/Gemini 3 ST 10.6	WHV153	MW	B5LH/Gemini 3 ST 10.6	WS64	NP	Streetlite WF 8.8
WHV79	C	B5LH/Gemini 3 ST 10.6	WHV154	MW	B5LH/Gemini 3 ST 10.6	WVL3	SW	B7TL/Gemini 10.1
WHV80	C	B5LH/Gemini 3 ST 10.6	WHV155	MW	B5LH/Gemini 3 ST 10.6	WVL18	SW	B7TL/Gemini 10.1
WHV81	AL	B5LH/Gemini 3 ST 10.6	WHV156	MW	B5LH/Gemini 3 ST 10.6	WVL24	Q	B7TL/Gemini 10.1
WHV82	AL	B5LH/Gemini 3 ST 10.6	WHV157	MW	B5LH/Gemini 3 ST 10.6	WVL25	Q	B7TL/Gemini 10.1
WHV83	AL	B5LH/Gemini 3 ST 10.6	WHV158	AF	B5LH/Gemini 3 ST 10.6	WVL27	Q	B7TL/Gemini 10.1
WHV84	AL	B5LH/Gemini 3 ST 10.6	WHV159	AF	B5LH/Gemini 3 ST 10.6	WVL29	AF	B7TL/Gemini 10.1
WHV85	AL	B5LH/Gemini 3 ST 10.6	WHV160	AF	B5LH/Gemini 3 ST 10.6	WVL30	AF	B7TL/Gemini 10.1
WHV86	AL	B5LH/Gemini 3 ST 10.6	WHV161	AF	B5LH/Gemini 3 ST 10.6	WVL32	AF	B7TL/Gemini 10.1
WHV87	AL	B5LH/Gemini 3 ST 10.6	WHV162	AF	B5LH/Gemini 3 ST 10.6	WVL38	AF	B7TL/Gemini 10.1
WHV88	AL	B5LH/Gemini 3 ST 10.6	WHV163	AF	B5LH/Gemini 3 ST 10.6	WVL39	AF	B7TL/Gemini 10.1
WHV89	AL	B5LH/Gemini 3 ST 10.6	WHV164	AF	B5LH/Gemini 3 ST 10.6	WVL49	AF	B7TL/Gemini 10.1
WHV90	AL	B5LH/Gemini 3 ST 10.6	WHV165	AF	B5LH/Gemini 3 ST 10.6	WVL54	AF	B7TL/Gemini 10.1
WHV91	AL	B5LH/Gemini 3 ST 10.6	WHV166	AF	B5LH/Gemini 3 ST 10.6	WVL55	AF	B7TL/Gemini 10.1
WHV92	AL	B5LH/Gemini 3 ST 10.6	WHV167	AF	B5LH/Gemini 3 ST 10.6	WVL64	AF	B7TL/Gemini 10.1
WHV93	AL	B5LH/Gemini 3 ST 10.6	WHY1	Q	Electrocity 10.4	WVL75	SW	B7TL/Gemini 10.1
WHV94	AL	B5LH/Gemini 3 ST 10.6	WHY2	Q	Electrocity 10.4	WVL79	NP	B7TL/Gemini 10.1
WHV95	AL	B5LH/Gemini 3 ST 10.6	WHY3	Q	Electrocity 10.4	WVL82	BV	B7TL/Gemini 10.1
WHV96	AL	B5LH/Gemini 3 ST 10.6	WHY4	Q	Electrocity 10.4	WVL84	NX	B7TL/Gemini 10.1
WHV97	AL	B5LH/Gemini 3 ST 10.6	WHY5	Q	Electrocity 10.4	WVL92	SW	B7TL/Gemini 10.1
WHV98	AL	B5LH/Gemini 3 ST 10.6	WHY6	Q	Electrocity 10.4	WVL96	Q	B7TL/Gemini 10.1
WHV99	AL	B5LH/Gemini 3 ST 10.6	WHY7	Q	Electrocity 10.4	WVL98	Q	B7TL/Gemini 10.1
WHV100	AL	B5LH/Gemini 3 ST 10.6	WHY8	Q	Electrocity 10.3	WVL102	AL	B7TL/Gemini 10.1
WHV101	AL	B5LH/Gemini 3 ST 10.6	WHY9	Q	Electrocity 10.3	WVL103	NX	B7TL/Gemini 10.1
WHV102	AL	B5LH/Gemini 3 ST 10.6	WHY10	Q	Electrocity 10.3	WVL107	SW	B7TL/Gemini 10.1
WHV103	AL	B5LH/Gemini 3 ST 10.6	WHY11	Q	Electrocity 10.3	WVL108	BX	B7TL/Gemini 10.1
WHV104	AL	B5LH/Gemini 3 ST 10.6	WHY12	Q	Electrocity 10.3	WVL109	NP	B7TL/Gemini 10.1
WHV105	A	B5LH/Gemini 3 ST 10.6	WHY13	Q	Electrocity 10.3	WVL110	NP	B7TL/Gemini 10.1
WHV106	A	B5LH/Gemini 3 ST 10.6	WS1	RR	Streetlite WF 8.8	WVL111	NP	B7TL/Gemini 10.1
WHV107	A	B5LH/Gemini 3 ST 10.6	WS2	RR	Streetlite WF 8.8	WVL112	NP	B7TL/Gemini 10.1
WHV108	A	B5LH/Gemini 3 ST 10.6	WS3	RR	Streetlite WF 8.8	WVL113	RR	B7TL/Gemini 10.1
WHV109	A	B5LH/Gemini 3 ST 10.6	WS4	RR	Streetlite WF 8.8	WVL114	RR	B7TL/Gemini 10.1
WHV110	A	B5LH/Gemini 3 ST 10.6	WS5	RR	Streetlite WF 8.8	WVL115	RR	B7TL/Gemini 10.1
WHV111	MW	B5LH/Gemini 3 ST 10.6	WS6	RR	Streetlite WF 8.8	WVL116	RR	B7TL/Gemini 10.1
WHV112	AF	B5LH/Gemini 3 ST 10.6	WS7	RR	Streetlite WF 8.8	WVL117	RR	B7TL/Gemini 10.1
WHV113	AF	B5LH/Gemini 3 ST 10.6	WS8	RR	Streetlite WF 8.8	WVL118	BV	B7TL/Gemini 10.1
WHV114	AF	B5LH/Gemini 3 ST 10.6	WS9	RR	Streetlite WF 8.8	WVL119	BX	B7TL/Gemini 10.1
WHV115	AF	B5LH/Gemini 3 ST 10.6	WS10	AL	Streetlite DF 10.8	WVL120	BX	B7TL/Gemini 10.1
WHV116	AF	B5LH/Gemini 3 ST 10.6	WS11	AL	Streetlite DF 10.8	WVL121	BX	B7TL/Gemini 10.1
WHV117	AF	B5LH/Gemini 3 ST 10.6	WS12	AL	Streetlite DF 10.8	WVL137	Q	B7TL/Gemini 10.1
WHV118	AF	B5LH/Gemini 3 ST 10.6	WS13	AL	Streetlite DF 10.8	WVL138	Q	B7TL/Gemini 10.1
WHV119	AF	B5LH/Gemini 3 ST 10.6	WS14	AL	Streetlite DF 10.8	WVL139	Q	B7TL/Gemini 10.1
WHV120	AF	B5LH/Gemini 3 ST 10.6	WS15	AL	Streetlite DF 10.8	WVL141	Q	B7TL/Gemini 10.1
WHV121	AF	B5LH/Gemini 3 ST 10.6	WS16	AL	Streetlite DF 10.8	WVL144	Q	B7TL/Gemini 10.1
WHV122	AF	B5LH/Gemini 3 ST 10.6	WS17	AL	Streetlite DF 10.8	WVL148	Q	B7TL/Gemini 10.1
WHV123	AF	B5LH/Gemini 3 ST 10.6	WS18	AL	Streetlite DF 10.8	WVL151	Q	B7TL/Gemini 10.1
WHV124	AF	B5LH/Gemini 3 ST 10.6	WS19	AL	Streetlite DF 10.8	WVL152	AL	B7TL/Gemini 10.1
WHV125	AF	B5LH/Gemini 3 ST 10.6	WS20	AL	Streetlite DF 10.8	WVL153	AF	B7TL/Gemini 10.1

Go-Ahead

No.	G.	Type	No.	G.	Type	No.	G.	Type
WVL154	AF	B7TL/Gemini 10.1	WVL255	Q	B7TL/Gemini 10.1	WVL330	BX	B9TL/Gemini 2 10.4
WVL160	AF	B7TL/Gemini 10.1	WVL256	Q	B7TL/Gemini 10.1	WVL331	BX	B9TL/Gemini 2 10.4
WVL161	AF	B7TL/Gemini 10.1	WVL257	Q	B7TL/Gemini 10.1	WVL332	PM	B9TL/Gemini 2 10.4
WVL163	AF	B7TL/Gemini 10.1	WVL258	Q	B7TL/Gemini 10.1	WVL333	PM	B9TL/Gemini 2 10.4
WVL164	AF	B7TL/Gemini 10.1	WVL259	Q	B7TL/Gemini 10.1	WVL334	RR	B9TL/Gemini 2 10.4
WVL165	AF	B7TL/Gemini 10.1	WVL260	Q	B7TL/Gemini 10.1	WVL335	RR	B9TL/Gemini 2 10.4
WVL167	AF	B7TL/Gemini 10.1	WVL261	Q	B7TL/Gemini 10.1	WVL336	RR	B9TL/Gemini 2 10.4
WVL169	AF	B7TL/Gemini 10.1	WVL262	Q	B7TL/Gemini 10.1	WVL337	RR	B9TL/Gemini 2 10.4
WVL170	AF	B7TL/Gemini 10.1	WVL263	Q	B7TL/Gemini 10.1	WVL338	RR	B9TL/Gemini 2 10.4
WVL174	AF	B7TL/Gemini 10.1	WVL264	Q	B7TL/Gemini 10.1	WVL339	RR	B9TL/Gemini 2 10.4
WVL177	AF	B7TL/Gemini 10.1	WVL265	Q	B7TL/Gemini 10.1	WVL340	RR	B9TL/Gemini 2 10.4
WVL180	AF	B7TL/Gemini 10.1	WVL266	Q	B7TL/Gemini 10.1	WVL341	RR	B9TL/Gemini 2 10.4
WVL188	AF	B7TL/Gemini 10.1	WVL267	Q	B7TL/Gemini 10.1	WVL342	RR	B9TL/Gemini 2 10.4
WVL189	NP	B7TL/Gemini 10.1	WVL268	Q	B7TL/Gemini 10.1	WVL343	RR	B9TL/Gemini 2 10.4
WVL190	NP	B7TL/Gemini 10.1	WVL269	Q	B7TL/Gemini 10.1	WVL344	RR	B9TL/Gemini 2 10.4
WVL191	NP	B7TL/Gemini 10.1	WVL270	Q	B7TL/Gemini 10.1	WVL345	RR	B9TL/Gemini 2 10.4
WVL192	NP	B7TL/Gemini 10.1	WVL271	Q	B7TL/Gemini 10.1	WVL346	RR	B9TL/Gemini 2 10.4
WVL193	NP	B7TL/Gemini 10.1	WVL273	BX	B7TL/Gemini 10.1	WVL347	RR	B9TL/Gemini 2 10.4
WVL194	NP	B7TL/Gemini 10.1	WVL274	NX	B9TL/Gemini 2 10.4	WVL348	RR	B9TL/Gemini 2 10.4
WVL195	NP	B7TL/Gemini 10.1	WVL275	NX	B9TL/Gemini 2 10.4	WVL349	RR	B9TL/Gemini 2 10.4
WVL196	NP	B7TL/Gemini 10.1	WVL276	NX	B9TL/Gemini 2 10.4	WVL350	NX	B9TL/Gemini 2 10.4
WVL197	NP	B7TL/Gemini 10.1	WVL277	NX	B9TL/Gemini 2 10.4	WVL351	NX	B9TL/Gemini 2 10.4
WVL198	NP	B7TL/Gemini 10.1	WVL278	NX	B9TL/Gemini 2 10.4	WVL352	NX	B9TL/Gemini 2 10.4
WVL199	NP	B7TL/Gemini 10.1	WVL279	NX	B9TL/Gemini 2 10.4	WVL353	NX	B9TL/Gemini 2 10.4
WVL200	NP	B7TL/Gemini 10.1	WVL280	NX	B9TL/Gemini 2 10.4	WVL354	NX	B9TL/Gemini 2 10.4
WVL201	NP	B7TL/Gemini 10.1	WVL281	NX	B9TL/Gemini 2 10.4	WVL355	NX	B9TL/Gemini 2 10.4
WVL202	NP	B7TL/Gemini 10.1	WVL282	NX	B9TL/Gemini 2 10.4	WVL356	NX	B9TL/Gemini 2 10.4
WVL203	NP	B7TL/Gemini 10.1	WVL283	NX	B9TL/Gemini 2 10.4	WVL357	NX	B9TL/Gemini 2 10.4
WVL204	NP	B7TL/Gemini 10.1	WVL284	NX	B9TL/Gemini 2 10.4	WVL358	NP	B9TL/Gemini 2 10.4
WVL205	NP	B7TL/Gemini 10.1	WVL285	NX	B9TL/Gemini 2 10.4	WVL359	NP	B9TL/Gemini 2 10.4
WVL206	AL	B7TL/Gemini 10.1	WVL286	NX	B9TL/Gemini 2 10.4	WVL360	AL	B9TL/Gemini 2 10.4
WVL207	AL	B7TL/Gemini 10.1	WVL287	NX	B9TL/Gemini 2 10.4	WVL361	A	B9TL/Gemini 2 10.4
WVL208	AL	B7TL/Gemini 10.1	WVL288	NX	B9TL/Gemini 2 10.4	WVL362	A	B9TL/Gemini 2 10.4
WVL209	AL	B7TL/Gemini 10.1	WVL289	NX	B9TL/Gemini 2 10.4	WVL363	A	B9TL/Gemini 2 10.4
WVL210	AL	B7TL/Gemini 10.1	WVL290	NX	B9TL/Gemini 2 10.4	WVL364	SW	B9TL/Gemini 2 10.4
WVL211	AL	B7TL/Gemini 10.1	WVL291	NX	B9TL/Gemini 2 10.4	WVL365	A	B9TL/Gemini 2 10.4
WVL212	MB	B7TL/Gemini 10.1	WVL292	NX	B9TL/Gemini 2 10.4	WVL366	C	B9TL/Gemini 2 10.4
WVL213	MB	B7TL/Gemini 10.1	WVL293	NX	B9TL/Gemini 2 10.4	WVL367	NP	B9TL/Gemini 2 10.4
WVL214	MB	B7TL/Gemini 10.1	WVL294	NX	B9TL/Gemini 2 10.4	WVL368	BX	B9TL/Gemini 2 10.4
WVL215	MB	B7TL/Gemini 10.1	WVL295	NX	B9TL/Gemini 2 10.4	WVL369	BX	B9TL/Gemini 2 10.4
WVL216	MB	B7TL/Gemini 10.1	WVL296	NX	B9TL/Gemini 2 10.4	WVL370	BX	B9TL/Gemini 2 10.4
WVL217	MB	B7TL/Gemini 10.1	WVL297	NX	B9TL/Gemini 2 10.4	WVL371	BX	B9TL/Gemini 2 10.4
WVL218	MB	B7TL/Gemini 10.1	WVL298	NX	B9TL/Gemini 2 10.4	WVL372	BX	B9TL/Gemini 2 10.4
WVL219	MB	B7TL/Gemini 10.1	WVL299	NX	B9TL/Gemini 2 10.4	WVL373	BX	B9TL/Gemini 2 10.4
WVL220	MB	B7TL/Gemini 10.1	WVL300	NX	B9TL/Gemini 2 10.4	WVL374	BX	B9TL/Gemini 2 10.4
WVL222	MB	B7TL/Gemini 10.1	WVL301	NX	B9TL/Gemini 2 10.4	WVL375	BX	B9TL/Gemini 2 10.4
WVL223	MB	B7TL/Gemini 10.1	WVL302	NX	B9TL/Gemini 2 10.4	WVL376	BX	B9TL/Gemini 2 10.4
WVL224	MB	B7TL/Gemini 10.1	WVL303	BX	B9TL/Gemini 2 10.4	WVL377	BX	B9TL/Gemini 2 10.4
WVL225	MB	B7TL/Gemini 10.1	WVL304	BX	B9TL/Gemini 2 10.4	WVL378	BX	B9TL/Gemini 2 10.4
WVL226	MB	B7TL/Gemini 10.1	WVL305	BX	B9TL/Gemini 2 10.4	WVL379	BX	B9TL/Gemini 2 10.4
WVL227	MB	B7TL/Gemini 10.1	WVL306	BX	B9TL/Gemini 2 10.4	WVL380	SW	B9TL/Gemini 2 10.4
WVL228	MB	B7TL/Gemini 10.1	WVL307	BX	B9TL/Gemini 2 10.4	WVL381	SW	B9TL/Gemini 2 10.4
WVL229	MB	B7TL/Gemini 10.1	WVL308	BX	B9TL/Gemini 2 10.4	WVL382	SW	B9TL/Gemini 2 10.4
WVL230	MB	B7TL/Gemini 10.1	WVL309	BX	B9TL/Gemini 2 10.4	WVL383	SW	B9TL/Gemini 2 10.4
WVL231	MB	B7TL/Gemini 10.1	WVL310	BX	B9TL/Gemini 2 10.4	WVL384	SW	B9TL/Gemini 2 10.4
WVL232	MB	B7TL/Gemini 10.1	WVL311	BX	B9TL/Gemini 2 10.4	WVL385	SW	B9TL/Gemini 2 10.4
WVL233	MB	B7TL/Gemini 10.1	WVL312	BX	B9TL/Gemini 2 10.4	WVL386	NX	B9TL/Gemini 2 10.4
WVL234	NX	B7TL/Gemini 10.1	WVL313	BX	B9TL/Gemini 2 10.4	WVL387	NX	B9TL/Gemini 2 10.4
WVL235	NX	B7TL/Gemini 10.1	WVL314	BX	B9TL/Gemini 2 10.4	WVL388	NX	B9TL/Gemini 2 10.4
WVL236	NX	B7TL/Gemini 10.1	WVL315	BX	B9TL/Gemini 2 10.4	WVL389	NX	B9TL/Gemini 2 10.4
WVL237	C	B7TL/Gemini 10.1	WVL316	BX	B9TL/Gemini 2 10.4	WVL390	NX	B9TL/Gemini 2 10.4
WVL238	C	B7TL/Gemini 10.1	WVL317	BX	B9TL/Gemini 2 10.4	WVL391	NX	B9TL/Gemini 2 10.4
WVL239	C	B7TL/Gemini 10.1	WVL318	BX	B9TL/Gemini 2 10.4	WVL392	NX	B9TL/Gemini 2 10.4
WVL240	C	B7TL/Gemini 10.1	WVL319	BX	B9TL/Gemini 2 10.4	WVL393	NX	B9TL/Gemini 2 10.4
WVL241	MB	B7TL/Gemini 10.1	WVL320	BX	B9TL/Gemini 2 10.4	WVL394	NX	B9TL/Gemini 2 10.4
WVL246	AL	B7TL/Gemini 10.1	WVL321	BX	B9TL/Gemini 2 10.4	WVL395	NX	B9TL/Gemini 2 10.4
WVL247	AL	B7TL/Gemini 10.1	WVL322	BX	B9TL/Gemini 2 10.4	WVL396	NX	B9TL/Gemini 2 10.4
WVL248	AL	B7TL/Gemini 10.1	WVL323	BX	B9TL/Gemini 2 10.4	WVL397	NX	B9TL/Gemini 2 10.4
WVL249	RR	B7TL/Gemini 10.1	WVL324	BX	B9TL/Gemini 2 10.4	WVL398	NX	B9TL/Gemini 2 10.4
WVL250	RR	B7TL/Gemini 10.1	WVL325	BX	B9TL/Gemini 2 10.4	WVL399	NX	B9TL/Gemini 2 10.4
WVL251	Q	B7TL/Gemini 10.1	WVL326	BX	B9TL/Gemini 2 10.4	WVL400	NX	B9TL/Gemini 2 10.4
WVL252	Q	B7TL/Gemini 10.1	WVL327	BX	B9TL/Gemini 2 10.4	WVL401	NX	B9TL/Gemini 2 10.4
WVL253	Q	B7TL/Gemini 10.1	WVL328	BX	B9TL/Gemini 2 10.4	WVL402	NX	B9TL/Gemini 2 10.4
WVL254	Q	B7TL/Gemini 10.1	WVL329	BX	B9TL/Gemini 2 10.4	WVL403	NX	B9TL/Gemini 2 10.4

No.	G.	Type	No.	G.	Type	No.	G.	Type
WVL404	NX	B9TL/Gemini 2 10.4	WVL458	NP	B9TL/Gemini 2 (EC) 10.5	WVN2	NP	B9TL/Gemini 2 10.4
WVL405	NX	B9TL/Gemini 2 10.4	WVL459	NP	B9TL/Gemini 2 (EC) 10.5	WVN3	NP	B9TL/Gemini 2 10.4
WVL406	NX	B9TL/Gemini 2 10.4	WVL460	NP	B9TL/Gemini 2 (EC) 10.5	WVN4	NP	B9TL/Gemini 2 10.4
WVL407	NX	B9TL/Gemini 2 10.4	WVL461	NP	B9TL/Gemini 2 (EC) 10.5	WVN5	NP	B9TL/Gemini 2 10.4
WVL408	NX	B9TL/Gemini 2 10.4	WVL462	NP	B9TL/Gemini 2 (EC) 10.5	WVN6	NP	B9TL/Gemini 2 10.4
WVL409	NX	B9TL/Gemini 2 10.4	WVL463	NP	B9TL/Gemini 2 (EC) 10.5	WVN7	NP	B9TL/Gemini 2 10.4
WVL410	NX	B9TL/Gemini 2 10.4	WVL464	NP	B9TL/Gemini 2 (EC) 10.5	WVN8	NP	B9TL/Gemini 2 10.4
WVL411	NX	B9TL/Gemini 2 10.4	WVL465	NP	B9TL/Gemini 2 (EC) 10.5	WVN9	NP	B9TL/Gemini 2 10.4
WVL412	NX	B9TL/Gemini 2 10.4	WVL466	NP	B9TL/Gemini 2 (EC) 10.5	WVN10	NP	B9TL/Gemini 2 10.4
WVL413	RR	B9TL/Gemini 2 10.4	WVL467	NP	B9TL/Gemini 2 (EC) 10.5	WVN11	NP	B9TL/Gemini 2 10.4
WVL414	RR	B9TL/Gemini 2 10.4	WVL468	RR	B9TL/Gemini 2 (EC) 10.5	WVN12	NP	B9TL/Gemini 2 10.4
WVL415	RR	B9TL/Gemini 2 10.4	WVL469	RR	B9TL/Gemini 2 (EC) 10.5	WVN13	NP	B9TL/Gemini 2 10.4
WVL416	RR	B9TL/Gemini 2 10.4	WVL470	RR	B9TL/Gemini 2 (EC) 10.5	WVN14	NP	B9TL/Gemini 2 10.4
WVL417	RR	B9TL/Gemini 2 10.4	WVL471	RR	B9TL/Gemini 2 (EC) 10.5	WVN15	NP	B9TL/Gemini 2 10.4
WVL418	RR	B9TL/Gemini 2 10.4	WVL472	RR	B9TL/Gemini 2 (EC) 10.5	WVN16	NP	B9TL/Gemini 2 10.4
WVL419	RR	B9TL/Gemini 2 10.4	WVL473	RR	B9TL/Gemini 2 (EC) 10.5	WVN17	NP	B9TL/Gemini 2 10.4
WVL420	RR	B9TL/Gemini 2 10.4	WVL474	RR	B9TL/Gemini 2 (EC) 10.5	WVN18	NP	B9TL/Gemini 2 10.4
WVL421	RR	B9TL/Gemini 2 10.4	WVL475	RR	B9TL/Gemini 2 (EC) 10.5	WVN19	NP	B9TL/Gemini 2 10.4
WVL422	SI	B9TL/Gemini 2 10.4	WVL476	RR	B9TL/Gemini 2 (EC) 10.5	WVN20	NP	B9TL/Gemini 2 10.4
WVL423	SI	B9TL/Gemini 2 10.4	WVL477	RR	B9TL/Gemini 2 (EC) 10.5	WVN21	NP	B9TL/Gemini 2 10.4
WVL424	SI	B9TL/Gemini 2 10.4	WVL478	RR	B9TL/Gemini 2 (EC) 10.5	WVN22	NP	B9TL/Gemini 2 10.4
WVL425	SI	B9TL/Gemini 2 10.4	WVL479	RR	B9TL/Gemini 2 (EC) 10.5	WVN23	NP	B9TL/Gemini 2 10.4
WVL426	SI	B9TL/Gemini 2 10.4	WVL480	RR	B9TL/Gemini 2 (EC) 10.5	WVN24	NP	B9TL/Gemini 2 10.4
WVL427	SI	B9TL/Gemini 2 10.4	WVL481	NP	B9TL/Gemini 2 (EC) 10.5	WVN25	NP	B9TL/Gemini 2 10.4
WVL428	SI	B9TL/Gemini 2 10.4	WVL482	NP	B9TL/Gemini 2 (EC) 10.5	WVN26	NP	B9TL/Gemini 2 10.4
WVL429	SI	B9TL/Gemini 2 10.4	WVL483	NP	B9TL/Gemini 2 (EC) 10.5	WVN27	NP	B9TL/Gemini 2 10.4
WVL430	SI	B9TL/Gemini 2 10.4	WVL484	NP	B9TL/Gemini 2 (EC) 10.5	WVN28	NP	B9TL/Gemini 2 10.4
WVL431	SI	B9TL/Gemini 2 10.4	WVL485	NP	B9TL/Gemini 2 (EC) 10.5	WVN29	NP	B9TL/Gemini 2 10.4
WVL432	RR	B9TL/Gemini 2 10.4	WVL486	NP	B9TL/Gemini 2 (EC) 10.5	WVN30	NP	B9TL/Gemini 2 10.4
WVL433	SI	B9TL/Gemini 2 10.4	WVL487	NP	B9TL/Gemini 2 (EC) 10.5	WVN31	NP	B9TL/Gemini 2 10.4
WVL434	SI	B9TL/Gemini 2 10.4	WVL488	NP	B9TL/Gemini 2 (EC) 10.5	WVN32	NP	B9TL/Gemini 2 10.4
WVL435	AF	B9TL/Gemini 2 10.4	WVL489	NP	B9TL/Gemini 2 (EC) 10.5	WVN33	NP	B9TL/Gemini 2 10.4
WVL436	SW	B9TL/Gemini 2 10.4	WVL490	NP	B9TL/Gemini 2 (EC) 10.5	WVN34	NP	B9TL/Gemini 2 10.4
WVL437	SW	B9TL/Gemini 2 10.4	WVL491	NP	B9TL/Gemini 2 (EC) 10.5	WVN35	NP	B9TL/Gemini 2 10.4
WVL438	SW	B9TL/Gemini 2 10.4	WVL492	NP	B9TL/Gemini 2 (EC) 10.5	WVN36	NP	B9TL/Gemini 2 10.4
WVL439	SW	B9TL/Gemini 2 10.4	WVL493	NP	B9TL/Gemini 2 (EC) 10.5	WVN37	NP	B9TL/Gemini 2 10.4
WVL440	A	B9TL/Gemini 2 10.4	WVL494	NP	B9TL/Gemini 2 (EC) 10.5	WVN38	NP	B9TL/Gemini 2 10.4
WVL441	A	B9TL/Gemini 2 10.4	WVL495	NP	B9TL/Gemini 2 (EC) 10.5	WVN39	NP	B9TL/Gemini 2 10.4
WVL442	A	B9TL/Gemini 2 10.4	WVL496	AF	B9TL/Gemini 2 (EC) 10.5	WVN40	NP	B9TL/Gemini 2 10.4
WVL443	A	B9TL/Gemini 2 10.4	WVL497	AF	B9TL/Gemini 2 (EC) 10.5	WVN41	NP	B9TL/Gemini 2 10.4
WVL444	A	B9TL/Gemini 2 10.4	WVL498	AF	B9TL/Gemini 2 (EC) 10.5	WVN42	NP	B9TL/Gemini 2 10.4
WVL445	A	B9TL/Gemini 2 10.4	WVL499	AF	B9TL/Gemini 2 (EC) 10.5	WVN43	NP	B9TL/Gemini 2 10.4
WVL446	A	B9TL/Gemini 2 10.4	WVL500	AF	B9TL/Gemini 2 (EC) 10.5	WVN44	NP	B9TL/Gemini 2 10.4
WVL447	A	B9TL/Gemini 2 10.4	WVL501	AF	B9TL/Gemini 2 (EC) 10.5	WVN45	NP	B9TL/Gemini 2 10.4
WVL448	NP	B9TL/Gemini 2 10.4	WVL502	AF	B9TL/Gemini 2 (EC) 10.5	WVN46	NP	B9TL/Gemini 2 (EC) 10.5
WVL449	NP	B9TL/Gemini 2 10.4	WVL503	AL	B9TL/Gemini 2 (EC) 10.5	WVN47	NP	B9TL/Gemini 2 (EC) 10.5
WVL450	NP	B9TL/Gemini 2 10.4	WVL504	AL	B9TL/Gemini 2 (EC) 10.5	WVN48	NP	B9TL/Gemini 2 (EC) 10.5
WVL451	RR	B9TL/Gemini 2 10.4	WVL505	AL	B9TL/Gemini 2 (EC) 10.5	WVN49	NP	B9TL/Gemini 2 (EC) 10.5
WVL452	RR	B9TL/Gemini 2 10.4	WVL506	AL	B9TL/Gemini 2 (EC) 10.5	WVN50	NP	B9TL/Gemini 2 (EC) 10.5
WVL453	RR	B9TL/Gemini 2 10.4	WVL507	AF	B9TL/Gemini 2 (EC) 10.5	WVN51	NP	B9TL/Gemini 2 (EC) 10.5
WVL454	RR	B9TL/Gemini 2 10.4	WVL508	AF	B9TL/Gemini 2 (EC) 10.5	WVN52	NP	B9TL/Gemini 2 (EC) 10.5
WVL455	BX	B9TL/Gemini 2 10.4	WVL509	C	B5TL/Gemini 3 (E6) 10.6	WVN53	NP	B9TL/Gemini 2 (EC) 10.5
WVL456	BX	B9TL/Gemini 2 10.4	WVL510	C	B5TL/Gemini 3 (E6) 10.6			
WVL457	NP	B9TL/Gemini 2 (EC) 10.5	WVN1	NP	B9TL/Gemini 2 10.4			

Metroline

No.	G.	Type	No.	G.	Type	No.	G.	Type
BYD1471	AC	K10 Electric D/D 10.2	DE1029	W	E200/E200 10.2	DE1322	KC	E20D/E200 10.2
BYD1472	AC	K10 Electric D/D 10.2	DE1030	W	E200/E200 10.2	DE1323	KC	E20D/E200 10.2
BYD1473	AC	K10 Electric D/D 10.2	DE1031	W	E200/E200 10.2	DE1324	KC	E20D/E200 10.2
BYD1474	AC	K10 Electric D/D 10.2	DE1032	W	E200/E200 10.2	DE1325	KC	E20D/E200 10.2
BYD1475	AC	K10 Electric D/D 10.2	DE1033	W	E200/E200 10.2	DE1326	KC	E20D/E200 10.2
DE859	W	E200/E200 10.2	DE1115	W	E200/E200 10.2	DE1327	KC	E20D/E200 10.2
DE860	W	E200/E200 10.2	DE1116	W	E200/E200 10.2	DE1328	KC	E20D/E200 10.2
DE861	W	E200/E200 10.2	DE1117	W	E200/E200 10.2	DE1329	KC	E20D/E200 10.2
DE862	W	E200/E200 10.2	DE1118	W	E200/E200 10.2	DE1330	KC	E20D/E200 10.2
DE863	W	E200/E200 10.2	DE1119	W	E200/E200 10.2	DE1331	KC	E20D/E200 10.2
DE864	W	E200/E200 10.2	DE1120	W	E200/E200 10.2	DE1332	KC	E20D/E200 10.2
DE865	W	E200/E200 10.2	DE1121	W	E200/E200 10.2	DE1333	KC	E20D/E200 10.2
DE866	W	E200/E200 10.2	DE1122	W	E200/E200 10.2	DE1334	KC	E20D/E200 10.2
DE867	W	E200/E200 10.2	DE1123	W	E200/E200 10.2	DE1335	KC	E20D/E200 10.2
DE868	W	E200/E200 10.2	DE1124	W	E200/E200 10.2	DE1336	KC	E20D/E200 10.2
DE869	W	E200/E200 10.2	DE1125	W	E200/E200 10.2	DE1583	HS	E200/E200 10.2
DE870	W	E200/E200 10.2	DE1126	W	E200/E200 10.2	DE1584	UX	E200/E200 10.2
DE871	W	E200/E200 10.2	DE1127	W	E200/E200 10.2	DE1585	UX	E200/E200 10.2
DE872	W	E200/E200 10.2	DE1128	W	E200/E200 10.2	DE1586	UX	E200/E200 10.2
DE873	W	E200/E200 10.2	DE1129	W	E200/E200 10.2	DE1587	HS	E200/E200 10.2
DE874	W	E200/E200 10.2	DE1130	W	E200/E200 10.2	DE1588	HS	E200/E200 10.2
DE875	W	E200/E200 10.2	DE1131	W	E200/E200 10.2	DE1589	UX	E200/E200 10.2
DE876	W	E200/E200 10.2	DE1132	W	E200/E200 10.2	DE1590	UX	E200/E200 10.2
DE877	W	E200/E200 10.2	DE1133	W	E200/E200 10.2	DE1591	UX	E200/E200 10.2
DE952	PA	E200/E200 10.2	DE1134	W	E200/E200 10.2	DE1592	UX	E200/E200 10.2
DE953	AH	E200/E200 10.2	DE1135	W	E200/E200 10.2	DE1593	UX	E200/E200 10.2
DE954	PA	E200/E200 10.2	DE1136	W	E200/E200 10.2	DE1594	UX	E200/E200 10.2
DE955	PA	E200/E200 10.2	DE1137	W	E200/E200 10.2	DE1595	UX	E200/E200 10.2
DE956	AH	E200/E200 10.2	DE1138	W	E200/E200 10.2	DE1596	UX	E200/E200 10.2
DE957	W	E200/E200 10.2	DE1139	W	E200/E200 10.2	DE1597	HS	E200/E200 10.2
DE958	PA	E200/E200 10.2	DE1140	W	E200/E200 10.2	DE1598	HS	E200/E200 10.2
DE959	AH	E200/E200 10.2	DE1141	W	E200/E200 10.2	DE1599	HS	E200/E200 10.2
DE960	CW	E200/E200 10.2	DE1142	W	E200/E200 10.2	DE1600	ON	E200/E200 10.2
DE993	AH	E200/E200 10.2	DE1143	W	E200/E200 10.2	DE1601	UX	E200/E200 10.2
DE994	AH	E200/E200 10.2	DE1144	W	E200/E200 10.2	DE1602	UX	E200/E200 10.2
DE995	AH	E200/E200 10.2	DE1145	W	E200/E200 10.2	DE1603	WJ	E200/E200 10.2
DE996	AH	E200/E200 10.2	DE1146	W	E200/E200 10.2	DE1604	UX	E200/E200 10.2
DE997	AH	E200/E200 10.2	DE1147	W	E200/E200 10.2	DE1605	HS	E200/E200 10.2
DE998	AH	E200/E200 10.2	DE1148	W	E200/E200 10.2	DE1606	HS	E200/E200 10.2
DE999	KC	E200/E200 10.2	DE1149	W	E200/E200 10.2	DE1607	HS	E200/E200 10.2
DE1000	AH	E200/E200 10.2	DE1150	W	E200/E200 10.2	DE1608	G	E200/E200 10.2
DE1001	AH	E200/E200 10.2	DE1151	KC	E200/E200 10.2	DE1609	G	E200/E200 10.2
DE1002	AH	E200/E200 10.2	DE1152	KC	E200/E200 10.2	DE1610	UX	E200/E200 10.2
DE1003	AH	E200/E200 10.2	DE1153	KC	E200/E200 10.2	DE1611	G	E200/E200 10.2
DE1004	AH	E200/E200 10.2	DE1154	KC	E200/E200 10.2	DE1612	CW	E200/E200 10.2
DE1005	AH	E200/E200 10.2	DE1155	KC	E200/E200 10.2	DE1613	WJ	E200/E200 10.2
DE1006	AH	E200/E200 10.2	DE1156	KC	E200/E200 10.2	DE1614	WJ	E200/E200 10.2
DE1007	AH	E200/E200 10.2	DE1157	KC	E200/E200 10.2	DE1615	WJ	E200/E200 10.2
DE1008	AH	E200/E200 10.2	DE1158	KC	E200/E200 10.2	DE1616	WJ	E200/E200 10.2
DE1009	AH	E200/E200 10.2	DE1159	KC	E200/E200 10.2	DE1617	WJ	E200/E200 10.2
DE1010	AH	E200/E200 10.2	DE1160	KC	E200/E200 10.2	DE1618	WJ	E200/E200 10.2
DE1011	AH	E200/E200 10.2	DE1161	KC	E200/E200 10.2	DE1619	WJ	E200/E200 10.2
DE1012	AH	E200/E200 10.2	DE1162	KC	E200/E200 10.2	DE1620	WJ	E200/E200 10.2
DE1013	AH	E200/E200 10.2	DE1163	KC	E200/E200 10.2	DE1621	WJ	E200/E200 10.2
DE1014	AH	E200/E200 10.2	DE1164	KC	E200/E200 10.2	DE1622	WJ	E200/E200 10.2
DE1015	W	E200/E200 10.2	DE1165	KC	E200/E200 10.2	DE1623	WJ	E200/E200 10.2
DE1016	W	E200/E200 10.2	DE1166	KC	E200/E200 10.2	DE1624	WJ	E200/E200 10.2
DE1017	W	E200/E200 10.2	DE1167	KC	E200/E200 10.2	DE1625	WJ	E200/E200 10.2
DE1018	W	E200/E200 10.2	DE1168	KC	E200/E200 10.2	DE1626	WJ	E200/E200 10.2
DE1019	W	E200/E200 10.2	DE1169	KC	E200/E200 10.2	DE1627	WJ	E200/E200 10.2
DE1020	W	E200/E200 10.2	DE1170	KC	E200/E200 10.2	DE1628	WJ	E200/E200 10.2
DE1021	W	E200/E200 10.2	DE1171	KC	E200/E200 10.2	DE1629	WJ	E200/E200 10.2
DE1022	W	E200/E200 10.2	DE1172	W	E200/E200 10.2	DE1630	WJ	E200/E200 10.2
DE1023	W	E200/E200 10.2	DE1173	W	E200/E200 10.2	DE1631	WJ	E200/E200 10.2
DE1024	W	E200/E200 10.2	DE1174	W	E200/E200 10.2	DE1632	WJ	E200/E200 10.2
DE1025	W	E200/E200 10.2	DE1318	KC	E20D/E200 10.2	DE1633	WJ	E200/E200 10.2
DE1026	W	E200/E200 10.2	DE1319	KC	E20D/E200 10.2	DE1634	WJ	E200/E200 10.2
DE1027	W	E200/E200 10.2	DE1320	KC	E20D/E200 10.2	DE1635	WJ	E200/E200 10.2
DE1028	W	E200/E200 10.2	DE1321	KC	E20D/E200 10.2	DE1636	WJ	E200/E200 10.2

No.	G.	Type	No.	G.	Type	No.	G.	Type
DE1637	WJ	E200/E200 10.2	DE1808	UX	E200/E200 10.2	DEL2161	UX	E20D/E200MMC 10.9
DE1638	WJ	E200/E200 10.2	DE1809	HS	E200/E200 10.2	DEL2162	UX	E20D/E200MMC 10.9
DE1639	WJ	E200/E200 10.2	DE1810	G	E200/E200 10.2	DEL2163	UX	E20D/E200MMC 10.9
DE1640	WJ	E200/E200 10.2	DE1811	G	E200/E200 10.2	DEL2164	UX	E20D/E200MMC 10.9
DE1641	WJ	E200/E200 10.2	DE1812	UX	E200/E200 10.2	DEL2244	AH	E20D/E200MMC 10.9
DE1642	WJ	E200/E200 10.2	DE1813	UX	E200/E200 10.2	DEL2245	AH	E20D/E200MMC 10.9
DE1643	WJ	E200/E200 10.2	DE1814	UX	E200/E200 10.2	DEL2246	AH	E20D/E200MMC 10.9
DE1644	WJ	E200/E200 10.2	DE1815	G	E200/E200 10.2	DEL2247	AH	E20D/E200MMC 10.9
DE1645	WJ	E200/E200 10.2	DE1816	UX	E200/E200 10.2	DEL2248	AH	E20D/E200MMC 10.9
DE1646	WJ	E200/E200 10.2	DE1895	HS	E200/E200 10.2	DEL2249	AH	E20D/E200MMC 10.9
DE1647	ON	E200/E200 10.2	DE1896	G	E200/E200 10.2	DEL2250	AH	E20D/E200MMC 10.9
DE1648	WJ	E200/E200 10.2	DE1897	G	E200/E200 10.2	DEL2251	AH	E20D/E200MMC 10.9
DE1649	WJ	E200/E200 10.2	DE1898	G	E200/E200 10.2	DEL2252	AH	E20D/E200MMC 10.9
DE1650	WJ	E200/E200 10.2	DE1899	G	E200/E200 10.2	DEL2253	AH	E20D/E200MMC 10.9
DE1651	WJ	E200/E200 10.2	DE1900	G	E200/E200 10.2	DEL2254	AH	E20D/E200MMC 10.9
DE1652	WJ	E200/E200 10.2	DE1901	G	E200/E200 10.2	DEL2255	AH	E20D/E200MMC 10.9
DE1653	WJ	E200/E200 10.2	DE1902	G	E200/E200 10.2	DEL2256	AH	E20D/E200MMC 10.9
DE1654	WJ	E200/E200 10.2	DE1903	G	E200/E200 10.2	DEL2257	AH	E20D/E200MMC 10.9
DE1655	WJ	E200/E200 10.2	DE1904	G	E200/E200 10.2	DEL2258	AH	E20D/E200MMC 10.9
DE1656	WJ	E200/E200 10.2	DE1905	G	E200/E200 10.2	DEL2259	AH	E20D/E200MMC 10.9
DE1657	WJ	E200/E200 10.2	DE1906	G	E200/E200 10.2	DEL2260	AH	E20D/E200MMC 10.9
DE1658	WJ	E200/E200 10.2	DE1907	G	E200/E200 10.2	DEL2261	AH	E20D/E200MMC 10.9
DE1659	WJ	E200/E200 10.2	DE1908	G	E200/E200 10.2	DEL2262	AH	E20D/E200MMC 10.9
DE1660	WJ	E200/E200 10.2	DE1909	G	E200/E200 10.2	DEL2263	AH	E20D/E200MMC 10.9
DE1661	WJ	E200/E200 10.2	DE1910	G	E200/E200 10.2	DEL2264	AH	E20D/E200MMC 10.9
DE1662	WJ	E200/E200 10.2	DE1911	G	E200/E200 10.2	DEL2265	AH	E20D/E200MMC 10.9
DE1663	ON	E200/E200 10.2	DE1958	ON	E20D/E200 10.2	DEM1337	PB	E20D/E200 9.6
DE1664	WJ	E200/E200 10.2	DE1959	ON	E20D/E200 10.2	DEM1338	PB	E20D/E200 9.6
DE1665	ON	E200/E200 10.2	DE1960	ON	E20D/E200 10.2	DEM1339	PB	E20D/E200 9.6
DE1666	ON	E200/E200 10.2	DE1961	ON	E20D/E200 10.2	DEM1340	PB	E20D/E200 9.6
DE1667	ON	E200/E200 10.2	DE1962	ON	E20D/E200 10.2	DEM1341	PB	E20D/E200 9.6
DE1668	ON	E200/E200 10.2	DE1963	ON	E20D/E200 10.2	DEM1342	PB	E20D/E200 9.6
DE1669	ON	E200/E200 10.2	DE1964	ON	E20D/E200 10.2	DEM1343	PB	E20D/E200 9.6
DE1670	ON	E200/E200 10.2	DE1965	ON	E20D/E200 10.2	DEM1344	PB	E20D/E200 9.6
DE1671	ON	E200/E200 10.2	DE1966	ON	E20D/E200 10.2	DEM1345	PB	E20D/E200 9.6
DE1672	ON	E200/E200 10.2	DE1967	ON	E20D/E200 10.2	DEM1346	PB	E20D/E200 9.6
DE1673	ON	E200/E200 10.2	DE1968	ON	E20D/E200 10.2	DEM1347	PB	E20D/E200 9.6
DE1674	ON	E200/E200 10.2	DE1969	ON	E20D/E200 10.2	DEM1348	PB	E20D/E200 9.6
DE1675	G	E200/E200 10.2	DEL1970	WJ	E20D/E200 10.8	DEM1349	PB	E20D/E200 9.6
DE1676	G	E200/E200 10.2	DEL1971	WJ	E20D/E200 10.8	DEM1350	PB	E20D/E200 9.6
DE1678	G	E200/E200 10.2	DEL1972	WJ	E20D/E200 10.8	DEM1351	PB	E20D/E200 9.6
DE1679	G	E200/E200 10.2	DEL1973	WJ	E20D/E200 10.8	DEM1352	PB	E20D/E200 9.6
DE1681	G	E200/E200 10.2	DEL1974	WJ	E20D/E200 10.8	DEM1353	PB	E20D/E200 9.6
DE1683	G	E200/E200 10.2	DEL1975	WJ	E20D/E200 10.8	DEM1354	PB	E20D/E200 9.6
DE1684	G	E200/E200 10.2	DEL1976	WJ	E20D/E200 10.8	DEM1355	PB	E20D/E200 9.6
DE1685	G	E200/E200 10.2	DEL1977	WJ	E20D/E200 10.8	DEM1356	PB	E20D/E200 9.6
DE1687	G	E200/E200 10.2	DEL1978	WJ	E20D/E200 10.8	DEM1357	PB	E20D/E200 9.6
DE1692	G	E200/E200 10.2	DEL1979	WJ	E20D/E200 10.8	DEM1358	PB	E20D/E200 9.6
DE1693	G	E200/E200 10.2	DEL1980	WJ	E20D/E200 10.8	DEM1359	PB	E20D/E200 9.6
DE1694	G	E200/E200 10.2	DEL2062	CW	E20D/E200 10.8	DEM1912	ON	E20D/E200 9.6
DE1783	G	E200/E200 10.2	DEL2063	CW	E20D/E200 10.8	DEM1913	ON	E20D/E200 9.6
DE1784	G	E200/E200 10.2	DEL2064	CW	E20D/E200 10.8	DEM1914	ON	E20D/E200 9.6
DE1785	G	E200/E200 10.2	DEL2065	CW	E20D/E200 10.8	DEM1915	ON	E20D/E200 9.6
DE1786	G	E200/E200 10.2	DEL2066	CW	E20D/E200 10.8	DEM1916	ON	E20D/E200 9.6
DE1787	G	E200/E200 10.2	DEL2067	CW	E20D/E200 10.8	DEM1917	ON	E20D/E200 9.6
DE1788	G	E200/E200 10.2	DEL2068	CW	E20D/E200 10.8	DEM1918	ON	E20D/E200 9.6
DE1789	G	E200/E200 10.2	DEL2069	CW	E20D/E200 10.8	DES795	PB	E200/E200 8.9
DE1790	G	E200/E200 10.2	DEL2070	CW	E20D/E200 10.8	DES797	PB	E200/E200 8.9
DE1791	G	E200/E200 10.2	DEL2071	CW	E20D/E200 10.8	DES799	PB	E200/E200 8.9
DE1792	G	E200/E200 10.2	DEL2145	UX	E20D/E200 10.8	DES800	PB	E200/E200 8.9
DE1793	G	E200/E200 10.2	DEL2146	UX	E20D/E200 10.8	DES801	PB	E200/E200 8.9
DE1794	G	E200/E200 10.2	DEL2147	UX	E20D/E200 10.8	DLD693	KC	Dart/Pointer 2 10.1
DE1795	G	E200/E200 10.2	DEL2148	UX	E20D/E200 10.8	DLD694	KC	Dart/Pointer 2 10.1
DE1796	G	E200/E200 10.2	DEL2149	UX	E20D/E200 10.8	DLD695	KC	Dart/Pointer 2 10.1
DE1797	G	E200/E200 10.2	DEL2150	UX	E20D/E200 10.8	DLD696	KC	Dart/Pointer 2 10.1
DE1798	UX	E200/E200 10.2	DEL2151	UX	E20D/E200 10.8	DLD697	KC	Dart/Pointer 2 10.1
DE1799	HS	E200/E200 10.2	DEL2152	UX	E20D/E200 10.8	DLD698	KC	Dart/Pointer 2 10.1
DE1800	UX	E200/E200 10.2	DEL2153	UX	E20D/E200 10.8	DLD699	KC	Dart/Pointer 2 10.1
DE1801	UX	E200/E200 10.2	DEL2154	UX	E20D/E200 10.8	DLD700	KC	Dart/Pointer 2 10.1
DE1802	UX	E200/E200 10.2	DEL2155	UX	E20D/E200MMC 10.9	DLD701	KC	Dart/Pointer 2 10.1
DE1803	UX	E200/E200 10.2	DEL2156	UX	E20D/E200MMC 10.9	DLD703	KC	Dart/Pointer 2 10.1
DE1804	UX	E200/E200 10.2	DEL2157	UX	E20D/E200MMC 10.9	DLD704	KC	Dart/Pointer 2 10.1
DE1805	HS	E200/E200 10.2	DEL2158	UX	E20D/E200MMC 10.9	DLD705	KC	Dart/Pointer 2 10.1
DE1806	UX	E200/E200 10.2	DEL2159	UX	E20D/E200MMC 10.9	DLD706	KC	Dart/Pointer 2 10.1
DE1807	UX	E200/E200 10.2	DEL2160	UX	E20D/E200MMC 10.9			

Metroline

No.	G.	Type	No.	G.	Type	No.	G.	Type
DLD707	KC	Dart/Pointer 2 10.1	LT116	HT	NRM 11.3	LT793	W	NRM (E6) 11.3
DLD708	KC	Dart/Pointer 2 10.1	LT117	HT	NRM 11.3	LT794	W	NRM (E6) 11.3
DLD709	KC	Dart/Pointer 2 10.1	LT190	W	NRM (E6) 11.3	LT795	W	NRM (E6) 11.3
DLD710	KC	Dart/Pointer 2 10.1	LT543	W	NRM (E6) 11.3	LT796	W	NRM (E6) 11.3
DLD711	KC	Dart/Pointer 2 10.1	LT544	W	NRM (E6) 11.3	LT797	W	NRM (E6) 11.3
DM961	AH	E200/Evolution 10.4	LT545	W	NRM (E6) 11.3	LT798	W	NRM (E6) 11.3
DM962	AH	E200/Evolution 10.4	LT546	W	NRM (E6) 11.3	LT799	W	NRM (E6) 11.3
DM963	AH	E200/Evolution 10.4	LT547	W	NRM (E6) 11.3	LT800	W	NRM (E6) 11.3
DM964	AH	E200/Evolution 10.4	LT548	W	NRM (E6) 11.3	LT801	W	NRM (E6) 11.3
DM965	AH	E200/Evolution 10.4	LT549	W	NRM (E6) 11.3	LT802	W	NRM (E6) 11.3
DM966	AH	E200/Evolution 10.4	LT550	W	NRM (E6) 11.3	LT803	W	NRM (E6) 11.3
DM967	AH	E200/Evolution 10.4	LT551	W	NRM (E6) 11.3	LT804	W	NRM (E6) 11.3
DM968	AH	E200/Evolution 10.4	LT552	W	NRM (E6) 11.3	LT805	W	NRM (E6) 11.3
DM969	AH	E200/Evolution 10.4	LT553	W	NRM (E6) 11.3	LT806	W	NRM (E6) 11.3
DM970	AH	E200/Evolution 10.4	LT554	W	NRM (E6) 11.3	LT807	W	NRM (E6) 11.3
DP1009	PA	Dart/Pointer 10.1	LT555	W	NRM (E6) 11.3	LT808	W	NRM (E6) 11.3
DP1010	PA	Dart/Pointer 10.1	LT556	W	NRM (E6) 11.3	LT809	W	NRM (E6) 11.3
DP1011	PA	Dart/Pointer 10.1	LT557	W	NRM (E6) 11.3	LT810	W	NRM (E6) 11.3
DP1012	PA	Dart/Pointer 10.1	LT558	W	NRM (E6) 11.3	LT811	W	NRM (E6) 11.3
DP1013	PA	Dart/Pointer 10.1	LT559	W	NRM (E6) 11.3	SEL739	PA	N230/Olympus 10.8
LT8	HT	NRM (E6) 11.3	LT560	W	NRM (E6) 11.3	SEL740	PA	N230/Olympus 10.8
LT9	HT	NRM 11.3	LT561	W	NRM (E6) 11.3	SEL741	PA	N230/Olympus 10.8
LT10	HT	NRM 11.3	LT562	W	NRM (E6) 11.3	SEL742	PA	N230/Olympus 10.8
LT11	HT	NRM 11.3	LT563	W	NRM (E6) 11.3	SEL743	PA	N230/Olympus 10.8
LT12	HT	NRM 11.3	LT641	W	NRM (E6) 11.3	SEL744	PA	N230/Olympus 10.8
LT13	HT	NRM 11.3	LT642	W	NRM (E6) 11.3	SEL745	PA	N230/Olympus 10.8
LT14	HT	NRM 11.3	LT643	W	NRM (E6) 11.3	SEL746	PA	N230/Olympus 10.8
LT15	HT	NRM 11.3	LT644	W	NRM (E6) 11.3	SEL747	PA	N230/Olympus 10.8
LT16	HT	NRM 11.3	LT645	W	NRM (E6) 11.3	SEL748	PA	N230/Olympus 10.8
LT17	HT	NRM 11.3	LT646	W	NRM (E6) 11.3	SEL749	PA	N230/Olympus 10.8
LT18	HT	NRM 11.3	LT647	W	NRM (E6) 11.3	SEL750	PA	N230/Olympus 10.8
LT19	HT	NRM 11.3	LT648	W	NRM (E6) 11.3	SEL751	PA	N230/Olympus 10.8
LT20	HT	NRM 11.3	LT649	W	NRM (E6) 11.3	SEL752	PA	N230/Olympus 10.8
LT21	HT	NRM 11.3	LT650	W	NRM (E6) 11.3	SEL753	PA	N230/Olympus 10.8
LT22	HT	NRM 11.3	LT651	W	NRM (E6) 11.3	SEL754	PA	N230/Olympus 10.8
LT23	HT	NRM 11.3	LT652	W	NRM (E6) 11.3	SEL755	PA	N230/Olympus 10.8
LT24	HT	NRM 11.3	LT653	W	NRM (E6) 11.3	SEL756	PA	N230/Olympus 10.8
LT25	HT	NRM 11.3	LT654	W	NRM (E6) 11.3	SEL757	PA	N230/Olympus 10.8
LT26	HT	NRM 11.3	LT655	W	NRM (E6) 11.3	SEL758	PA	N230/Olympus 10.8
LT27	HT	NRM 11.3	LT656	W	NRM (E6) 11.3	SEL759	PA	N230/Olympus 10.8
LT28	HT	NRM 11.3	LT657	W	NRM (E6) 11.3	SEL760	PA	N230/Olympus 10.8
LT29	HT	NRM 11.3	LT658	W	NRM (E6) 11.3	SEL761	PA	N230/Olympus 10.8
LT30	KC	NRM 11.3	LT659	W	NRM (E6) 11.3	SEL762	PA	N230/Olympus 10.8
LT31	HT	NRM 11.3	LT660	W	NRM (E6) 11.3	SEL763	PA	N230/Olympus 10.8
LT32	HT	NRM 11.3	LT661	W	NRM (E6) 11.3	SEL764	PA	N230/Olympus 10.8
LT33	HT	NRM 11.3	LT662	W	NRM (E6) 11.3	SEL803	PA	N230/Olympus 10.8
LT34	HT	NRM 11.3	LT663	W	NRM (E6) 11.3	SEL804	PA	N230/Olympus 10.8
LT35	HT	NRM 11.3	LT745	HT	NRM (E6) 11.3	SEL805	PA	N230/Olympus 10.8
LT36	HT	NRM 11.3	LT746	HT	NRM (E6) 11.3	SEL806	PA	N230/Olympus 10.8
LT37	HT	NRM 11.3	LT747	HT	NRM (E6) 11.3	SEL807	PA	N230/Olympus 10.8
LT38	HT	NRM 11.3	LT748	HT	NRM (E6) 11.3	SEL808	PA	N230/Olympus 10.8
LT39	HT	NRM 11.3	LT749	HT	NRM (E6) 11.3	SEL809	PA	N230/Olympus 10.8
LT40	HT	NRM 11.3	LT750	HT	NRM (E6) 11.3	SN1919	HS	N230/OmniCity 10.8
LT95	HT	NRM 11.3	LT751	HT	NRM (E6) 11.3	SN1920	HS	N230/OmniCity 10.8
LT96	HT	NRM 11.3	LT752	HT	NRM (E6) 11.3	SN1921	HS	N230/OmniCity 10.8
LT97	HT	NRM 11.3	LT753	HT	NRM (E6) 11.3	SN1922	HS	N230/OmniCity 10.8
LT98	HT	NRM 11.3	LT754	HT	NRM (E6) 11.3	SN1923	HS	N230/OmniCity 10.8
LT99	HT	NRM 11.3	LT755	HT	NRM (E6) 11.3	SN1924	HS	N230/OmniCity 10.8
LT100	HT	NRM 11.3	LT756	HT	NRM (E6) 11.3	SN1925	HS	N230/OmniCity 10.8
LT101	HT	NRM 11.3	LT757	HT	NRM (E6) 11.3	SN1926	HS	N230/OmniCity 10.8
LT102	HT	NRM 11.3	LT758	HT	NRM (E6) 11.3	SN1927	HS	N230/OmniCity 10.8
LT103	HT	NRM 11.3	LT759	HT	NRM (E6) 11.3	SN1928	HS	N230/OmniCity 10.8
LT104	HT	NRM 11.3	LT760	HT	NRM (E6) 11.3	SN1929	HS	N230/OmniCity 10.8
LT105	HT	NRM 11.3	LT761	HT	NRM (E6) 11.3	SN1930	HS	N230/OmniCity 10.8
LT106	HT	NRM 11.3	LT762	HT	NRM (E6) 11.3	SN1931	HS	N230/OmniCity 10.8
LT107	HT	NRM 11.3	LT763	HT	NRM (E6) 11.3	SN1932	HS	N230/OmniCity 10.8
LT108	HT	NRM 11.3	LT764	HT	NRM (E6) 11.3	SN1933	HS	N230/OmniCity 10.8
LT109	HT	NRM 11.3	LT765	HT	NRM (E6) 11.3	SN1934	HS	N230/OmniCity 10.8
LT110	HT	NRM 11.3	LT766	HT	NRM (E6) 11.3	SN1935	HS	N230/OmniCity 10.8
LT111	HT	NRM 11.3	LT767	HT	NRM (E6) 11.3	SN1936	HS	N230/OmniCity 10.8
LT112	HT	NRM 11.3	LT789	W	NRM (E6) 11.3	SN1937	HS	N230/OmniCity 10.8
LT113	HT	NRM 11.3	LT790	W	NRM (E6) 11.3	SN1938	HS	N230/OmniCity 10.8
LT114	HT	NRM 11.3	LT791	W	NRM (E6) 11.3	SN1939	HS	N230/OmniCity 10.8
LT115	HT	NRM 11.3	LT792	W	NRM (E6) 11.3	SN1940	HS	N230/OmniCity 10.8

No.	G.	Type	No.	G.	Type	No.	G.	Type
SN1941	HS	N230/OmniCity 10.8	TE732	EW	Trident/E400 10.1	TE931	PB	Trident/E400 10.1
SN1942	HS	N230/OmniCity 10.8	TE733	EW	Trident/E400 10.1	TE932	PB	Trident/E400 10.1
SN1943	HS	N230/OmniCity 10.8	TE734	EW	Trident/E400 10.1	TE933	PB	Trident/E400 10.1
SN1944	HS	N230/OmniCity 10.8	TE735	EW	Trident/E400 10.1	TE934	PB	Trident/E400 10.1
SN1945	HS	N230/OmniCity 10.8	TE736	EW	Trident/E400 10.1	TE935	PB	Trident/E400 10.1
SN1946	HS	N230/OmniCity 10.8	TE737	EW	Trident/E400 10.1	TE936	PB	Trident/E400 10.1
SN1947	HS	N230/OmniCity 10.8	TE738	EW	Trident/E400 10.1	TE937	PB	Trident/E400 10.1
SN1948	HS	N230/OmniCity 10.8	TE828	EW	Trident/E400 10.1	TE938	PB	Trident/E400 10.1
SN1949	HS	N230/OmniCity 10.8	TE829	EW	Trident/E400 10.1	TE939	PB	Trident/E400 10.1
SN1950	HS	N230/OmniCity 10.8	TE830	EW	Trident/E400 10.1	TE940	PB	Trident/E400 10.1
SN1951	HS	N230/OmniCity 10.8	TE831	EW	Trident/E400 10.1	TE941	PB	Trident/E400 10.1
SN1952	HS	N230/OmniCity 10.8	TE832	EW	Trident/E400 10.1	TE942	PB	Trident/E400 10.1
SN1953	HS	N230/OmniCity 10.8	TE833	EW	Trident/E400 10.1	TE943	PB	Trident/E400 10.1
SN1954	HS	N230/OmniCity 10.8	TE834	EW	Trident/E400 10.1	TE944	PB	Trident/E400 10.1
SN1955	HS	N230/OmniCity 10.8	TE835	EW	Trident/E400 10.1	TE945	PB	Trident/E400 10.1
SN1956	HS	N230/OmniCity 10.8	TE836	EW	Trident/E400 10.1	TE946	PB	Trident/E400 10.1
SN1957	HS	N230/OmniCity 10.8	TE837	EW	Trident/E400 10.1	TE947	PB	Trident/E400 10.1
ST812	HT	NRM (E6) 10.2	TE838	EW	Trident/E400 10.1	TE948	PB	Trident/E400 10.1
TA641	W	Trident/ALX400 9.9	TE839	EW	Trident/E400 10.1	TE949	PB	Trident/E400 10.1
TA642	W	Trident/ALX400 9.9	TE840	EW	Trident/E400 10.1	TE950	PB	Trident/E400 10.1
TA643	W	Trident/ALX400 9.9	TE841	EW	Trident/E400 10.1	TE951	PB	Trident/E400 10.1
TA645	W	Trident/ALX400 9.9	TE842	EW	Trident/E400 10.1	TE976	EW	Trident/E400 10.1
TA648	W	Trident/ALX400 9.9	TE843	EW	Trident/E400 10.1	TE977	EW	Trident/E400 10.1
TA649	W	Trident/ALX400 9.9	TE844	EW	Trident/E400 10.1	TE978	EW	Trident/E400 10.1
TA653	W	Trident/ALX400 9.9	TE845	EW	Trident/E400 10.1	TE979	EW	Trident/E400 10.1
TA657	W	Trident/ALX400 9.9	TE846	EW	Trident/E400 10.1	TE980	EW	Trident/E400 10.1
TA659	W	Trident/ALX400 9.9	TE847	EW	Trident/E400 10.1	TE981	EW	Trident/E400 10.1
TE665	HT	Trident/E400 10.1	TE878	EW	Trident/E400 10.1	TE982	EW	Trident/E400 10.1
TE666	HT	Trident/E400 10.1	TE879	EW	Trident/E400 10.1	TE983	EW	Trident/E400 10.1
TE667	HT	Trident/E400 10.1	TE880	EW	Trident/E400 10.1	TE984	EW	Trident/E400 10.1
TE668	HT	Trident/E400 10.1	TE881	EW	Trident/E400 10.1	TE985	EW	Trident/E400 10.1
TE669	HT	Trident/E400 10.1	TE882	EW	Trident/E400 10.1	TE986	EW	Trident/E400 10.1
TE670	HT	Trident/E400 10.1	TE883	EW	Trident/E400 10.1	TE987	EW	Trident/E400 10.1
TE671	HT	Trident/E400 10.1	TE884	EW	Trident/E400 10.1	TE988	EW	Trident/E400 10.1
TE672	HT	Trident/E400 10.1	TE885	EW	Trident/E400 10.1	TE989	EW	Trident/E400 10.1
TE673	HT	Trident/E400 10.1	TE886	EW	Trident/E400 10.1	TE990	EW	Trident/E400 10.1
TE674	HT	Trident/E400 10.1	TE887	EW	Trident/E400 10.1	TE991	EW	Trident/E400 10.1
TE675	HT	Trident/E400 10.1	TE888	EW	Trident/E400 10.1	TE992	EW	Trident/E400 10.1
TE676	HT	Trident/E400 10.1	TE889	EW	Trident/E400 10.1	TE1073	HT	Trident/E400 10.1
TE677	HT	Trident/E400 10.1	TE890	EW	Trident/E400 10.1	TE1074	PB	Trident/E400 10.1
TE678	HT	Trident/E400 10.1	TE891	EW	Trident/E400 10.1	TE1075	HT	Trident/E400 10.1
TE679	HT	Trident/E400 10.1	TE892	EW	Trident/E400 10.1	TE1076	HT	Trident/E400 10.1
TE680	HT	Trident/E400 10.1	TE893	EW	Trident/E400 10.1	TE1077	HT	Trident/E400 10.1
TE681	HT	Trident/E400 10.1	TE894	PB	Trident/E400 10.1	TE1078	HT	Trident/E400 10.1
TE682	HT	Trident/E400 10.1	TE895	PB	Trident/E400 10.1	TE1079	HT	Trident/E400 10.1
TE683	HT	Trident/E400 10.1	TE896	PB	Trident/E400 10.1	TE1080	HT	Trident/E400 10.1
TE684	HT	Trident/E400 10.1	TE897	EW	Trident/E400 10.1	TE1081	HT	Trident/E400 10.1
TE685	HT	Trident/E400 10.1	TE898	PB	Trident/E400 10.1	TE1082	HT	Trident/E400 10.1
TE686	HT	Trident/E400 10.1	TE899	PB	Trident/E400 10.1	TE1083	HT	Trident/E400 10.1
TE687	HT	Trident/E400 10.1	TE900	PB	Trident/E400 10.1	TE1084	HT	Trident/E400 10.1
TE688	HT	Trident/E400 10.1	TE901	PB	Trident/E400 10.1	TE1085	HT	Trident/E400 10.1
TE689	HT	Trident/E400 10.1	TE902	PB	Trident/E400 10.1	TE1086	HT	Trident/E400 10.1
TE690	HT	Trident/E400 10.1	TE903	PB	Trident/E400 10.1	TE1087	HT	Trident/E400 10.1
TE691	HT	Trident/E400 10.1	TE904	PB	Trident/E400 10.1	TE1088	PB	Trident/E400 10.1
TE692	HT	Trident/E400 10.1	TE905	PB	Trident/E400 10.1	TE1089	HT	Trident/E400 10.1
TE712	EW	Trident/E400 10.1	TE906	PB	Trident/E400 10.1	TE1090	PB	Trident/E400 10.1
TE713	EW	Trident/E400 10.1	TE907	PB	Trident/E400 10.1	TE1091	PB	Trident/E400 10.1
TE714	EW	Trident/E400 10.1	TE908	PB	Trident/E400 10.1	TE1092	PB	Trident/E400 10.1
TE715	EW	Trident/E400 10.1	TE909	PB	Trident/E400 10.1	TE1093	PB	Trident/E400 10.1
TE716	EW	Trident/E400 10.1	TE910	PB	Trident/E400 10.1	TE1094	PB	Trident/E400 10.1
TE717	EW	Trident/E400 10.1	TE911	PB	Trident/E400 10.1	TE1095	PB	Trident/E400 10.1
TE718	EW	Trident/E400 10.1	TE912	PB	Trident/E400 10.1	TE1096	PB	Trident/E400 10.1
TE719	EW	Trident/E400 10.1	TE913	PB	Trident/E400 10.1	TE1097	PB	Trident/E400 10.1
TE720	EW	Trident/E400 10.1	TE914	PB	Trident/E400 10.1	TE1098	PB	Trident/E400 10.1
TE721	EW	Trident/E400 10.1	TE920	HT	Trident/E400 10.1	TE1099	PB	Trident/E400 10.1
TE722	EW	Trident/E400 10.1	TE921	PB	Trident/E400 10.1	TE1100	HT	Trident/E400 10.1
TE723	EW	Trident/E400 10.1	TE922	PB	Trident/E400 10.1	TE1101	PB	Trident/E400 10.1
TE724	EW	Trident/E400 10.1	TE923	PB	Trident/E400 10.1	TE1102	PB	Trident/E400 10.1
TE725	EW	Trident/E400 10.1	TE924	PB	Trident/E400 10.1	TE1103	HT	Trident/E400 10.1
TE726	EW	Trident/E400 10.1	TE925	PB	Trident/E400 10.1	TE1104	PB	Trident/E400 10.1
TE727	EW	Trident/E400 10.1	TE926	PB	Trident/E400 10.1	TE1307	HT	E40D/E400 (EC) 10.2
TE728	EW	Trident/E400 10.1	TE927	PB	Trident/E400 10.1	TE1308	HT	E40D/E400 (EC) 10.2
TE729	EW	Trident/E400 10.1	TE928	PB	Trident/E400 10.1	TE1309	HT	E40D/E400 (EC) 10.2
TE730	EW	Trident/E400 10.1	TE929	PB	Trident/E400 10.1	TE1310	HT	E40D/E400 (EC) 10.2
TE731	EW	Trident/E400 10.1	TE930	PB	Trident/E400 10.1	TE1311	HT	E40D/E400 (EC) 10.2

Metroline

No.	G.	Type	No.	G.	Type	No.	G.	Type
TE1312	HT	E40D/E400 (EC) 10.2	TE1742	UX	Trident/E400 10.1	TEH1452	W	E40H/E400 (EC) 10.2
TE1313	HT	E40D/E400 (EC) 10.2	TE1743	UX	Trident/E400 10.1	TEH1453	W	E40H/E400 (EC) 10.2
TE1314	W	E40D/E400 (EC) 10.2	TE1744	UX	Trident/E400 10.1	TEH1454	W	E40H/E400 (EC) 10.2
TE1315	HT	E40D/E400 (EC) 10.2	TE1745	UX	Trident/E400 10.1	TEH1455	W	E40H/E400 (EC) 10.2
TE1316	HT	E40D/E400 (EC) 10.2	TE1746	UX	Trident/E400 10.1	TEH1456	W	E40H/E400 (EC) 10.2
TE1317	HT	E40D/E400 (EC) 10.2	TE1747	UX	Trident/E400 10.1	TEH1457	W	E40H/E400 (EC) 10.2
TE1420	PB	E40D/E400 (EC) 10.2	TE1748	UX	Trident/E400 10.1	TEH1458	W	E40H/E400 (EC) 10.2
TE1421	PB	E40D/E400 (EC) 10.2	TE1749	UX	Trident/E400 10.1	TEH1459	W	E40H/E400 (EC) 10.2
TE1422	PB	E40D/E400 (EC) 10.2	TE1750	UX	Trident/E400 10.1	TEH1460	W	E40H/E400 (EC) 10.2
TE1423	PB	E40D/E400 (EC) 10.2	TE1751	UX	Trident/E400 10.1	TEH1461	W	E40H/E400 (EC) 10.2
TE1424	PB	E40D/E400 (EC) 10.2	TE1981	G	E40D/E400 (EC) 10.2	TEH1462	W	E40H/E400 (EC) 10.2
TE1425	PB	E40D/E400 (EC) 10.2	TE1982	G	E40D/E400 (EC) 10.2	TEH1463	W	E40H/E400 (EC) 10.2
TE1426	PB	E40D/E400 (EC) 10.2	TE1983	G	E40D/E400 (EC) 10.2	TEH1464	W	E40H/E400 (EC) 10.2
TE1427	PB	E40D/E400 (EC) 10.2	TE1984	G	E40D/E400 (EC) 10.2	TEH1465	W	E40H/E400 (EC) 10.2
TE1428	PB	E40D/E400 (EC) 10.2	TE1985	G	E40D/E400 (EC) 10.2	TEH1466	W	E40H/E400 (EC) 10.2
TE1429	PB	E40D/E400 (EC) 10.2	TE1986	G	E40D/E400 (EC) 10.2	TEH1467	W	E40H/E400 (EC) 10.2
TE1430	PB	E40D/E400 (EC) 10.2	TE1987	G	E40D/E400 (EC) 10.2	TEH2072	W	E40H/E400MMC 10.35
TE1431	PB	E40D/E400 (EC) 10.2	TE1988	G	E40D/E400 (EC) 10.2	TEH2073	W	E40H/E400MMC 10.35
TE1432	PB	E40D/E400 (EC) 10.2	TE1989	G	E40D/E400 (EC) 10.2	TEH2074	W	E40H/E400MMC 10.35
TE1433	PB	E40D/E400 (EC) 10.2	TE1990	G	E40D/E400 (EC) 10.2	TEH2075	W	E40H/E400MMC 10.35
TE1434	PB	E40D/E400 (EC) 10.2	TE1991	G	E40D/E400 (EC) 10.2	TEH2076	W	E40H/E400MMC 10.35
TE1435	PB	E40D/E400 (EC) 10.2	TE1992	G	E40D/E400 (EC) 10.2	TEH2077	W	E40H/E400MMC 10.35
TE1436	PB	E40D/E400 (EC) 10.2	TE1993	G	E40D/E400 (EC) 10.2	TEH2078	W	E40H/E400MMC 10.35
TE1437	PB	E40D/E400 (EC) 10.2	TE1994	G	E40D/E400 (EC) 10.2	TEH2079	W	E40H/E400MMC 10.35
TE1438	PB	E40D/E400 (EC) 10.2	TE1995	G	E40D/E400 (EC) 10.2	TEH2080	W	E40H/E400MMC 10.35
TE1439	PB	E40D/E400 (EC) 10.2	TE1996	G	E40D/E400 (EC) 10.2	TEH2081	W	E40H/E400MMC 10.35
TE1440	PB	E40D/E400 (EC) 10.2	TE1997	G	E40D/E400 (EC) 10.2	TEH2082	W	E40H/E400MMC 10.35
TE1441	PB	E40D/E400 (EC) 10.2	TE1998	G	E40D/E400 (EC) 10.2	TEH2083	W	E40H/E400MMC 10.35
TE1442	PB	E40D/E400 (EC) 10.2	TE1999	G	E40D/E400 (EC) 10.2	TEH2084	W	E40H/E400MMC 10.35
TE1443	PB	E40D/E400 (EC) 10.2	TE2000	G	E40D/E400 (EC) 10.2	TEH2085	W	E40H/E400MMC 10.35
TE1444	PB	E40D/E400 (EC) 10.2	TEH915	W	Trident/E400H 10.1	TEH2086	W	E40H/E400MMC 10.35
TE1445	PB	E40D/E400 (EC) 10.2	TEH916	W	Trident/E400H 10.1	TEH2087	W	E40H/E400MMC 10.35
TE1446	PB	E40D/E400 (EC) 10.2	TEH917	W	Trident/E400H 10.1	VP466	HD	B7TL/President 10.0
TE1447	PB	E40D/E400 (EC) 10.2	TEH918	W	Trident/E400H 10.1	VP468	HD	B7TL/President 10.0
TE1448	PB	E40D/E400 (EC) 10.2	TEH919	W	Trident/E400H 10.1	VP469	HD	B7TL/President 10.0
TE1571	UX	Trident/E400 10.1	TEH1105	W	Trident/E400H 10.1	VP470	HD	B7TL/President 10.0
TE1572	UX	Trident/E400 10.1	TEH1106	W	Trident/E400H 10.1	VP471	HD	B7TL/President 10.0
TE1573	UX	Trident/E400 10.1	TEH1107	W	Trident/E400H 10.1	VP472	HD	B7TL/President 10.0
TE1574	UX	Trident/E400 10.1	TEH1108	W	Trident/E400H 10.1	VP474	UX	B7TL/President 10.0
TE1575	UX	Trident/E400 10.1	TEH1109	W	Trident/E400H 10.1	VP475	UX	B7TL/President 10.0
TE1576	UX	Trident/E400 10.1	TEH1110	W	Trident/E400H 10.1	VP476	UX	B7TL/President 10.0
TE1577	UX	Trident/E400 10.1	TEH1111	W	Trident/E400H 10.1	VP477	UX	B7TL/President 10.0
TE1578	UX	Trident/E400 10.1	TEH1112	W	Trident/E400H 10.1	VP478	UX	B7TL/President 10.0
TE1579	UX	Trident/E400 10.1	TEH1113	W	Trident/E400H 10.1	VP479	UX	B7TL/President 10.0
TE1580	UX	Trident/E400 10.1	TEH1114	W	Trident/E400H 10.1	VP481	UX	B7TL/President 10.0
TE1581	UX	Trident/E400 10.1	TEH1217	W	E40H/E400 (EC) 10.2	VP482	UX	B7TL/President 10.0
TE1582	UX	Trident/E400 10.1	TEH1218	W	E40H/E400 (EC) 10.2	VP483	HT	B7TL/President 10.0
TE1715	G	Trident/E400 10.1	TEH1219	W	E40H/E400 (EC) 10.2	VP485	HD	B7TL/President 10.0
TE1716	G	Trident/E400 10.1	TEH1220	W	E40H/E400 (EC) 10.2	VP486	HD	B7TL/President 10.0
TE1717	G	Trident/E400 10.1	TEH1221	W	E40H/E400 (EC) 10.2	VP489	HT	B7TL/President 10.0
TE1718	G	Trident/E400 10.1	TEH1222	W	E40H/E400 (EC) 10.2	VP490	HT	B7TL/President 10.0
TE1719	G	Trident/E400 10.1	TEH1223	W	E40H/E400 (EC) 10.2	VP491	HT	B7TL/President 10.0
TE1720	G	Trident/E400 10.1	TEH1224	W	E40H/E400 (EC) 10.2	VP492	HT	B7TL/President 10.0
TE1721	G	Trident/E400 10.1	TEH1225	W	E40H/E400 (EC) 10.2	VP493	AC	B7TL/President 10.0
TE1722	G	Trident/E400 10.1	TEH1226	W	E40H/E400 (EC) 10.2	VP494	HT	B7TL/President 10.0
TE1723	G	Trident/E400 10.1	TEH1227	W	E40H/E400 (EC) 10.2	VP495	HT	B7TL/President 10.0
TE1724	G	Trident/E400 10.1	TEH1228	W	E40H/E400 (EC) 10.2	VP496	HT	B7TL/President 10.0
TE1725	G	Trident/E400 10.1	TEH1229	W	E40H/E400 (EC) 10.2	VP497	HT	B7TL/President 10.0
TE1726	HS	Trident/E400 10.1	TEH1230	W	E40H/E400 (HS) 10.2	VP498	HT	B7TL/President 10.0
TE1727	G	Trident/E400 10.1	TEH1231	W	E40H/E400 (EC) 10.2	VP499	HT	B7TL/President 10.0
TE1728	G	Trident/E400 10.1	TEH1232	W	E40H/E400 (EC) 10.2	VP500	HT	B7TL/President 10.0
TE1729	G	Trident/E400 10.1	TEH1233	W	E40H/E400 (EC) 10.2	VP501	HT	B7TL/President 10.0
TE1730	G	Trident/E400 10.1	TEH1234	W	E40H/E400 (EC) 10.2	VP502	HT	B7TL/President 10.0
TE1731	G	Trident/E400 10.1	TEH1235	W	E40H/E400 (EC) 10.2	VP503	HT	B7TL/President 10.0
TE1732	G	Trident/E400 10.1	TEH1236	W	E40H/E400 (EC) 10.2	VP504	AC	B7TL/President 10.0
TE1733	G	Trident/E400 10.1	TEH1237	W	E40H/E400 (EC) 10.2	VP505	AC	B7TL/President 10.0
TE1734	G	Trident/E400 10.1	TEH1238	W	E40H/E400 (EC) 10.2	VP506	AC	B7TL/President 10.0
TE1735	G	Trident/E400 10.1	TEH1239	W	E40H/E400 (EC) 10.2	VP507	UX	B7TL/President 10.0
TE1736	G	Trident/E400 10.1	TEH1240	W	E40H/E400 (EC) 10.2	VP508	AC	B7TL/President 10.0
TE1737	G	Trident/E400 10.1	TEH1241	W	E40H/E400 (EC) 10.2	VP509	AC	B7TL/President 10.0
TE1738	G	Trident/E400 10.1	TEH1242	W	E40H/E400 (EC) 10.2	VP510	HT	B7TL/President 10.0
TE1739	G	Trident/E400 10.1	TEH1449	W	E40H/E400 (EC) 10.2	VP511	HT	B7TL/President 10.0
TE1740	G	Trident/E400 10.1	TEH1450	W	E40H/E400 (EC) 10.2	VP512	HT	B7TL/President 10.0
TE1741	G	Trident/E400 10.1	TEH1451	W	E40H/E400 (EC) 10.2	VP513	HT	B7TL/President 10.0

No.	G.	Type	No.	G.	Type	No.	G.	Type
VP514	AC	B7TL/President 10.0	VP608	UX	B7TL/President 10.0	VW1055	AH	B9TL/Gemini 2 10.4
VP515	AC	B7TL/President 10.0	VP609	UX	B7TL/President 10.0	VW1056	AH	B9TL/Gemini 2 10.4
VP516	AC	B7TL/President 10.0	VP610	UX	B7TL/President 10.0	VW1057	AH	B9TL/Gemini 2 10.4
VP517	AC	B7TL/President 10.0	VP611	UX	B7TL/President 10.0	VW1058	AH	B9TL/Gemini 2 10.4
VP518	AC	B7TL/President 10.0	VP612	UX	B7TL/President 10.0	VW1059	AH	B9TL/Gemini 2 10.4
VP519	AC	B7TL/President 10.0	VP613	HD	B7TL/President 10.0	VW1060	AH	B9TL/Gemini 2 10.4
VP520	AC	B7TL/President 10.0	VP614	HD	B7TL/President 10.0	VW1061	AH	B9TL/Gemini 2 10.4
VP521	AC	B7TL/President 10.0	VP615	HD	B7TL/President 10.0	VW1062	AH	B9TL/Gemini 2 10.4
VP522	AC	B7TL/President 10.0	VP616	HD	B7TL/President 10.0	VW1063	AH	B9TL/Gemini 2 10.4
VP523	AC	B7TL/President 10.0	VP617	HD	B7TL/President 10.0	VW1064	AH	B9TL/Gemini 2 10.4
VP524	AC	B7TL/President 10.0	VP618	HD	B7TL/President 10.0	VW1065	AH	B9TL/Gemini 2 10.4
VP525	AC	B7TL/President 10.0	VP619	HD	B7TL/President 10.0	VW1066	AH	B9TL/Gemini 2 10.4
VP526	AC	B7TL/President 10.0	VP620	HD	B7TL/President 10.0	VW1067	AH	B9TL/Gemini 2 10.4
VP527	AC	B7TL/President 10.0	VP621	HD	B7TL/President 10.0	VW1068	AH	B9TL/Gemini 2 10.4
VP528	AC	B7TL/President 10.0	VP622	HD	B7TL/President 10.0	VW1069	AH	B9TL/Gemini 2 10.4
VP529	AC	B7TL/President 10.0	VP623	HD	B7TL/President 10.0	VW1070	AH	B9TL/Gemini 2 10.4
VP530	AC	B7TL/President 10.0	VP624	HS	B7TL/President 10.0	VW1071	AH	B9TL/Gemini 2 10.4
VP531	AC	B7TL/President 10.0	VP625	HD	B7TL/President 10.0	VW1072	AH	B9TL/Gemini 2 10.4
VP532	AC	B7TL/President 10.0	VP626	HD	B7TL/President 10.0	VW1175	PA	B9TL/Gemini 2 10.4
VP533	AC	B7TL/President 10.0	VP627	HD	B7TL/President 10.0	VW1176	PA	B9TL/Gemini 2 10.4
VP534	AC	B7TL/President 10.0	VP628	HD	B7TL/President 10.0	VW1177	PA	B9TL/Gemini 2 10.4
VP535	AC	B7TL/President 10.0	VPL581	HT	B7TL/President 10.6	VW1178	PA	B9TL/Gemini 2 10.4
VP536	AC	B7TL/President 10.0	VPL582	HT	B7TL/President 10.6	VW1179	PA	B9TL/Gemini 2 10.4
VP537	AC	B7TL/President 10.0	VPL583	HT	B7TL/President 10.6	VW1180	PA	B9TL/Gemini 2 10.4
VP538	AC	B7TL/President 10.0	VPL584	HT	B7TL/President 10.6	VW1181	PA	B9TL/Gemini 2 10.4
VP539	AC	B7TL/President 10.0	VPL585	HT	B7TL/President 10.6	VW1182	PA	B9TL/Gemini 2 10.4
VP540	AC	B7TL/President 10.0	VPL586	HT	B7TL/President 10.6	VW1183	PA	B9TL/Gemini 2 10.4
VP541	AC	B7TL/President 10.0	VPL587	HT	B7TL/President 10.6	VW1184	PA	B9TL/Gemini 2 10.4
VP542	AC	B7TL/President 10.0	VPL588	HT	B7TL/President 10.6	VW1185	PA	B9TL/Gemini 2 10.4
VP543	AC	B7TL/President 10.0	VPL589	HT	B7TL/President 10.6	VW1186	PA	B9TL/Gemini 2 10.4
VP544	AC	B7TL/President 10.0	VPL590	HT	B7TL/President 10.6	VW1187	PA	B9TL/Gemini 2 10.4
VP545	AC	B7TL/President 10.0	VPL591	HT	B7TL/President 10.6	VW1188	PA	B9TL/Gemini 2 10.4
VP546	AC	B7TL/President 10.0	VPL592	HT	B7TL/President 10.6	VW1189	PA	B9TL/Gemini 2 10.4
VP547	AC	B7TL/President 10.0	VPL593	HT	B7TL/President 10.6	VW1190	PA	B9TL/Gemini 2 10.4
VP548	AC	B7TL/President 10.0	VPL594	HT	B7TL/President 10.6	VW1191	PA	B9TL/Gemini 2 10.4
VP549	AC	B7TL/President 10.0	VPL595	HT	B7TL/President 10.6	VW1192	PA	B9TL/Gemini 2 10.4
VP550	AC	B7TL/President 10.0	VPL596	HT	B7TL/President 10.6	VW1193	PA	B9TL/Gemini 2 10.4
VP551	AC	B7TL/President 10.0	VPL597	HT	B7TL/President 10.6	VW1194	PA	B9TL/Gemini 2 10.4
VP552	AC	B7TL/President 10.0	VPL598	HT	B7TL/President 10.6	VW1195	PA	B9TL/Gemini 2 10.4
VP553	AC	B7TL/President 10.0	VPL599	HT	B7TL/President 10.6	VW1196	PA	B9TL/Gemini 2 10.4
VP554	AC	B7TL/President 10.0	VPL600	HT	B7TL/President 10.6	VW1197	PA	B9TL/Gemini 2 10.4
VP555	AC	B7TL/President 10.0	VPL601	HT	B7TL/President 10.6	VW1198	PA	B9TL/Gemini 2 10.4
VP556	AC	B7TL/President 10.0	VPL602	HT	B7TL/President 10.6	VW1199	PA	B9TL/Gemini 2 10.4
VP556	AC	B7TL/President 10.0	VPL603	HT	B7TL/President 10.6	VW1200	PV	B9TL/Gemini 2 10.4
VP557	AC	B7TL/President 10.0	VPL629	HT	B7TL/President 10.6	VW1201	PV	B9TL/Gemini 2 10.4
VP557	AC	B7TL/President 10.0	VPL630	HT	B7TL/President 10.6	VW1202	PV	B9TL/Gemini 2 10.4
VP558	AC	B7TL/President 10.0	VPL631	HT	B7TL/President 10.6	VW1203	PV	B9TL/Gemini 2 10.4
VP558	AC	B7TL/President 10.0	VPL632	HT	B7TL/President 10.6	VW1204	PV	B9TL/Gemini 2 10.4
VP559	AC	B7TL/President 10.0	VPL633	HT	B7TL/President 10.6	VW1205	PV	B9TL/Gemini 2 (EC) 10.5
VP560	AC	B7TL/President 10.0	VPL634	HT	B7TL/President 10.6	VW1206	PV	B9TL/Gemini 2 (EC) 10.5
VP561	AC	B7TL/President 10.0	VPL635	HT	B7TL/President 10.6	VW1207	PV	B9TL/Gemini 2 (EC) 10.5
VP562	AC	B7TL/President 10.0	VPL636	HT	B7TL/President 10.6	VW1208	PV	B9TL/Gemini 2 (EC) 10.5
VP563	AC	B7TL/President 10.0	VPL637	HT	B7TL/President 10.6	VW1209	PV	B9TL/Gemini 2 (EC) 10.5
VP564	AC	B7TL/President 10.0	VW1034	AH	B9TL/Gemini 2 10.4	VW1210	PV	B9TL/Gemini 2 (EC) 10.5
VP565	AC	B7TL/President 10.0	VW1035	AH	B9TL/Gemini 2 10.4	VW1211	PA	B9TL/Gemini 2 (EC) 10.5
VP566	AC	B7TL/President 10.0	VW1036	AH	B9TL/Gemini 2 10.4	VW1212	AH	B9TL/Gemini 2 (EC) 10.5
VP567	AC	B7TL/President 10.0	VW1037	AH	B9TL/Gemini 2 10.4	VW1213	AH	B9TL/Gemini 2 (EC) 10.5
VP568	AC	B7TL/President 10.0	VW1038	AH	B9TL/Gemini 2 10.4	VW1214	AH	B9TL/Gemini 2 (EC) 10.5
VP569	AC	B7TL/President 10.0	VW1039	AH	B9TL/Gemini 2 10.4	VW1215	AH	B9TL/Gemini 2 (EC) 10.5
VP570	AC	B7TL/President 10.0	VW1040	AH	B9TL/Gemini 2 10.4	VW1216	AH	B9TL/Gemini 2 (EC) 10.5
VP571	AC	B7TL/President 10.0	VW1041	AH	B9TL/Gemini 2 10.4	No.		
VP572	AC	B7TL/President 10.0	VW1042	AH	B9TL/Gemini 2 10.4	VW1243	ON	B9TL/Gemini 2 (EC) 10.5
VP573	AC	B7TL/President 10.0	VW1043	AH	B9TL/Gemini 2 10.4	VW1244	ON	B9TL/Gemini 2 (EC) 10.5
VP574	AC	B7TL/President 10.0	VW1044	AH	B9TL/Gemini 2 10.4	VW1245	ON	B9TL/Gemini 2 (EC) 10.5
VP575	AC	B7TL/President 10.0	VW1045	AH	B9TL/Gemini 2 10.4	VW1246	ON	B9TL/Gemini 2 (EC) 10.5
VP576	AC	B7TL/President 10.0	VW1046	AH	B9TL/Gemini 2 10.4	VW1247	ON	B9TL/Gemini 2 (EC) 10.5
VP577	AC	B7TL/President 10.0	VW1047	AH	B9TL/Gemini 2 10.4	VW1248	ON	B9TL/Gemini 2 (EC) 10.5
VP578	AC	B7TL/President 10.0	VW1048	AH	B9TL/Gemini 2 10.4	VW1249	AH	B9TL/Gemini 2 (EC) 10.5
VP579	AC	B7TL/President 10.0	VW1049	AH	B9TL/Gemini 2 10.4	VW1250	AH	B9TL/Gemini 2 (EC) 10.5
VP580	AC	B7TL/President 10.0	VW1050	AH	B9TL/Gemini 2 10.4	VW1251	AH	B9TL/Gemini 2 (EC) 10.5
VP604	UX	B7TL/President 10.0	VW1051	AH	B9TL/Gemini 2 10.4	VW1252	AH	B9TL/Gemini 2 (EC) 10.5
VP605	UX	B7TL/President 10.0	VW1052	AH	B9TL/Gemini 2 10.4	VW1253	AH	B9TL/Gemini 2 (EC) 10.5
VP606	UX	B7TL/President 10.0	VW1053	AH	B9TL/Gemini 2 10.4	VW1254	AH	B9TL/Gemini 2 (EC) 10.5
VP607	UX	B7TL/President 10.0	VW1054	AH	B9TL/Gemini 2 10.4	VW1255	AH	B9TL/Gemini 2 (EC) 10.5
						VW1256	AH	B9TL/Gemini 2 (EC) 10.5

Metroline

No.	G.	Type
VW1257	HT	B9TL/Gemini 2 (EC) 10.5
VW1258	AH	B9TL/Gemini 2 (EC) 10.5
VW1259	AH	B9TL/Gemini 2 (EC) 10.5
VW1260	AH	B9TL/Gemini 2 (EC) 10.5
VW1261	ON	B9TL/Gemini 2 (EC) 10.5
VW1262	AH	B9TL/Gemini 2 (EC) 10.5
VW1263	AH	B9TL/Gemini 2 (EC) 10.5
VW1264	HT	B9TL/Gemini 2 (EC) 10.5
VW1265	ON	B9TL/Gemini 2 (EC) 10.5
VW1266	HT	B9TL/Gemini 2 (EC) 10.5
VW1267	ON	B9TL/Gemini 2 (EC) 10.5
VW1268	HT	B9TL/Gemini 2 (EC) 10.5
VW1269	HT	B9TL/Gemini 2 (EC) 10.5
VW1270	ON	B9TL/Gemini 2 (EC) 10.5
VW1271	HT	B9TL/Gemini 2 (EC) 10.5
VW1272	HT	B9TL/Gemini 2 (EC) 10.5
VW1273	HT	B9TL/Gemini 2 (EC) 10.5
VW1274	ON	B9TL/Gemini 2 (EC) 10.5
VW1275	ON	B9TL/Gemini 2 (EC) 10.5
VW1276	ON	B9TL/Gemini 2 (EC) 10.5
VW1277	HT	B9TL/Gemini 2 (EC) 10.5
VW1278	ON	B9TL/Gemini 2 (EC) 10.5
VW1279	HT	B9TL/Gemini 2 (EC) 10.5
VW1280	HT	B9TL/Gemini 2 (EC) 10.5
VW1281	HT	B9TL/Gemini 2 (EC) 10.5
VW1282	HT	B9TL/Gemini 2 (EC) 10.5
VW1283	HT	B9TL/Gemini 2 (EC) 10.5
VW1284	HT	B9TL/Gemini 2 (EC) 10.5
VW1285	HT	B9TL/Gemini 2 (EC) 10.5
VW1286	HT	B9TL/Gemini 2 (EC) 10.5
VW1287	HT	B9TL/Gemini 2 (EC) 10.5
VW1288	HT	B9TL/Gemini 2 (EC) 10.5
VW1289	HT	B9TL/Gemini 2 (EC) 10.5
VW1290	HT	B9TL/Gemini 2 (EC) 10.5
VW1291	HT	B9TL/Gemini 2 (EC) 10.5
VW1292	HT	B9TL/Gemini 2 (EC) 10.5
VW1293	HT	B9TL/Gemini 2 (EC) 10.5
VW1294	HT	B9TL/Gemini 2 (EC) 10.5
VW1295	HT	B9TL/Gemini 2 (EC) 10.5
VW1296	HT	B9TL/Gemini 2 (EC) 10.5
VW1297	HT	B9TL/Gemini 2 (EC) 10.5
VW1298	HT	B9TL/Gemini 2 (EC) 10.5
VW1299	HT	B9TL/Gemini 2 (EC) 10.5
VW1300	HT	B9TL/Gemini 2 (EC) 10.5
VW1301	HT	B9TL/Gemini 2 (EC) 10.5
VW1302	HT	B9TL/Gemini 2 (EC) 10.5
VW1303	HT	B9TL/Gemini 2 (EC) 10.5
VW1304	HT	B9TL/Gemini 2 (EC) 10.5
VW1305	HT	B9TL/Gemini 2 (EC) 10.5
VW1306	HT	B9TL/Gemini 2 (EC) 10.5
VW1365	PV	B9TL/Gemini 2 (EC) 10.5
VW1366	PV	B9TL/Gemini 2 (EC) 10.5
VW1367	PV	B9TL/Gemini 2 (EC) 10.5
VW1368	PV	B9TL/Gemini 2 (EC) 10.5
VW1369	PV	B9TL/Gemini 2 (EC) 10.5
VW1370	PV	B9TL/Gemini 2 (EC) 10.5
VW1371	PV	B9TL/Gemini 2 (EC) 10.5
VW1372	PV	B9TL/Gemini 2 (EC) 10.5
VW1373	PV	B9TL/Gemini 2 (EC) 10.5
VW1374	PV	B9TL/Gemini 2 (EC) 10.5
VW1375	PV	B9TL/Gemini 2 (EC) 10.5
VW1376	PV	B9TL/Gemini 2 (EC) 10.5
VW1377	PV	B9TL/Gemini 2 (EC) 10.5
VW1378	HT	B9TL/Gemini 2 (EC) 10.5
VW1379	HT	B9TL/Gemini 2 (EC) 10.5
VW1380	HT	B9TL/Gemini 2 (EC) 10.5
VW1381	HT	B9TL/Gemini 2 (EC) 10.5
VW1382	HT	B9TL/Gemini 2 (EC) 10.5
VW1383	HT	B9TL/Gemini 2 (EC) 10.5
VW1384	HT	B9TL/Gemini 2 (EC) 10.5
VW1385	HT	B9TL/Gemini 2 (EC) 10.5
VW1386	HT	B9TL/Gemini 2 (EC) 10.5
VW1387	HT	B9TL/Gemini 2 (EC) 10.5
VW1388	HT	B9TL/Gemini 2 (EC) 10.5

No.	G.	Type
VW1389	PV	B9TL/Gemini 2 (EC) 10.5
VW1390	PV	B9TL/Gemini 2 (EC) 10.5
VW1391	PV	B9TL/Gemini 2 (EC) 10.5
VW1392	PV	B9TL/Gemini 2 (EC) 10.5
VW1393	PV	B9TL/Gemini 2 (EC) 10.5
VW1394	PV	B9TL/Gemini 2 (EC) 10.5
VW1395	PV	B9TL/Gemini 2 (EC) 10.5
VW1396	PV	B9TL/Gemini 2 (EC) 10.5
VW1397	PV	B9TL/Gemini 2 (EC) 10.5
VW1398	AH	B9TL/Gemini 2 (EC) 10.5
VW1399	AC	B9TL/Gemini 2 (EC) 10.5
VW1400	AC	B9TL/Gemini 2 (EC) 10.5
VW1401	AC	B9TL/Gemini 2 (EC) 10.5
VW1402	AC	B9TL/Gemini 2 (EC) 10.5
VW1403	AC	B9TL/Gemini 2 (EC) 10.5
VW1404	AC	B9TL/Gemini 2 (EC) 10.5
VW1405	AC	B9TL/Gemini 2 (EC) 10.5
VW1406	AC	B9TL/Gemini 2 (EC) 10.5
VW1407	AC	B9TL/Gemini 2 (EC) 10.5
VW1468	HT	B9TL/Gemini 2 (EC) 10.5
VW1560	UX	B7TL/Gemini 10.1
VW1561	UX	B7TL/Gemini 10.1
VW1562	UX	B7TL/Gemini 10.1
VW1563	UX	B7TL/Gemini 10.1
VW1564	UX	B7TL/Gemini 10.1
VW1565	UX	B7TL/Gemini 10.1
VW1566	UX	B7TL/Gemini 10.1
VW1567	UX	B7TL/Gemini 10.1
VW1568	UX	B7TL/Gemini 10.1
VW1569	UX	B7TL/Gemini 10.1
VW1570	UX	B7TL/Gemini 10.1
VW1752	ON	B9TL/Gemini 2 10.4
VW1753	ON	B9TL/Gemini 2 10.4
VW1754	ON	B9TL/Gemini 2 10.4
VW1755	ON	B9TL/Gemini 2 10.4
VW1756	ON	B9TL/Gemini 2 10.4
VW1757	ON	B9TL/Gemini 2 10.4
VW1758	ON	B9TL/Gemini 2 10.4
VW1759	ON	B9TL/Gemini 2 10.4
VW1760	ON	B9TL/Gemini 2 10.4
VW1761	ON	B9TL/Gemini 2 10.4
VW1762	ON	B9TL/Gemini 2 10.4
VW1763	ON	B9TL/Gemini 2 10.4
VW1764	ON	B9TL/Gemini 2 10.4
VW1765	ON	B9TL/Gemini 2 10.4
VW1766	ON	B9TL/Gemini 2 10.4
VW1767	ON	B9TL/Gemini 2 10.4
VW1768	ON	B9TL/Gemini 2 10.4
VW1769	ON	B9TL/Gemini 2 10.4
VW1770	ON	B9TL/Gemini 2 10.4
VW1771	ON	B9TL/Gemini 2 10.4
VW1772	ON	B9TL/Gemini 2 10.4
VW1773	ON	B9TL/Gemini 2 10.4
VW1774	ON	B9TL/Gemini 2 10.4
VW1775	ON	B9TL/Gemini 2 10.4
VW1776	ON	B9TL/Gemini 2 10.4
VW1777	ON	B9TL/Gemini 2 10.4
VW1778	ON	B9TL/Gemini 2 10.4
VW1779	ON	B9TL/Gemini 2 10.4
VW1780	ON	B9TL/Gemini 2 10.4
VW1781	ON	B9TL/Gemini 2 10.4
VW1782	ON	B9TL/Gemini 2 10.4
VW1817	HS	B9TL/Gemini 2 10.4
VW1818	HS	B9TL/Gemini 2 10.4
VW1819	HS	B9TL/Gemini 2 10.4
VW1820	HS	B9TL/Gemini 2 10.4
VW1821	HS	B9TL/Gemini 2 10.4
VW1822	HS	B9TL/Gemini 2 10.4
VW1823	HS	B9TL/Gemini 2 10.4
VW1824	HS	B9TL/Gemini 2 10.4
VW1825	HS	B9TL/Gemini 2 10.4
VW1826	HS	B9TL/Gemini 2 10.4
VW1827	HS	B9TL/Gemini 2 10.4
VW1828	HS	B9TL/Gemini 2 10.4

No.	G.	Type
VW1829	HS	B9TL/Gemini 2 10.4
VW1830	HS	B9TL/Gemini 2 10.4
VW1831	HS	B9TL/Gemini 2 10.4
VW1832	HS	B9TL/Gemini 2 10.4
VW1833	HS	B9TL/Gemini 2 10.4
VW1834	HS	B9TL/Gemini 2 10.4
VW1835	HS	B9TL/Gemini 2 10.4
VW1836	HS	B9TL/Gemini 2 10.4
VW1837	HS	B9TL/Gemini 2 10.4
VW1838	HS	B9TL/Gemini 2 10.4
VW1839	HS	B9TL/Gemini 2 10.4
VW1840	HS	B9TL/Gemini 2 10.4
VW1841	ON	B9TL/Gemini 2 10.4
VW1842	ON	B9TL/Gemini 2 10.4
VW1843	ON	B9TL/Gemini 2 10.4
VW1844	AH	B9TL/Gemini 2 10.4
VW1845	AH	B9TL/Gemini 2 10.4
VW1846	WJ	B9TL/Gemini 2 10.4
VW1847	WJ	B9TL/Gemini 2 10.4
VW1848	WJ	B9TL/Gemini 2 10.4
VW1849	WJ	B9TL/Gemini 2 10.4
VW1850	WJ	B9TL/Gemini 2 10.4
VW1851	WJ	B9TL/Gemini 2 10.4
VW1852	WJ	B9TL/Gemini 2 10.4
VW1853	WJ	B9TL/Gemini 2 10.4
VW1854	WJ	B9TL/Gemini 2 10.4
VW1855	WJ	B9TL/Gemini 2 10.4
VW1856	WJ	B9TL/Gemini 2 10.4
VW1857	WJ	B9TL/Gemini 2 10.4
VW1858	WJ	B9TL/Gemini 2 10.4
VW1859	WJ	B9TL/Gemini 2 10.4
VW1860	WJ	B9TL/Gemini 2 10.4
VW1861	WJ	B9TL/Gemini 2 10.4
VW1862	WJ	B9TL/Gemini 2 10.4
VW1863	WJ	B9TL/Gemini 2 10.4
VW1864	WJ	B9TL/Gemini 2 10.4
VW1865	WJ	B9TL/Gemini 2 10.4
VW1866	WJ	B9TL/Gemini 2 10.4
VW1867	WJ	B9TL/Gemini 2 10.4
VW1868	WJ	B9TL/Gemini 2 10.4
VW1869	WJ	B9TL/Gemini 2 10.4
VW1870	WJ	B9TL/Gemini 2 10.4
VW1871	WJ	B9TL/Gemini 2 10.4
VW1872	WJ	B9TL/Gemini 2 10.4
VW1873	WJ	B9TL/Gemini 2 10.4
VW1874	WJ	B9TL/Gemini 2 10.4
VW1875	WJ	B9TL/Gemini 2 10.4
VW1876	WJ	B9TL/Gemini 2 10.4
VW1877	WJ	B9TL/Gemini 2 10.4
VW1878	WJ	B9TL/Gemini 2 10.4
VW1879	WJ	B9TL/Gemini 2 10.4
VW1880	WJ	B9TL/Gemini 2 10.4
VW1881	WJ	B9TL/Gemini 2 10.4
VW1882	WJ	B9TL/Gemini 2 10.4
VW1883	WJ	B9TL/Gemini 2 10.4
VW1884	WJ	B9TL/Gemini 2 10.4
VW1885	WJ	B9TL/Gemini 2 10.4
VW1886	WJ	B9TL/Gemini 2 10.4
VW1887	WJ	B9TL/Gemini 2 10.4
VW1888	WJ	B9TL/Gemini 2 10.4
VW1889	WJ	B9TL/Gemini 2 10.4
VW1890	WJ	B9TL/Gemini 2 10.4
VW1891	WJ	B9TL/Gemini 2 10.4
VW1892	WJ	B9TL/Gemini 2 10.4
VW1893	WJ	B9TL/Gemini 2 10.4
VW1894	WJ	B9TL/Gemini 2 10.4
VWH1360	AC	B5LH/Gemini 2 (EC) 10.5
VWH1361	AC	B5LH/Gemini 2 (EC) 10.5
VWH1362	AC	B5LH/Gemini 2 (EC) 10.5
VWH1363	AC	B5LH/Gemini 2 (EC) 10.5
VWH1364	AC	B5LH/Gemini 2 (EC) 10.5
VWH1408	AC	B5LH/Gemini 2 (EC) 10.5
VWH1409	AC	B5LH/Gemini 2 (EC) 10.5
VWH1410	AC	B5LH/Gemini 2 (EC) 10.5

No.	G.	Type	No.	G.	Type	No.	G.	Type
VWH1411	AC	B5LH/Gemini 2 (EC) 10.5	VWH2061	PB	B5LH/Gemini 3 10.5	VWH2178	UX	B5LH/Gemini 3 ST 10.6
VWH1412	AC	B5LH/Gemini 2 (EC) 10.5	VWH2088	AC	B5LH/Gemini 3 10.5	VWH2179	UX	B5LH/Gemini 3 ST 10.6
VWH1413	AC	B5LH/Gemini 2 (EC) 10.5	VWH2089	AC	B5LH/Gemini 3 10.5	VWH2180	UX	B5LH/Gemini 3 ST 10.6
VWH1414	AC	B5LH/Gemini 2 (EC) 10.5	VWH2090	AC	B5LH/Gemini 3 10.5	VWH2181	UX	B5LH/Gemini 3 ST 10.6
VWH1415	AC	B5LH/Gemini 2 (EC) 10.5	VWH2091	AC	B5LH/Gemini 3 10.5	VWH2182	UX	B5LH/Gemini 3 ST 10.6
VWH1416	AC	B5LH/Gemini 2 (EC) 10.5	VWH2092	AC	B5LH/Gemini 3 10.5	VWH2183	UX	B5LH/Gemini 3 ST 10.6
VWH1417	AC	B5LH/Gemini 2 (EC) 10.5	VWH2093	AC	B5LH/Gemini 3 10.5	VWH2184	UX	B5LH/Gemini 3 ST 10.6
VWH1418	AC	B5LH/Gemini 2 (EC) 10.5	VWH2094	PB	B5LH/Gemini 3 10.5	VWH2185	UX	B5LH/Gemini 3 ST 10.6
VWH1419	AC	B5LH/Gemini 2 (EC) 10.5	VWH2095	AC	B5LH/Gemini 3 10.5	VWH2186	UX	B5LH/Gemini 3 ST 10.6
VWH2001	PV	B5LH/Gemini 3 10.5	VWH2096	AC	B5LH/Gemini 3 10.5	VWH2187	HD	B5LH/Gemini 3 ST 10.6
VWH2002	PV	B5LH/Gemini 3 10.5	VWH2097	PB	B5LH/Gemini 3 10.5	VWH2188	HD	B5LH/Gemini 3 ST 10.6
VWH2003	PV	B5LH/Gemini 3 10.5	VWH2098	AC	B5LH/Gemini 3 10.5	VWH2189	HD	B5LH/Gemini 3 ST 10.6
VWH2004	PV	B5LH/Gemini 3 10.5	VWH2099	AC	B5LH/Gemini 3 10.5	VWH2190	HD	B5LH/Gemini 3 ST 10.6
VWH2005	PV	B5LH/Gemini 3 10.5	VWH2100	AC	B5LH/Gemini 3 10.5	VWH2191	HD	B5LH/Gemini 3 ST 10.6
VWH2006	PV	B5LH/Gemini 3 10.5	VWH2101	AC	B5LH/Gemini 3 10.5	VWH2192	HD	B5LH/Gemini 3 ST 10.6
VWH2007	PV	B5LH/Gemini 3 10.5	VWH2102	AC	B5LH/Gemini 3 10.5	VWH2193	HD	B5LH/Gemini 3 ST 10.6
VWH2008	PV	B5LH/Gemini 3 10.5	VWH2103	AC	B5LH/Gemini 3 10.5	VWH2194	HD	B5LH/Gemini 3 ST 10.6
VWH2009	PV	B5LH/Gemini 3 10.5	VWH2104	AC	B5LH/Gemini 3 10.5	VWH2195	HD	B5LH/Gemini 3 ST 10.6
VWH2010	PV	B5LH/Gemini 3 10.5	VWH2105	AC	B5LH/Gemini 3 10.5	VWH2196	HD	B5LH/Gemini 3 ST 10.6
VWH2011	PV	B5LH/Gemini 3 10.5	VWH2106	AC	B5LH/Gemini 3 10.5	VWH2197	HD	B5LH/Gemini 3 ST 10.6
VWH2012	PV	B5LH/Gemini 3 10.5	VWH2107	AC	B5LH/Gemini 3 10.5	VWH2198	HD	B5LH/Gemini 3 ST 10.6
VWH2013	PV	B5LH/Gemini 3 10.5	VWH2108	AC	B5LH/Gemini 3 10.5	VWH2199	HD	B5LH/Gemini 3 ST 10.6
VWH2014	PV	B5LH/Gemini 3 10.5	VWH2109	AC	B5LH/Gemini 3 10.5	VWH2200	HD	B5LH/Gemini 3 ST 10.6
VWH2015	PV	B5LH/Gemini 3 10.5	VWH2110	AC	B5LH/Gemini 3 10.5	VWH2201	HD	B5LH/Gemini 3 ST 10.6
VWH2016	PV	B5LH/Gemini 3 10.5	VWH2111	AC	B5LH/Gemini 3 10.5	VWH2202	HD	B5LH/Gemini 3 ST 10.6
VWH2017	PV	B5LH/Gemini 3 10.5	VWH2112	AC	B5LH/Gemini 3 10.5	VWH2203	HD	B5LH/Gemini 3 ST 10.6
VWH2018	PV	B5LH/Gemini 3 10.5	VWH2113	AC	B5LH/Gemini 3 10.5	VWH2204	HD	B5LH/Gemini 3 ST 10.6
VWH2019	PV	B5LH/Gemini 3 10.5	VWH2114	AC	B5LH/Gemini 3 10.5	VWH2205	HD	B5LH/Gemini 3 ST 10.6
VWH2020	PV	B5LH/Gemini 3 10.5	VWH2115	AC	B5LH/Gemini 3 10.5	VWH2206	HD	B5LH/Gemini 3 ST 10.6
VWH2021	PV	B5LH/Gemini 3 10.5	VWH2116	AC	B5LH/Gemini 3 10.5	VWH2207	HD	B5LH/Gemini 3 ST 10.6
VWH2022	PV	B5LH/Gemini 3 10.5	VWH2117	AC	B5LH/Gemini 3 10.5	VWH2208	HD	B5LH/Gemini 3 ST 10.6
VWH2023	PV	B5LH/Gemini 3 10.5	VWH2118	AC	B5LH/Gemini 3 10.5	VWH2209	HD	B5LH/Gemini 3 ST 10.6
VWH2024	PV	B5LH/Gemini 3 10.5	VWH2119	AC	B5LH/Gemini 3 10.5	VWH2210	HD	B5LH/Gemini 3 ST 10.6
VWH2025	PB	B5LH/Gemini 3 10.5	VWH2120	AC	B5LH/Gemini 3 10.5	VWH2211	HD	B5LH/Gemini 3 ST 10.6
VWH2026	PB	B5LH/Gemini 3 10.5	VWH2121	AC	B5LH/Gemini 3 10.5	VWH2212	HD	B5LH/Gemini 3 ST 10.6
VWH2027	PB	B5LH/Gemini 3 10.5	VWH2122	WJ	B5LH/Gemini 3 ST 10.6	VWH2213	HD	B5LH/Gemini 3 ST 10.6
VWH2028	PB	B5LH/Gemini 3 10.5	VWH2123	WJ	B5LH/Gemini 3 ST 10.6	VWH2214	HD	B5LH/Gemini 3 ST 10.6
VWH2029	PB	B5LH/Gemini 3 10.5	VWH2124	WJ	B5LH/Gemini 3 ST 10.6	VWH2215	HD	B5LH/Gemini 3 ST 10.6
VWH2030	PB	B5LH/Gemini 3 10.5	VWH2125	WJ	B5LH/Gemini 3 ST 10.6	VWH2216	HD	B5LH/Gemini 3 ST 10.6
VWH2031	PB	B5LH/Gemini 3 10.5	VWH2126	WJ	B5LH/Gemini 3 ST 10.6	VWH2217	HD	B5LH/Gemini 3 ST 10.6
VWH2032	PB	B5LH/Gemini 3 10.5	VWH2127	WJ	B5LH/Gemini 3 ST 10.6	VWH2218	HD	B5LH/Gemini 3 ST 10.6
VWH2033	PB	B5LH/Gemini 3 10.5	VWH2128	WJ	B5LH/Gemini 3 ST 10.6	VWH2219	HD	B5LH/Gemini 3 ST 10.6
VWH2034	PB	B5LH/Gemini 3 10.5	VWH2129	WJ	B5LH/Gemini 3 ST 10.6	VWH2220	HD	B5LH/Gemini 3 ST 10.6
VWH2035	PB	B5LH/Gemini 3 10.5	VWH2130	WJ	B5LH/Gemini 3 ST 10.6	VWH2221	HD	B5LH/Gemini 3 ST 10.6
VWH2036	PB	B5LH/Gemini 3 10.5	VWH2131	WJ	B5LH/Gemini 3 ST 10.6	VWH2222	HD	B5LH/Gemini 3 ST 10.6
VWH2037	PB	B5LH/Gemini 3 10.5	VWH2132	WJ	B5LH/Gemini 3 ST 10.6	VWH2223	HD	B5LH/Gemini 3 ST 10.6
VWH2038	PB	B5LH/Gemini 3 10.5	VWH2133	WJ	B5LH/Gemini 3 ST 10.6	VWH2224	HD	B5LH/Gemini 3 ST 10.6
VWH2039	PB	B5LH/Gemini 3 10.5	VWH2134	WJ	B5LH/Gemini 3 ST 10.6	VWH2225	HD	B5LH/Gemini 3 ST 10.6
VWH2040	PB	B5LH/Gemini 3 10.5	VWH2135	WJ	B5LH/Gemini 3 ST 10.6	VWH2226	HD	B5LH/Gemini 3 ST 10.6
VWH2041	PB	B5LH/Gemini 3 10.5	VWH2136	WJ	B5LH/Gemini 3 ST 10.6	VWH2227	HD	B5LH/Gemini 3 ST 10.6
VWH2042	PB	B5LH/Gemini 3 10.5	VWH2137	WJ	B5LH/Gemini 3 ST 10.6	VWH2228	HD	B5LH/Gemini 3 ST 10.6
VWH2043	PB	B5LH/Gemini 3 10.5	VWH2138	WJ	B5LH/Gemini 3 ST 10.6	VWH2229	HD	B5LH/Gemini 3 ST 10.6
VWH2044	PB	B5LH/Gemini 3 10.5	VWH2139	WJ	B5LH/Gemini 3 ST 10.6	VWH2230	HD	B5LH/Gemini 3 ST 10.6
VWH2045	PB	B5LH/Gemini 3 10.5	VWH2140	WJ	B5LH/Gemini 3 ST 10.6	VWH2231	HD	B5LH/Gemini 3 ST 10.6
VWH2046	PB	B5LH/Gemini 3 10.5	VWH2141	WJ	B5LH/Gemini 3 ST 10.6	VWH2232	HD	B5LH/Gemini 3 ST 10.6
VWH2047	PB	B5LH/Gemini 3 10.5	VWH2142	WJ	B5LH/Gemini 3 ST 10.6	VWH2233	HD	B5LH/Gemini 3 ST 10.6
VWH2048	PB	B5LH/Gemini 3 10.5	VWH2143	WJ	B5LH/Gemini 3 ST 10.6	VWH2234	HD	B5LH/Gemini 3 ST 10.6
VWH2049	PB	B5LH/Gemini 3 10.5	VWH2144	WJ	B5LH/Gemini 3 ST 10.6	VWH2235	HD	B5LH/Gemini 3 ST 10.6
VWH2050	PB	B5LH/Gemini 3 10.5	VWH2167	UX	B5LH/Gemini 3 ST 10.6	VWH2236	HD	B5LH/Gemini 3 ST 10.6
VWH2051	PB	B5LH/Gemini 3 10.5	VWH2168	UX	B5LH/Gemini 3 ST 10.6	VWH2237	HD	B5LH/Gemini 3 ST 10.6
VWH2052	PB	B5LH/Gemini 3 10.5	VWH2169	UX	B5LH/Gemini 3 ST 10.6	VWH2238	HD	B5LH/Gemini 3 ST 10.6
VWH2053	PB	B5LH/Gemini 3 10.5	VWH2170	UX	B5LH/Gemini 3 ST 10.6	VWH2239	HD	B5LH/Gemini 3 ST 10.6
VWH2054	PB	B5LH/Gemini 3 10.5	VWH2171	UX	B5LH/Gemini 3 ST 10.6	VWH2240	HD	B5LH/Gemini 3 ST 10.6
VWH2055	PB	B5LH/Gemini 3 10.5	VWH2172	UX	B5LH/Gemini 3 ST 10.6	VWH2241	HD	B5LH/Gemini 3 ST 10.6
VWH2056	PB	B5LH/Gemini 3 10.5	VWH2173	UX	B5LH/Gemini 3 ST 10.6	VWH2242	HD	B5LH/Gemini 3 ST 10.6
VWH2057	PB	B5LH/Gemini 3 10.5	VWH2174	UX	B5LH/Gemini 3 ST 10.6	VWH2243	HD	B5LH/Gemini 3 ST 10.6
VWH2058	PB	B5LH/Gemini 3 10.5	VWH2175	UX	B5LH/Gemini 3 ST 10.6			
VWH2059	PB	B5LH/Gemini 3 10.5	VWH2176	UX	B5LH/Gemini 3 ST 10.6			
VWH2060	PB	B5LH/Gemini 3 10.5	VWH2177	UX	B5LH/Gemini 3 ST 10.6			

Quality Line

No.	G.	Type	No.	G.	Type	No.	G.	Type
DD01	EB	Trident/E400 10.1	MCS08	EB	Citaro 10.8	OPL08	EB	Solo SR 9.7
DD02	EB	Trident/E400 10.1	MCS09	EB	Citaro 10.8	OV01	EB	Versa 11.1
DD03	EB	Trident/E400 10.1	MCS10	EB	Citaro 10.8	OV02	EB	Versa 11.1
DD04	EB	Trident/E400 10.1	OC01	EB	MetroCity 10.6	OV03	EB	Versa 11.1
DD05	EB	Trident/E400 10.1	OM01	EB	MetroCity 9.9	OV04	EB	Versa 11.1
DD06	EB	Trident/E400 10.1	OM02	EB	MetroCity 9.9	OV05	EB	Versa 11.1
DD07	EB	Trident/E400 10.1	OM03	EB	MetroCity 9.9	OV06	EB	Versa 11.1
DD08	EB	Trident/E400 10.1	OM04	EB	MetroCity 9.9	OV07	EB	Versa 11.1
DD09	EB	Trident/E400 10.1	OM05	EB	MetroCity 9.9	OV08	EB	Versa 11.1
DD10	EB	Trident/E400 10.1	OM06	EB	MetroCity 9.9	OV09	EB	Versa 11.1
DD11	EB	E40D/E400 (EC) 10.2	OM07	EB	MetroCity 9.9	OV10	EB	Versa 11.1
DD12	EB	E40D/E400 (EC) 10.2	OM08	EB	MetroCity 9.9	OV11	EB	Versa 11.1
DD13	EB	E40D/E400 (EC) 10.2	OM09	EB	MetroCity 9.9	OV12	EB	Versa 11.1
DD14	EB	E40D/E400 (E6) 10.35	OM10	EB	MetroCity 9.9	OV13	EB	Versa 11.1
DD15	EB	E40D/E400 (E6) 10.35	OM11	EB	MetroCity 9.9	SD52	EB	E200/East Lancs 9.0
DD16	EB	E40D/E400 (E6) 10.35	OM12	EB	MetroCity 9.9	SD53	EB	E200/East Lancs 9.0
DD17	EB	E40D/E400 (E6) 10.35	OM13	EB	MetroCity 9.9	SD54	EB	E20D/E200 8.9
DD18	EB	E40D/E400 (E6) 10.35	OP23	EB	Solo 8.8	SD55	EB	E20D/E200 8.9
MCL01	EB	Citaro 12.0	OP24	EB	Solo 8.8	SD56	EB	E20D/E200 8.9
MCL08	EB	Citaro Single Door 12.0	OP25	EB	Solo 8.8	SD57	EB	E20D/E200 8.9
MCL09	EB	Citaro Single Door 12.0	OP26	EB	Solo 8.8	SD58	EB	E20D/E200 8.9
MCL10	EB	Citaro Single Door 12.0	OP27	EB	Solo 8.8	SD59	EB	E20D/E200 8.9
MCL11	EB	Citaro Single Door 12.0	OP28	EB	Solo 8.8	SD60	EB	E20D/E200 8.9
MCL12	EB	Citaro Single Door 12.0	OP29	EB	Solo 8.8	WS01	EB	Streetlite WF 8.8
MCL13	EB	Citaro Single Door 12.0	OP30	EB	Solo 8.8	WS02	EB	Streetlite WF 8.8
MCL14	EB	Citaro Single Door 12.0	OP31	EB	Solo 8.8	WS03	EB	Streetlite WF 8.8
MCL15	EB	Citaro Single Door 12.0	OP32	EB	Solo 8.8	WS04	EB	Streetlite WF 8.8
MCL16	EB	Citaro Single Door 12.0	OP33	EB	Solo 8.8	WS05	EB	Streetlite WF 8.8
MCL17	EB	Citaro Single Door 12.0	OP34	EB	Solo SR 9.0	WS06	EB	Streetlite WF 8.8
MCS01	EB	Citaro 10.8	OPL01	EB	Solo SR 9.7	WS07	EB	Streetlite WF 8.8
MCS02	EB	Citaro 10.8	OPL02	EB	Solo SR 9.7	WS08	EB	Streetlite WF 8.8
MCS03	EB	Citaro 10.8	OPL03	EB	Solo SR 9.7	WS09	EB	Streetlite WF 8.8
MCS04	EB	Citaro 10.8	OPL04	EB	Solo SR 9.7	WS10	EB	Streetlite WF 8.8
MCS05	EB	Citaro 10.8	OPL05	EB	Solo SR 9.7	WS11	EB	Streetlite WF 8.8
MCS06	EB	Citaro 10.8	OPL06	EB	Solo SR 9.7			
MCS07	EB	Citaro 10.8	OPL07	EB	Solo SR 9.7			

Short Mercedes Citaro MCS05 works the 413 in Sutton. *Ken Carr*

RATP-Dev London

No.	G.	Type	No.	G.	Type	No.	G.	Type
ADE40401	AV	E40D/E400 (EC) 10.2	ADE40471	PK	E40D/E400 (EC) 10.2	DE20017	PK	E200/E200 10.2
ADE40402	AV	E40D/E400 (EC) 10.2	ADE40472	PK	E40D/E400 (EC) 10.2	DE20018	PK	E200/E200 10.2
ADE40403	AV	E40D/E400 (EC) 10.2	ADE40473	PK	E40D/E400 (EC) 10.2	DE20019	BT	E200/E200 10.2
ADE40404	AV	E40D/E400 (EC) 10.2	ADH45001	V	Trident/E400H 10.1	DE20020	S	E200/E200 10.2
ADE40405	AV	E40D/E400 (EC) 10.2	ADH45002	V	Trident/E400H 10.1	DE20021	BT	E200/E200 10.2
ADE40406	AV	E40D/E400 (EC) 10.2	ADH45003	S	Trident/E400H 10.1	DE20022	HH	E200/E200 10.2
ADE40407	AV	E40D/E400 (EC) 10.2	ADH45004	S	Trident/E400H 10.1	DE20023	FW	E200/E200 10.2
ADE40408	AV	E40D/E400 (EC) 10.2	ADH45005	S	Trident/E400H 10.1	DE20024	FW	E200/E200 10.2
ADE40409	AV	E40D/E400 (EC) 10.2	ADH45006	S	Trident/E400H 10.1	DE20025	FW	E200/E200 10.2
ADE40410	AV	E40D/E400 (EC) 10.2	ADH45007	S	Trident/E400H 10.1	DE20026	FW	E200/E200 10.2
ADE40411	AV	E40D/E400 (EC) 10.2	ADH45008	S	Trident/E400H 10.1	DE20027	FW	E200/E200 10.2
ADE40412	AV	E40D/E400 (EC) 10.2	ADH45009	S	Trident/E400H 10.1	DE20028	FW	E200/E200 10.2
ADE40413	AV	E40D/E400 (EC) 10.2	ADH45010	S	Trident/E400H 10.1	DE20029	FW	E200/E200 10.2
ADE40414	AV	E40D/E400 (EC) 10.2	ADH45011	S	Trident/E400H 10.1	DE20030	FW	E200/E200 10.2
ADE40415	AV	E40D/E400 (EC) 10.2	ADH45012	S	Trident/E400H 10.1	DE20031	FW	E200/E200 10.2
ADE40416	AV	E40D/E400 (EC) 10.2	ADH45013	S	Trident/E400H 10.1	DE20032	S	E200/E200 10.2
ADE40417	AV	E40D/E400 (EC) 10.2	ADH45014	S	Trident/E400H 10.1	DE20033	SO	E200/E200 10.2
ADE40418	AV	E40D/E400 (EC) 10.2	ADH45015	S	Trident/E400H 10.1	DE20034	S	E200/E200 10.2
ADE40419	AV	E40D/E400 (EC) 10.2	ADH45016	S	Trident/E400H 10.1	DE20035	S	E200/E200 10.2
ADE40420	AV	E40D/E400 (EC) 10.2	ADH45017	S	Trident/E400H 10.1	DE20036	SO	E200/E200 10.2
ADE40421	AV	E40D/E400 (EC) 10.2	ADH45018	S	Trident/E400H 10.1	DE20037	S	E200/E200 10.2
ADE40422	AV	E40D/E400 (EC) 10.2	ADH45019	S	Trident/E400H 10.1	DE20038	S	E200/E200 10.2
ADE40423	AV	E40D/E400 (EC) 10.2	ADH45020	S	Trident/E400H 10.1	DE20039	S	E200/E200 10.2
ADE40424	AV	E40D/E400 (EC) 10.2	ADH45021	S	Trident/E400H 10.1	DE20040	S	E200/E200 10.2
ADE40425	AV	E40D/E400 (EC) 10.2	ADH45022	S	Trident/E400H 10.1	DE20041	S	E200/E200 10.2
ADE40426	AV	E40D/E400 (EC) 10.2	ADH45023	V	E40H/E400 (EC) 10.2	DE20042	S	E200/E200 10.2
ADE40427	AV	E40D/E400 (EC) 10.2	ADH45024	V	E40H/E400 (EC) 10.2	DE20043	S	E200/E200 10.2
ADE40428	AV	E40D/E400 (EC) 10.2	ADH45025	V	E40H/E400 (EC) 10.2	DE20044	S	E200/E200 10.2
ADE40429	AV	E40D/E400 (EC) 10.2	ADH45026	V	E40H/E400 (EC) 10.2	DE20045	S	E200/E200 10.2
ADE40430	AV	E40D/E400 (EC) 10.2	ADH45027	V	E40H/E400 (EC) 10.2	DE20046	SO	E200/E200 10.2
ADE40431	AV	E40D/E400 (EC) 10.2	ADH45028	V	E40H/E400 (EC) 10.2	DE20047	SO	E200/E200 10.2
ADE40432	AV	E40D/E400 (EC) 10.2	ADH45029	V	E40H/E400 (EC) 10.2	DE20048	S	E200/E200 10.2
ADE40433	AV	E40D/E400 (EC) 10.2	ADH45030	V	E40H/E400 (EC) 10.2	DE20049	S	E200/E200 10.2
ADE40434	AV	E40D/E400 (EC) 10.2	ADH45031	V	E40H/E400 (EC) 10.2	DE20050	SO	E200/E200 10.2
ADE40435	AV	E40D/E400 (EC) 10.2	ADH45032	V	E40H/E400 (EC) 10.2	DE20051	SO	E200/E200 10.2
ADE40436	AV	E40D/E400 (EC) 10.2	ADH45033	V	E40H/E400 (EC) 10.2	DE20052	BT	E200/E200 10.2
ADE40437	AV	E40D/E400 (EC) 10.2	ADH45034	V	E40H/E400 (EC) 10.2	DE20053	SO	E200/E200 10.2
ADE40438	AV	E40D/E400 (EC) 10.2	ADH45035	V	E40H/E400 (EC) 10.2	DE20054	SO	E200/E200 10.2
ADE40439	AV	E40D/E400 (EC) 10.2	ADH45036	V	E40H/E400 (EC) 10.2	DE20055	SO	E200/E200 10.2
ADE40440	AV	E40D/E400 (EC) 10.2	ADH45037	V	E40H/E400 (EC) 10.2	DE20056	SO	E200/E200 10.2
ADE40441	AV	E40D/E400 (EC) 10.2	ADH45038	V	E40H/E400 (EC) 10.2	DE20057	TV	E200/E200 10.2
ADE40442	AV	E40D/E400 (EC) 10.2	ADH45039	V	E40H/E400 (EC) 10.2	DE20058	TV	E200/E200 10.2
ADE40443	AV	E40D/E400 (EC) 10.2	ADH45040	V	E40H/E400 (EC) 10.2	DE20059	TV	E200/E200 10.2
ADE40444	AV	E40D/E400 (EC) 10.2	ADH45041	V	E40H/E400 (EC) 10.2	DE20060	TV	E200/E200 10.2
ADE40445	EP	E40D/E400 (EC) 10.2	ADH45042	V	E40H/E400 (EC) 10.2	DE20061	TV	E200/E200 10.2
ADE40446	PK	E40D/E400 (EC) 10.2	ADH45043	V	E40H/E400 (EC) 10.2	DE20062	TV	E200/E200 10.2
ADE40447	PK	E40D/E400 (EC) 10.2	ADH45044	V	E40H/E400 (EC) 10.2	DE20063	TV	E200/E200 10.2
ADE40448	PK	E40D/E400 (EC) 10.2	ADH45045	V	E40H/E400 (EC) 10.2	DE20064	TV	E200/E200 10.2
ADE40449	PK	E40D/E400 (EC) 10.2	ADH45046	V	E40H/E400 (EC) 10.2	DE20065	TV	E200/E200 10.2
ADE40450	PK	E40D/E400 (EC) 10.2	ADH45047	V	E40H/E400 (EC) 10.2	DE20066	TV	E200/E200 10.2
ADE40451	PK	E40D/E400 (EC) 10.2	ADH45048	V	E40H/E400 (EC) 10.2	DE20067	TV	E200/E200 10.2
ADE40452	PK	E40D/E400 (EC) 10.2	ADH45049	V	E40H/E400 (EC) 10.2	DE20068	HH	E200/E200 10.2
ADE40453	PK	E40D/E400 (EC) 10.2	ADH45050	V	E40H/E400 (EC) 10.2	DE20069	HH	E200/E200 10.2
ADE40454	PK	E40D/E400 (EC) 10.2	ADH45051	V	E40H/E400 (EC) 10.2	DE20070	HH	E200/E200 10.2
ADE40455	PK	E40D/E400 (EC) 10.2	DE20001	BT	E200/E200 10.2	DE20071	HH	E200/E200 10.2
ADE40456	PK	E40D/E400 (EC) 10.2	DE20002	BT	E200/E200 10.2	DE20072	FW	E200/E200 10.2
ADE40457	PK	E40D/E400 (EC) 10.2	DE20003	BT	E200/E200 10.2	DE20073	FW	E200/E200 10.2
ADE40458	PK	E40D/E400 (EC) 10.2	DE20004	BT	E200/E200 10.2	DE20074	S	E200/E200 10.2
ADE40459	PK	E40D/E400 (EC) 10.2	DE20005	BT	E200/E200 10.2	DE20075	PK	E200/E200 10.2
ADE40460	PK	E40D/E400 (EC) 10.2	DE20006	BT	E200/E200 10.2	DE20076	PK	E200/E200 10.2
ADE40461	PK	E40D/E400 (EC) 10.2	DE20007	BT	E200/E200 10.2	DE20077	PK	E200/E200 10.2
ADE40462	PK	E40D/E400 (EC) 10.2	DE20008	BT	E200/E200 10.2	DE20078	PK	E200/E200 10.2
ADE40463	PK	E40D/E400 (EC) 10.2	DE20009	BT	E200/E200 10.2	DE20079	PK	E200/E200 10.2
ADE40464	PK	E40D/E400 (EC) 10.2	DE20010	BT	E200/E200 10.2	DE20080	PK	E200/E200 10.2
ADE40465	PK	E40D/E400 (EC) 10.2	DE20011	BT	E200/E200 10.2	DE20081	PK	E200/E200 10.2
ADE40466	PK	E40D/E400 (EC) 10.2	DE20012	BT	E200/E200 10.2	DE20082	PK	E200/E200 10.2
ADE40467	PK	E40D/E400 (EC) 10.2	DE20013	BT	E200/E200 10.2	DE20083	PK	E200/E200 10.2
ADE40468	PK	E40D/E400 (EC) 10.2	DE20014	BT	E200/E200 10.2	DE20084	S	E200/E200 10.2
ADE40469	PK	E40D/E400 (EC) 10.2	DE20015	BT	E200/E200 10.2	DE20085	S	E200/E200 10.2
ADE40470	PK	E40D/E400 (EC) 10.2	DE20016	BT	E200/E200 10.2	DE20086	S	E200/E200 10.2

RATP-Dev London

No.	G.	Type	No.	G.	Type	No.	G.	Type
DE20087	S	E200/E200 10.2	DE20175	SO	E200/E200 10.2	DPS30677	S	Dart/Pointer 2 10.2
DE20088	S	E200/E200 10.2	DE20176	SO	E200/E200 10.2	DPS30678	HH	Dart/Pointer 2 10.2
DE20089	S	E200/E200 10.2	DE20177	SO	E200/E200 10.2	DPS30679	S	Dart/Pointer 2 10.2
DE20090	S	E200/E200 10.2	DE20178	SO	E200/E200 10.2	DPS30680	S	Dart/Pointer 2 10.2
DE20091	S	E200/E200 10.2	DE20179	SO	E200/E200 10.2	DPS30681	AV	Dart/Pointer 2 10.2
DE20092	S	E200/E200 10.2	DE20180	SO	E200/E200 10.2	DPS30682	TV	Dart/Pointer 2 10.2
DE20093	S	E200/E200 10.2	DE20181	SO	E200/E200 10.2	DPS30683	TV	Dart/Pointer 2 10.2
DE20094	S	E200/E200 10.2	DE20182	SO	E200/E200 10.2	DPS30684	TV	Dart/Pointer 2 10.2
DE20095	S	E200/E200 10.2	DE20183	SO	E200/E200 10.2	DPS30685	TV	Dart/Pointer 2 10.2
DE20096	S	E200/E200 10.2	DE20184	SO	E200/E200 10.2	DPS30686	AV	Dart/Pointer 2 10.2
DE20097	S	E200/E200 10.2	DE20185	SO	E200/E200 10.2	DPS30687	AV	Dart/Pointer 2 10.2
DE20098	S	E200/E200 10.2	DE20186	SO	E200/E200 10.2	DPS30688	TV	Dart/Pointer 2 10.2
DE20099	S	E200/E200 10.2	DE20187	SO	E200/E200 10.2	DPS30689	AV	Dart/Pointer 2 10.2
DE20100	S	E200/E200 10.2	DE20188	SO	E200/E200 10.2	DPS30690	AV	Dart/Pointer 2 10.2
DE20101	S	E200/E200 10.2	DE20189	SO	E200/E200 10.2	DPS30691	AV	Dart/Pointer 2 10.2
DE20102	S	E200/E200 10.2	DE20190	SO	E200/E200 10.2	DPS30692	S	Dart/Pointer 2 10.2
DE20103	S	E200/E200 10.2	DE20191	SO	E200/E200 10.2	DPS30693	S	Dart/Pointer 2 10.2
DE20104	S	E200/E200 10.2	DE20192	SO	E200/E200 10.2	DPS30694	TV	Dart/Pointer 2 10.2
DE20105	S	E200/E200 10.2	DE20193	SO	E200/E200 10.2	DPS30701	S	Dart/Pointer 10.1
DE20106	S	E200/E200 10.2	DE20194	SO	E200/E200 10.2	DPS30702	S	Dart/Pointer 10.1
DE20107	S	E200/E200 10.2	DE20195	SO	E200/E200 10.2	DPS30703	S	Dart/Pointer 10.1
DE20108	S	E200/E200 10.2	DE20196	SO	E200/E200 10.2	DPS30704	S	Dart/Pointer 10.1
DE20109	FW	E200/E200 10.2	DE20197	SO	E200/E200 10.2	DPS30705	S	Dart/Pointer 10.1
DE20110	FW	E200/E200 10.2	DE20198	SO	E200/E200 10.2	DPS30706	S	Dart/Pointer 10.1
DE20111	FW	E200/E200 10.2	DE20199	SO	E200/E200 10.2	DPS30707	S	Dart/Pointer 10.1
DE20112	FW	E200/E200 10.2	DLE30001	AV	E200/E200 10.8	DPS30708	HH	Dart/Pointer 10.1
DE20113	FW	E200/E200 10.2	DLE30002	AV	E200/E200 10.8	DPS30709	HH	Dart/Pointer 10.1
DE20114	FW	E200/E200 10.2	DLE30003	AV	E200/E200 10.8	DPS30710	HH	Dart/Pointer 10.1
DE20115	FW	E200/E200 10.2	DLE30004	AV	E200/E200 10.8	DPS30711	HH	Dart/Pointer 10.1
DE20116	FW	E200/E200 10.2	DLE30005	AV	E200/E200 10.8	DPS30712	HH	Dart/Pointer 10.1
DE20117	FW	E200/E200 10.2	DLE30006	AV	E200/E200 10.8	DPS30713	HH	Dart/Pointer 10.1
DE20118	FW	E200/E200 10.2	DLE30007	AV	E200/E200 10.8	DPS30714	HH	Dart/Pointer 10.1
DE20119	FW	E200/E200 10.2	DLE30008	AV	E200/E200 10.8	DPS30715	HH	Dart/Pointer 10.1
DE20120	FW	E200/E200 10.2	DLE30009	AV	E200/E200 10.8	DPS30716	HH	Dart/Pointer 10.1
DE20121	FW	E200/E200 10.2	DLE30010	AV	E200/E200 10.8	DPS30717	HH	Dart/Pointer 10.1
DE20122	FW	E200/E200 10.2	DLE30011	AV	E200/E200 10.8	DPS30718	HH	Dart/Pointer 10.1
DE20123	FW	E200/E200 10.2	DLE30012	AV	E200/E200 10.8	DPS30719	S	Dart/Pointer 10.1
DE20124	FW	E200/E200 10.2	DLE30013	AV	E200/E200 10.8	DPS30720	S	Dart/Pointer 10.1
DE20125	FW	E200/E200 10.2	DLE30014	AV	E200/E200 10.8	DPS30721	S	Dart/Pointer 10.1
DE20126	FW	E200/E200 10.2	DLE30015	AV	E200/E200 10.8	DPS30722	TV	Dart/Pointer 10.1
DE20127	FW	E200/E200 10.2	DLE30016	AV	E200/E200 10.8	DPS30724	HH	Dart/Pointer 10.1
DE20128	FW	E200/E200 10.2	DLE30017	AV	E200/E200 10.8	DPS30725	HH	Dart/Pointer 10.1
DE20129	TV	E20D/E200MMC 10.9	DLE30018	AV	E200/E200 10.8	DPS30726	HH	Dart/Pointer 10.1
DE20130	TV	E20D/E200MMC 10.9	DLE30019	AV	E200/E200 10.8	DPS30727	HH	Dart/Pointer 10.1
DE20131	TV	E20D/E200MMC 10.9	DLE30020	AV	E200/E200 10.8	HDE25001	FW	E200H/E200 10.2
DE20132	TV	E20D/E200MMC 10.9	DLE30021	AV	E200/E200 10.8	HDE25002	FW	E200H/E200 10.2
DE20133	TV	E20D/E200MMC 10.9	DLE30022	AV	E200/E200 10.8	HDE25003	FW	E200H/E200 10.2
DE20134	TV	E20D/E200MMC 10.9	DLE30023	AV	E200/E200 10.8	HDE25004	FW	E200H/E200 10.2
DE20135	TV	E20D/E200MMC 10.9	DLE30024	FW	E200/E200 10.8	HDE25005	FW	E200H/E200 10.2
DE20136	TV	E20D/E200MMC 10.9	DLE30025	FW	E200/E200 10.8	LT69	V	NRM 11.3
DE20137	TV	E20D/E200MMC 10.9	DLE30026	SO	E20D/E200 10.8	LT70	V	NRM 11.3
DE20138	TV	E20D/E200MMC 10.9	DPS30628	HH	Dart/Pointer 2 10.2	LT71	V	NRM 11.3
DE20139	TV	E20D/E200MMC 10.9	DPS30630	SO	Dart/Pointer 2 10.2	LT72	V	NRM 11.3
DE20140	TV	E20D/E200MMC 10.9	DPS30636	SO	Dart/Pointer 2 10.2	LT73	V	NRM 11.3
DE20141	TV	E20D/E200MMC 10.9	DPS30639	S	Dart/Pointer 2 10.2	LT74	V	NRM 11.3
DE20142	TV	E20D/E200MMC 10.9	DPS30640	S	Dart/Pointer 2 10.2	LT75	V	NRM 11.3
DE20157	BT	E200/E200 10.2	DPS30648	S	Dart/Pointer 2 10.2	LT76	V	NRM 11.3
DE20158	BT	E200/E200 10.2	DPS30649	S	Dart/Pointer 2 10.2	LT77	V	NRM 11.3
DE20159	BT	E200/E200 10.2	DPS30650	S	Dart/Pointer 2 10.2	LT78	V	NRM 11.3
DE20160	BT	E200/E200 10.2	DPS30651	S	Dart/Pointer 2 10.2	LT79	V	NRM 11.3
DE20161	BT	E200/E200 10.2	DPS30652	S	Dart/Pointer 2 10.2	LT80	V	NRM 11.3
DE20162	BT	E200/E200 10.2	DPS30653	S	Dart/Pointer 2 10.2	LT81	V	NRM 11.3
DE20163	BT	E200/E200 10.2	DPS30655	PK	Dart/Pointer 2 10.2	LT82	V	NRM 11.3
DE20164	BT	E200/E200 10.2	DPS30659	S	Dart/Pointer 2 10.2	LT83	V	NRM 11.3
DE20165	BT	E200/E200 10.2	DPS30661	S	Dart/Pointer 2 10.2	LT84	V	NRM 11.3
DE20166	BT	E200/E200 10.2	DPS30663	TV	Dart/Pointer 2 10.2	LT85	V	NRM 11.3
DE20167	BT	E200/E200 10.2	DPS30664	SO	Dart/Pointer 2 10.2	LT86	V	NRM 11.3
DE20168	BT	E200/E200 10.2	DPS30668	PK	Dart/Pointer 2 10.2	LT87	V	NRM 11.3
DE20169	BT	E200/E200 10.2	DPS30669	S	Dart/Pointer 2 10.2	LT88	V	NRM 11.3
DE20170	BT	E200/E200 10.2	DPS30671	S	Dart/Pointer 2 10.2	LT89	V	NRM 11.3
DE20171	BT	E200/E200 10.2	DPS30672	S	Dart/Pointer 2 10.2	LT90	V	NRM 11.3
DE20172	SO	E200/E200 10.2	DPS30673	S	Dart/Pointer 2 10.2	LT91	V	NRM 11.3
DE20173	SO	E200/E200 10.2	DPS30674	S	Dart/Pointer 2 10.2	LT92	V	NRM 11.3
DE20174	SO	E200/E200 10.2	DPS30675	S	Dart/Pointer 2 10.2	LT93	V	NRM 11.3

No.	G.	Type	No.	G.	Type	No.	G.	Type
LT94	V	NRM 11.3	OT30207	AV	Tempo 12.0	SLE40650	FW	N94/OmniDekka 10.6
LT120	S	NRM 11.3	OT30208	AV	Tempo 12.0	SLE40651	FW	N94/OmniDekka 10.6
LT121	S	NRM 11.3	OT30209	AV	Tempo 12.0	SLE40653	FW	N94/OmniDekka 10.6
LT122	S	NRM 11.3	OT30210	AV	Tempo 12.0	SLE40654	FW	N94/OmniDekka 10.6
LT123	S	NRM 11.3	OT30211	AV	Tempo 12.0	SLE40655	FW	N94/OmniDekka 10.6
LT124	S	NRM 11.3	OT30212	AV	Tempo 12.0	SLE40656	FW	N94/OmniDekka 10.6
LT125	S	NRM 11.3	OT30213	AV	Tempo 12.0	SLE40657	FW	N94/OmniDekka 10.6
LT126	S	NRM 11.3	OT30214	AV	Tempo 12.0	SLE40658	FW	N94/OmniDekka 10.6
LT127	S	NRM 11.3	OT30215	AV	Tempo 12.0	SLE40659	FW	N94/OmniDekka 10.6
LT128	S	NRM 11.3	OT30216	AV	Tempo 12.0	SLE40660	FW	N94/OmniDekka 10.6
LT129	S	NRM 11.3	OV30001	FW	Versa 10.4	SLE40661	FW	N94/OmniDekka 10.6
LT130	S	NRM 11.3	OV30002	FW	Versa 10.4	SLE40662	FW	N94/OmniDekka 10.6
LT131	S	NRM 11.3	OV30003	FW	Versa 10.4	SLE40663	FW	N94/OmniDekka 10.6
LT132	S	NRM 11.3	OV30004	FW	Versa 10.4	SLE40664	FW	N94/OmniDekka 10.6
LT133	S	NRM 11.3	OV30005	FW	Versa 10.4	SP40001	AV	N94/OmniCity 10.7
LT134	S	NRM 11.3	OV30006	FW	Versa 10.4	SP40002	AV	N94/OmniCity 10.7
LT135	S	NRM 11.3	OV30007	FW	Versa 10.4	SP40003	AV	N94/OmniCity 10.7
LT136	S	NRM 11.3	OV30008	FW	Versa 10.4	SP40004	AV	N94/OmniCity 10.7
LT137	S	NRM 11.3	OV30009	FW	Versa 10.4	SP40005	AV	N94/OmniCity 10.7
LT138	S	NRM 11.3	OV30010	FW	Versa 10.4	SP40006	AV	N94/OmniCity 10.7
LT139	S	NRM 11.3	OV30011	FW	Versa 10.4	SP40007	AV	N94/OmniCity 10.7
LT140	S	NRM 11.3	OV30012	FW	Versa 10.4	SP40008	AV	N94/OmniCity 10.7
LT141	S	NRM 11.3	OV30013	FW	Versa 10.4	SP40009	AV	N94/OmniCity 10.7
LT142	S	NRM 11.3	OV30014	FW	Versa 10.4	SP40010	AV	N94/OmniCity 10.7
LT143	S	NRM 11.3	OV30015	FW	Versa 10.4	SP40011	AV	N94/OmniCity 10.7
LT144	S	NRM 11.3	OV30016	FW	Versa 10.4	SP40012	AV	N94/OmniCity 10.7
LT145	S	NRM 11.3	OV30017	FW	Versa 10.4	SP40013	AV	N94/OmniCity 10.7
LT146	S	NRM 11.3	OV30018	FW	Versa 10.4	SP40014	AV	N94/OmniCity 10.7
LT147	S	NRM 11.3	OV30019	PK	Versa 10.4	SP40015	AV	N94/OmniCity 10.7
LT148	V	NRM 11.3	OV30020	PK	Versa 10.4	SP40016	TV	N230/OmniCity 10.8
LT149	V	NRM 11.3	OV30021	PK	Versa 10.4	SP40017	TV	N230/OmniCity 10.8
LT150	V	NRM 11.3	OV30022	PK	Versa 10.4	SP40018	TV	N230/OmniCity 10.8
LT151	V	NRM 11.3	OV30023	PK	Versa 10.4	SP40019	TV	N230/OmniCity 10.8
LT152	V	NRM 11.3	OV30024	PK	Versa 10.4	SP40020	TV	N230/OmniCity 10.8
LT153	V	NRM 11.3	OV30025	PK	Versa 10.4	SP40021	TV	N230/OmniCity 10.8
LT154	V	NRM 11.3	OV30026	PK	Versa 10.4	SP40022	TV	N230/OmniCity 10.8
LT155	V	NRM 11.3	OV30101	PK	Versa 10.4	SP40023	AV	N230/OmniCity 10.8
LT156	V	NRM 11.3	OV30102	PK	Versa 10.4	SP40024	AV	N230/OmniCity 10.8
LT157	V	NRM 11.3	OV30103	PK	Versa 10.4	SP40025	TV	N230/OmniCity 10.8
LT158	V	NRM 11.3	OV30104	PK	Versa 10.4	SP40026	TV	N230/OmniCity 10.8
LT159	V	NRM 11.3	OV30105	PK	Versa 10.4	SP40027	AV	N230/OmniCity 10.8
LT160	V	NRM 11.3	OV30106	PK	Versa 10.4	SP40028	TV	N230/OmniCity 10.8
LT161	V	NRM 11.3	OV30107	PK	Versa 10.4	SP40029	TV	N230/OmniCity 10.8
LT162	V	NRM 11.3	OV30108	PK	Versa 10.4	SP40030	TV	N230/OmniCity 10.8
LT163	V	NRM 11.3	OV30109	PK	Versa 10.4	SP40031	TV	N230/OmniCity 10.8
LT164	V	NRM 11.3	OV30110	PK	Versa 10.4	SP40032	TV	N230/OmniCity 10.8
LT165	V	NRM 11.3	SDE20201	PK	E200/E200 8.9	SP40033	TV	N230/OmniCity 10.8
LT166	V	NRM 11.3	SDE20202	PK	E200/E200 8.9	SP40034	AV	N230/OmniCity 10.8
LT167	V	NRM 11.3	SDE20203	PK	E200/E200 8.9	SP40035	AV	N230/OmniCity 10.8
LT168	V	NRM 11.3	SDE20204	PK	E200/E200 8.9	SP40036	TV	N230/OmniCity 10.8
LT169	V	NRM 11.3	SDE20205	PK	E200/E200 8.9	SP40037	TV	N230/OmniCity 10.8
LT170	V	NRM 11.3	SDE20206	TV	E200/E200 8.9	SP40038	FW	N230/OmniCity 10.8
LT171	V	NRM 11.3	SDE20207	TV	E200/E200 8.9	SP40039	FW	N230/OmniCity 10.8
LT174	V	NRM 11.3	SDE20208	TV	E200/E200 8.9	SP40040	FW	N230/OmniCity 10.8
LT175	V	NRM 11.3	SDE20209	TV	E200/E200 8.9	SP40041	AV	N230/OmniCity 10.8
LT460	S	NRM (E6) 11.3	SDE20210	TV	E200/E200 8.9	SP40042	AV	N230/OmniCity 10.8
LT461	V	NRM (E6) 11.3	SDE20211	PK	E200/E200 8.9	SP40043	AV	N230/OmniCity 10.8
MCL30301	AV	Citaro 12.0	SDE20214	PK	E200/E200 8.9	SP40044	AV	N230/OmniCity 10.8
MCL30302	AV	Citaro 12.0	SLE40621	BT	N94/OmniDekka 10.6	SP40045	AV	N230/OmniCity 10.8
MCL30303	AV	Citaro 12.0	SLE40624	BT	N94/OmniDekka 10.6	SP40046	AV	N230/OmniCity 10.8
MCL30304	AV	Citaro 12.0	SLE40625	BT	N94/OmniDekka 10.6	SP40047	AV	N230/OmniCity 10.8
MCL30305	AV	Citaro 12.0	SLE40626	BT	N94/OmniDekka 10.6	SP40048	AV	N230/OmniCity 10.8
MCL30306	AV	Citaro 12.0	SLE40629	BT	N94/OmniDekka 10.6	SP40049	AV	N230/OmniCity 10.8
MCL30307	AV	Citaro 12.0	SLE40631	BT	N94/OmniDekka 10.6	SP40050	AV	N230/OmniCity 10.8
OCE37001	AV	MetroCity EV 10.6	SLE40635	BT	N94/OmniDekka 10.6	SP40051	AV	N230/OmniCity 10.8
OCE37002	AV	MetroCity EV 10.6	SLE40636	BT	N94/OmniDekka 10.6	SP40052	FW	N230/OmniCity 10.8
OCE37003	AV	MetroCity EV 10.6	SLE40640	BT	N94/OmniDekka 10.6	SP40053	FW	N230/OmniCity 10.8
OCE37004	AV	MetroCity EV 10.6	SLE40643	BT	N94/OmniDekka 10.6	SP40054	FW	N230/OmniCity 10.8
OT30201	AV	Tempo 12.0	SLE40644	BT	N94/OmniDekka 10.6	SP40055	FW	N230/OmniCity 10.8
OT30202	AV	Tempo 12.0	SLE40645	FW	N94/OmniDekka 10.6	SP40056	FW	N230/OmniCity 10.8
OT30203	AV	Tempo 12.0	SLE40646	FW	N94/OmniDekka 10.6	SP40057	FW	N230/OmniCity 10.8
OT30204	AV	Tempo 12.0	SLE40647	FW	N94/OmniDekka 10.6	SP40058	FW	N230/OmniCity 10.8
OT30205	AV	Tempo 12.0	SLE40648	FW	N94/OmniDekka 10.6	SP40059	FW	N230/OmniCity 10.8
OT30206	AV	Tempo 12.0	SLE40649	FW	N94/OmniDekka 10.6	SP40060	FW	N230/OmniCity 10.8

RATP-Dev London

No.	G.	Type	No.	G.	Type	No.	G.	Type
SP40061	FW	N230/OmniCity 10.8	SP40135	V	N230/OmniCity 10.8	TA40218	TV	Trident/ALX400 9.9
SP40062	FW	N230/OmniCity 10.8	SP40136	V	N230/OmniCity 10.8	TA40220	TV	Trident/ALX400 9.9
SP40063	FW	N230/OmniCity 10.8	SP40137	V	N230/OmniCity 10.8	TA40221	HH	Trident/ALX400 9.9
SP40064	FW	N230/OmniCity 10.8	SP40138	V	N230/OmniCity 10.8	TA40222	AV	Trident/ALX400 9.9
SP40065	FW	N230/OmniCity 10.8	SP40139	V	N230/OmniCity 10.8	TA40223	PK	Trident/ALX400 9.9
SP40066	FW	N230/OmniCity 10.8	SP40140	V	N230/OmniCity 10.8	TA40224	FW	Trident/ALX400 9.9
SP40067	FW	N230/OmniCity 10.8	SP40141	V	N230/OmniCity 10.8	TA40225	TV	Trident/ALX400 9.9
SP40068	SO	N230/OmniCity 10.8	SP40142	V	N230/OmniCity 10.8	TA40229	FW	Trident/ALX400 9.9
SP40069	SO	N230/OmniCity 10.8	SP40143	V	N230/OmniCity 10.8	TA40230	AV	Trident/ALX400 9.9
SP40070	SO	N230/OmniCity 10.8	SP40144	V	N230/OmniCity 10.8	TA40231	TV	Trident/ALX400 9.9
SP40071	SO	N230/OmniCity 10.8	SP40145	V	N230/OmniCity 10.8	TA40232	FW	Trident/ALX400 9.9
SP40072	SO	N230/OmniCity 10.8	SP40146	V	N230/OmniCity 10.8	TA40234	AV	Trident/ALX400 9.9
SP40073	SO	N230/OmniCity 10.8	SP40147	V	N230/OmniCity 10.8	TA40235	AV	Trident/ALX400 9.9
SP40074	BT	N230/OmniCity 10.8	SP40148	V	N230/OmniCity 10.8	TA40236	PK	Trident/ALX400 9.9
SP40075	SO	N230/OmniCity 10.8	SP40149	V	N230/OmniCity 10.8	TA40237	TV	Trident/ALX400 9.9
SP40076	SO	N230/OmniCity 10.8	SP40150	V	N230/OmniCity 10.8	TA40238	TV	Trident/ALX400 9.9
SP40077	SO	N230/OmniCity 10.8	SP40151	V	N230/OmniCity 10.8	TA40239	PK	Trident/ALX400 9.9
SP40078	SO	N230/OmniCity 10.8	SP40152	V	N230/OmniCity 10.8	TA40240	TV	Trident/ALX400 9.9
SP40079	SO	N230/OmniCity 10.8	SP40153	V	N230/OmniCity 10.8	TA40242	AV	Trident/ALX400 9.9
SP40080	SO	N230/OmniCity 10.8	SP40154	V	N230/OmniCity 10.8	TA40243	FW	Trident/ALX400 9.9
SP40081	SO	N230/OmniCity 10.8	SP40155	V	N230/OmniCity 10.8	TA40244	TV	Trident/ALX400 9.9
SP40082	SO	N230/OmniCity 10.8	SP40156	V	N230/OmniCity 10.8	TA40245	AV	Trident/ALX400 9.9
SP40083	SO	N230/OmniCity 10.8	SP40157	V	N230/OmniCity 10.8	TA40246	AV	Trident/ALX400 9.9
SP40084	SO	N230/OmniCity 10.8	SP40158	V	N230/OmniCity 10.8	TA40247	TV	Trident/ALX400 9.9
SP40085	BT	N230/OmniCity 10.8	SP40159	V	N230/OmniCity 10.8	TA40248	TV	Trident/ALX400 9.9
SP40086	BT	N230/OmniCity 10.8	SP40160	V	N230/OmniCity 10.8	TA40249	HH	Trident/ALX400 9.9
SP40087	BT	N230/OmniCity 10.8	SP40161	V	N230/OmniCity 10.8	TA40250	AV	Trident/ALX400 9.9
SP40088	FW	N230/OmniCity 10.8	SP40162	V	N230/OmniCity 10.8	TA40313	TV	Trident/ALX400 9.9
SP40089	FW	N230/OmniCity 10.8	SP40163	FW	N230/OmniCity 10.8	TA40316	FW	Trident/ALX400 9.9
SP40090	FW	N230/OmniCity 10.8	SP40164	FW	N230/OmniCity 10.8	TA40318	TV	Trident/ALX400 9.9
SP40091	FW	N230/OmniCity 10.8	SP40165	AV	N230/OmniCity 10.8	TA40320	TV	Trident/ALX400 9.9
SP40092	FW	N230/OmniCity 10.8	SP40166	AV	N230/OmniCity 10.8	TLA40321	AV	Trident/ALX400 10.5
SP40093	FW	N230/OmniCity 10.8	SP40167	AV	N230/OmniCity 10.8	TLA40322	AV	Trident/ALX400 10.5
SP40094	FW	N230/OmniCity 10.8	SP40168	AV	N230/OmniCity 10.8	TLA40323	FW	Trident/ALX400 10.5
SP40095	FW	N230/OmniCity 10.8	SP40169	AV	N230/OmniCity 10.8	TLA40324	FW	Trident/ALX400 10.5
SP40096	TV	N230/OmniCity 10.8	SP40170	AV	N230/OmniCity 10.8	TLA40325	AV	Trident/ALX400 10.5
SP40097	TV	N230/OmniCity 10.8	SP40171	AV	N230/OmniCity 10.8	TLA40326	HH	Trident/ALX400 10.5
SP40098	TV	N230/OmniCity 10.8	SP40172	AV	N230/OmniCity 10.8	TLA40327	HH	Trident/ALX400 10.5
SP40099	TV	N230/OmniCity 10.8	SP40173	AV	N230/OmniCity 10.8	TLA40328	HH	Trident/ALX400 10.5
SP40100	TV	N230/OmniCity 10.8	SP40174	AV	N230/OmniCity 10.8	VH45101	BT	B5LH/Gemini 2 (EC) 10.5
SP40101	TV	N230/OmniCity 10.8	SP40175	AV	N230/OmniCity 10.8	VH45102	AV	B5LH/Gemini 2 (EC) 10.5
SP40102	FW	N230/OmniCity 10.8	SP40176	AV	N230/OmniCity 10.8	VH45103	BT	B5LH/Gemini 2 (EC) 10.5
SP40103	TV	N230/OmniCity 10.8	SP40177	AV	N230/OmniCity 10.8	VH45104	BT	B5LH/Gemini 2 (EC) 10.5
SP40104	TV	N230/OmniCity 10.8	SP40178	AV	N230/OmniCity 10.8	VH45105	BT	B5LH/Gemini 2 (EC) 10.5
SP40105	TV	N230/OmniCity 10.8	SP40179	AV	N230/OmniCity 10.8	VH45106	BT	B5LH/Gemini 2 (EC) 10.5
SP40106	TV	N230/OmniCity 10.8	SP40180	AV	N230/OmniCity 10.8	VH45107	BT	B5LH/Gemini 2 (EC) 10.5
SP40107	TV	N230/OmniCity 10.8	SP40181	AV	N230/OmniCity 10.8	VH45108	BT	B5LH/Gemini 2 (EC) 10.5
SP40108	TV	N230/OmniCity 10.8	SP40182	AV	N230/OmniCity 10.8	VH45109	BT	B5LH/Gemini 2 (EC) 10.5
SP40109	FW	N230/OmniCity 10.8	SP40183	AV	N230/OmniCity 10.8	VH45110	BT	B5LH/Gemini 2 (EC) 10.5
SP40110	FW	N230/OmniCity 10.8	SP40184	AV	N230/OmniCity 10.8	VH45111	BT	B5LH/Gemini 2 (EC) 10.5
SP40111	FW	N230/OmniCity 10.8	SP40185	AV	N230/OmniCity 10.8	VH45112	BT	B5LH/Gemini 2 (EC) 10.5
SP40112	FW	N230/OmniCity 10.8	SP40186	AV	N230/OmniCity 10.8	VH45113	BT	B5LH/Gemini 2 (EC) 10.5
SP40113	FW	N230/OmniCity 10.8	SP40187	AV	N230/OmniCity 10.8	VH45114	BT	B5LH/Gemini 2 (EC) 10.5
SP40114	FW	N230/OmniCity 10.8	SP40188	AV	N230/OmniCity 10.8	VH45115	BT	B5LH/Gemini 2 (EC) 10.5
SP40115	FW	N230/OmniCity 10.8	SP40189	AV	N230/OmniCity 10.8	VH45116	BT	B5LH/Gemini 2 (EC) 10.5
SP40116	FW	N230/OmniCity 10.8	SP40190	AV	N230/OmniCity 10.8	VH45117	BT	B5LH/Gemini 2 (EC) 10.5
SP40117	FW	N230/OmniCity 10.8	SP40191	AV	N230/OmniCity 10.8	VH45118	BT	B5LH/Gemini 2 (EC) 10.5
SP40118	FW	N230/OmniCity 10.8	SP40192	HH	N230/OmniCity 10.8	VH45119	BT	B5LH/Gemini 2 (EC) 10.5
SP40119	FW	N230/OmniCity 10.8	SP40193	HH	N230/OmniCity 10.8	VH45120	BT	B5LH/Gemini 2 (EC) 10.5
SP40120	FW	N230/OmniCity 10.8	SP40194	HH	N230/OmniCity 10.8	VH45121	BT	B5LH/Gemini 2 (EC) 10.5
SP40121	FW	N230/OmniCity 10.8	SP40195	HH	N230/OmniCity 10.8	VH45122	BT	B5LH/Gemini 2 (EC) 10.5
SP40122	FW	N230/OmniCity 10.8	SP40196	HH	N230/OmniCity 10.8	VH45123	BT	B5LH/Gemini 2 (EC) 10.5
SP40123	FW	N230/OmniCity 10.8	SP40197	HH	N230/OmniCity 10.8	VH45124	HH	B5LH/Gemini 3 10.5
SP40124	FW	N230/OmniCity 10.8	SP40198	HH	N230/OmniCity 10.8	VH45125	HH	B5LH/Gemini 3 10.5
SP40125	FW	N230/OmniCity 10.8	SP40199	HH	N230/OmniCity 10.8	VH45126	HH	B5LH/Gemini 3 10.5
SP40126	FW	N230/OmniCity 10.8	SP40200	HH	N230/OmniCity 10.8	VH45127	HH	B5LH/Gemini 3 10.5
SP40127	FW	N230/OmniCity 10.8	SP40201	HH	N230/OmniCity 10.8	VH45128	HH	B5LH/Gemini 3 10.5
SP40128	FW	N230/OmniCity 10.8	SP40202	HH	N230/OmniCity 10.8	VH45129	HH	B5LH/Gemini 3 10.5
SP40129	FW	N230/OmniCity 10.8	SP40203	HH	N230/OmniCity 10.8	VH45130	HH	B5LH/Gemini 3 10.5
SP40130	FW	N230/OmniCity 10.8	SP40204	HH	N230/OmniCity 10.8	VH45131	HH	B5LH/Gemini 3 10.5
SP40131	FW	N230/OmniCity 10.8	SP40205	HH	N230/OmniCity 10.8	VH45132	HH	B5LH/Gemini 3 10.5
SP40132	FW	N230/OmniCity 10.8	SP40206	HH	N230/OmniCity 10.8	VH45133	HH	B5LH/Gemini 3 10.5
SP40133	FW	N230/OmniCity 10.8	TA40213	FW	Trident/ALX400 9.9	VH45134	HH	B5LH/Gemini 3 10.5
SP40134	V	N230/OmniCity 10.8	TA40214	TV	Trident/ALX400 9.9	VH45135	HH	B5LH/Gemini 3 10.5

No.	G.	Type	No.	G.	Type	No.	G.	Type
VH45136	HH	B5LH/Gemini 3 10.5	VH45164	FW	B5LH/Gemini 3 ST 10.6	VH45192	S	B5LH/Gemini 3 ST 10.6
VH45137	HH	B5LH/Gemini 3 10.5	VH45165	FW	B5LH/Gemini 3 ST 10.6	VH45193	S	B5LH/Gemini 3 ST 10.6
VH45138	HH	B5LH/Gemini 3 10.5	VH45166	FW	B5LH/Gemini 3 ST 10.6	VH45194	S	B5LH/Gemini 3 ST 10.6
VH45139	HH	B5LH/Gemini 3 10.5	VH45167	TV	B5LH/Gemini 3 ST 10.6	VH45195	S	B5LH/Gemini 3 ST 10.6
VH45140	HH	B5LH/Gemini 3 10.5	VH45168	TV	B5LH/Gemini 3 ST 10.6	VH45196	S	B5LH/Gemini 3 ST 10.6
VH45141	HH	B5LH/Gemini 3 10.5	VH45169	TV	B5LH/Gemini 3 ST 10.6	VH45197	S	B5LH/Gemini 3 ST 10.6
VH45142	HH	B5LH/Gemini 3 10.5	VH45170	TV	B5LH/Gemini 3 ST 10.6	VH45198	S	B5LH/Gemini 3 ST 10.6
VH45143	HH	B5LH/Gemini 3 10.5	VH45171	TV	B5LH/Gemini 3 ST 10.6	VH45199	S	B5LH/Gemini 3 ST 10.6
VH45144	HH	B5LH/Gemini 3 10.5	VH45172	TV	B5LH/Gemini 3 ST 10.6	VH45200	S	B5LH/Gemini 3 ST 10.6
VH45145	HH	B5LH/Gemini 3 10.5	VH45173	TV	B5LH/Gemini 3 ST 10.6	VH45201	NC	B5LH/Gemini 3 ST 10.6
VH45146	HH	B5LH/Gemini 3 10.5	VH45174	TV	B5LH/Gemini 3 ST 10.6	VH45202	NC	B5LH/Gemini 3 ST 10.6
VH45147	HH	B5LH/Gemini 3 10.5	VH45175	TV	B5LH/Gemini 3 ST 10.6	VHR45203	BT	B5LH/SRM 10.6
VH45148	HH	B5LH/Gemini 3 10.5	VH45176	TV	B5LH/Gemini 3 ST 10.6	VHR45204	BT	B5LH/SRM 10.6
VH45149	HH	B5LH/Gemini 3 10.5	VH45177	TV	B5LH/Gemini 3 ST 10.6	VHR45205	BT	B5LH/SRM 10.6
VH45150	HH	B5LH/Gemini 3 10.5	VH45178	TV	B5LH/Gemini 3 ST 10.6	VHR45206	BT	B5LH/SRM 10.6
VH45151	HH	B5LH/Gemini 3 10.5	VH45179	TV	B5LH/Gemini 3 ST 10.6	VHR45207	BT	B5LH/SRM 10.6
VH45152	HH	B5LH/Gemini 3 10.5	VH45180	TV	B5LH/Gemini 3 ST 10.6	VHR45208	BT	B5LH/SRM 10.6
VH45153	BT	B5LH/Gemini 3 ST 10.6	VH45181	TV	B5LH/Gemini 3 ST 10.6	VLE40515	TV	B7TL/Vyking 11.0
VH45154	BT	B5LH/Gemini 3 ST 10.6	VH45182	TV	B5LH/Gemini 3 ST 10.6	VLE40518	BT	B7TL/Vyking 11.0
VH45155	BT	B5LH/Gemini 3 ST 10.6	VH45183	FW	B5LH/Gemini 3 ST 10.6	VLE40522	BT	B7TL/Vyking 11.0
VH45156	BT	B5LH/Gemini 3 ST 10.6	VH45184	FW	B5LH/Gemini 3 ST 10.6	VLE40523	BT	B7TL/Vyking 11.0
VH45157	BT	B5LH/Gemini 3 ST 10.6	VH45185	FW	B5LH/Gemini 3 ST 10.6	VLP40718	BT	B7TL/President 10.6
VH45158	BT	B5LH/Gemini 3 ST 10.6	VH45186	FW	B5LH/Gemini 3 ST 10.6	VLP40719	BT	B7TL/President 10.6
VH45159	BT	B5LH/Gemini 3 ST 10.6	VH45187	S	B5LH/Gemini 3 ST 10.6	VLP40720	BT	B7TL/President 10.6
VH45160	BT	B5LH/Gemini 3 ST 10.6	VH45188	S	B5LH/Gemini 3 ST 10.6	VLP40722	BT	B7TL/President 10.6
VH45161	BT	B5LH/Gemini 3 ST 10.6	VH45189	S	B5LH/Gemini 3 ST 10.6	VLP40725	BT	B7TL/President 10.6
VH45162	TV	B5LH/Gemini 3 ST 10.6	VH45190	S	B5LH/Gemini 3 ST 10.6	VLP40726	BT	B7TL/President 10.6
VH45163	FW	B5LH/Gemini 3 ST 10.6	VH45191	S	B5LH/Gemini 3 ST 10.6	VLP40727	BT	B7TL/President 10.6

VHR45204 runs through Harrow on the H14. Normally these can be found on route 183. However, they do spill onto other routes. *Tommy Cooling*

Stagecoach

No.	G.	Type	No.	G.	Type	No.	G.	Type
10101	WH	E40D/E400 (EC) 10.2	10170	RM	E40D/E400 (EC) 10.2	10334	NS	E40D/E400MMC 10.35
10102	WH	E40D/E400 (EC) 10.2	10171	RM	E40D/E400 (EC) 10.2	10335	NS	E40D/E400MMC 10.35
10103	WH	E40D/E400 (EC) 10.2	10172	T	E40D/E400 (EC) 10.2	10336	NS	E40D/E400MMC 10.35
10104	WH	E40D/E400 (EC) 10.2	10173	T	E40D/E400 (EC) 10.2	10337	NS	E40D/E400MMC 10.35
10105	WH	E40D/E400 (EC) 10.2	10174	T	E40D/E400 (EC) 10.2	10338	NS	E40D/E400MMC 10.35
10106	WH	E40D/E400 (EC) 10.2	10175	T	E40D/E400 (EC) 10.2	10339	NS	E40D/E400MMC 10.35
10107	WH	E40D/E400 (EC) 10.2	10176	T	E40D/E400 (EC) 10.2	10340	NS	E40D/E400MMC 10.35
10108	WH	E40D/E400 (EC) 10.2	10177	T	E40D/E400 (EC) 10.2	10341	NS	E40D/E400MMC 10.35
10109	WH	E40D/E400 (EC) 10.2	10178	T	E40D/E400 (EC) 10.2	10342	NS	E40D/E400MMC 10.35
10110	WH	E40D/E400 (EC) 10.2	10179	T	E40D/E400 (EC) 10.2	10343	NS	E40D/E400MMC 10.35
10111	WH	E40D/E400 (EC) 10.2	10180	T	E40D/E400 (EC) 10.2	10344	NS	E40D/E400MMC 10.35
10112	WH	E40D/E400 (EC) 10.2	10181	T	E40D/E400 (EC) 10.2	10345	NS	E40D/E400MMC 10.35
10113	T	E40D/E400 (EC) 10.2	10182	T	E40D/E400 (EC) 10.2	10346	NS	E40D/E400MMC 10.35
10114	T	E40D/E400 (EC) 10.2	10183	T	E40D/E400 (EC) 10.2	10347	NS	E40D/E400MMC 10.35
10115	T	E40D/E400 (EC) 10.2	10184	TB	E40D/E400 (EC) 10.2	10348	TL	E40D/E400MMC 10.35
10116	T	E40D/E400 (EC) 10.2	10185	TB	E40D/E400 (EC) 10.2	10349	TL	E40D/E400MMC 10.35
10117	T	E40D/E400 (EC) 10.2	10186	TB	E40D/E400 (EC) 10.2	10350	TL	E40D/E400MMC 10.35
10118	T	E40D/E400 (EC) 10.2	10187	TB	E40D/E400 (EC) 10.2	12128	T	E40H/E400 (EC) 10.2
10119	T	E40D/E400 (EC) 10.2	10188	TB	E40D/E400 (EC) 10.2	12129	T	E40H/E400 (EC) 10.2
10120	T	E40D/E400 (EC) 10.2	10189	TB	E40D/E400 (EC) 10.2	12130	T	E40H/E400 (EC) 10.2
10121	T	E40D/E400 (EC) 10.2	10190	TB	E40D/E400 (EC) 10.2	12131	T	E40H/E400 (EC) 10.2
10122	T	E40D/E400 (EC) 10.2	10191	TB	E40D/E400 (EC) 10.2	12132	T	E40H/E400 (EC) 10.2
10123	T	E40D/E400 (EC) 10.2	10192	TB	E40D/E400 (EC) 10.2	12133	T	E40H/E400 (EC) 10.2
10124	TL	E40D/E400 (EC) 10.2	10193	TB	E40D/E400 (EC) 10.2	12134	T	E40H/E400 (EC) 10.2
10125	TL	E40D/E400 (EC) 10.2	10194	TB	E40D/E400 (EC) 10.2	12135	T	E40H/E400 (EC) 10.2
10126	TL	E40D/E400 (EC) 10.2	10195	TB	E40D/E400 (EC) 10.2	12136	T	E40H/E400 (EC) 10.2
10127	TL	E40D/E400 (EC) 10.2	10196	PD	E40D/E400 (EC) 10.2	12137	T	E40H/E400 (EC) 10.2
10128	TL	E40D/E400 (EC) 10.2	10197	TL	E40D/400 (E6) 10.35	12138	T	E40H/E400 (EC) 10.2
10129	TL	E40D/E400 (EC) 10.2	10198	TL	E40D/400 (E6) 10.35	12139	T	E40H/E400 (EC) 10.2
10130	TL	E40D/E400 (EC) 10.2	10199	TL	E40D/400 (E6) 10.35	12140	T	E40H/E400 (EC) 10.2
10131	TL	E40D/E400 (EC) 10.2	10200	TL	E40D/400 (E6) 10.35	12141	T	E40H/E400 (EC) 10.2
10132	TL	E40D/E400 (EC) 10.2	10201	TL	E40D/400 (E6) 10.35	12142	T	E40H/E400 (EC) 10.2
10133	TL	E40D/E400 (EC) 10.2	10202	TL	E40D/400 (E6) 10.35	12143	T	E40H/E400 (EC) 10.2
10134	TL	E40D/E400 (EC) 10.2	10203	TL	E40D/400 (E6) 10.35	12144	T	E40H/E400 (EC) 10.2
10135	TL	E40D/E400 (EC) 10.2	10204	TL	E40D/400 (E6) 10.35	12145	T	E40H/E400 (EC) 10.2
10136	TL	E40D/E400 (EC) 10.2	10205	TL	E40D/400 (E6) 10.35	12146	T	E40H/E400 (EC) 10.2
10137	TL	E40D/E400 (EC) 10.2	10301	NS	E40D/E400MMC 10.35	12147	T	E40H/E400 (EC) 10.2
10138	TL	E40D/E400 (EC) 10.2	10302	NS	E40D/E400MMC 10.35	12148	T	E40H/E400 (EC) 10.2
10139	TB	E40D/E400 (EC) 10.2	10303	NS	E40D/E400MMC 10.35	12149	T	E40H/E400 (EC) 10.2
10140	TB	E40D/E400 (EC) 10.2	10304	NS	E40D/E400MMC 10.35	12150	T	E40H/E400 (EC) 10.2
10141	TB	E40D/E400 (EC) 10.2	10305	NS	E40D/E400MMC 10.35	12151	T	E40H/E400 (EC) 10.2
10142	TB	E40D/E400 (EC) 10.2	10306	NS	E40D/E400MMC 10.35	12152	T	E40H/E400 (EC) 10.2
10143	TB	E40D/E400 (EC) 10.2	10307	NS	E40D/E400MMC 10.35	12153	T	E40H/E400 (EC) 10.2
10144	TB	E40D/E400 (EC) 10.2	10308	BK	E40D/E400MMC 10.35	12261	TL	E40H/E400 (E6) 10.35
10145	TB	E40D/E400 (EC) 10.2	10309	BK	E40D/E400MMC 10.35	12262	TL	E40H/E400 (E6) 10.35
10146	TB	E40D/E400 (EC) 10.2	10310	BK	E40D/E400MMC 10.35	12263	TL	E40H/E400 (E6) 10.35
10147	TB	E40D/E400 (EC) 10.2	10311	BK	E40D/E400MMC 10.35	12264	TL	E40H/E400 (E6) 10.35
10148	TB	E40D/E400 (EC) 10.2	10312	BK	E40D/E400MMC 10.35	12265	TL	E40H/E400 (E6) 10.35
10149	TB	E40D/E400 (EC) 10.2	10313	BK	E40D/E400MMC 10.35	12266	TL	E40H/E400 (E6) 10.35
10150	TB	E40D/E400 (EC) 10.2	10314	BK	E40D/E400MMC 10.35	12267	TL	E40H/E400 (E6) 10.35
10151	TB	E40D/E400 (EC) 10.2	10315	BK	E40D/E400MMC 10.35	12268	TL	E40H/E400 (E6) 10.35
10152	TB	E40D/E400 (EC) 10.2	10316	BK	E40D/E400MMC 10.35	12269	TL	E40H/E400 (E6) 10.35
10153	TB	E40D/E400 (EC) 10.2	10317	BK	E40D/E400MMC 10.35	12270	TL	E40H/E400 (E6) 10.35
10154	TB	E40D/E400 (EC) 10.2	10318	BK	E40D/E400MMC 10.35	12271	TL	E40H/E400 (E6) 10.35
10155	RM	E40D/E400 (EC) 10.2	10319	BK	E40D/E400MMC 10.35	12272	TL	E40H/E400 (E6) 10.35
10156	RM	E40D/E400 (EC) 10.2	10320	BK	E40D/E400MMC 10.35	12273	TL	E40H/E400 (E6) 10.35
10157	RM	E40D/E400 (EC) 10.2	10321	BK	E40D/E400MMC 10.35	12274	TL	E40H/E400 (E6) 10.35
10158	RM	E40D/E400 (EC) 10.2	10322	BK	E40D/E400MMC 10.35	12275	TL	E40H/E400 (E6) 10.35
10159	RM	E40D/E400 (EC) 10.2	10323	BK	E40D/E400MMC 10.35	12276	TL	E40H/E400 (E6) 10.35
10160	RM	E40D/E400 (EC) 10.2	10324	BK	E40D/E400MMC 10.35	12277	TL	E40H/E400 (E6) 10.35
10161	RM	E40D/E400 (EC) 10.2	10325	BK	E40D/E400MMC 10.35	12278	TL	E40H/E400 (E6) 10.35
10162	RM	E40D/E400 (EC) 10.2	10326	BK	E40D/E400MMC 10.35	12279	TL	E40H/E400 (E6) 10.35
10163	RM	E40D/E400 (EC) 10.2	10327	BK	E40D/E400MMC 10.35	12280	TL	E40H/E400 (E6) 10.35
10164	TB	E40D/E400 (EC) 10.2	10328	BK	E40D/E400MMC 10.35	12281	TL	E40H/E400 (E6) 10.35
10165	RM	E40D/E400 (EC) 10.2	10329	BK	E40D/E400MMC 10.35	12282	TL	E40H/E400 (E6) 10.35
10166	RM	E40D/E400 (EC) 10.2	10330	BK	E40D/E400MMC 10.35	12283	TL	E40H/E400 (E6) 10.35
10167	RM	E40D/E400 (EC) 10.2	10331	BK	E40D/E400MMC 10.35	12284	TL	E40H/E400 (E6) 10.35
10168	RM	E40D/E400 (EC) 10.2	10332	BK	E40D/E400MMC 10.35	12285	TL	E40H/E400 (E6) 10.35
10169	RM	E40D/E400 (EC) 10.2	10333	NS	E40D/E400MMC 10.35	12286	TL	E40H/E400 (E6) 10.35

No.	G.	Type	No.	G.	Type	No.	G.	Type
12287	TL	E40H/E400 (E6) 10.35	12361	PD	E40H/E400 (E6) 10.35	13010	PD	B5LH/Gemini 3 10.5
12288	TL	E40H/E400 (E6) 10.35	12362	PD	E40H/E400 (E6) 10.35	13011	PD	B5LH/Gemini 3 10.5
12289	TL	E40H/E400 (E6) 10.35	12363	PD	E40H/E400 (E6) 10.35	13012	PD	B5LH/Gemini 3 10.5
12290	TL	E40H/E400 (E6) 10.35	12364	PD	E40H/E400 (E6) 10.35	13013	PD	B5LH/Gemini 3 10.5
12291	TL	E40H/E400 (E6) 10.35	12365	PD	E40H/E400MMC 10.35	13014	PD	B5LH/Gemini 3 10.5
12292	TL	E40H/E400 (E6) 10.35	12366	PD	E40H/E400MMC 10.35	13015	PD	B5LH/Gemini 3 10.5
12293	PD	E40H/E400 (E6) 10.35	12367	PD	E40H/E400MMC 10.35	13016	PD	B5LH/Gemini 3 10.5
12294	PD	E40H/E400 (E6) 10.35	12368	PD	E40H/E400MMC 10.35	13017	PD	B5LH/Gemini 3 10.5
12295	PD	E40H/E400 (E6) 10.35	12369	PD	E40H/E400MMC 10.35	13018	PD	B5LH/Gemini 3 10.5
12296	PD	E40H/E400 (E6) 10.35	12370	PD	E40H/E400MMC 10.35	13019	PD	B5LH/Gemini 3 10.5
12297	PD	E40H/E400 (E6) 10.35	12371	PD	E40H/E400MMC 10.35	13020	PD	B5LH/Gemini 3 10.5
12298	PD	E40H/E400 (E6) 10.35	12372	PD	E40H/E400MMC 10.35	13021	PD	B5LH/Gemini 3 10.5
12299	PD	E40H/E400 (E6) 10.35	12373	PD	E40H/E400MMC 10.35	13022	PD	B5LH/Gemini 3 10.5
12300	PD	E40H/E400 (E6) 10.35	12374	PD	E40H/E400MMC 10.35	13023	PD	B5LH/Gemini 3 10.5
12301	PD	E40H/E400 (E6) 10.35	12375	PD	E40H/E400MMC 10.35	13024	PD	B5LH/Gemini 3 10.5
12302	PD	E40H/E400 (E6) 10.35	12376	PD	E40H/E400MMC 10.35	13025	PD	B5LH/Gemini 3 10.5
12303	PD	E40H/E400 (E6) 10.35	12377	PD	E40H/E400MMC 10.35	13026	PD	B5LH/Gemini 3 10.5
12304	BW	E40H/E400 (E6) 10.35	12378	PD	E40H/E400MMC 10.35	13027	PD	B5LH/Gemini 3 10.5
12305	BW	E40H/E400 (E6) 10.35	12379	PD	E40H/E400MMC 10.35	13028	PD	B5LH/Gemini 3 10.5
12306	BW	E40H/E400 (E6) 10.35	12380	PD	E40H/E400MMC 10.35	13029	PD	B5LH/Gemini 3 10.5
12307	BW	E40H/E400 (E6) 10.35	12381	PD	E40H/E400MMC 10.35	13030	PD	B5LH/Gemini 3 10.5
12308	BW	E40H/E400 (E6) 10.35	12382	PD	E40H/E400MMC 10.35	13031	PD	B5LH/Gemini 3 10.5
12309	BW	E40H/E400 (E6) 10.35	12383	PD	E40H/E400MMC 10.35	13032	PD	B5LH/Gemini 3 10.5
12310	BW	E40H/E400 (E6) 10.35	12384	PD	E40H/E400MMC 10.35	13061	PD	B5LH/E400MMC 10.5
12311	BW	E40H/E400 (E6) 10.35	12385	PD	E40H/E400MMC 10.35	13062	PD	B5LH/E400MMC 10.5
12312	BW	E40H/E400 (E6) 10.35	12386	PD	E40H/E400MMC 10.35	13063	PD	B5LH/E400MMC 10.5
12313	BW	E40H/E400 (E6) 10.35	12387	PD	E40H/E400MMC 10.35	13064	PD	B5LH/E400MMC 10.5
12314	BW	E40H/E400 (E6) 10.35	12388	PD	E40H/E400MMC 10.35	13065	PD	B5LH/E400MMC 10.5
12315	BW	E40H/E400 (E6) 10.35	12389	PD	E40H/E400MMC 10.35	13066	PD	B5LH/E400MMC 10.5
12316	BW	E40H/E400 (E6) 10.35	12390	PD	E40H/E400MMC 10.35	13067	PD	B5LH/E400MMC 10.5
12317	BW	E40H/E400 (E6) 10.35	12391	PD	E40H/E400MMC 10.35	13068	PD	B5LH/E400MMC 10.5
12318	BW	E40H/E400 (E6) 10.35	12392	PD	E40H/E400MMC 10.35	13069	PD	B5LH/E400MMC 10.5
12319	BW	E40H/E400 (E6) 10.35	12393	PD	E40H/E400MMC 10.35	13070	PD	B5LH/E400MMC 10.5
12320	BW	E40H/E400 (E6) 10.35	12394	PD	E40H/E400MMC 10.35	13071	PD	B5LH/E400MMC 10.5
12321	BW	E40H/E400 (E6) 10.35	12395	PD	E40H/E400MMC 10.35	13072	PD	B5LH/E400MMC 10.5
12322	BW	E40H/E400 (E6) 10.35	12396	PD	E40H/E400MMC 10.35	13073	PD	B5LH/E400MMC 10.5
12323	BW	E40H/E400 (E6) 10.35	12397	PD	E40H/E400MMC 10.35	13074	PD	B5LH/E400MMC 10.5
12324	BW	E40H/E400 (E6) 10.35	12398	PD	E40H/E400MMC 10.35	13075	PD	B5LH/E400MMC 10.5
12325	BW	E40H/E400 (E6) 10.35	12399	PD	E40H/E400MMC 10.35	13076	PD	B5LH/E400MMC 10.5
12326	BW	E40H/E400 (E6) 10.35	12400	PD	E40H/E400MMC 10.35	13077	PD	B5LH/E400MMC 10.5
12327	BW	E40H/E400 (E6) 10.35	12401	TL	E40H/E400MMC 10.35	13078	PD	B5LH/E400MMC 10.5
12328	BW	E40H/E400 (E6) 10.35	12402	PD	E40H/E400MMC 10.35	13079	PD	B5LH/E400MMC 10.5
12329	BW	E40H/E400 (E6) 10.35	12403	BW	E40H/E400MMC 10.35	13080	PD	B5LH/E400MMC 10.5
12330	BW	E40H/E400 (E6) 10.35	12404	BW	E40H/E400MMC 10.35	13081	PD	B5LH/E400MMC 10.5
12331	BW	E40H/E400 (E6) 10.35	12405	BW	E40H/E400MMC 10.35	13082	TL	B5LH/E400MMC 10.5
12332	BW	E40H/E400 (E6) 10.35	12406	BW	E40H/E400MMC 10.35	13083	TL	B5LH/E400MMC 10.5
12333	BW	E40H/E400 (E6) 10.35	12407	BW	E40H/E400MMC 10.35	13084	TL	B5LH/E400MMC 10.5
12334	PD	E40H/E400 (E6) 10.35	12408	BW	E40H/E400MMC 10.35	13085	TL	B5LH/E400MMC 10.5
12335	PD	E40H/E400 (E6) 10.35	12409	BW	E40H/E400MMC 10.35	13086	TL	B5LH/E400MMC 10.5
12336	PD	E40H/E400 (E6) 10.35	12410	BW	E40H/E400MMC 10.35	13087	TL	B5LH/E400MMC 10.5
12337	PD	E40H/E400 (E6) 10.35	12411	BW	E40H/E400MMC 10.35	13088	TL	B5LH/E400MMC 10.5
12338	PD	E40H/E400 (E6) 10.35	12412	BW	E40H/E400MMC 10.35	13089	TL	B5LH/E400MMC 10.5
12339	PD	E40H/E400 (E6) 10.35	12413	BW	E40H/E400MMC 10.35	13090	TL	B5LH/E400MMC 10.5
12340	PD	E40H/E400 (E6) 10.35	12414	BW	E40H/E400MMC 10.35	13091	TL	B5LH/E400MMC 10.5
12341	PD	E40H/E400 (E6) 10.35	12415	BW	E40H/E400MMC 10.35	13092	TL	B5LH/E400MMC 10.5
12342	PD	E40H/E400 (E6) 10.35	12416	BW	E40H/E400MMC 10.35	13093	TL	B5LH/E400MMC 10.5
12343	PD	E40H/E400 (E6) 10.35	12417	BW	E40H/E400MMC 10.35	13094	TL	B5LH/E400MMC 10.5
12344	PD	E40H/E400 (E6) 10.35	12418	BW	E40H/E400MMC 10.35	13095	TL	B5LH/E400MMC 10.5
12345	PD	E40H/E400 (E6) 10.35	12419	BW	E40H/E400MMC 10.35	13096	TL	B5LH/E400MMC 10.5
12346	PD	E40H/E400 (E6) 10.35	12420	BW	E40H/E400MMC 10.35	13097	TL	B5LH/E400MMC 10.5
12347	PD	E40H/E400 (E6) 10.35	12421	BW	E40H/E400MMC 10.35	13098	TL	B5LH/E400MMC 10.5
12348	PD	E40H/E400 (E6) 10.35	12422	BW	E40H/E400MMC 10.35	13099	TL	B5LH/E400MMC 10.5
12349	PD	E40H/E400 (E6) 10.35	12423	BW	E40H/E400MMC 10.35	13100	TL	B5LH/E400MMC 10.5
12350	PD	E40H/E400 (E6) 10.35	12424	BW	E40H/E400MMC 10.35	13101	TL	B5LH/E400MMC 10.5
12351	PD	E40H/E400 (E6) 10.35	12425	BW	E40H/E400MMC 10.35	13102	TL	B5LH/E400MMC 10.5
12352	PD	E40H/E400 (E6) 10.35	13001	PD	B5LH/Gemini 3 10.5	15001	RM	N230/OmniCity 10.8
12353	PD	E40H/E400 (E6) 10.35	13002	PD	B5LH/Gemini 3 10.5	15002	RM	N230/OmniCity 10.8
12354	PD	E40H/E400 (E6) 10.35	13003	PD	B5LH/Gemini 3 10.5	15003	RM	N230/OmniCity 10.8
12355	PD	E40H/E400 (E6) 10.35	13004	PD	B5LH/Gemini 3 10.5	15004	RM	N230/OmniCity 10.8
12356	PD	E40H/E400 (E6) 10.35	13005	PD	B5LH/Gemini 3 10.5	15005	RM	N230/OmniCity 10.8
12357	PD	E40H/E400 (E6) 10.35	13006	PD	B5LH/Gemini 3 10.5	15006	RM	N230/OmniCity 10.8
12358	PD	E40H/E400 (E6) 10.35	13007	PD	B5LH/Gemini 3 10.5	15007	RM	N230/OmniCity 10.8
12359	PD	E40H/E400 (E6) 10.35	13008	PD	B5LH/Gemini 3 10.5	15008	RM	N230/OmniCity 10.8
12360	PD	E40H/E400 (E6) 10.35	13009	PD	B5LH/Gemini 3 10.5	15009	RM	N230/OmniCity 10.8

Stagecoach

No.	G.	Type	No.	G.	Type	No.	G.	Type
15010	RM	N230/OmniCity 10.8	15085	WH	N230/OmniCity 10.8	17848	WH	Trident/ALX400 10.5
15011	RM	N230/OmniCity 10.8	15086	WH	N230/OmniCity 10.8	17849	WH	Trident/ALX400 10.5
15012	RM	N230/OmniCity 10.8	15087	WH	N230/OmniCity 10.8	17850	RM	Trident/ALX400 10.5
15014	RM	N230/OmniCity 10.8	15088	WH	N230/OmniCity 10.8	17851	WH	Trident/ALX400 10.5
15015	RM	N230/OmniCity 10.8	15089	WH	N230/OmniCity 10.8	17852	BK	Trident/ALX400 10.5
15016	RM	N230/OmniCity 10.8	15090	WH	N230/OmniCity 10.8	17853	BK	Trident/ALX400 10.5
15017	RM	N230/OmniCity 10.8	15091	WH	N230/OmniCity 10.8	17855	BK	Trident/ALX400 10.5
15018	RM	N230/OmniCity 10.8	15092	WH	N230/OmniCity 10.8	17856	WH	Trident/ALX400 10.5
15019	RM	N230/OmniCity 10.8	15093	WH	N230/OmniCity 10.8	17857	TB	Trident/ALX400 10.5
15020	RM	N230/OmniCity 10.8	15094	WH	N230/OmniCity 10.8	17858	NS	Trident/ALX400 10.5
15021	RM	N230/OmniCity 10.8	15095	WH	N230/OmniCity 10.8	17859	NS	Trident/ALX400 10.5
15022	RM	N230/OmniCity 10.8	15096	PD	N230/OmniCity 10.8	17860	PD	Trident/ALX400 10.5
15023	RM	N230/OmniCity 10.8	15097	BW	N230/OmniCity 10.8	17861	PD	Trident/ALX400 10.5
15024	RM	N230/OmniCity 10.8	15098	BW	N230/OmniCity 10.8	17862	PD	Trident/ALX400 10.5
15025	RM	N230/OmniCity 10.8	15099	BW	N230/OmniCity 10.8	17863	PD	Trident/ALX400 10.5
15026	RM	N230/OmniCity 10.8	15100	BW	N230/OmniCity 10.8	17864	TB	Trident/ALX400 10.5
15027	RM	N230/OmniCity 10.8	15101	BW	N230/OmniCity 10.8	17865	WH	Trident/ALX400 10.5
15028	RM	N230/OmniCity 10.8	15102	WH	N230/OmniCity 10.8	17866	TB	Trident/ALX400 10.5
15029	RM	N230/OmniCity 10.8	15103	WH	N230/OmniCity 10.8	17873	WH	Trident/ALX400 10.5
15030	RM	N230/OmniCity 10.8	15104	BW	N230/OmniCity 10.8	17875	WH	Trident/ALX400 10.5
15031	RM	N230/OmniCity 10.8	15105	BW	N230/OmniCity 10.8	17876	TL	Trident/ALX400 10.5
15032	RM	N230/OmniCity 10.8	15106	BW	N230/OmniCity 10.8	17877	TL	Trident/ALX400 10.5
15033	RM	N230/OmniCity 10.8	15107	BW	N230/OmniCity 10.8	17878	BK	Trident/ALX400 10.5
15034	RM	N230/OmniCity 10.8	15108	BW	N230/OmniCity 10.8	17880	BK	Trident/ALX400 10.5
15035	RM	N230/OmniCity 10.8	15109	BW	N230/OmniCity 10.8	17881	BK	Trident/ALX400 10.5
15036	RM	N230/OmniCity 10.8	15110	BW	N230/OmniCity 10.8	17882	BK	Trident/ALX400 10.5
15037	RM	N230/OmniCity 10.8	15111	WH	N230/OmniCity 10.8	17883	BK	Trident/ALX400 10.5
15038	WH	N230/OmniCity 10.8	15112	BW	N230/OmniCity 10.8	17884	BK	Trident/ALX400 10.5
15039	BW	N230/OmniCity 10.8	15113	BW	N230/OmniCity 10.8	17885	BK	Trident/ALX400 10.5
15040	BW	N230/OmniCity 10.8	15114	BW	N230/OmniCity 10.8	17886	BK	Trident/ALX400 10.5
15041	WH	N230/OmniCity 10.8	15115	BW	N230/OmniCity 10.8	17887	BK	Trident/ALX400 10.5
15042	WH	N230/OmniCity 10.8	15116	BW	N230/OmniCity 10.8	17888	BK	Trident/ALX400 10.5
15043	WH	N230/OmniCity 10.8	15117	BW	N230/OmniCity 10.8	17889	WH	Trident/ALX400 10.5
15044	WH	N230/OmniCity 10.8	15118	BW	N230/OmniCity 10.8	17890	WH	Trident/ALX400 10.5
15045	WH	N230/OmniCity 10.8	15119	BW	N230/OmniCity 10.8	17891	WH	Trident/ALX400 10.5
15046	WH	N230/OmniCity 10.8	17749	PD	Trident/ALX400 10.5	17893	TL	Trident/ALX400 10.5
15047	WH	N230/OmniCity 10.8	17750	T	Trident/ALX400 10.5	17894	NS	Trident/ALX400 10.5
15048	WH	N230/OmniCity 10.8	17779	TB	Trident/ALX400 10.5	17896	PD	Trident/ALX400 10.5
15049	PD	N230/OmniCity 10.8	17780	TB	Trident/ALX400 10.5	17897	BK	Trident/ALX400 10.5
15050	PD	N230/OmniCity 10.8	17788	BK	Trident/ALX400 10.5	17898	TB	Trident/ALX400 10.5
15051	PD	N230/OmniCity 10.8	17791	NS	Trident/ALX400 10.5	17899	TB	Trident/ALX400 10.5
15052	PD	N230/OmniCity 10.8	17795	TB	Trident/ALX400 10.5	17900	TB	Trident/ALX400 10.5
15053	PD	N230/OmniCity 10.8	17796	PD	Trident/ALX400 10.5	17901	BK	Trident/ALX400 10.5
15054	PD	N230/OmniCity 10.8	17799	WH	Trident/ALX400 10.5	17902	BK	Trident/ALX400 10.5
15055	PD	N230/OmniCity 10.8	17811	T	Trident/ALX400 10.5	17903	WH	Trident/ALX400 10.5
15056	PD	N230/OmniCity 10.8	17813	TL	Trident/ALX400 10.5	17904	BK	Trident/ALX400 10.5
15057	PD	N230/OmniCity 10.8	17814	TL	Trident/ALX400 10.5	17905	WH	Trident/ALX400 10.5
15058	PD	N230/OmniCity 10.8	17815	WH	Trident/ALX400 10.5	17906	WH	Trident/ALX400 10.5
15059	PD	N230/OmniCity 10.8	17816	WH	Trident/ALX400 10.5	17907	WH	Trident/ALX400 10.5
15060	PD	N230/OmniCity 10.8	17817	WH	Trident/ALX400 10.5	17908	WH	Trident/ALX400 10.5
15061	PD	N230/OmniCity 10.8	17818	PD	Trident/ALX400 10.5	17923	WH	Trident/ALX400 10.5
15062	PD	N230/OmniCity 10.8	17820	WH	Trident/ALX400 10.5	17924	WH	Trident/ALX400 10.5
15063	PD	N230/OmniCity 10.8	17821	WH	Trident/ALX400 10.5	17927	WH	Trident/ALX400 10.5
15064	PD	N230/OmniCity 10.8	17822	WH	Trident/ALX400 10.5	17928	WH	Trident/ALX400 10.5
15065	PD	N230/OmniCity 10.8	17823	TL	Trident/ALX400 10.5	17929	WH	Trident/ALX400 10.5
15066	PD	N230/OmniCity 10.8	17824	TL	Trident/ALX400 10.5	17930	WH	Trident/ALX400 10.5
15067	PD	N230/OmniCity 10.8	17825	TL	Trident/ALX400 10.5	17931	WH	Trident/ALX400 10.5
15068	PD	N230/OmniCity 10.8	17826	WH	Trident/ALX400 10.5	17932	WH	Trident/ALX400 10.5
15069	PD	N230/OmniCity 10.8	17827	WH	Trident/ALX400 10.5	17933	WH	Trident/ALX400 10.5
15070	PD	N230/OmniCity 10.8	17828	WH	Trident/ALX400 10.5	17934	WH	Trident/ALX400 10.5
15071	PD	N230/OmniCity 10.8	17831	TB	Trident/ALX400 10.5	17935	WH	Trident/ALX400 10.5
15072	PD	N230/OmniCity 10.8	17832	TB	Trident/ALX400 10.5	17936	WH	Trident/ALX400 10.5
15073	RM	N230/OmniCity 10.8	17833	PD	Trident/ALX400 10.5	17937	WH	Trident/ALX400 10.5
15074	WH	N230/OmniCity 10.8	17834	WH	Trident/ALX400 10.5	17938	WH	Trident/ALX400 10.5
15075	WH	N230/OmniCity 10.8	17836	T	Trident/ALX400 10.5	17939	WH	Trident/ALX400 10.5
15076	WH	N230/OmniCity 10.8	17837	BK	Trident/ALX400 10.5	17940	RM	Trident/ALX400 10.5
15077	WH	N230/OmniCity 10.8	17838	PD	Trident/ALX400 10.5	17941	WH	Trident/ALX400 10.5
15078	WH	N230/OmniCity 10.8	17840	PD	Trident/ALX400 10.5	17944	WH	Trident/ALX400 10.5
15079	WH	N230/OmniCity 10.8	17841	TB	Trident/ALX400 10.5	17951	BK	Trident/ALX400 10.5
15080	WH	N230/OmniCity 10.8	17842	PD	Trident/ALX400 10.5	17952	BK	Trident/ALX400 10.5
15081	WH	N230/OmniCity 10.8	17843	PD	Trident/ALX400 10.5	17953	BK	Trident/ALX400 10.5
15082	WH	N230/OmniCity 10.8	17844	TB	Trident/ALX400 10.5	17955	BK	Trident/ALX400 10.5
15083	WH	N230/OmniCity 10.8	17845	TB	Trident/ALX400 10.5	17956	BK	Trident/ALX400 10.5
15084	WH	N230/OmniCity 10.8	17847	WH	Trident/ALX400 10.5	17958	BK	Trident/ALX400 10.5

No.	G.	Type	No.	G.	Type	No.	G.	Type
17959	BK	Trident/ALX400 10.5	18458	WH	Trident/ALX400 10.5	19733	RM	Trident/E400 10.1
17960	BK	Trident/ALX400 10.5	18459	WH	Trident/ALX400 10.5	19734	RM	Trident/E400 10.1
17961	BK	Trident/ALX400 10.5	18460	WH	Trident/ALX400 10.5	19735	NS	Trident/E400 10.1
17962	BK	Trident/ALX400 10.5	18461	WH	Trident/ALX400 10.5	19736	NS	Trident/E400 10.1
17963	BK	Trident/ALX400 10.5	18462	WH	Trident/ALX400 10.5	19737	NS	Trident/E400 10.1
17976	NS	Trident/ALX400 9.9	18463	TL	Trident/ALX400 10.5	19738	NS	Trident/E400 10.1
17977	NS	Trident/ALX400 9.9	18464	TL	Trident/ALX400 10.5	19739	NS	Trident/E400 10.1
17978	NS	Trident/ALX400 9.9	18465	RM	Trident/ALX400 10.5	19740	NS	Trident/E400 10.1
17979	NS	Trident/ALX400 9.9	18466	RM	Trident/ALX400 10.5	19741	NS	Trident/E400 10.1
17980	NS	Trident/ALX400 9.9	18467	NS	Trident/ALX400 10.5	19742	PD	Trident/E400 10.1
17981	NS	Trident/ALX400 9.9	18468	NS	Trident/ALX400 10.5	19743	WH	Trident/E400 10.1
17982	NS	Trident/ALX400 9.9	18469	NS	Trident/ALX400 10.5	19744	WH	Trident/E400 10.1
17983	NS	Trident/ALX400 9.9	18470	NS	Trident/ALX400 10.5	19745	WH	Trident/E400 10.1
17984	NS	Trident/ALX400 9.9	18471	NS	Trident/ALX400 10.5	19746	PD	Trident/E400 10.1
17985	NS	Trident/ALX400 9.9	18472	NS	Trident/ALX400 10.5	19747	PD	Trident/E400 10.1
17988	WH	Trident/ALX400 9.9	18473	NS	Trident/ALX400 10.5	19748	NS	Trident/E400 10.1
17989	WH	Trident/ALX400 9.9	18474	NS	Trident/ALX400 10.5	19749	NS	Trident/E400 10.1
17990	RM	Trident/ALX400 9.9	18475	NS	Trident/ALX400 10.5	19750	NS	Trident/E400 10.1
17991	WH	Trident/ALX400 9.9	18476	NS	Trident/ALX400 10.5	19751	NS	Trident/E400 10.1
17992	WH	Trident/ALX400 9.9	18477	NS	Trident/ALX400 10.5	19752	NS	Trident/E400 10.1
17993	WH	Trident/ALX400 9.9	18478	NS	Trident/ALX400 10.5	19753	NS	Trident/E400 10.1
17994	WH	Trident/ALX400 9.9	18479	NS	Trident/ALX400 10.5	19754	NS	Trident/E400 10.1
17995	NS	Trident/ALX400 9.9	18480	NS	Trident/ALX400 10.5	19755	PD	Trident/E400 10.1
17996	WH	Trident/ALX400 9.9	18481	BK	Trident/ALX400 10.5	19756	BK	Trident/E400 10.1
17997	WH	Trident/ALX400 9.9	18482	BK	Trident/ALX400 10.5	19757	BK	Trident/E400 10.1
17998	BK	Trident/ALX400 9.9	18483	BK	Trident/ALX400 10.5	19758	BK	Trident/E400 10.1
17999	BK	Trident/ALX400 9.9	18484	BK	Trident/ALX400 10.5	19759	BK	Trident/E400 10.1
18201	BK	Trident/ALX400 10.5	18485	TB	Trident/ALX400 10.5	19760	BK	Trident/E400 10.1
18202	BK	Trident/ALX400 10.5	18486	TB	Trident/ALX400 10.5	19761	BK	Trident/E400 10.1
18203	NS	Trident/ALX400 10.5	18487	TB	Trident/ALX400 10.5	19762	BK	Trident/E400 10.1
18204	WH	Trident/ALX400 10.5	18488	TB	Trident/ALX400 10.5	19763	BK	Trident/E400 10.1
18205	NS	Trident/ALX400 10.5	18489	TB	Trident/ALX400 10.5	19764	BK	Trident/E400 10.1
18206	WH	Trident/ALX400 10.5	18490	TB	Trident/ALX400 10.5	19765	BK	Trident/E400 10.1
18207	NS	Trident/ALX400 10.5	18491	TB	Trident/ALX400 10.5	19766	BK	Trident/E400 10.1
18208	BK	Trident/ALX400 10.5	18492	TB	Trident/ALX400 10.5	19767	BK	Trident/E400 10.1
18209	T	Trident/ALX400 10.5	18493	TB	Trident/ALX400 10.5	19768	NS	Trident/E400 10.1
18210	RM	Trident/ALX400 10.5	18494	TB	Trident/ALX400 10.5	19769	NS	Trident/E400 10.1
18211	WH	Trident/ALX400 10.5	18495	TB	Trident/ALX400 10.5	19770	NS	Trident/E400 10.1
18212	WH	Trident/ALX400 10.5	18496	BK	Trident/ALX400 10.5	19771	NS	Trident/E400 10.1
18213	TB	Trident/ALX400 10.5	18497	BK	Trident/ALX400 10.5	19772	NS	Trident/E400 10.1
18214	RM	Trident/ALX400 10.5	18498	BK	Trident/ALX400 10.5	19773	BK	Trident/E400 10.1
18215	TB	Trident/ALX400 10.5	18499	BK	Trident/ALX400 10.5	19774	BK	Trident/E400 10.1
18216	BK	Trident/ALX400 10.5	19000	RM	Trident/E400 10.8	19775	BK	Trident/E400 10.1
18217	BK	Trident/ALX400 10.5	19131	TB	Trident/E400 10.8	19776	BK	Trident/E400 10.1
18218	T	Trident/ALX400 10.5	19132	TB	Trident/E400 10.8	19777	BK	Trident/E400 10.1
18219	PD	Trident/ALX400 10.5	19133	TB	Trident/E400 10.8	19778	BK	Trident/E400 10.1
18220	WH	Trident/ALX400 10.5	19134	TB	Trident/E400 10.8	19779	BK	Trident/E400 10.1
18257	WH	Trident/ALX400 10.5	19135	TB	Trident/E400 10.8	19780	BK	Trident/E400 10.1
18258	WH	Trident/ALX400 10.5	19136	TB	Trident/E400 10.8	19781	BK	Trident/E400 10.1
18259	WH	Trident/ALX400 10.5	19137	TB	Trident/E400 10.8	19782	BK	Trident/E400 10.1
18260	WH	Trident/ALX400 10.5	19138	TB	Trident/E400 10.8	19783	BK	Trident/E400 10.1
18261	WH	Trident/ALX400 10.5	19139	TB	Trident/E400 10.8	19784	BK	Trident/E400 10.1
18262	WH	Trident/ALX400 10.5	19140	TB	Trident/E400 10.8	19785	T	Trident/E400 10.1
18263	WH	Trident/ALX400 10.5	19711	RM	Trident/E400 10.1	19786	RM	Trident/E400 10.1
18264	WH	Trident/ALX400 10.5	19712	RM	Trident/E400 10.1	19787	RM	Trident/E400 10.1
18265	WH	Trident/ALX400 10.5	19713	RM	Trident/E400 10.1	19788	RM	Trident/E400 10.1
18266	WH	Trident/ALX400 10.5	19714	RM	Trident/E400 10.1	19789	RM	Trident/E400 10.1
18267	WH	Trident/ALX400 10.5	19715	RM	Trident/E400 10.1	19790	RM	Trident/E400 10.1
18268	WH	Trident/ALX400 10.5	19716	RM	Trident/E400 10.1	19791	RM	Trident/E400 10.1
18269	WH	Trident/ALX400 10.5	19717	RM	Trident/E400 10.1	19792	RM	Trident/E400 10.1
18270	WH	Trident/ALX400 10.5	19718	RM	Trident/E400 10.1	19793	RM	Trident/E400 10.1
18271	WH	Trident/ALX400 10.5	19719	RM	Trident/E400 10.1	19794	T	Trident/E400 10.1
18272	WH	Trident/ALX400 10.5	19720	RM	Trident/E400 10.1	19795	T	Trident/E400 10.1
18273	WH	Trident/ALX400 10.5	19721	RM	Trident/E400 10.1	19796	T	Trident/E400 10.1
18274	WH	Trident/ALX400 10.5	19722	RM	Trident/E400 10.1	19797	T	Trident/E400 10.1
18275	WH	Trident/ALX400 10.5	19723	RM	Trident/E400 10.1	19798	T	Trident/E400 10.1
18276	WH	Trident/ALX400 10.5	19724	RM	Trident/E400 10.1	19799	TB	Trident/E400 10.1
18277	WH	Trident/ALX400 10.5	19725	RM	Trident/E400 10.1	19800	TB	Trident/E400 10.1
18451	RM	Trident/ALX400 10.5	19726	RM	Trident/E400 10.1	19801	TL	Trident/E400 10.1
18452	RM	Trident/ALX400 10.5	19727	RM	Trident/E400 10.1	19802	TB	Trident/E400 10.1
18453	RM	Trident/ALX400 10.5	19728	RM	Trident/E400 10.1	19803	TB	Trident/E400 10.1
18454	RM	Trident/ALX400 10.5	19729	RM	Trident/E400 10.1	19804	NS	Trident/E400 10.1
18455	TL	Trident/ALX400 10.5	19730	RM	Trident/E400 10.1	19805	NS	Trident/E400 10.1
18456	WH	Trident/ALX400 10.5	19731	RM	Trident/E400 10.1	19806	NS	Trident/E400 10.1
18457	WH	Trident/ALX400 10.5	19732	RM	Trident/E400 10.1	19807	NS	Trident/E400 10.1

Stagecoach

No.	G.	Type	No.	G.	Type	No.	G.	Type
19808	NS	Trident/E400 10.1	23111	TB	Citaro 12.0	36313	TL	E200/E200 10.8
19809	NS	Trident/E400 10.1	23112	TB	Citaro 12.0	36314	TL	E200/E200 8.9
19810	NS	Trident/E400 10.1	25310	BK	Versa 10.4	36315	TL	E200/E200 8.9
19811	NS	Trident/E400 10.1	25311	BK	Versa 10.4	36316	TL	E200/E200 8.9
19812	NS	Trident/E400 10.1	25312	BK	Versa 10.4	36317	TL	E200/E200 8.9
19813	NS	Trident/E400 10.1	25313	BK	Versa 10.4	36318	TL	E200/E200 8.9
19814	NS	Trident/E400 10.1	25314	BK	Versa 10.4	36319	TL	E200/E200 8.9
19815	NS	Trident/E400 10.1	34359	TL	Dart/Pointer 10.1	36320	TL	E200/E200 8.9
19816	NS	Trident/E400 10.1	34370	TL	Dart/Pointer 8.8	36321	TL	E200/E200 8.9
19817	NS	Trident/E400 10.1	34372	PD	Dart/Pointer 8.8	36322	TL	E200/E200 8.9
19818	NS	Trident/E400 10.1	34377	PD	Dart/Pointer 9.3	36323	TL	E200/E200 8.9
19819	NS	Trident/E400 10.1	34378	PD	Dart/Pointer 9.3	36324	TL	E200/E200 8.9
19820	NS	Trident/E400 10.1	34379	PD	Dart/Pointer 9.3	36325	TL	E200/E200 8.9
19821	NS	Trident/E400 10.1	34380	PD	Dart/Pointer 9.3	36326	TL	E200/E200 8.9
19822	NS	Trident/E400 10.1	34381	PD	Dart/Pointer 9.3	36327	PD	E200/E200 9.3
19823	NS	Trident/E400 10.1	34382	PD	Dart/Pointer 9.3	36328	PD	E200/E200 9.3
19824	NS	Trident/E400 10.1	34383	PD	Dart/Pointer 9.3	36329	PD	E200/E200 9.3
19825	NS	Trident/E400 10.1	34384	PD	Dart/Pointer 9.3	36330	PD	E200/E200 9.3
19826	NS	Trident/E400 10.1	34385	PD	Dart/Pointer 9.3	36331	PD	E200/E200 9.3
19827	NS	Trident/E400 10.1	34386	PD	Dart/Pointer 9.3	36332	PD	E200/E200 9.3
19828	RM	Trident/E400 10.1	34388	TL	Dart/Pointer 10.1	36333	PD	E200/E200 9.3
19829	RM	Trident/E400 10.1	34390	TL	Dart/Pointer 10.1	36334	PD	E200/E200 9.3
19830	RM	Trident/E400 10.1	34391	TL	Dart/Pointer 10.1	36335	PD	E200/E200 9.3
19831	RM	Trident/E400 10.1	34392	TL	Dart/Pointer 10.1	36336	PD	E200/E200 9.3
19832	RM	Trident/E400 10.1	34393	TL	Dart/Pointer 10.1	36337	PD	E200/E200 9.3
19833	RM	Trident/E400 10.1	34395	TL	Dart/Pointer 10.1	36338	TL	E200/E200 10.8
19834	RM	Trident/E400 10.1	34396	TL	Dart/Pointer 10.1	36339	TL	E200/E200 10.8
19835	TB	E40D/E400 (EC) 10.2	34397	TL	Dart/Pointer 10.1	36340	TL	E200/E200 10.8
19836	TL	E40D/E400 (EC) 10.2	34551	TL	Dart/Pointer 10.1	36341	TL	E200/E200 10.8
19837	TL	E40D/E400 (EC) 10.2	34552	TL	Dart/Pointer 10.1	36342	TL	E200/E200 10.8
19838	TL	E40D/E400 (EC) 10.2	34553	TL	Dart/Pointer 10.1	36343	TL	E200/E200 10.8
19839	TL	E40D/E400 (EC) 10.2	34554	TL	Dart/Pointer 10.1	36344	TL	E200/E200 10.8
19840	TL	E40D/E400 (EC) 10.2	34557	TL	Dart/Pointer 10.1	36345	WH	E200/E200 10.2
19841	TL	E40D/E400 (EC) 10.2	34558	TL	Dart/Pointer 10.1	36346	BK	E200/E200 10.2
19842	TL	E40D/E400 (EC) 10.2	34559	TL	Dart/Pointer 10.1	36347	BK	E200/E200 10.2
19843	TL	E40D/E400 (EC) 10.2	34560	TL	Dart/Pointer 10.1	36348	TL	E200/E200 10.2
19844	TL	E40D/E400 (EC) 10.2	36261	TL	E200/E200 10.2	36349	WH	E200/E200 10.2
19845	TL	E40D/E400 (EC) 10.2	36262	TL	E200/E200 10.2	36350	WH	E200/E200 10.2
19846	TL	E40D/E400 (EC) 10.2	36263	NS	E200/E200 10.2	36351	WH	E200/E200 10.2
19847	WH	E40D/E400 (EC) 10.2	36264	NS	E200/E200 10.2	36352	WH	E200/E200 10.2
19848	WH	E40D/E400 (EC) 10.2	36265	NS	E200/E200 10.2	36353	WH	E200/E200 10.2
19849	WH	E40D/E400 (EC) 10.2	36267	NS	E200/E200 10.2	36354	WH	E200/E200 10.2
19850	WH	E40D/E400 (EC) 10.2	36280	BK	E200/E200 10.2	36355	WH	E200/E200 10.2
19851	WH	E40D/E400 (EC) 10.2	36281	BK	E200/E200 10.2	36356	WH	E200/E200 10.2
19852	WH	E40D/E400 (EC) 10.2	36282	BK	E200/E200 10.2	36357	WH	E200/E200 10.2
19853	WH	E40D/E400 (EC) 10.2	36283	BK	E200/E200 10.2	36358	WH	E200/E200 10.2
19854	WH	E40D/E400 (EC) 10.2	36284	BK	E200/E200 10.2	36359	WH	E200/E200 10.2
19855	WH	E40D/E400 (EC) 10.2	36285	BK	E200/E200 10.2	36360	WH	E200/E200 10.2
19856	WH	E40D/E400 (EC) 10.2	36286	BK	E200/E200 10.2	36361	WH	E200/E200 10.2
19857	WH	E40D/E400 (EC) 10.2	36287	BK	E200/E200 10.2	36362	WH	E200/E200 10.2
19858	WH	E40D/E400 (EC) 10.2	36288	BK	E200/E200 10.2	36363	WH	E200/E200 10.2
19859	WH	E40D/E400 (EC) 10.2	36289	BK	E200/E200 10.2	36364	WH	E200/E200 10.2
19860	WH	E40D/E400 (EC) 10.2	36290	BK	E200/E200 10.2	36365	WH	E200/E200 10.2
19861	WH	E40D/E400 (EC) 10.2	36291	BK	E200/E200 10.2	36366	WH	E200/E200 10.2
19862	WH	E40D/E400 (EC) 10.2	36292	BK	E200/E200 10.2	36367	WH	E200/E200 10.2
19863	WH	E40D/E400 (EC) 10.2	36293	BK	E200/E200 10.2	36368	WH	E200/E200 10.2
19864	WH	E40D/E400 (EC) 10.2	36294	BK	E200/E200 10.2	36369	WH	E200/E200 10.2
19865	WH	E40D/E400 (EC) 10.2	36295	BK	E200/E200 10.2	36370	WH	E200/E200 10.2
19866	WH	E40D/E400 (EC) 10.2	36296	BK	E200/E200 10.2	36371	WH	E200/E200 10.2
19867	WH	E40D/E400 (EC) 10.2	36297	BK	E200/E200 10.2	36372	BK	E200/E200 10.2
19868	WH	E40D/E400 (EC) 10.2	36298	BK	E200/E200 10.2	36373	BK	E200/E200 10.2
19869	WH	E40D/E400 (EC) 10.2	36299	BK	E200/E200 10.2	36374	TL	E200/E200 10.2
19870	WH	E40D/E400 (EC) 10.2	36301	BK	E200/E200 8.9	36375	BK	E200/E200 10.2
19871	WH	E40D/E400 (EC) 10.2	36302	BK	E200/E200 8.9	36528	TL	E20D/E200 8.9
23101	TB	Citaro 12.0	36303	BK	E200/E200 8.9	36529	TL	E20D/E200 8.9
23102	TB	Citaro 12.0	36304	BK	E200/E200 8.9	36530	TL	E20D/E200 8.9
23103	TB	Citaro 12.0	36305	BK	E200/E200 8.9	36531	TL	E20D/E200 8.9
23104	TB	Citaro 12.0	36306	BK	E200/E200 8.9	36532	TL	E20D/E200 8.9
23105	TB	Citaro 12.0	36307	BK	E200/E200 8.9	36533	TL	E20D/E200 8.9
23106	TB	Citaro 12.0	36308	BK	E200/E200 8.9	36534	TL	E20D/E200 8.9
23107	TB	Citaro 12.0	36309	TL	E200/E200 10.8	36535	TL	E20D/E200 8.9
23108	TB	Citaro 12.0	36310	TL	E200/E200 10.8	36536	TL	E20D/E200 8.9
23109	TB	Citaro 12.0	36311	TL	E200/E200 10.8	36537	TL	E20D/E200 8.9
23110	TB	Citaro 12.0	36312	TL	E200/E200 10.8	36538	TL	E20D/E200 8.9

No.	G.	Type	No.	G.	Type	No.	G.	Type
36539	TL	E20D/E200 8.9	36628	TL	E20D/E200MMC 9.0	LT315	T	NRM (E6) 11.3
36540	TL	E20D/E200 8.9	36629	TL	E20D/E200MMC 9.0	LT316	T	NRM (E6) 11.3
36541	TB	E20D/E200 10.2	36630	TL	E20D/E200MMC 9.0	LT357	T	NRM (E6) 11.3
36542	TB	E20D/E200 10.2	36631	TL	E20D/E200MMC 9.0	LT358	T	NRM (E6) 11.3
36543	TB	E20D/E200 10.2	36632	BK	E20D/E200MMC 9.0	LT359	T	NRM (E6) 11.3
36544	TB	E20D/E200 10.2	36633	BK	E20D/E200MMC 9.0	LT360	T	NRM (E6) 11.3
36545	TB	E20D/E200 10.2	36634	BK	E20D/E200MMC 9.0	LT361	T	NRM (E6) 11.3
36546	TB	E20D/E200 10.2	36635	BK	E20D/E200MMC 9.0	LT362	T	NRM (E6) 11.3
36547	TB	E20D/E200 10.2	36636	BK	E20D/E200MMC 9.0	LT363	T	NRM (E6) 11.3
36548	TB	E20D/E200 10.2	36637	BK	E20D/E200MMC 9.0	LT364	T	NRM (E6) 11.3
36549	TB	E20D/E200 10.2	36638	BK	E20D/E200MMC 9.0	LT365	T	NRM (E6) 11.3
36550	TB	E20D/E200 10.2	36639	BK	E20D/E200MMC 9.0	LT366	T	NRM (E6) 11.3
36551	TB	E20D/E200 10.2	36640	BK	E20D/E200MMC 9.0	LT367	T	NRM (E6) 11.3
36552	TB	E20D/E200 10.2	36641	TL	E20D/E200MMC 10.4	LT368	T	NRM (E6) 11.3
36553	TB	E20D/E200 10.2	36642	TL	E20D/E200MMC 10.4	LT369	T	NRM (E6) 11.3
36554	TB	E20D/E200 10.2	36643	TL	E20D/E200MMC 10.4	LT370	T	NRM (E6) 11.3
36555	PD	E20D/E200 9.6	36644	TL	E20D/E200MMC 10.4	LT371	T	NRM (E6) 11.3
36556	BK	E20D/E200 10.8	36645	TL	E20D/E200MMC 10.4	LT372	T	NRM (E6) 11.3
36557	BK	E20D/E200 10.8	36646	TL	E20D/E200MMC 10.4	LT373	T	NRM (E6) 11.3
36558	BK	E20D/E200 10.8	36647	TL	E20D/E200MMC 10.4	LT374	T	NRM (E6) 11.3
36559	BK	E20D/E200 10.8	36648	TL	E20D/E200MMC 10.4	LT375	T	NRM (E6) 11.3
36560	RM	E20D/E200 10.8	36649	TL	E20D/E200MMC 10.4	LT376	T	NRM (E6) 11.3
36561	RM	E20D/E200 10.8	36650	TL	E20D/E200MMC 10.4	LT377	T	NRM (E6) 11.3
36562	RM	E20D/E200 10.8	36651	TL	E20D/E200MMC 10.4	LT378	T	NRM (E6) 11.3
36563	RM	E20D/E200 10.8	36652	TL	E20D/E200MMC 10.4	LT379	T	NRM (E6) 11.3
36564	RM	E20D/E200 10.8	36653	TL	E20D/E200MMC 10.4	LT380	T	NRM (E6) 11.3
36565	RM	E20D/E200 10.8	36654	TL	E20D/E200MMC 10.4	LT381	T	NRM (E6) 11.3
36566	RM	E20D/E200 10.8	36655	TL	E20D/E200MMC 10.4	LT382	T	NRM (E6) 11.3
36567	RM	E20D/E200 10.8	36656	TL	E20D/E200MMC 10.4	LT383	T	NRM (E6) 11.3
36568	RM	E20D/E200 10.8	36657	WH	E20D/E200MMC 10.4	LT384	T	NRM (E6) 11.3
36569	RM	E20D/E200 10.8	36658	BK	E20D/E200MMC 10.4	LT385	T	NRM (E6) 11.3
36570	RM	E20D/E200 10.8	36659	BK	E20D/E200MMC 10.4	LT386	T	NRM (E6) 11.3
36571	RM	E20D/E200 10.8	36660	BK	E20D/E200MMC 10.4	LT387	T	NRM (E6) 11.3
36572	RM	E20D/E200 10.8	36661	BK	E20D/E200MMC 10.4	LT388	T	NRM (E6) 11.3
36573	RM	E20D/E200 10.8	36662	BK	E20D/E200MMC 10.4	LT389	T	NRM (E6) 11.3
36574	RM	E20D/E200 10.8	36663	BK	E20D/E200MMC 10.4	LT390	T	NRM (E6) 11.3
36575	RM	E20D/E200 10.8	36664	BK	E20D/E200MMC 10.4	LT391	BW	NRM (E6) 11.3
36576	RM	E20D/E200 10.8	36665	BK	E20D/E200MMC 10.4	LT392	BW	NRM (E6) 11.3
36577	RM	E20D/E200 10.8	LT239	BW	NRM 11.3	LT393	BW	NRM (E6) 11.3
36578	RM	E20D/E200 10.8	LT240	BW	NRM 11.3	LT394	BW	NRM (E6) 11.3
36579	RM	E20D/E200 10.8	LT241	BW	NRM 11.3	LT395	BW	NRM (E6) 11.3
36580	RM	E20D/E200 10.8	LT242	BW	NRM 11.3	LT396	BW	NRM (E6) 11.3
36581	TB	E20D/E200 8.9	LT243	BW	NRM 11.3	LT397	BW	NRM (E6) 11.3
36582	TB	E20D/E200 8.9	LT244	BW	NRM 11.3	LT398	BW	NRM (E6) 11.3
36583	TB	E20D/E200 8.9	LT245	BW	NRM 11.3	LT399	BW	NRM (E6) 11.3
36584	TL	E20D/E200 8.9	LT246	BW	NRM 11.3	LT400	BW	NRM (E6) 11.3
36585	TL	E20D/E200 8.9	LT247	BW	NRM 11.3	LT401	BW	NRM (E6) 11.3
36586	TL	E20D/E200 8.9	LT248	BW	NRM 11.3	LT402	BW	NRM (E6) 11.3
36587	TL	E20D/E200 8.9	LT249	BW	NRM 11.3	LT403	BW	NRM (E6) 11.3
36601	NS	E20D/E200MMC 10.9	LT250	BW	NRM 11.3	LT404	BW	NRM (E6) 11.3
36602	NS	E20D/E200MMC 10.9	LT251	BW	NRM 11.3	LT405	BW	NRM (E6) 11.3
36603	NS	E20D/E200MMC 10.9	LT252	BW	NRM 11.3	LT406	BW	NRM (E6) 11.3
36604	NS	E20D/E200MMC 10.9	LT253	BW	NRM 11.3	LT407	BW	NRM (E6) 11.3
36605	NS	E20D/E200MMC 10.9	LT254	BW	NRM 11.3	LT408	BW	NRM (E6) 11.3
36606	NS	E20D/E200MMC 10.9	LT255	BW	NRM 11.3	LT409	BW	NRM (E6) 11.3
36607	NS	E20D/E200MMC 10.9	LT256	BW	NRM 11.3	LT410	BW	NRM (E6) 11.3
36608	NS	E20D/E200MMC 10.9	LT257	BW	NRM 11.3	LT411	BW	NRM (E6) 11.3
36609	TB	E20D/E200MMC 9.0	LT258	BW	NRM 11.3	LT412	BW	NRM (E6) 11.3
36610	TB	E20D/E200MMC 9.0	LT259	BW	NRM 11.3	LT413	BW	NRM (E6) 11.3
36611	TB	E20D/E200MMC 9.0	LT260	BW	NRM 11.3	LT414	BW	NRM (E6) 11.3
36612	TB	E20D/E200MMC 9.0	LT261	BW	NRM 11.3	LT415	BW	NRM (E6) 11.3
36613	TB	E20D/E200MMC 9.0	LT262	BW	NRM 11.3	LT416	BW	NRM (E6) 11.3
36614	TB	E20D/E200MMC 9.0	LT263	BW	NRM 11.3	LT462	BW	NRM (E6) 11.3
36615	TB	E20D/E200MMC 9.0	LT264	BW	NRM 11.3	LT463	T	NRM (E6) 11.3
36616	TB	E20D/E200MMC 9.0	LT265	BW	NRM 11.3	RM324	WH	Routemaster
36617	TB	E20D/E200MMC 9.0	LT266	BW	NRM 11.3	RM652	WH	Routemaster
36618	TB	E20D/E200MMC 9.0	LT267	BW	NRM 11.3	RM871	WH	Routemaster
36619	TB	E20D/E200MMC 9.0	LT268	BW	NRM 11.3	RM1933	WH	Routemaster
36620	TB	E20D/E200MMC 9.0	LT269	BW	NRM 11.3	RM1941	WH	Routemaster
36621	TB	E20D/E200MMC 9.0	LT270	BW	NRM 11.3	RM1968	WH	Routemaster
36622	TL	E20D/E200MMC 9.0	LT271	BW	NRM 11.3	RM2050	WH	Routemaster
36623	TL	E20D/E200MMC 9.0	LT272	BW	NRM 11.3	RM2060	WH	Routemaster
36624	TL	E20D/E200MMC 9.0	LT312	T	NRM (E6) 11.3			
36625	TL	E20D/E200MMC 9.0	LT313	T	NRM (E6) 11.3			
36627	TL	E20D/E200MMC 9.0	LT314	T	NRM (E6) 11.3			

Sullivan Buses

No.	G.	Type	No.	G.	Type	No.	G.	Type
AE11	SM	E20D/E200 10.2	AE27	SM	E20D/E200MMC 9.75	ELV5	SM	B7TL/Vyking 11.0
AE12	SM	E20D/E200 10.2	DS50	SM	N230/OmniCity 10.8M	ELV6	SM	B7TL/Vyking 10.4
AE13	SM	E20D/E200 10.2	DS51	SM	N230/OmniCity 10.8M	ELV8	SM	B7TL/Vyking 11.0
AE14	SM	E20D/E200 10.2	DS52	SM	N230/OmniCity 10.8M	ELV9	SM	B7TL/Vyking 11.0
AE15	SM	E20D/E200 10.2	DS53	SM	N230/OmniCity 10.8M	ELV10	SM	B7TL/Vyking 11.0
AE16	SM	E20D/E200 10.2	E40	SM	Trident/E400 10.1	PDL26	SM	Trident/President 9.9
AE20	SM	E20D/E200MMC 9.75	E41	SM	Trident/E400 10.1	TPL926	SM	Trident/President 10.5
AE21	SM	E20D/E200MMC 9.75	E42	SM	Trident/E400 10.1	TPL927	SM	Trident/President 10.5
AE22	SM	E20D/E200MMC 9.75	E43	SM	Trident/E400 10.1	WVL2	SM	B7TL/Gemini 10.6
AE23	SM	E20D/E200MMC 9.75	E44	SM	Trident/E400 10.1	WVL3	SM	B7TL/Gemini 10.6
AE24	SM	E20D/E200MMC 9.75	ELV2	SM	B7TL/Vyking 10.4	WVL4	SM	B7TL/Gemini 10.6
AE25	SM	E20D/E200MMC 9.75	ELV3	SM	B7TL/Vyking 10.4			
AE26	SM	E20D/E200MMC 9.75	ELV4	SM	B7TL/Vyking 10.4			

Sullivans have eight Enviro 200 MMCs for use on route W9. All feature the same style moquette as the Enviro400 Citys. AE26 heads along Church Street in Enfield. *Mark Mcwalter*

Uno

No.	G.	Type
601	HF	E20D/E200 8.9M
602	HF	E20D/E200 8.9M
603	HF	E20D/E200 8.9M
604	HF	E20D/E200 8.9M

Tower Transit

No.	G.	Type	No.	G.	Type	No.	G.	Type
DH38501	LI	E400 VE 10.5	DMV44228	LI	E20D/E200 10.8	DN33648	LI	Trident/E400 10.1
DH38502	LI	E400 VE 10.5	DMV44229	LI	E20D/E200 10.8	DN33649	LI	Trident/E400 10.1
DH38503	LI	E400 VE 10.5	DMV44230	LI	E20D/E200 10.8	DN33650	LI	Trident/E400 10.1
DM44167	LI	E200/E200 9.3	DMV44231	LI	E20D/E200 10.8	DN33651	LI	Trident/E400 10.1
DM44168	LI	E200/E200 9.3	DMV44232	LI	E20D/E200 10.8	DN33652	LI	Trident/E400 10.1
DM44169	LI	E200/E200 9.3	DMV44233	LI	E20D/E200 10.8	DN33653	LI	Trident/E400 10.1
DM44170	LI	E200/E200 9.3	DMV44234	LI	E20D/E200 10.8	DN33654	LI	Trident/E400 10.1
DM44260	LI	E20D/E200 9.6	DMV44235	LI	E20D/E200 10.8	DN33655	LI	Trident/E400 10.1
DM44261	LI	E20D/E200 9.6	DMV44236	LI	E20D/E200 10.8	DN33776	LI	E40D/E400 (EC) 10.2
DM44262	LI	E20D/E200 9.6	DMV44250	LI	E20D/E200 10.8	DN33777	LI	E40D/E400 (EC) 10.2
DM44263	LI	E20D/E200 9.6	DMV44251	LI	E20D/E200 10.8	DN33778	X	E40D/E400 (EC) 10.2
DM44264	LI	E20D/E200 9.6	DMV44252	LI	E20D/E200 10.8	DN33779	LI	E40D/E400 (EC) 10.2
DM44265	LI	E20D/E200 9.6	DMV44253	LI	E20D/E200 10.8	DN33780	LI	E40D/E400 (EC) 10.2
DM44266	LI	E20D/E200 9.6	DMV44254	LI	E20D/E200 10.8	DN33781	LI	E40D/E400 (EC) 10.2
DM44267	LI	E20D/E200 9.6	DMV44255	LI	E20D/E200 10.8	DN33782	LI	E40D/E400 (EC) 10.2
DM44268	LI	E20D/E200 9.6	DMV44256	LI	E20D/E200 10.8	DN33783	X	E40D/E400 (EC) 10.2
DM44269	LI	E20D/E200 9.6	DMV44257	LI	E20D/E200 10.8	DN33784	LI	E40D/E400 (EC) 10.2
DM44270	LI	E20D/E200 9.6	DMV44258	LI	E20D/E200 10.8	DN33785	LI	E40D/E400 (EC) 10.2
DM45115	LI	E20D/E200 9.6	DMV44259	LI	E20D/E200 10.8	DN33786	X	E40D/E400 (EC) 10.2
DM45116	LI	E20D/E200 9.6	DMV45101	LI	E20D/E200 10.8	DN33787	X	E40D/E400 (EC) 10.2
DM45117	LI	E20D/E200 9.6	DMV45102	LI	E20D/E200 10.8	DN33789	LI	E40D/E400 (EC) 10.2
DM45118	LI	E20D/E200 9.6	DMV45103	LI	E20D/E200 10.8	DN33790	LI	E40D/E400 (EC) 10.2
DM45119	LI	E20D/E200 9.6	DMV45104	LI	E20D/E200 10.8	DN33791	LI	E40D/E400 (EC) 10.2
DM45120	LI	E20D/E200 9.6	DMV45105	LI	E20D/E200 10.8	DN33792	LI	E40D/E400 (EC) 10.2
DML44171	LI	E200/E200 10.2	DMV45106	LI	E20D/E200 10.8	DN33793	LI	E40D/E400 (EC) 10.2
DML44172	LI	E200/E200 10.2	DMV45107	LI	E20D/E200 10.8	DN33794	LI	E40D/E400 (EC) 10.2
DML44173	LI	E200/E200 10.2	DMV45108	LI	E20D/E200 10.8	DN33795	LI	E40D/E400 (EC) 10.2
DML44174	LI	E200/E200 10.2	DMV45109	LI	E20D/E200 10.8	DN33796	LI	E40D/E400 (EC) 10.2
DML44175	LI	E200/E200 10.2	DMV45110	LI	E20D/E200 10.8	DN33797	LI	E40D/E400 (EC) 10.2
DML44176	LI	E200/E200 10.2	DMV45111	LI	E20D/E200 10.8	DN33798	LI	E40D/E400 (EC) 10.2
DML44177	LI	E200/E200 10.2	DMV45112	LI	E20D/E200 10.8	DNH39111	X	E40H/E400 (EC) 10.2
DML44178	LI	E200/E200 10.2	DMV45113	LI	E20D/E200 10.8	DNH39112	X	E40H/E400 (EC) 10.2
DML44279	LI	E20D/E200 10.2	DMV45114	LI	E20D/E200 10.8	DNH39113	X	E40H/E400 (EC) 10.2
DML44280	LI	E20D/E200 10.2	DN33612	LI	Trident/E400 10.1	DNH39114	X	E40H/E400 (EC) 10.2
DML44281	LI	E20D/E200 10.2	DN33613	LI	Trident/E400 10.1	DNH39115	X	E40H/E400 (EC) 10.2
DML44282	X	E20D/E200 10.2	DN33614	LI	Trident/E400 10.1	DNH39116	X	E40H/E400 (EC) 10.2
DML44283	LI	E20D/E200 10.2	DN33615	LI	Trident/E400 10.1	DNH39117	X	E40H/E400 (EC) 10.2
DML44284	LI	E20D/E200 10.2	DN33616	LI	Trident/E400 10.1	DNH39118	X	E40H/E400 (EC) 10.2
DML44285	LI	E20D/E200 10.2	DN33617	LI	Trident/E400 10.1	DNH39119	X	E40H/E400 (EC) 10.2
DML44286	LI	E20D/E200 10.2	DN33618	LI	Trident/E400 10.1	DNH39120	X	E40H/E400 (EC) 10.2
DML44287	LI	E20D/E200 10.2	DN33619	LI	Trident/E400 10.1	DNH39121	X	E40H/E400 (EC) 10.2
DML44288	LI	E20D/E200 10.2	DN33620	LI	Trident/E400 10.1	DNH39122	X	E40H/E400 (EC) 10.2
DML44289	LI	E20D/E200 10.2	DN33621	LI	Trident/E400 10.1	DNH39123	X	E40H/E400 (EC) 10.2
DML44290	X	E20D/E200 10.2	DN33622	LI	Trident/E400 10.1	DNH39124	X	E40H/E400 (EC) 10.2
DML44291	X	E20D/E200 10.2	DN33623	LI	Trident/E400 10.1	DNH39125	X	E40H/E400 (EC) 10.2
DML44292	X	E20D/E200 10.2	DN33624	LI	Trident/E400 10.1	DNH39126	X	E40H/E400 (EC) 10.2
DML44313	X	E20D/E200 10.2	DN33625	LI	Trident/E400 10.1	DNH39127	X	E40H/E400 (EC) 10.2
DML44314	X	E20D/E200 10.2	DN33626	LI	Trident/E400 10.1	DNH39128	X	E40H/E400 (EC) 10.2
DML44315	X	E20D/E200 10.2	DN33627	LI	Trident/E400 10.1	DNH39129	X	E40H/E400 (EC) 10.2
DML44316	X	E20D/E200 10.2	DN33628	LI	Trident/E400 10.1	DNH39130	X	E40H/E400 (EC) 10.2
DML44317	X	E20D/E200 10.2	DN33629	LI	Trident/E400 10.1	DNH39131	X	E40H/E400 (EC) 10.2
DML44318	X	E20D/E200 10.2	DN33630	LI	Trident/E400 10.1	DNH39132	X	E40H/E400 (EC) 10.2
DML44319	X	E20D/E200 10.2	DN33631	LI	Trident/E400 10.1	MV38201	X	B5LH/Evosetti 10.6
DML44320	X	E20D/E200 10.2	DN33632	LI	Trident/E400 10.1	MV38202	X	B5LH/Evosetti 10.6
DML44321	X	E20D/E200 10.2	DN33633	LI	Trident/E400 10.1	MV38203	X	B5LH/Evosetti 10.6
DML44322	X	E20D/E200 10.2	DN33634	LI	Trident/E400 10.1	MV38204	X	B5LH/Evosetti 10.6
DML44323	X	E20D/E200 10.2	DN33635	LI	Trident/E400 10.1	MV38205	X	B5LH/Evosetti 10.6
DML44324	X	E20D/E200 10.2	DN33636	LI	Trident/E400 10.1	MV38206	X	B5LH/Evosetti 10.6
DML44325	X	E20D/E200 10.2	DN33637	LI	Trident/E400 10.1	MV38207	X	B5LH/Evosetti 10.6
DML44326	X	E20D/E200 10.2	DN33638	LI	Trident/E400 10.1	MV38208	X	B5LH/Evosetti 10.6
DML44327	X	E20D/E200 10.2	DN33639	LI	Trident/E400 10.1	MV38209	X	B5LH/Evosetti 10.6
DML44328	X	E20D/E200 10.2	DN33640	LI	Trident/E400 10.1	MV38210	X	B5LH/Evosetti 10.6
DMV44221	LI	E20D/E200 10.8	DN33641	LI	Trident/E400 10.1	MV38211	X	B5LH/Evosetti 10.6
DMV44222	LI	E20D/E200 10.8	DN33642	LI	Trident/E400 10.1	MV38212	X	B5LH/Evosetti 10.6
DMV44223	LI	E20D/E200 10.8	DN33643	LI	Trident/E400 10.1	MV38213	X	B5LH/Evosetti 10.6
DMV44224	LI	E20D/E200 10.8	DN33644	LI	Trident/E400 10.1	MV38214	X	B5LH/Evosetti 10.6
DMV44225	LI	E20D/E200 10.8	DN33645	LI	Trident/E400 10.1	MV38215	X	B5LH/Evosetti 10.6
DMV44226	LI	E20D/E200 10.8	DN33646	LI	Trident/E400 10.1	MV38216	X	B5LH/Evosetti 10.6
DMV44227	LI	E20D/E200 10.8	DN33647	LI	Trident/E400 10.1	MV38217	X	B5LH/Evosetti 10.6

Tower Transit

No.	G.	Type	No.	G.	Type	No.	G.	Type
MV38218	X	B5LH/Evosetti 10.6	VN36105	LI	B9TL/Gemini 2 10.4	VN37854	LI	B9TL/Gemini 2 10.4
MV38219	X	B5LH/Evosetti 10.6	VN36106	LI	B9TL/Gemini 2 10.4	VN37855	LI	B9TL/Gemini 2 10.4
MV38220	X	B5LH/Evosetti 10.6	VN36107	LI	B9TL/Gemini 2 10.4	VN37859	LI	B9TL/Gemini 2 10.4
MV38221	X	B5LH/Evosetti 10.6	VN36108	LI	B9TL/Gemini 2 10.4	VN37860	LI	B9TL/Gemini 2 10.4
MV38222	X	B5LH/Evosetti 10.6	VN36109	LI	B9TL/Gemini 2 10.4	VN37861	LI	B9TL/Gemini 2 10.4
MV38223	X	B5LH/Evosetti 10.6	VN36110	LI	B9TL/Gemini 2 10.4	VN37862	LI	B9TL/Gemini 2 10.4
MV38224	X	B5LH/Evosetti 10.6	VN36111	LI	B9TL/Gemini 2 10.4	VN37863	LI	B9TL/Gemini 2 10.4
MV38225	X	B5LH/Evosetti 10.6	VN36112	LI	B9TL/Gemini 2 10.4	VN37864	LI	B9TL/Gemini 2 10.4
MV38226	X	B5LH/Evosetti 10.6	VN36113	LI	B9TL/Gemini 2 10.4	VN37943	LI	B9TL/Gemini 2 10.4
MV38227	X	B5LH/Evosetti 10.6	VN36114	LI	B9TL/Gemini 2 10.4	VN37952	AS	B9TL/Gemini 2 (EC) 10.5
MV38228	X	B5LH/Evosetti 10.6	VN36115	LI	B9TL/Gemini 2 10.4	VN37953	LI	B9TL/Gemini 2 (EC) 10.5
MV38229	X	B5LH/Evosetti 10.6	VN36116	LI	B9TL/Gemini 2 10.4	VN37954	LI	B9TL/Gemini 2 (EC) 10.5
MV38230	X	B5LH/Evosetti 10.6	VN36117	LI	B9TL/Gemini 2 10.4	VN37955	AS	B9TL/Gemini 2 (EC) 10.5
MV38231	X	B5LH/Evosetti 10.6	VN36118	LI	B9TL/Gemini 2 10.4	VN37956	X	B9TL/Gemini 2 (EC) 10.5
MV38232	X	B5LH/Evosetti 10.6	VN36119	LI	B9TL/Gemini 2 10.4	VN37957	LI	B9TL/Gemini 2 (EC) 10.5
MV38233	X	B5LH/Evosetti 10.6	VN36120	LI	B9TL/Gemini 2 10.4	VN37958	LI	B9TL/Gemini 2 (EC) 10.5
MV38234	X	B5LH/Evosetti 10.6	VN36121	LI	B9TL/Gemini 2 10.4	VN37959	LI	B9TL/Gemini 2 (EC) 10.5
MV38235	LI	B5LH/Evosetti 10.6	VN36122	LI	B9TL/Gemini 2 10.4	VN37960	X	B9TL/Gemini 2 (EC) 10.5
MV38236	LI	B5LH/Evosetti 10.6	VN36123	LI	B9TL/Gemini 2 10.4	VN37961	LI	B9TL/Gemini 2 (EC) 10.5
MV38237	LI	B5LH/Evosetti 10.6	VN36124	LI	B9TL/Gemini 2 10.4	VN37962	AS	B9TL/Gemini 2 (EC) 10.5
MV38238	LI	B5LH/Evosetti 10.6	VN36125	LI	B9TL/Gemini 2 10.4	VN37963	AS	B9TL/Gemini 2 (EC) 10.5
MV38239	LI	B5LH/Evosetti 10.6	VN36126	LI	B9TL/Gemini 2 10.4	VN37964	AS	B9TL/Gemini 2 (EC) 10.5
MV38240	LI	B5LH/Evosetti 10.6	VN36127	LI	B9TL/Gemini 2 10.4	VN37965	AS	B9TL/Gemini 2 (EC) 10.5
MV38241	LI	B5LH/Evosetti 10.6	VN36128	LI	B9TL/Gemini 2 10.4	VN37966	AS	B9TL/Gemini 2 (EC) 10.5
MV38242	LI	B5LH/Evosetti 10.6	VN36129	LI	B9TL/Gemini 2 10.4	VN37967	AS	B9TL/Gemini 2 (EC) 10.5
MV38243	LI	B5LH/Evosetti 10.6	VN36130	LI	B9TL/Gemini 2 10.4	VN37968	AS	B9TL/Gemini 2 (EC) 10.5
MV38244	LI	B5LH/Evosetti 10.6	VN36131	LI	B9TL/Gemini 2 10.4	VN37969	AS	B9TL/Gemini 2 (EC) 10.5
MV38245	LI	B5LH/Evosetti 10.6	VN36132	LI	B9TL/Gemini 2 10.4	VN37970	AS	B9TL/Gemini 2 (EC) 10.5
MV38246	LI	B5LH/Evosetti 10.6	VN36133	LI	B9TL/Gemini 2 10.4	VN37971	AS	B9TL/Gemini 2 (EC) 10.5
MV38247	LI	B5LH/Evosetti 10.6	VN36134	LI	B9TL/Gemini 2 10.4	VN37972	AS	B9TL/Gemini 2 (EC) 10.5
MV38248	LI	B5LH/Evosetti 10.6	VN36135	LI	B9TL/Gemini 2 10.4	VN37973	AS	B9TL/Gemini 2 (EC) 10.5
MV38249	LI	B5LH/Evosetti 10.6	VN36136	LI	B9TL/Gemini 2 10.4	VN37974	AS	B9TL/Gemini 2 (EC) 10.5
MV38250	LI	B5LH/Evosetti 10.6	VN36137	LI	B9TL/Gemini 2 10.4	VN37975	AS	B9TL/Gemini 2 (EC) 10.5
MV38251	LI	B5LH/Evosetti 10.6	VN36138	LI	B9TL/Gemini 2 10.4	VN37976	AS	B9TL/Gemini 2 (EC) 10.5
VH38101	LI	B5LH/Gemini 3 10.5	VN36139	LI	B9TL/Gemini 2 10.4	VN37977	AS	B9TL/Gemini 2 (EC) 10.5
VH38102	LI	B5LH/Gemini 3 10.5	VN36140	LI	B9TL/Gemini 2 10.4	VN37978	AS	B9TL/Gemini 2 (EC) 10.5
VH38103	LI	B5LH/Gemini 3 10.5	VN36141	LI	B9TL/Gemini 2 10.4	VN37979	AS	B9TL/Gemini 2 (EC) 10.5
VH38104	LI	B5LH/Gemini 3 10.5	VN36142	LI	B9TL/Gemini 2 10.4	VN37980	AS	B9TL/Gemini 2 (EC) 10.5
VH38105	LI	B5LH/Gemini 3 10.5	VN36143	LI	B9TL/Gemini 2 10.4	VN37981	AS	B9TL/Gemini 2 (EC) 10.5
VH38106	LI	B5LH/Gemini 3 10.5	VN36144	LI	B9TL/Gemini 2 10.4	VN37982	AS	B9TL/Gemini 2 (EC) 10.5
VH38107	LI	B5LH/Gemini 3 10.5	VN36145	LI	B9TL/Gemini 2 10.4	VN37983	AS	B9TL/Gemini 2 (EC) 10.5
VH38108	LI	B5LH/Gemini 3 10.5	VN36146	LI	B9TL/Gemini 2 10.4	VN37984	AS	B9TL/Gemini 2 (EC) 10.5
VH38109	LI	B5LH/Gemini 3 10.5	VN36147	LI	B9TL/Gemini 2 10.4	VN37988	AS	B9TL/Gemini 2 (EC) 10.5
VH38110	LI	B5LH/Gemini 3 10.5	VN36148	LI	B9TL/Gemini 2 10.4	VN37989	AS	B9TL/Gemini 2 (EC) 10.5
VH38111	LI	B5LH/Gemini 3 10.5	VN36149	LI	B9TL/Gemini 2 10.4	VN37990	AS	B9TL/Gemini 2 (EC) 10.5
VH38112	AS	B5LH/Gemini 3 ST 10.5	VN36150	LI	B9TL/Gemini 2 10.4	VN37991	AS	B9TL/Gemini 2 (EC) 10.5
VH38113	AS	B5LH/Gemini 3 ST 10.5	VN36151	LI	B9TL/Gemini 2 10.4	VN37992	AS	B9TL/Gemini 2 (EC) 10.5
VH38114	AS	B5LH/Gemini 3 ST 10.5	VN36152	LI	B9TL/Gemini 2 10.4	VN37993	AS	B9TL/Gemini 2 (EC) 10.5
VH38115	AS	B5LH/Gemini 3 ST 10.5	VN36153	LI	B9TL/Gemini 2 10.4	VN37994	LI	B9TL/Gemini 2 (EC) 10.5
VH38116	AS	B5LH/Gemini 3 ST 10.5	VN36154	LI	B9TL/Gemini 2 10.4	VN37995	LI	B9TL/Gemini 2 (EC) 10.5
VH38117	AS	B5LH/Gemini 3 ST 10.5	VN36155	LI	B9TL/Gemini 2 10.4	VN37996	LI	B9TL/Gemini 2 (EC) 10.5
VH38118	AS	B5LH/Gemini 3 ST 10.5	VN36156	LI	B9TL/Gemini 2 10.4	VNW32362	AS	B7TL/Gemini 10.1
VH38119	AS	B5LH/Gemini 3 ST 10.5	VN36157	LI	B9TL/Gemini 2 10.4	VNW32364	AS	B7TL/Gemini 10.1
VH38120	AS	B5LH/Gemini 3 ST 10.5	VN36158	LI	B9TL/Gemini 2 10.4	VNW32366	AS	B7TL/Gemini 10.1
VH38121	AS	B5LH/Gemini 3 ST 10.5	VN36159	LI	B9TL/Gemini 2 10.4	VNW32367	AS	B7TL/Gemini 10.1
VH38122	AS	B5LH/Gemini 3 ST 10.5	VN36160	LI	B9TL/Gemini 2 10.4	VNW32369	AS	B7TL/Gemini 10.1
VH38123	AS	B5LH/Gemini 3 ST 10.5	VN36161	LI	B9TL/Gemini 2 10.4	VNW32371	AS	B7TL/Gemini 10.1
VH38124	AS	B5LH/Gemini 3 ST 10.5	VN36162	LI	B9TL/Gemini 2 10.4	VNW32372	AS	B7TL/Gemini 10.1
VH38125	AS	B5LH/Gemini 3 ST 10.5	VN36163	LI	B9TL/Gemini 2 10.4	VNW32373	AS	B7TL/Gemini 10.1
VH38126	AS	B5LH/Gemini 3 ST 10.5	VN36164	LI	B9TL/Gemini 2 10.4	VNW32375	AS	B7TL/Gemini 10.1
VH38127	AS	B5LH/Gemini 3 ST 10.5	VN36165	LI	B9TL/Gemini 2 10.4	VNW32376	AS	B7TL/Gemini 10.1
VH38128	AS	B5LH/Gemini 3 ST 10.5	VN36291	AS	B9TL/Gemini 2 (EC) 10.5	VNW32377	AS	B7TL/Gemini 10.1
VH38129	AS	B5LH/Gemini 3 ST 10.5	VN36292	AS	B9TL/Gemini 2 (EC) 10.5	VNW32378	AS	B7TL/Gemini 10.1
VH38130	AS	B5LH/Gemini 3 ST 10.5	VN36293	LI	B9TL/Gemini 2 (EC) 10.5	VNW32379	AS	B7TL/Gemini 10.1
VH38131	AS	B5LH/Gemini 3 ST 10.5	VN36294	AS	B9TL/Gemini 2 (EC) 10.5	VNW32380	AS	B7TL/Gemini 10.1
VH38132	AS	B5LH/Gemini 3 ST 10.5	VN36295	AS	B9TL/Gemini 2 (EC) 10.5	VNW32381	AS	B7TL/Gemini 10.1
VH38133	AS	B5LH/Gemini 3 ST 10.5	VN37842	LI	B9TL/Gemini 2 10.4	VNW32383	AS	B7TL/Gemini 10.1
VH38134	AS	B5LH/Gemini 3 ST 10.5	VN37844	LI	B9TL/Gemini 2 10.4	VNW32385	AS	B7TL/Gemini 10.1
VH38135	AS	B5LH/Gemini 3 ST 10.5	VN37847	LI	B9TL/Gemini 2 10.4	VNW32386	AS	B7TL/Gemini 10.1
VH38136	AS	B5LH/Gemini 3 ST 10.5	VN37849	LI	B9TL/Gemini 2 10.4	VNW32387	AS	B7TL/Gemini 10.1
VN36101	LI	B9TL/Gemini 2 10.4	VN37850	LI	B9TL/Gemini 2 10.4	VNW32388	AS	B7TL/Gemini 10.1
VN36102	LI	B9TL/Gemini 2 10.4	VN37851	LI	B9TL/Gemini 2 10.4	VNW32389	AS	B7TL/Gemini 10.1
VN36103	LI	B9TL/Gemini 2 10.4	VN37852	LI	B9TL/Gemini 2 10.4	VNW32390	AS	B7TL/Gemini 10.1
VN36104	LI	B9TL/Gemini 2 10.4	VN37853	LI	B9TL/Gemini 2 10.4			

No.	G.	Type	No.	G.	Type	No.	G.	Type
VNW32391	AS	B7TL/Gemini 10.1	VNW32413	AS	B7TL/Gemini 10.1	WN35004	AS	Gemini 2DL 10.4
VNW32392	AS	B7TL/Gemini 10.1	VNW32414	AS	B7TL/Gemini 10.1	WSH62991	LI	SB200/Pulsar 2 11.9
VNW32393	AS	B7TL/Gemini 10.1	VNW32415	AS	B7TL/Gemini 10.1	WSH62992	LI	SB200/Pulsar 2 11.9
VNW32394	AS	B7TL/Gemini 10.1	VNW32416	AS	B7TL/Gemini 10.1	WSH62993	LI	SB200/Pulsar 2 11.9
VNW32395	AS	B7TL/Gemini 10.1	VNW32417	AS	B7TL/Gemini 10.1	WSH62994	LI	SB200/Pulsar 2 11.9
VNW32396	AS	B7TL/Gemini 10.1	VNW32419	AS	B7TL/Gemini 10.1	WSH62995	LI	SB200/Pulsar 2 11.9
VNW32397	AS	B7TL/Gemini 10.1	VNW32420	AS	B7TL/Gemini 10.1	WSH62996	LI	SB200/Pulsar 2 11.9
VNW32398	AS	B7TL/Gemini 10.1	VNW32421	AS	B7TL/Gemini 10.1	WSH62997	LI	SB200/Pulsar 2 11.9
VNW32399	AS	B7TL/Gemini 10.1	VNW32422	AS	B7TL/Gemini 10.1	WSH62998	LI	SB200/Pulsar 2 11.9
VNW32400	AS	B7TL/Gemini 10.1	VNW32423	AS	B7TL/Gemini 10.1	WV46101	LI	Streetlite DF (E6) 10.8
VNW32401	AS	B7TL/Gemini 10.1	VNW32424	AS	B7TL/Gemini 10.1	WV46102	LI	Streetlite DF (E6) 10.8
VNW32402	AS	B7TL/Gemini 10.1	VNW32425	AS	B7TL/Gemini 10.1	WV46103	LI	Streetlite DF (E6) 10.8
VNW32403	AS	B7TL/Gemini 10.1	VNW32426	AS	B7TL/Gemini 10.1	WV46104	LI	Streetlite DF (E6) 10.8
VNW32405	AS	B7TL/Gemini 10.1	VNW32427	AS	B7TL/Gemini 10.1	WV46105	LI	Streetlite DF (E6) 10.8
VNW32406	AS	B7TL/Gemini 10.1	VNW32428	AS	B7TL/Gemini 10.1	WV46106	LI	Streetlite DF (E6) 10.8
VNW32407	AS	B7TL/Gemini 10.1	VNW32429	LI	B7TL/Gemini 10.1	WV46107	LI	Streetlite DF (E6) 10.8
VNW32408	AS	B7TL/Gemini 10.1	VNW32430	LI	B7TL/Gemini 10.1	WV46108	LI	Streetlite DF (E6) 10.8
VNW32409	AS	B7TL/Gemini 10.1	WL44700	LI	Streetlite DF 10.2	WV46109	LI	Streetlite DF (E6) 10.8
VNW32410	AS	B7TL/Gemini 10.1	WN35001	AS	Gemini 2DL 10.4	WV46110	LI	Streetlite DF (E6) 10.8
VNW32411	AS	B7TL/Gemini 10.1	WN35002	AS	Gemini 2DL 10.4	WV46111	LI	Streetlite DF (E6) 10.8
VNW32412	AS	B7TL/Gemini 10.1	WN35003	AS	Gemini 2DL 10.4			

DH38501 is one of three Virtual Electric Enviro400s based at Lea Interchange for use on route 69. It awaits its next duty at Canning Town. *Michael J. McClelland*

On Order

No.	G.	Type	No.	G.	Type	No.	G.	Type
SULLIVAN BUSES			LT960		NRM (E6) 11.3	LT981		NRM (E6) 11.3
E70	SM	E40D/E400MMC 10.35	LT961		NRM (E6) 11.3	LT982		NRM (E6) 11.3
E71	SM	E40D/E400MMC 10.35	LT962		NRM (E6) 11.3	LT983		NRM (E6) 11.3
E72	SM	E40D/E400MMC 10.35	LT963		NRM (E6) 11.3	LT984		NRM (E6) 11.3
E73	SM	E40D/E400MMC 10.35	LT964		NRM (E6) 11.3	LT985		NRM (E6) 11.3
E74	SM	E40D/E400MMC 10.35	LT965		NRM (E6) 11.3	LT986		NRM (E6) 11.3
E75	SM	E40D/E400MMC 10.35	LT966		NRM (E6) 11.3	LT987		NRM (E6) 11.3
E76	SM	E40D/E400MMC 10.35	LT967		NRM (E6) 11.3	LT988		NRM (E6) 11.3
E77	SM	E40D/E400MMC 10.35	LT968		NRM (E6) 11.3	LT989		NRM (E6) 11.3
E78	SM	E40D/E400MMC 10.35	LT969		NRM (E6) 11.3	LT990		NRM (E6) 11.3
E79	SM	E40D/E400MMC 10.35	LT970		NRM (E6) 11.3	LT991		NRM (E6) 11.3
E80	SM	E40D/E400MMC 10.35	LT971		NRM (E6) 11.3	LT992		NRM (E6) 11.3
E81	SM	E40D/E400MMC 10.35	LT972		NRM (E6) 11.3	LT993		NRM (E6) 11.3
			LT973		NRM (E6) 11.3	LT994		NRM (E6) 11.3
NEW ROUTEMASTERS			LT974		NRM (E6) 11.3	LT995		NRM (E6) 11.3
LT954		NRM (E6) 11.3	LT975		NRM (E6) 11.3	LT996		NRM (E6) 11.3
LT955		NRM (E6) 11.3	LT976		NRM (E6) 11.3	LT997		NRM (E6) 11.3
LT956		NRM (E6) 11.3	LT977		NRM (E6) 11.3	LT998		NRM (E6) 11.3
LT957		NRM (E6) 11.3	LT978		NRM (E6) 11.3	LT999		NRM (E6) 11.3
LT958		NRM (E6) 11.3	LT979		NRM (E6) 11.3	LT1000		NRM (E6) 11.3
LT959		NRM (E6) 11.3	LT980		NRM (E6) 11.3			

Codes For LVF

Operator Codes:

Abellio	TLN
Arriva	AL
CT Plus	CTP
Go-Ahead	GAL
Metroline	ML
Quality Line	EP
RATP-Dev London	RTP
Stagecoach	SLN
Sullivan Buses	SB
Tower Transit	TT
Uno	UNO

Other Useful Codes

ZA	List new
ZB	List ads
ZC	Marble arch stops
ZD	Paliament Square stops
ZE	Hyde Park Corner stops
ZF	Trafalgar Square stops
ZG	Elephant and Castle stops
ZH	List NRM ads
ZI	List non NRM ads
ZJ	List Recent ads

Notes